OLIGARCHY *in* AMERICA

RHETORIC, CULTURE, AND SOCIAL CRITIQUE

SERIES EDITOR

John Louis Lucaites

EDITORIAL BOARD

Jeffrey A. Bennett
Carole Blair
Joshua Gunn
Robert Hariman
Debra Hawhee
Claire Sisco King
Steven Mailloux
Raymie E. McKerrow
Toby Miller
Phaedra C. Pezzullo
Austin Sarat
Janet Staiger
Barbie Zelizer

OLIGARCHY
in AMERICA

POWER, JUSTICE, AND
THE RULE OF THE FEW

LUKE WINSLOW

THE UNIVERSITY OF ALABAMA PRESS   *Tuscaloosa*

The University of Alabama Press
Tuscaloosa, Alabama 35487-0380
uapress.ua.edu

Copyright © 2024 by the University of Alabama Press
All rights reserved.

Inquiries about reproducing material from this work should
be addressed to the University of Alabama Press.

Typeface: Plantin

Cover design: Lori Lynch

Cataloging-in-Publication data is available from the Library of Congress.
ISBN: 978-0-8173-2206-9 (cloth)
ISBN: 978-0-8173-6154-9 (paper)
E-ISBN: 978-0-8173-6524-0

Contents

Preface | ix

Introduction | 1

1. The Rhetoric of Democratic Oligarchy | 12
2. Survival of the Fittest and the Rhetoric of Herbert Spencer | 32
3. Natural Law and the Rhetoric of Andrew Carnegie | 46
4. The Road to Oligarchy and the Rhetoric of Friedrich Hayek | 61
5. Judicial Oligarchy and the Rhetoric of James J. Kilpatrick | 78
6. Cultivating Political Power and the Rhetoric of Lewis F. Powell | 98
7. The Laws of Science and the Rhetoric of Milton Friedman | 118
8. Conjoint Depletion and the Rhetoric of James M. Buchanan | 135
9. The Science of Success and the Rhetoric of Charles Koch | 151
10. Class Consciousness and the Rhetoric of Tucker Carlson | 171

Conclusion: The Oligarchy We Deserve | 189

Acknowledgments | 201

Appendix: Theorizing Democratic Oligarchy | 203

Notes | 211

References | 275

Index | 293

Preface

ON AN EPISODE OF THE TV SERIES *COMEDIANS IN CARS GETTING COFFEE*, Jerry Seinfeld admitted he had no idea what oligarchy meant: "To me it sounds like a butter," he said. Imitating the formal voice of a TV pitchman, he suggested, "Try oligarchy on your toast. It has less saturated fat."

Seinfeld is not alone. Oligarchy is one of the most widely used yet least well-understood concepts in American public argument. Our discursive deficiencies were amplified in February 2022 when Vladimir Putin and the Russian military invaded Ukraine. According to Google Trends, online searches for the term exploded. "Russian oligarchs" emerged as a handy shortcut for explaining a perplexing geopolitical event. In that context, "oligarch" referred to a group of men leveraging their status as Kremlin insiders and party apparatchiks for economic gain.[1] Ultra-rich Russians came to be called "oligarchs," as they enjoined the Russian government in defending and enhancing their wealth. "Oligarchy" was applied smoothly to Roman Abramovich, Boris Berezovsky, and Alexander Smolensky, but less so to Jeff Bezos, Bill Gates, and Charles Koch. Donald Trump and Fred Smith were "billionaires." Viktor Vekselberg was an "oligarch." But what's the difference? And why does it seem like oligarchy is unique to eastern Europe and foreign to the United States?

This book argues that oligarchy is a defining but understudied feature of American democracy. As a discrete governing logic, I introduce the term "democratic oligarchy" to describe the marriage of economic wealth with political power through the symbolic acquisition of democratic consent. In what follows, I seek to locate this definition in the distinguishing boundaries and features of American democracy, examine the rhetoricity of those features in public discourse and affective circularities, and then link those features to systematic and generalizable principles informing the rhetorical dimensions of our lives.[2]

American democracy seems to be at an inflection point. Public conversations are filled with lamentations and eulogies as American democracy hangs in the balance.[3] One goal of this book is to redirect those lamentations by suggesting that democratic oligarchy says less about the survival of democracy, writ large, than it does about our capacity to communicate productively about the discursive core of American democracy, including Enlightenment understandings of self-rule and open debate, shared prosperity prompted by market economies, and the ability of strong civic and economic institutions to lubricate a market economy as a generator of wealth and security.[4] Jeremy Engels proposed a familiar way to begin such an inquiry by recommending that if we want to get our minds right, a good place to start is by getting our language right. Thinking at one higher level of abstraction, if we want to improve our society, we will have to change our language, our rhetoric, our ways of relating to ourselves and our fellow citizens, through discourse.[5] Such is the purpose of this book.

OLIGARCHY *in* AMERICA

Introduction

DURING THE 2016 US PRESIDENTIAL CAMPAIGN, DONALD TRUMP promised middle-class tax relief by passing legislation lowering the business tax from 35 to 15 percent.[1] But after Trump won, and with Republican majorities in Congress, his promises went unfulfilled during his first year in office. Until Fred Smith got involved. A graduate of Yale, the founder and CEO of FedEx, and an ex-Marine, Fred Smith also wanted Trump to cut taxes. But Smith did more than complain when Trump did not. Smith actually wrote his own tax plan, cutting the corporate tax rate from 35 to 20 percent and allowing businesses to write off new investments.[2] Smith's tax plan promised to spark a resurgence of business investment in America. Increased investment would then benefit both the CEOs and the American public, because businesses would innovate, expand, and hire. "The fundamental problem with the U.S. tax code is that it punishes investment," Smith said. "And at the end of the day, investment is what produces high-paying jobs. If you make the United States a better place to invest, there is no question in my mind that we would see a renaissance of capital investment, a growth in G.D.P. and an increase in income for our blue-collar workforce in the United States."[3]

Smith framed his tax plan as an altruistic mechanism benefiting ordinary Americans. "Investment is the only way to make blue-collar workers, people that don't have college degrees, more productive and have more income," he said.[4] When taxes are cut, corporations like FedEx start investing more in America, the economy grows, and everyone is better off. Smith employed a sports metaphor aligned with Trump's America First message: "It's just like us playing basketball. And on our end of the court, we're playing with a 12-foot basket, and everybody else that we compete with around the world is shooting on a 10-foot basket." Smith's basketball metaphor highlighted fears of a rigged global competition limiting American innovation and supremacy. He affirmed the link among tax cuts, corporate investment, and increased wages for the "blue-collar workforce." And he explained away the self-serving impact of his tax plan by tying together economic justice and the belief that, in America, everyone has the chance to be a FedEx shareholder.[5]

By 2017, Fred Smith's tax plan had become law, and he reaped the rewards: Before the new tax cuts, FedEx paid an effective tax rate of 34 percent, or $1.5 billion in taxes. After the tax cuts, instead of owing the federal government $1.5 billion in taxes, FedEx had a negative tax rate and the federal government ended up owing FedEx money. But FedEx did not use the savings to spark investment, as Fred Smith promised. Investment declined after the tax cuts passed. Instead, FedEx increased its dividends and stock buybacks to push up its stock price.

We have no shortage of provocative and colorful names to describe an economic and political system serving the interests of billionaires like Fred Smith. The purpose of *Oligarchy in America* is to highlight the limitations of our extant conceptual tools, and then redress this gap by defining oligarchy, locating its distinctive features in public argument, and tracing the development of its emergence as a distinctive governing logic. My methodological goal is to light up a synthetic pathway forward allowing for an ontological critique of the American political economy, transcending instrumentalist naivete and ideological futility and illuminating the genealogical level of power relations by discursively tracking affective modalities through symbolic and discursive appeals.[6] More simply, understanding oligarchy in America requires focused attention on both the thought leaders articulating oligarchic arguments *and* the discursive source of slow, subtle, and hard-to-pin-down public arguments generated by the think tanks, foundations, and educational systems. Going forward, I assume that the rhetorical potency of a discrete oligarchic class cannot come from persuading the public to accept their unpopular policies. The discipline of rhetoric is not well-equipped to make those causal connections anyway.[7] Theorizing oligarchy requires understanding the *rhetoricity* preceding and operating independently of symbolic intervention.[8]

Defining Democratic Oligarchy

The etymology of oligarchy comes from the Greek, meaning "rule of the few."[9] But left unexplained in that etymology is how oligarchy differs from other political systems also concentrating the rule of the few, including plutocracy, autocracy, monarchy, and fascism. Also left unexplained by "rule of the few" is how oligarchy compares to more common terms, such as conservative, liberal, or libertarian.

Recall Fred Smith. His alliance with a Republican president makes sense. Fred Smith is no liberal progressive. Beyond higher tax rates and more regulation, liberal economic policy is premised on the public's willingness to let Smith make a lot of money, as long as the benefits are shared. But if rising tides do not lift all our boats, Smith is exposed to the masses' capricious whims. His FedEx drivers and their allies can retaliate at the ballot box and redistribute his wealth. Classical liberalism does not maximize his profitability either. Because Smith cannot enjoin the government on his behalf, a lucrative source of wealth is left untapped. But the conservative and libertarian economic systems associated with the political Right are also not ideal for Smith. Conservative nostalgia is as impractical as it is unprofitable. And the focus on social issues distracts from making money. Libertarianism's minimal taxes and regulations may attract Smith's attention, and without the social baggage. But when put into practice, libertarianism's anarchist leanings would leave FedEx without publicly educated supply-chain managers and publicly maintained roads. Further, Smith is worth more than $4 billion not because he outperformed his competition in a free market. He is well aware that a free market allows for new competitors, shifting consumer preferences, and market fluctuations. A lucrative market needs robust monitoring and protection. There is no better entity than the state, with its immense symbolic, legal, and coercive resources, to do just that.[10]

In her book *Plutocrats*, Chrystia Freeland details the overlap and divergence between oligarchy and plutocracy by showing how the emergence of a class of the global super-rich is aided as their economic might grows in relation to their political muscle.[11] Freeland details how massive wealth can grow almost inevitably from the rent-seeking efforts of the ultra-rich when they control political machinations. In his book *The 9.9 Percent*, Matthew Stewart describes a rigged economic game, in large part, because a new aristocratic class is enjoining the state to protect and enhance their wealth.[12] In each case, plutocracy and aristocracy describe an outcome in which wealth and power are concentrated into the hands of a select few. To supplement those terms, democratic oligarchy explains less the end result and more the process by which economic and political power are married. More than a governing logic or a set of wealth-concentrating policies, democratic oligarchy describes how American oligarchs acquire the consent of the American people to support a political economy oriented toward the interests of the wealthy. Unlike plutocracy or aristocracy, democratic oligarchy is not a fixed endpoint or a coherent governing logic reducible to rent-seeking actions or regressive tax policies. Democracies can be oligarchic or anti-oligarchic, just as democracies can be liberal or illiberal. Accordingly, it is not conceptually useful to try to draw a line between Fred Smith, who is an oligarch, and his FedEx truck drivers, who are not. Instead, democratic oligarchy is theorized as an inventional resource, a culture of political organization, explaining power concentration in complementary and incommensurate ways while also highlighting the undertheorized interventions of the state in American democracy.

As a resource of rhetorical invention, democratic oligarchy is defined by an institutional arrangement in which the ultra-rich create a discrete class consciousness based on leveraging the state to accumulate wealth. The constitutive features of an oligarchic class consciousness are marked by the assumption that the primary purpose of the state is to protect and maximize the economic interests of a discrete capitalist ruling class.[13] Clyde Barrow finds evidence of ruling-class domination in the degree to which the affluent exercise decisive influence over state policy and to which a capitalist class shapes the state apparatus through interlocking positions of governmental, coercive, and administrative authority.[14] The result is an observable, differentiated, and incommensurate class of affluent individuals united by the defense of a political order affording class privileges through the ownership and control of economic life based on an advantageous relationship with the state.[15] But the coherence of an oligarchic class is not limited to economic constitutive parameters. A set of discrete cultural values—even noneconomic linkages, cultural affiliations, lifestyles, common experiences, and social interactions—form a discursive substructure of class cohesion.[16]

To note the presence of a discrete class consciousness among the ultra-rich in America can sound tone-deaf, cynical, and even unpatriotic. In contrast, references to "the middle class" or "the working class" are common in public conversations, along with the specific social formation and observable characteristics marking a middle-class or working-class identity.[17] Plus, capitalist market rivalries are supposed to limit the solidarity, cohesion, and consciousness of a discrete ruling class.[18] But despite the potential for rivalries among the ultra-rich, there is what Barrow calls a clear pattern of coordination between elites based on the perception of a range of common interests "distinct from the rest of society."[19] In the end, the rich are especially class conscious, even if they are subtle about it, because the rich need class consciousness to defend a social order affording them wealth and power.[20]

By braiding together disparate systems of power, an oligarchic class consciousness highlights the difference between democratic oligarchs and those who are just really rich by drawing a conceptual distinction between wealth and income.[21] *Income* explains the ability to purchase day-to-day necessities, like the cost of jet fuel or crown molding in a London apartment. By contrast, *wealth* is more readily deployed for political influence. Not all high-income individuals are oligarchs. An almost-certainly apocryphal story has it that when F. Scott Fitzgerald tried to explain to Ernest Hemingway that the rich are different than you and me, Hemingway cut him off by saying, "Yes, they have more money." Advancing that conversation, oligarchs are different than you and me, but not just because they have more money. Oligarchs are different because they use that money to bridge the economic-political chasm in a way the rest of us cannot. Plus, not all oligarchs are high-income. Amazon paid Jeff Bezos a base salary of $81,840 in 2019 and 2020, but that income does not account for his political influence.[22]

A second way democratic oligarchy affirms and extends our extant vocabulary is by highlighting the institutional setup where the ultra-rich can leverage the state's unique infrastructure, educational, and political resources to accumulate wealth.[23] With profit maximization as the telos, the oligarchic-oriented enlist the state to maximize profit, rather than eschew its capacities for the ideological purity demanded by membership in the political Right. Instead of seeking to drown the government in the bathtub, oligarchs use the state to defend and enhance their wealth and power.

Democratic oligarchy is distinguished by a marked ambivalence toward majoritarian democracy, free market capitalism, and the size and scope of federal and state governmental institutions. Like Fred Smith, the oligarchs examined here did not become rich by competing on a level playing field. And they did not reorient the American political landscape by passively accepting the capriciousness of majoritarian democracy. Oligarchy is not reliant on the market or the masses. Oligarchs understand, as much as any liberal progressive, the state's importance. The state and the market are inextricably bound. In fact, there is no Right/Left ideological seesaw: Instead, there is a tangled web of political economy, marked by a complex confluence of state policy and corporate machinations.[24]

Democratic oligarchy is not limited to military and police actions, lawmakers, political parties, or electoral politics, and thus, military and the police, lawmakers, political parties, or electoral politics will not be my primary focus. Instead, democratic oligarchy maintains a nominal absence from political authority—an absence highlighting democratic oligarchy's rhetorical distinctiveness. In the United States, oligarchs use what looks like the absence of authority to cover indirect political actions. Oligarchs cannot be voted out of office. Oligarchs do not need their own standing armies, and oligarchs do not need to rely on crime syndicates. Oligarchs do not need to bribe judges because they are already legally protected.[25]

There are exceptions. Vladimir Putin has crossed the chasm between economic and political power. The US Congress is the wealthiest in human history, and ultra-rich Americans like Pete du Pont, Nelson Rockefeller, David Koch, Michael Bloomberg, and Donald Trump have used their wealth to run for political office. But the rationale for their formal position of power only illustrates the indirect exercise of oligarchy.[26] Putin and Trump may be very rich, but they do not justify their nominal positions of power based on their own self-interest. They lead as an act of public service.[27]

Democratic oligarchy influences American democracy without direct control of the state apparatus. Unlike an English monarchy or African kleptocracy, democratic oligarchy's ability to shape public policy is dependent on its ability to organize class interests within the political system and deploy resources toward influencing the representative systems, institutions, and individuals who do shape policy.[28] Consider the difference between oligarchy and an autocratic dictatorship. American liberal democracy is not marked by an oligarchic class directly making money from government-owned or government-regulated companies, like in Russia, because in the United States, oligarchy is subtly embedded in the political system.[29] But before democratic oligarchy focuses on downstream legislative policies, it intervenes upstream into the *machinations* of power concentration. This distinction draws from Aristotle, whose conceptualization of oligarchy focuses more on how rulers are selected and less on what rulers do once in office.[30] The upstream inventions are important to consider at the outset because democratic oligarchy will often appear to be a contradictory political philosophy and an incoherent governing logic. Democratic oligarchy will seem to be selectively, sporadically, and inconsistently applied, in large part because oligarchy is more focused on maximizing the strategic flexibility of the few who should rule and less focused on how they should rule. For this reason, I avoid conceptualizing democracy and oligarchy as separate spheres.[31]

I am also careful about drawing rigid distinctions between democratic oligarchy and conservatism. Although public conversations often unite the ultra-rich like Fred Smith and the political Right, those conversations assume a fictive political-ideological axis.[32] I concede useful points of conceptual entailment across democratic oligarchy and the Right. George Will, in his 2018 book *The Conservative Sensibility*, defines the term "conservative" by asking what conservatives seek to conserve.[33] He concisely answers his own question: Conservatives seek to conserve the American founding. Will goes on to describe the clear mission of American conservatism as articulating and demonstrating the continuing pertinence of the Founder's thinking.[34] In turn, conservatives seek to prune the functions of the state, reducing regulation, lowering taxes, localizing control, and prioritizing fiscal discipline. George Will writes, "The law's primary purposes are to keep the peace and facilitate quotidian transactions—to resolve disputes and regularize behaviors and expectations. The law is not supposed to be salvific; it is not written to perfect either the individual or the community."[35] In action, the political impact of conservatism is a pruned state marked by limited government designed to reorient the state toward an earlier historical moment when the strong and free competed without the interference of a meddling government bureaucracy. Likewise, democratic oligarchy affirms the strict hierarchies at the foundation of these accounts. Overlapping assumptions include belief in a natural human hierarchy and that hell is the result of trying to be wiser than the divine.[36] The capacity to generate capital raises one's status on the power hierarchy, as those who can generate the most capital are considered the most human.[37] As Foley writes, each citizen is an *oikonomon*, a self-sufficient economic agent with the duty to take care of themselves.[38] To the victor go the spoils, and so, increased risk signifies increased opportunity and increased humanity, and the market reflects the final score. Because capital generation correlates to one's humanity, persistent inequalities are encouraged.[39] The Right's aversion to equality and egalitarianism resonates with democratic oligarchy's preferred power hierarchies.

But with these overlaps noted, I want to suggest that democratic oligarchy offers a conceptually, theoretically, and politically distinct perspective on the American political economy. Democratic oligarchy rejects the individualistic metaphysics assigned to the political Right in exchange for a discrete class consciousness of the ultra-rich seeking to enlist the state to maximize profits. Democratic oligarchy maintains limited loyalty to laissez-faire economics and free market capitalism. Unlike Edmund Burke's conservatism, democratic oligarchy reflects selective allegiance to a free market's ability to reward the winners and punish the losers. And unlike Russell Kirk and George Will, democratic oligarchy maintains limited loyalty to the country's framers and to the social and cultural traditionalism of the family, community, or church.

Conservative populism thinks institutions suppress "the people" and thus positions its outlook in an antagonistic relationship with the federal government. Conservative populism thinks the political establishment's discrimination and suppression of the people is unjust. In contrast, democratic oligarchy enlists institutions for the precise purpose of discriminating against the people. For example, William F. Buckley famously urged the nascent conservative movement to stand athwart history and yell stop. Democratic oligarchy assumes if you are forced to stand athwart and yell at the forward march of history, then something must be wrong with you.[40] Paul Johnson also marries conservative and neoliberal critiques of central planning to differentiate those systems from the Left.[41] Osnos includes a movement to "delegitimate federal power" as part of the libertarian fringe.[42] In contrast, democratic oligarchy seeks to control central planning and legitimate the federal power of the state to ensure just power hierarchies.

Finally, consider the diverging political subjectivities produced by democratic oligarchy and the familiar concepts on the political Right. Engels argues the neoliberal art of government produces political acquiescence, and Johnson suggests "conservative populism drains the polity of democratic potential."[43] To be sure, democratic oligarchy, at times, affirms political apathy; but as I will show in the case study chapters, democratic oligarchy also inspires an active political subjectivity based not on individual material self-interest, but on ensuring just power hierarchies. As I will argue, oligarchy is willing to use history as a source of rhetorical invention but never feels bound to maintain ideological purity when profit maximization demands purity be compromised.

Oligarchy, Democracy, and Symbolic Consent

Most fascist dictatorships and plutocratic autocracies are propped up by a monopoly on resources, especially the capacity to commit violence. Democratic oligarchy is understated in comparison, serving a biopolitical function by enticing a particular subjectivity that is free to choose another political-economic system.[44] Ordinary Americans who are not ultra-rich are induced and invited—but not coerced—to accept the "natural subordination" of a social order and political system that is not in their interests.[45] This ideological effort involves the aggregation of perceived interests across class lines, to be sure, but also the congealing of political formations across economic blocs and the coordination and fusing of cultural interests and values.[46] Never limited to public policy, ideological influence and normative loyalty is secured through political myths, national symbols, and rituals of participation far beyond fiscal or legal considerations.[47]

Recall that Fred Smith's self-serving political maneuvering was not illegal. Likewise, there is also nothing illegal about Apple setting up corporate fronts in Nevada to avoid paying taxes in California. In 2018, Facebook made $15 billion dollars in legal profit in Ireland, or roughly $10 million dollars for every Facebook employee based in Ireland. Although headquartered in New York City, Bristol Myers Squibb made nearly $5 billion of profit in Ireland, or about $7.5 million for each employee.[48] And GE is well within their legal rights to eliminate one-fifth of its workforce in the United States while accumulating $92 billion in offshore profit.[49] When the public becomes aware of such profits, corporations trot out a compelling defense: *They are obeying the law.* J. P. Morgan used the same defense one hundred years ago.[50] Corporations today deflect criticism by claiming to abide by the law and then urging the public to direct their wrath at a softer target: the federal government and its outdated tax code.[51] When tax documents were leaked showing how little Koch Industries paid in taxes, the Kochs' public relations team said that the company followed applicable tax laws.[52] Emmanuel Saez and Gabriel Zucman detailed a similar set of messages for Apple ("In Ireland and in every country where we operate, Apple follows the law and we pay all the taxes we owe") and Nike ("Nike fully complies with tax regulation"). When the CEO of Google was accused of avoiding his taxes, he said, "We encourage the OECD to actually solve these issues."[53]

Legal protection reveals a further distinction between democratic oligarchy and kleptocracy. Street criminals fear the police, but oligarchs rest easy because they are legally protected.[54] Oligarchic influence remains legal because oligarchs can recruit and fund compliant political candidates, influence the media, and punish states and local governments that are considering stronger regulation by threatening to relocate their operations.[55] The rent-seeking efforts of the oligarchic are also built atop a firm foundation of campaign contributions and political lobbying.[56] Lobbying and campaign contributions are legal. The First Amendment guarantees the right "to petition the Government for a redress of grievances." But lobbying and campaign contributions also reflect how the government advances the discrete interests of the ultra-rich by helping to siphon resources away from productive economic investments to zero-sum political victories benefiting a tiny slice of wealthy Americans.[57] Individual Uber drivers cannot afford lobbying services. Koch Industries can.[58]

The assumed analytic separation between the state and the market, and the economic and the political, is one reason oligarchy is poorly conceptualized in public conversations.[59] The ontology of the modern economy is often described as an ideological axis where folks on the political Right believe the social and economic conditions will allow individuals to make rational economic decisions; all the state needs to do is to maintain a level playing field so that economic actors can compete to maximize profits and accumulate resources.[60] As a result, what I describe as the oligarchic dimensions of American liberal democracy are left undertheorized, and the spatial and temporal positionality of the state is neglected.[61] This depiction of the state communicates an absence of rhetorical agency and positions the immense potential of the state outside rhetorical boundaries.[62] In turn, public conversation ends up focused on demarcating where the market ends and where the state begins or describing "interventions" in the market by autonomous governing mechanisms.[63] But portraying the government and market as being in opposition is as misguided as assuming "swim meet" is the opposite of "swimming pool," according to Matthew Stewart.[64] Likewise, "free market" and "unfettered" are not synonymous. Just as a free country can have criminal laws, a market economy can have social spending and robust regulations.[65] If words have consequences, we must take seriously the implications of this analytic separation, because, as Kenneth Burke wrote, "A yielding to the form prepares for assent to the matter identified with it."[66]

Conclusion

The case study chapters are organized to feature a rhetorical analysis of one rhetor. However, the focus of the analysis transcends one singular person in one singular historical moment. Influential rhetors emerge by knowing and appealing to our existing passions and prejudices.[67] Going forward, the focus of each chapter is on what Gunn describes as "relationships, on the connections between bodies, on the relation between publics and personae, on the links between relations among people and the forces of production (e.g., technology), and on the bond that an electorate imagines between itself and its leaders (a fantasy with consequences)."[68] The case study chapters are arranged chronologically and historically, beginning with Herbert Spencer in the 1850s and ending with Tucker Carlson in the 2020s. Each represents kairotic resonance, appropriate for a discrete historical moment.[69] But each rhetor also represents a genealogical development of oligarchic argument across time and space, reflecting larger systematic findings lending insight into deeper patterns of human connection and pattern recognition. For example, the broad scope, from Spencer to Carlson, will allow for the examination of fits and starts, oligarchic arguments, and anti-oligarchic reactions reflected in the pragmatic public policy implications for antitrust law during the Gilded Age, Civil Rights legislation, tax policies, funding for public schools, geopolitical relationships, property tax policy, and the state's willingness to use violence.

In the next chapter, I focus on defining and operationalizing democratic oligarchy as a vehicle for inductive theory building. Toward that end, I begin by positioning oligarchy's etymology in relation to democratic political theory. I do so by positioning public oligarchic arguments and policy within what Gunn calls the "ceaselessly and unrelentingly constituting [of] context."[70] I do not set out to uncover a set of political and cultural solutions to redress the pernicious impact of oligarchy on American democracy. I am a rhetorician, and in the spirit of immanent critique, my scope is narrower.[71] I focus on text and context, and argument and affect, to describe a political economy eluding tidy classification. While I leave it to more qualified scholars, activists, and policy wonks to detail the pragmatic alternative to oligarchy, I do employ the critical insights of rhetorical studies to better understand how we name, describe, and theorize our modern political economy. I turn to those critical insights now.

1

The Rhetoric of Democratic Oligarchy

DEMOCRATIC OLIGARCHY IS ATTRACTIVE TO WEALTHY ELITES BECAUSE it affirms the simplest, oldest, and most influential exercise in moral psychology: the rhetorical justification of selfishness. Far more interesting, then, is to consider why ordinary Americans whose lives are made more difficult by democratic oligarchy are attracted to it. To that end, I begin this chapter by putting democratic oligarchy in conversation with other voices exploring why people support ideas and policies at odds with their interests.

An Imperfect Synthesis

On the surface, democratic oligarchy's popular resonance contradicts what Gershberg and Illing call a "folk theory of democracy," defined by governing institutions oriented toward maximizing equality, universalizing inclusion, and the perfect synthesis between the interests of ordinary citizens and their elected leaders.[1] According to the folk theory of democracy, exclusion, inequality, and imperfect synthesis are incongruous deviations from democracy's telos, usually caused by some confluence of mass ignorance and ideological manipulation.[2] Scholars and public intellectuals often approach the political Right's sustained capacity to attract the support of middle- and working-class Americans from this perspective, such as in-depth studies of Kansas voters, evangelical Christians, the Tea Party, and lately, Donald J. Trump.[3]

In his 2004 book, *What's the Matter with Kansas*, Thomas Frank details how politicians in Kansas moved voters from reliable partisans of the New Deal to the conservative camp by featuring conservative values on the campaign trail, and then once in office, smashing the welfare state, reducing the taxes of corporations and the wealthy, and leaving a "a working-class movement that has done incalculable, historic harm to working-class people."[4] Frank takes as axiomatic that the duped Kansas voter and the man in the bread line weeping for the man lounging on his yacht reflect an "ideological triumph."[5] Frank drew the ideological conquest far beyond Kansas, pointing out that "the mystery of America" is the historical shift urging conservatives to erupt in revolt and call for more of the deregulation, privatization, and laissez-faire policies that caused their ruination in the first place.[6] In his more recent book, *Pity The Billionaire*, Frank also details conservatism's "dalliance with error" and decries the millions of Americans "increasingly separated from social reality."[7] More than deception alone, Frank writes, the Right has met its goals "by offering an idealism so powerful it clouds its partisans' perceptions of reality."[8] Frank deploys a set of brainwashing metaphors to illustrate his point, describing Glenn Beck's rhetoric as "like something from a brainwashing session as Lubyanka," the "lunacy of the rejuvenated Right," the "funhouse mirror of contemporary conservatism," and the "bald hypocrisy" of rhetors like Paul Ryan, which "should be obvious to anyone with an Internet connection."[9]

Rhetorical scholars also feature ideological manipulation in the political Right, including Jeremy Engels, who suggested most Kansans "think that when they vote Republican, they are resisting dominant regimes of power, that they are being subversive to the welfare state and the errors of big government." Although not bad people, Engels writes, Kansans are mistaken in their political loyalty.[10] Ralph Cintron faults the "loss of rational powers and clear-headedness" for the inability to notice the oppressive conditions that come with fetishizing democracy.[11] Paul Johnson describes a rhetorical form in which "conservatives have engineered an end-run around the tensions of liberal democratic life" allowing the Right to run away from the contradictions inherent in their political philosophy. Following Johnson's "end-run" football metaphor, it seems that instead of running between the tackles and openly confronting the oppressive implications of regressive tax policies and corrupting campaign finance laws, conservatism would rather evade the truth by running toward the sidelines. Johnson explores the rise of the Tea Party after the 2008 economic recession as an illustration of elite ideological conquest. Because mainstream media framed the Tea Party as an "electorally influential grassroots movement primarily concerned with an overreaching, fiscally irresponsible federal government," many Tea Party supporters were left ignorant of the influence of wealthy oligarchs on the movement, such as the Mercer and Koch families, along with well-resourced organizations like

FreedomWorks and Americans for Prosperity. In particular, Rick Santelli is revealed to be a carnival barking huckster representing ordinary Americans when, in fact, he was a member of the financial elite.[12] Johnson describes cynical attempts by Tea Party rhetors to "spoof public reason's thin capacities" to notice such incongruous influence.[13] Johnson also describes being "gobsmacked" that the Tea Party's shocking and preposterous argument worked.[14]

Because rhetoric is the key to enlightening ordinary Americans, it is understandable rhetorical scholars are keen on explaining democracy's imperfect synthesis as a product of ignorance and ideological manipulation. Drawing on the counter-hegemonic capacities of rhetorical criticism, rhetoricians are charged with educating and emancipating the masses, and—following Plato's allegory—venturing down into the darkness to unchain the imprisoned and lead them to the light.[15] To be sure, democratic oligarchy requires an ideological conquest marked by gathering the consent of the governed by convincing the public they are unfit to govern. Power concentrations are then justified based on the distinct capacities of the ruling elite, in sharp contrast with the deficiencies of ordinary people.[16] And yet, the oligarchy features of American democracy could not constitute a massive community for this long through ignorance and ideological manipulation alone.[17] The intensity, loyalty, and durability of democratic oligarchy points to a reservoir of rhetorical energy independent of, or at least incommensurate with, ignorance and manipulation.

Theorizing that reservoir begins with exploring the folk theory of democracy's conceptual flaws. From the ancient Greeks to the framers of the US Constitution, political theorists have understood that "the people" cannot be reduced to a referential and preexisting audience—as if every citizen were waiting together in the town square to elect politicians to perfectly synthesize their interests into law. Further, for more practical reasons, a healthy representative democracy could not be established based on the singular coherence of "the people." A perfectly synthetic democracy cannot guarantee stability against the threat of disorder, and thus, maximizing equality and universal inclusion has never been democracy's highest priority.[18]

Although democracy announces a belonging, it is always partial and incomplete.[19] Not everyone gets to belong, gets to vote, or gets to be a citizen. No matter how permissive, democracies target some for exclusion and others for inclusion according to agreed-upon standards of citizenship, age, loyalty, mental fitness, and criminal history.[20] As a result, democratic governments constrain the influence of the people by codifying power concentrations into minoritarian institutions, governing bodies, and formal constitutions.[21]

In Book 4 of the *Politics*, Aristotle explored who should control democratic institutions and why.[22] Aristotle assumed not everyone was qualified to deliberate, participate, and legislate. He was worried that diffusing too much political power would promote the mediocrity of the middling masses. He deemed it "an impossibility" for a city controlled by the non-elite to lead a "well-ordered government."[23] The rule of the "most numerous," according to Aristotle, was not unlike a despotic and tyrannical monarchy, because "both exercise despotic control over the better classes." The result, Aristotle feared, was a legislative assembly responsive to the whims of the multitudes and not the law.[24]

The framers of the US Constitution affirmed elite suspicion of universal representation. Alexander Hamilton expressed little interest in synthesizing popular references with political leadership, writing to George Washington, "It is long since I have learned to hold popular opinion of no value."[25] Ron Chernow describes Hamilton as "frightened by a sense of the fickle and fallible nature of the masses."[26] John Adams also assumed that it was delusional to look to "the people" as an infallible source of political wisdom.[27] "The fundamental Article of my political Creed," Adams wrote, "is that Despotism, or unlimited Sovereignty, or Absolute Power is the same in a popular Assembly, an Aristocratic Counsel, an Oligarchic Junto and single Emperor."[28] Any political system denying the obvious differences in individual human capacities would be built atop a "school of folly," Adams wrote. Inequality was humankind's natural condition. In a letter to Thomas Jefferson, Adams wrote, "Inequalities of Mind and Body are so established by God Almighty in the constitution of Human Nature that no Art or policy can ever plain them down to a level."[29] Adams also wrote that he had "never read Reasoning more absurd, Sophistry more gross in proof of Athanasian Creed, or Transubstantiation, than the subtle labors to demonstrate the Natural Equality of Mankind."[30] Adams warned against believing that "all men [are] born with equal powers and faculties and equal influence in society," calling that a "gross a fraud as ever was practiced by monks, by Devils, by Brahmins, by priests of the immortal Lama, or by the self-styled philosophers of the French Revolution."[31] He chose his examples intentionally, writing shortly after the French Revolution's bloody mass violence in the streets, executions at the guillotine, and the resulting rise of a despotic Napoleon Bonaparte.[32] But Adams was also an ambivalent American revolutionary, unsettled equally by the oppression of British rule and the disorder of the rebellious young nation.[33]

Although public conversations tend to unite "equality" with the framers, the Constitution actually contains significant guardrails against democracy.[34] The framers meant to force national majorities through a confluence of fractured authority and to mediate—even stymie—the will of ordinary people as much as possible. Without such restraints, unwise decision-making from the masses was not just possible—it was likely.[35] The durability of the US Constitution can be traced back to striking the right balance in the framers' faith in liberty for ordinary people but skepticism for mob rule, which is best contained by "an ironclad system of checks and balances," Chernow writes.[36]

Democracy and Symbolic Consent

Apart from the folk theory of democratic governance, political theorists have explored how the ruling elite can concentrate power without resorting to coercion and violence.[37] The consent of the middle classes was vital, because Aristotle assumed elite influence needed to coexist with democracy's arithmetic dominance. In other words, Aristotle knew a healthy democracy would always have an arithmetic problem. If the elite could not reconcile their numerical disadvantage, Aristotle wrote, then lofty "pronouncements about the constitution" would "entirely miss the points of practical utility."[38] A sound constitution and just laws were meaningless if public consent could not be gathered. "To have good laws enacted but not obey them does not constitute well-ordered government," Aristotle wrote. Consent must first be gathered when the constitution was created. Then consent must be gathered continuously as laws are enacted. Aristotle focused his advice on gathering public consent, suggesting that lawgivers "making the laws of an oligarchical character must keep the middle class in view." The elite could overcome the arithmetic problem and gather public consent through violent suppression. But Aristotle said it was better to gain consent through the symbolic exchange of meaning and influence.[39] Symbolic consent is inherent to democratic oligarchy, as universal suffrage has expanded since Aristotle's day and gathering the people's consent through public argument determines political rule.

Aristotle made the charge clear for power-hungry elites. He counseled, "bring forward an organization of such a sort that men will easily be persuaded and be able in the existing circumstances to take part in it." Aristotle recognized that every form of constitutional government would require "persuading people to accept it." The framers of the US Constitution agreed. Alexander Hamilton in Federalist #22 wrote, "The fabric of American empire ought to rest on the solid basis of the consent of the people."[40]

"Ought to" is the operative phrase. Hamilton was arguing for the moral superiority of consent-based governance while at the same time conceding democracy's indeterminacy. Like Aristotle, Hamilton conceded there are other ways to govern, including the exercise of raw political power. The moral underpinning in the phrase "ought to" points to the rhetorical spadework needed to gather the consent of the people while also limiting their power.

Elite intellectual, social, moral, and cultural superiority has historically underpinned the rhetorical justification for concentrating power.[41] Oligarchic consent depends on the belief that the wealthy's transcendent superiority ought to allow disproportionate influence on the political process.[42] Plato argued for a quasi-dictatorship in which the wisest were trained to rule over the lowly masses.[43] In other words, Aristotle was not alone in believing the rich were superior. In Alexander Hamilton's political vision, superior elites should be leading the inferior masses.[44] Hamilton pointed to wisdom, substance, and experience as qualities that should elevate some men over others.[45] Hamilton assumed elite superiority merited special treatment, writing of the rich, "That valuable class of citizens forms too important an organ of the general weal not to claim every practicable and reasonable exemption and indulgence."[46] In his famous Federalist #10, James Madison's starting point for political governance was that "people possess different natural endowments."[47] Madison added ambition to the recipe in Federalist #51, hoping power hierarchies could be justified as we "let ambition counter ambition."[48] In the nineteenth century, Edmund Burke also highlighted ambition as the quality by which superior men are elevated to their appointed place, holding together law and nature against a "world of madness, discord, vice, confusion, and unavailing sorrow."[49] In the early twentieth century, uplift suasion featured morality and education as the qualities of superior Black American leaders required to lift (supposedly) inferior Black Americans by reaching down and pulling up everyone else.[50]

While it makes sense why the rich believe their superiority should translate into economic and political influence, the widespread acceptance of elite superiority as a rationale for unequal political representation has long troubled political theorists, because the implications for governance so often lead to unrest, disorder, and violence. Put another way, elite rule is justified by promising to maintain order and stability; but as the historical record has shown, when elite rule causes unjustified power concentration, the masses will revolt. For example, John Adams worried the relentless pattern of history reflected in the French Revolution, along with the stagnant British aristocracies Adams reviled, highlighted a basic human orientation toward entrenched inequality, and Adams assumed inequality of wealth led inevitably to inequality of political power. America was not to be an exception. "There is no special providence of Americans," Adams wrote in *Defence*, noting that "Riches Grandeur, and Power will have the same effect upon Americans as it has upon European minds."[51]

For a venerated Founding Father, Adams's rhetoric is jarring and scandalous. But Adams understood the psychology of wealth and power better than Jefferson and Hamilton.[52] "In every society known to man, an aristocracy has risen up in the course of time, consisting of a few rich and honorable families who have united against both the people and the first magistrate," Adams wrote in *Defence*.[53] Adams went further by connecting the dots between aristocracy and oligarchy. Like "gravity in nature" or "the current in a river," material wealth in liberal democracies exert relentless pressure toward oligarchy, he wrote.[54] Rich Americans would be driven to acquire and display ever larger amounts of wealth.[55] The very-human desire to be loved and to be noticed would motivate political and economic stratification just like the European aristocrats the new nation was defining itself against.[56] Anticipating Thorstein Veblen's doctrine of "conspicuous consumption," Adams thought that without European titles, America's "moneyed aristocracy" would be prone to flamboyant displays of extravagant wealth to set themselves apart from their inferiors.[57] Maybe the American aristocracy would be based on wealth and not inherited bloodlines, but Adams worried that would be a distinction without a difference.

Adams anticipated the structural inequalities at the root of the first and second Gilded Ages. He also turned out to be prescient in linking aristocracy and oligarchy. He predicted that the ultra-rich in America would be motivated by the same logic that the ultra-rich everywhere else were: the elemental passions and primal instincts of European plutocratic aristocrats would create an oligarchic ruling class, mobilizing economic power to influence politics.[58]

Strong Government, Strong Institutions

As a countervailing force, Federalist framers like Hamilton and Adams proposed a robust federal government and a strong executive branch. Adams rejected Jefferson's concerns about centralized authority, evinced most vividly in the image of a corrupt and out-of-touch monarchy. Such concerns were misguided, Adams thought; the historical record actually showed that centralized branches of a strong government were the best defense against oligarchic inevitability.[59] Adams sought to attract competent citizens—apart from selfish gain—by enhancing the honorific status of public servants. Historian Joseph Ellis wrote that Adams, as vice president, was widely mocked for proposing that the American president be addressed as "His Majestic Mightiness."[60] But such pufferies affirmed Adams's anti-oligarchic aims because he wanted to attract and honor competent public service without relying on material rewards.

Not long after George Washington, John Adams, and Alexander Hamilton led the Federalists to victory over the anti-federalists, it became clear that strong centralized institutions were vital for preserving liberty and order, including a central bank, funded debt, federal taxation systems, and a customs service.[61] Adams's faith in the anti-oligarchic capacities of a strong federal government can be seen in American liberal democracy in the twentieth century. With some qualifications, it turned out that massive economic stratification and its concurrent political machinations could be restrained by a centralized federal government curbing the excesses of an oligarchic class.[62] Chernow detailed how Hamilton, in particular, bound together the country during the early years in a way Thomas Jefferson or James Madison never could because their abhorrence of centralized authority would turn revolutionary utopianism into perpetual unrest and disorder.[63]

A healthy democracy can counterbalance the gravitational pull of oligarchic power when it is controlled by public servants willing to police the economic and political boundaries.[64] The state assumes the unique legal and political capacity to influence and control the means of production, inducing investment and employment through incentives to workers and those who control productive assets.[65] Forms of representations in American democracy include universal suffrage, individual rights, the separation of power, formal constitutions, freedoms of expression, equal protection under the law, an independent judiciary, and the public character of deliberation and legislation forcing compromises from oligarchic-oriented elites.[66] Competition, antagonism, and compromise are magnified in the class struggles between workers and capital, with labor using their arithmetic advantages against capitalists' ability to leverage economies of scale and "counteract worker's organizations by concentrating and centralizing capital."[67] As a result, with the assistance of strong economic interventions, legal arrangements, and the tapping of the entire society's productive capacity, the state can shape public policy in the interests of ordinary Americans.

At its best, American democracy is marked by competent governmental administration.[68] Barrow describes "islands of administrative expertise in

American federal democracy" that expanded and improved social programs in the interests of ordinary Americans during the mid-twentieth century.[69] The caricature of the buffoonish federal employee or the pernicious deep-state conspirator marks our public conversations, but that caricature contradicts the reality of so many Americans filling administrative roles of professional expertise to influence government interventions against the interests of the elite.[70]

These islands of administrative expertise and technical competence reflect a contingent power struggle. American judges, for example, often reflect their own class origins by ruling disproportionately in favor of the interests of the affluent.[71] But there are also wide variations, including the presence of nondominant classes within the state apparatus affecting the content of public policy in the direction of non-elites. The lessons drawn from American judges, as a representative anecdote, must be tempered by the presence of nondominant classes in governmental administration who fulfill a sense of democratic purpose legitimating a desire to use the state to act in the interests of ordinary Americans.[72]

Ultimately, American democracy has no predetermined telos. As Engels writes, "There is nothing objective about how societies are structured, about who is on top and who is on bottom, about who is rich and who is poor, about who is included and who is excluded, about who can speak and who can't."[73] Democracy is a hope, a throw of the dice, or as Engels puts it, "democracy is a wager" because one cannot know how democratic politics will turn out.[74] Democracy is not a goal but a means, a potentiality, never secured or determined.[75] And thus, we cannot expect that the power concentrations produced by elite influence will always be mediated by funneling power to a strong federal government. Instead, the form and function of the state is determined by the struggle between the interests of ordinary Americans and the interests of elites.[76]

Elite influence on the form and function of the state lends insight into how majoritarian democracies can transform into totalitarian states, without relying on violence and coercion, by seizing on the populist strands existing within a democratic culture of communication to justify oligarchic concentrations of power and wealth.[77] In such situations, power is concentrated by producing an apolitical citizen-subject suspicious of collective action—a citizen who works hard, obeys the law, pays their taxes, and votes with their wallet but is otherwise politically acquiescent.[78] Apathy allows wealthy elites to then compensate for their numerical disadvantages through political interventions reorienting the state toward their interests. Frustrated by an ineffectual, corrupt state, ordinary Americans are then drawn to greater levels of apathy. It's just not worth it. Major transformations in American democracy during the mid-twentieth century have been traced back to this depoliticized subject.[79] Engels developed the term "resentment" to explain the confluence of apathy and anger as frustrated citizens are encouraged to shout, rage, and vent, but always within controlled forms—like an overzealous bumper car driver at the county fair.[80] Democratic activism is left toothless, the demos left fractured, and the public's numerical strength left weakened, producing in the end "widespread feelings of powerlessness," Engels writes.[81]

How do the conceptualizations of the form and function of the state allow us to observe oligarchy in America? Taken together, the historical record highlights how ordinary Americans can leverage democratic indeterminacy to align the form and function of their state with their material interests. Likewise, the immense resources of the ultra-rich can overcome their numerical disadvantages and shape the form and function of the state against the interests of ordinary people. Left undertheorized, however, is how and why ordinary people affect the form and function of the state, through democratic means, to concentrate power and wealth into the hands of the ultra-rich. The rhetoric of democratic oligarchy intervenes in this conceptual void.

Rhetorical Invention

If public arguments do not exist in a vacuum, rhetorical invention is the conceptual tool for translating that cliché into a fresh intellectual exploration. Beyond a vacuum, potent and resonant public arguments are *enlivened* within a rhetorical encounter, according to Sharon Crowley.[82] Drawing on Aristotle's formative definition of rhetoric, Crowley suggests that critics display the capacity to observe the available means of persuasion by considering how arguments are interpreted within discrete temporal and communal contexts. Taken together, Aristotle's definition of rhetoric and Crowley's contextual considerations of rhetorical invention carve out a vital role for the critic of public arguments, not just the rhetor. If the rhetor behind the podium, on the stage, or on the screen is akin to a factory manufacturing public arguments, then rhetorical invention is the tool the critic employs to analyze what arguments are selling and why, once they enter the marketplace. For example, consider how the term "justice" functions as an influential public argument in the rhetoric of democratic oligarchy. In a vacuum, justice is the mechanism for achieving a mutually agreeable and consensus-based social order in a world marked by dissensus and conflict.[83] Put more directly—but still in a vacuum—justice is getting what you deserve. But as an *enlivened* source of rhetorical invention, "getting" and "you" and "deserve" are each complex and textured symbols, interpreted in relation to pre-existing expectations and the unsettling subjectivity produced by assuming anyone gets what they deserve.[84] As Osnos asks, "Who, among us, deserves what we have—good or bad? How much are we, any of us, in control of our lives? And how did our collective choices lead us here?"[85]

Aristotle answered these big questions by assuming the rulers over human affairs should be based on merit, virtue, and wisdom so that the demos can be protected from the chaotic and unsuppressed whims of public opinion.[86] But in *Aristotle's Politics*, Garver highlights how a set of outdated and bigoted assumptions should remind us that Aristotle did not have American liberal democracy in mind when he wrote the *Politics*.[87] As we all do, Aristotle made judgments in line with the prejudices of his historical moment.[88] Aristotle reflected the elitism and bigotry of his day, leaving his symbolic rationales stale and unconvincing. For example, he drew an archaic causal link across political power, wealth, and "good birth." Consequently, he suggested the arithmetic problem endemic to democratic oligarchy could be redressed, and oligarchic political influence justified, by adopting the governing logic of a successful monarchy and concentrating power "based on the outstanding superiority of the man who is king." Accordingly, appeals to justice have long been put into action by monarchies based on the divine right of kings, and then later, patrician elites like William F. Buckley, Charles Koch, and Peter Thiel, who were raised to assume their "good birth," good breeding, and good bloodlines justified the rule of men like them over everyone else.[89] Buckley, Koch, and Thiel are not historical anomalies. Following Aristotle's definition of rhetoric, the divine right of kings and "good birth" were commonly *available* as temporal and communal resources for constructing arguments. Appeals to virtue, intelligence, industriousness, and courage in combat were also markers of one's capacity to rule.

Approaching democratic oligarchy from a rhetorical perspective complements the efforts of political and sociological theorists to conceptualize the form and function of the state by offering the critic a discrete set of inventional resources for analyzing the available means of persuasion undergirding democratic oligarchy. To that end, I explore three specific inventional resources undergirding democratic oligarchy.

Naturalism

In the following pages, the reader will notice how the rhetoric of democratic oligarchy features the accumulation of evidence uncovering a divine, objective, and causal link between *getting* and *deserving*. If justice is getting what you deserve, then you must deserve what you get; or else you do not deserve it. Democratic oligarchy pursues justice according to natural, divine, and objective appeals to justice, deservedness, and merit. Democratic oligarchy floats above emotional subjectivity, partisanship, and the tribal appeals so central to fascist power concentration so that, in the end, audience subjectivity exchanges contempt for the elites outside of one's social group for admiration and emulation. After all, there are no unearned privileges in a world marked by natural justice.

Naturalism imposes order on chaos. We are subject to nature's laws and, thus, positioned as passive, referential, and reactive subjects. Naturalism functions as a source of rhetorical invention, according to Kenneth Burke, as a "body of knowledge concerning 'causal' relationships [is] applied by analogy to the charting of natural phenomena."[90] Such bodies of knowledge function as rhetorical aquifers formed by the sediments of law, legality, and other forensic material, Burke wrote.

Drawing its public arguments from the language of Alexander von Humboldt, Thomas Malthus, and Charles Darwin, naturalism serves a sensemaking function by offering a vocabulary for stratification and power concentration taken from the unquestionable world of natural law. On the surface, the natural world's complexity, cruelty, and violence is papered over in the image of a quiet mountain stream or birds singing in a tree. Likewise, social stratification is mediated in the tranquility of voters casting their ballots on election day, presidential inauguration speeches, and the minutes taken from the annual meeting of the Federalist Society. *Americans do not want their president wearing fatigues.* But at the same time, the tranquility of democratic power concentrations belies a cutthroat struggle not unlike a Darwinian jungle.

Naturalism points to a relentless battle. Plants and animals limit each other's numbers in a long, continued contest for space and nourishment. Seeds, eggs, and spawn are produced in huge quantities, but only a fraction grow into maturity.[91] The natural world is not oriented toward maximizing equality or universal participation. Social stratification is no different. Conforming to temporal and communal expectations, the power concentrations and social stratification that can appear orderly and tranquil distract from the rotting carcasses of the unfit (mostly) kept out of view.

Along a causal chain, individuals are elevated according to a concrete set of material metrics. As a symbol system, economic wealth is the end result of a Darwinian contest sorting and stratifying the winners and losers.[92] Although the natural world is beyond human influence, democratic oligarchy relies on a discrete symbol system to show others the link between their deservedness and their rewards (akin to seventeenth-century Calvinist-Puritans using wealth to symbolize their divine standing without assuming they could influence an omnipotent and unchanging God). The overwhelming power of the natural world would not allow the unworthy to possess material rewards—at least not for long. And so, private property, electoral victories, the capacity for coercion, and the ability to influence the political system will emerge in the forthcoming pages as symbolic reflections of one's justified capacity to rule.

In the following chapters, the reader will also notice how the application of abstract natural discourses can be adjusted to meet the particular demands of social stratification—what Kenneth Burke called "casuistry."[93] In the nineteenth and early twentieth century, for example, naturalism relied on appeals to the divine, the mystical, and the mysterious. Later, as scientific epistemologies gained widespread acceptance, naturalism came to rely on the objective, disinterested, and empirical. Naturalism underpins this transformation.

The rhetors in my case study chapters assume the persona of an objecting truth teller floating above the fray. They do not use beaker jars or wear lab goggles, but their Nobel Prizes and computer models symbolize the discrete communal and temporal condition of a post-Darwinist understanding of both the natural and the social. The unfalsifiability of oligarchy's naturalism and the undeniable fact that the world holds no homeostatic orientation toward justice is mediated by the epistemological privilege that comes with articulating belief in naturalism. In other words, naturalism offers community members a political, legal, cultural, and economic interpretive mechanism for making sense of power concentrations. What's more, as a source of rhetorical invention, naturalism offers community members a vocabulary for translating the struggle of the natural world into the struggle of the social world.

Realism

If naturalism informs how the social order is held in place, then realism explains the mental faculty by which humans perceive a social order marked by clear rules, fixed meaning, and objective truth.[94] Realism is an epistemological philosophy defining truth against the Enlightenment's facile optimism, unbounded confidence in human progress, and cheap egalitarianism where the inferior no longer genuflect to their bettors. But realism is not anti-intellectual. Realism is a republican epistemology, assuming knowledge is accessible to everyone, regardless of training or education. Realism assumes individuals have a natural right to liberty of conscience free from social constructions and human control. Consciousness is referential.[95] The economists, lawyers, engineers, and journalists I explore next do not create reality; they *discover* it by shining a light into the darkness.

Realism makes sense of complicated moral challenges by drawing on preexisting cognitive machinery. Realism need not be a cerebral weighing of complicated social and cultural variables. Realism is rapid, automatic, and intuitive.[96] In *The Righteous Mind*, Jonathan Haidt ties the automatic, affective, and unconscious revulsion one might feel when faced with excrement or vultures to the automatic, affective, and unconscious faculty of human moral judgment. Realism activates moral outrage in a similar way and is capable of affecting a similar moral reaction in an individual faced with an incompetent authority figure taking their hard-earned money and giving it to a "non-producing, welfare collecting, single mother, crack baby producing future democrat," as Haidt puts it.[97]

The social implications in Haidt's example point to how realism functions also as a source of rhetorical invention, influencing political, legal, cultural, and even economic sense making. In the following case studies, realism will draw rhetorical strength from right-wing populist rhetoric. But the rhetors I examine are not unhinged zealots like Joseph McCarthy, Bull Connor, or George Wallace. Nor do the rhetors I examine resemble twenty-first-century populist political leaders like Rodrigo Duterte, Narendra Modi, or Jair Bolsonaro. Instead, the rhetors are highly erudite, well-educated, and intellectually accomplished scholars and thought leaders. Even so, they are each willing to use populism as a rhetorical tactic for combating the anti-oligarchy features of liberal democracy.[98]

Realism will also draw rhetorical strength from a vein of American Protestant Christianity in which the natural order is made vivid in the rhetorical dimensions of daily life through God's clear, objective, and timeless plan. But in an illustration of the republican accessibility of realism, God's plan is observable, without the need for formal religious instruction or a doctorate in theology. Realism's equality of epistemological access is affirmed in the history of Protestant Christianity defining itself against an elite priesthood using theological exclusivity to maintain control.[99]

CHAPTER 1

Finally, realism will draw rhetorical strength from American free market capitalism. Broadly, the American economy is sprawling and complicated; but locally, every American is supposed to be able to control their personal economic status because the American free enterprise system rewards those willing to conform to a discernible and accessible set of economic truths, including the law of supply and demand, market competition, and self-interest. When unadulterated, free markets assume a divine capacity to judge human worth according to God's plan and nature's laws. In turn, the American working class and poor are urged to cheer for the material wealth of their bosses as a divine, meritorious, and natural extension in the Great Chain of Being and to throw off the tyranny of closing the carried interest loophole as if they were throwing tea into the Boston Harbor.[100]

In the following case studies, the reader will notice a distinct oligarchic rhetoric produced by realism's capacity to reconcile elite superiority and epistemological accessibility. Realism reconciles this paradox through a bold, vernacular, and entertaining rhetoric. Each rhetor approaches democracy as a spectacle. Each rhetor is capable of turning performance into power and power into performance.[101] Each rhetor is a gifted translator, operating competently in the liminal space between the ignorance of the masses and the rarefied air of standing on the edge of Truth. And each rhetor is willing to leverage indeterminacy to cloak power acquisition in democratic trappings.[102] The reader will also notice how the rhetoric of oligarchic realism antagonizes political and social institutions by constituting a community in opposition to mainstream sources of institutional authority.

And yet, the community produced by realist rhetoric is not held in high regard by oligarchy's rhetors. Realism constitutes an audience familiar with the elite vocabulary of scientists, economists, lawyers, and engineers. But realism also constitutes an audience defined against complexity, nuance, and sophistication. If the test of first-rate intelligence is the ability to function while holding opposing ideas in mind, the test of first-rate realism is the ability to discover which ideas should be rejected and construct an identity in relation to the remaining objective Truth.

Consequentialism

As a source of rhetorical invention, consequentialism functions inductively, emerging as a forceful feature of public argument after the material evidence of one's deservedness is made clear. Democratic oligarchy urges us to observe power hierarchies *and then* justify them. This temporal distinction is well suited to modern democratic governing systems lacking a predetermined telos, because democracy demands only open channels of communication. Public arguments begin not with the qualities of ruling elites but only after the superiority of elites is evinced. Then, public argument uncovers characteristics like merit, virtue, and ambition to justify stratified resource distribution and unequal political representation. During the early years of his presidency, Donald Trump responded to critics highlighting his mistakes with the consequentialist retort: "I'm the president and you're not."[103] The subtext was clear: Trump's electoral victory offered a priori justification for what seemed to be foolish decision-making. Likewise, Richard Nixon expressed a consequentialist interpretation when he told journalist David Frost his actions were subject to a different legal standard because "when the president does it . . . that means that it is not illegal."[104] Long before Nixon, Aaron Burr recommended Alexander Hamilton use his growing military power to demolish the US Constitution. When Hamilton declined, citing his own moral qualms with such an autocratic maneuver, Burr reassured him, "General, all things are moral to great souls."[105]

Beyond singular political figures, Ibram Kendi's efforts to conceptualize racism offers a fresh illustration of consequentialist rhetoric. According to Kendi, the fraught labels "racist" and "racism" can be clarified by focusing on the direct material outcomes of actions and policies, not on psychology or intent.[106] If a law or policy harms Black Americans, then it is racist. Notice the temporal distinction. As a historian, Kendi discovered that economic oppression preceded racial oppression. Categories like "Black" developed as a post-hoc tool to locate and justify cheap labor.[107] The rhetoric of democratic oligarchy follows a similar temporal logic. If impartial power hierarchies are assumed, then law and policy can be judged on their consequential capacity to reward the deserving and punish the undeserving. The countermajoritarian features of American democracy are justified accordingly.

Consequentialism helps clarify how identity markers like race, ethnicity, gender, and class are interpreted in the rhetoric of democratic oligarchy. The reader will notice how the forthcoming case study chapters feature a motley crew of grade-school dropouts and Nobel Prize winners, anti-Semites and Jews, ultra-rich industrial tycoons and media personalities speaking for the working class. Consequentialism binds these disparate rhetors into a constitutive community because, in the rhetoric of democratic oligarchy, identity markers like race, ethnicity, gender, religion, and socioeconomic class are portrayed to be distracting, ancillary, and inconsequential in comparison to raw power. At the same time, the reader will also notice how the rhetoric of democratic oligarchy is especially attractive to rich white men and their allies. I draw from Charles W. Mills's 1997 book *The Racial Contract* to explain why. Mills positions white supremacy as a dominant but "unnamed political system" structuring established norms for the differential distribution of material wealth and opportunities, benefits and burdens, and rights and duties in the United States. While Mills focuses on race, his deft application of "contract talk" to political systems informs the rhetorical value of consequentialism in a liberal democracy marked by appeals to post-racialism. Mills argues that the "great virtue" of social contract theory is its ability to "provide seemingly straightforward answers both to factual questions about the origins and workings of society and government and normative questions about the justification of socioeconomic structures and political institutions."[108] Historically, white supremacy was built upon the accepted assumption that the creation of society requires the intervention of white people, positioned as advanced sociopolitical beings who are uniquely qualified to take over and run social systems for the betterment not only of themselves but of all the inferior non-whites, who are childlike and incapable of self-rule. Consequentialism provides the material evidence for white supremacist rule, in relation to gender and socioeconomic privilege, and transforming the possibility of a fair society into a nonideal contract propping up an unjust, exploitative society, marked by distinct power hierarchies.

Taken together, naturalism, realism, and consequentialism allow the rhetoric of democratic oligarchy to engage with extant political and economic theory and also to light up the real character of the world we are living in, including the corresponding discursive limitations of the Right/Left vocabulary dominating public conversations.

The Form and Function of the Oligarchic State

The natural "body of knowledge" Kenneth Burke described emerges as a potent source of rhetorical invention, as it evolves into highly bureaucratized legal and political institutions reflecting and shaping sensemaking capacities about responsibility, charity, grace, and deservedness. Reflecting the contingency of the state, appeals to the natural world can be "seized casuistically for the protection of special interests," Burke wrote. The result is an almost unquestioned bureaucratized heuristic for making sense of unequal social stratification—efficiently, effortlessly, and completely. As an illustration, Burke showed how monastic religious orders rely on appeals to naturalism for deciding what should be considered heresy and what should be considered orthodoxy.[109] Secular institutions are also constructed and affirmed by appeals to the objective, telic, and the divine, but also apolitical, impersonal, incontestable vocabularies of the natural world.

The state and its bureaucracies, institutions, laws, and governing rationales are constructed and affirmed according to the state's capacity to conform to the temporal and communal expectations of democratic oligarchy. In sharp contrast to the folk theory of democratic equality and egalitarian majoritarianism, institutions are evaluated based on their capacity to deny the undeserving both equal representation and shared prosperity. Instead, the state is charged with channeling representation and resources to the deserving.[110] The state does not exist to maximize equality; it exists to maximize a particular climate of stratified power relations by ensuring the ordinary and unexceptional do not get what they do not deserve. Democratic oligarchy rejects state efforts to intervene on behalf of the disempowered. Affirmative action policies, progressive tax laws, and wealth redistribution efforts are anathema because they reward the unworthy. In other words, the state should not level the playing field because the playing field should not be level. Likewise, universal participation and equality maximization are consequentially unjust because they use the state to channel power and resources from the deserving to the undeserving and, thus, each represent irrational adulterations of the laws of nature. Rather than provide welfare, race-equity policies, or progressive tax laws ensuring the marginalized can compete, the state is charged with producing jungle-like conditions so the fit and strong can be revealed.[111]

Democratic oligarchy demands a selective allegiance to democratic state institutions, including majoritarian governance, the courts, and the market. For example, "the market" will be described in the following pages as an impersonal, natural, lawlike touchstone oriented toward justice and unaffected by human capriciousness.[112] The second-by-second fluctuations of bond yields and exchange rates are incomprehensible to most, but beneath the complexity there is wonder, innocence, and purity, affirmed by references to the law of supply and demand and "the gravity of market laws."[113] Like an earthquake or hurricane, human economic subjects are framed in the rhetoric of democratic oligarchy as passive, referential, and reactive. The market acts upon us—not the other way around. Economic markets offer an objective metric for evaluating winners and losers. As the market stratifies, the rhetoric of democratic oligarchy urges the state to let nature run its course because economic crises, recessions, and depressions are as unavoidable in the social world as natural disasters are in the physical world. Positioned in relation to familiar arguments from the political Right, democratic oligarchy rejects government bailouts for the undeserving losers, because the natural forces of competition need to be able to thin the herd and separate the strong from the weak.

And yet, democratic oligarchy demands a flexible pragmatism in response to the market and the state. With naturalism, consequentialism, and realism at the core, the rhetoric of democratic oligarchy diverges from the conventions of conservatism and libertarianism by supporting active and robust state interventions when the natural forces of the market look to be punishing the winners and rewarding the losers. A rhetoric of economic exceptionalism will emerge in the following pages to defend democratic oligarchy against accusations of self-serving inconsistency. Scholars have noted how the state's monopoly on violence, responsibility to enforce contracts, and ensure sound currency can casuistically stretch to also justify robust interventions into a free market on behalf of the ultra-rich.[114] Democratic oligarchy features a unique temporal extension of the rhetoric of exceptionalism. Democratic oligarchy affirms the market as a natural and impartial metric for human stratification, but importantly, it assumes the forces of competition have already sorted and ranked the winners and losers. The scoreboard is frozen, the referees have left the field, and the fans are going home.

To better understand how democratic oligarchy functions as a coherent governing logic, consider how the logic of exceptionalism again lights up incommensurate differences between democratic oligarchy and more familiar labels for the political Right, including conservatism and libertarianism. The conventional governing logics associated with the political Right are ill-suited to ensuring the impartial power hierarchies democratic oligarchy demands. Instead, democratic oligarchy constitutes a community oriented toward supporting state institutions that rank, stratify, and reward in accordance with the demands of natural law, including the Supreme Court, political lobbying, and influential think tanks. Such support can be questioned as conditional and selective, but according to its proponents, it is not arbitrary, capricious, or reductively self-serving.[115]

Democratic oligarchy will concede inconsistent and selective loyalty to majoritarian democracy and its institutions. But democratic oligarchy will reject the accusation that it is unprincipled by appealing to an alternative moral framework—a framework that cannot be understood through a folk theory of democratic governance. In a world oriented toward naturalism, there are no ethics of prudence or forbearance. Ethical behavior is measured by what one can get away with.[116] Nothing more. For example, the rhetoric of democratic oligarchy will display a counterintuitive, begrudging respect for anyone and anything that can acquire material resources—from entrepreneurial welfare queens creatively enriching themselves by manipulating the state to multinational corporations shifting their corporate home bases to Ireland to pay lower taxes. In sharp relief, the rhetoric of democratic oligarchy will direct its most vociferous approbation to class traitors like Franklin Roosevelt, Earl Warren, Ralph Nader, and Barack Obama. The material wealth of these class traitors indicates they have conformed to the demands of the natural world. And yet, they embody the epitome of injustice by betraying their class in their efforts to transfer wealth and power to the undeserving.

Conclusion

As I began the chapter suggesting, it is unsurprising elites would affirm an interpretive mechanism supporting their power and privilege. If the rhetoric of democratic oligarchy only attracted the rich, it would produce familiar governing systems akin to conventional forms of monarchy, aristocracy, or plutocracy. Instead, the *democratic* dimension of this project points to its conceptual incommensurability, as ordinary, non-elites are encouraged to articulate their belief in a governing logic causing self-negation, disempowerment, suffering, and pain. What's more, the rhetoric of democratic oligarchy circumscribes ignorance and ideological manipulation. The public is not urged to deny their suffering and pain; nor does the public deny their exclusion from majoritarian democracy or the imperfect synthesis between their material interests and the interests of ruling elites. Instead, suffering is an act of altruism in service to an ordered and more just society. Further, the rhetorical resonance is amplified by localized material suffering. Individuals gain entrance into a community marked by the confidence that they are suffering for the pursuit of justice.

In the forthcoming case study chapters, notice how democratic oligarchy urges a confident and secure subjectivity in the face of material suffering. The arithmetic advantages of majoritarian democracy are neutered, appeals to equality eschewed, and universal participation unmotivating, unnatural, and unjust. For the ruling elite, it is lonely at the top but also satisfying, because universal justice is not measured by mass appeal. And although it can be lonely at the bottom too, the community of the collective holds no appeal. It is better to be a hungry lone wolf than an ignorant sheep.

2

Survival of the Fittest and the Rhetoric of Herbert Spencer

IN 1859, CHARLES DARWIN'S *ON THE ORIGIN OF SPECIES* CHANGED HOW we talked about the natural world by introducing terms like "adaptation," "evolution," and "natural selection" into public conversations. For the first time, the natural world was conceptualized as an organic whole woven together "as with a thousand threads." Darwin's entangled bank emerged as a representative anecdote as he described different kinds of plants, birds, insects, and worms living in dependent concert. But beneath the tranquility of Darwin's entangled bank, he described a relentless battle for survival marked by "hourly carnage" of animals preying on each other. For plant seeds and turtle eggs alike, survival of a species depended on the overproduction of offspring and, concurrently, the demise of the weak and unfit, ultimately providing what Darwin described as a "positive check" on natural selection, adaptation, and evolution. Brushing cruelty aside, Darwin described a natural struggle for survival "produced by laws acting upon us."[1]

Far beyond the natural world, Darwin also affected how the public thought and spoke about economic and political institutions in the second half of the nineteenth century. *On the Origin of Species* evolved into a transcendent source of social, political, and economic sense making because it aligned with the changing conditions of the industrial age.[2] Before Darwin, economic activity was thought to be the result of top-down direction by monarchs and feudal lords—not individual effort or competitive enterprise. Further, as Benjamin Friedman notes in *Religion and the Rise of Capitalism*, most people thought it was both impossible and undesirable to improve one's general standard of living. Social norms did sanction buying and selling, and one could borrow and lend, as long as prices and interest rates did not alter economic standing. But the Darwinian focus on individual competition, effort, and ability prompted many to reject the idea that economic status was divinely fixed. Instead of the teeth and claws of Darwin's natural selection, economic competition hinged on individual ability, effort, and ambition.[3]

In this way, Darwinian discourse transcended the natural world because natural selection aligned with the growing influence of Adam Smith on market competition. Although *The Wealth of Nations* was published in 1776, Darwin's description of competition's positive check provided a natural analogy for Smith's approach to market competition. Smith argued that private initiative, for no other reason than to advance personal interest, could produce mutually beneficial outcomes for all involved—an assumption that had been circulating for decades but grew into the conceptual core of western economic thinking only after Darwin's natural selection began circulating in public conversations.[4] Smith assumed market competition could motivate individuals, households, and large industrial corporations to maximize their well-being by maximizing their profitability.[5]

As a coherent, lawlike force, Darwin's natural selection influenced the form and function of the state.[6] Accordingly, political and social institutions should also be reoriented toward delivering the maximum benefit to the broadest public interest. A confluence of natural, economic, and religious discourse is assumed to then shape the form and function of the state. Market competition regulates itself, in the end, to work toward the good. Thus, many assume a reoriented state would be marked by a lean, minimal state apparatus, standing back so that unrestricted market competition could allow the strong and free to compete because, following Darwin and Smith, we will all be better off.[7] As a result, the lean government of the political Right emerges as a sensible public policy outgrowth to the natural wonders of a free market.

However, that policy outgrowth reflects a profoundly un-Darwinian misreading. In the second half of the nineteenth century, it became clear that individual effort and ability meant little in terms of influencing economic standing, compared to the capacities of the state. The individual abilities and efforts that were assumed to dictate the material rewards of Darwinian competition were mediated by the acquisition of raw political power, including monopolies and trusts, the accumulation of physical capital, land rents, and international trade laws. New and pressing questions were raised about the form and function of the state in the supposedly lawlike market economy of Darwin and Smith. Ultimately, the political economy was a natural, unquestioned force exerting lawlike influence upon humans; wealth stratification was a natural consequence of the strong and free succeeding in open competition; and political power was a mechanism for ensuring just power concentrations.

And yet, democracy maintains the potential to limit economic Darwinism. On Darwin's entangled bank, the overproduced turtle eggs cannot influence the political arrangements of the surviving turtles because the overproduced eggs will not survive. In American democracy, both the losers and the winners get to vote. Further, the losers—by definition—can claim numerical representation over the winners. The paradox of democratic oligarchy emerges again here. Without the "hourly carnage" of Darwin's natural selection, how can the strong and fit mediate their numerical disadvantages to justify the confluence of economic and political power?

In this chapter, I argue that shortly after Darwin transformed how the public talked about the natural world, a British philosopher named Herbert Spencer advanced Darwinian language to transform how the public talked about liberal democracy. Spencer was a syncretic thinker who gained worldwide fame for combining psychology, metaphysics, sociology, and biology into an influential program of political advocacy infused with normative science.[8] More specifically, Spencer linked Charles Darwin's evolution and adaptation theory to the changing political and economic structures of the nineteenth century. In so doing, Spencer laid the foundation for a century of conceptual economic incongruity.

Although linked with small-government conservatism today, Spencer's mission in life is better understood as an effort to protect the evolutionary gains civilization had achieved by preventing ordinary people from influencing political structures. In other words, Spencer sought to keep an inferior majority from forcing its will on a superior minority.[9] Spencer can be understood as the catalyst at the center of that alchemy.

Nature Will Be Obeyed

Herbert Spencer was a serious, eclectic polymath from Derbyshire, England, with dark piercing eyes, a bald head, and a robust neck beard. He was rarely seen in public in anything but a tuxedo, and he was a companion to the most brilliant minds of his day, including John Stuart Mill and Thomas Henry Huxley. His biographer, Mark Francis, describes Spencer as a "quintessentially English thinker of the Victorian period." But Spencer was also idolized in the United States, where he claimed more followers than either Karl Marx or Charles Darwin.[10]

Herbert Spencer wrote during an era of economic expansion previously unimaginable in human history.[11] Scarce resources no longer defined the human condition. Instead, the just administration of wealth imbued political organizations with the new moral responsibility to dictate who gets what and how much. Michel Foucault shows how, during Spencer's historical moment, "the market" began to appear as a natural and spontaneous mechanism governing the biopolitical dimensions of modern life.[12] Since then, influential economic rhetors like Adam Smith have been used to create a version of free market capitalism pulling participants "toward particular identifications within the system and [wherein] the supply and demand of exchange mobilizes the fluctuating energies of specific actions," according to Catherine Chaput.[13] Smith's approach aligned with the economic growth of the nineteenth century, but his approach to market competition also benefited from a massive shift in religious thinking away from Calvinist predestination and depravity and toward the assumption that God wanted humans to be happy and would be pleased if we could improve our economic conditions.[14] Garver highlights the freshness of Adam Smith's approach by tracing a more deterministic view of economic conditions back to Aristotle's day, when many assumed that "it was simply a given that some people are wealthy and others poor."[15] Adam Smith's optimistic prospect of human progress must be understood in contrast to the Greeks and Romans, who conceived of human history "as the reverse of progress"; the Middle Ages who "saw human history as merely cycling between periods of advance and regression"; and especially the Renaissance period, which marked a return to the "classical belief that human history was a story of decline."[16] In other words, Adam Smith's market economy was the product of a complex confluence of scientific, religious, and Enlightenment thinking—not just the magical powers of persuasion detailed in *The Wealth of Nations*.[17] Here we return to Spencer because the "market" that Foucault and Chaput describe was also influenced as Darwinian theories became metaphors for structuring political institutions and social organizations far beyond biology.

Within this kairotic moment, Herbert Spencer synthesized sociological, religious, and political messaging in alignment with the emerging realities of scientific knowledge.[18] Because he was among the first generation of scholars who possessed an exclusively scientific explanation of the universe, Spencer had a distinct first-mover advantage.[19] Spencer popularized the assumption that natural and divine laws governed the material world. In an 1852 letter, Spencer wrote that understanding a "true theory of humanity" comes only from studying "it in the facts you see around you and in the general laws of life."[20] In an 1859 letter, Spencer wrote that a "want of knowledge . . . needs a scientific setting forth of all organic processes as come under ordinary physical laws."[21] More than an inquiry into a specific subject, Spencer described his "system of philosophy" as *synthetic* because it "recognizes each derivate law of force as a demonstrable corollary from the ultimate law, the Persistence of Force. It is synthetic as proceeding consciously to the interpretation of phenomena as caused by a co-operation of forces conforming to these derivative laws." He continued to describe his synthetic philosophy as "proceeding to deduce from the general of the redistribution of matter and motion the successive orders of concrete phenomena in their ascending complexities," and, ultimately, informing "in its conception of the Universe as objective, since it regards the progress of things which bring about evolution as being itself a synthesis—a reaching of more and more complex products through successive increments of modifications."[22] Notice in Spencer's argument how Darwin's influence is reflected, especially in the suggestion that all living things, including human species and everything in the animal kingdom, progress toward an unspecified future. Spencer amplified the divine, however, suggesting that progress was determined by one's capacity to follow the laws of nature—and God. God had given humans an invariable set of natural laws based on the balanced and organic forces of the universe, and nature will be obeyed.[23]

Spencer's vision of progress assumed widespread rhetorical potency through the development and circulation of his famous phrase: *survival of the fittest*, which he described as the end "product of the laws of evolution."[24] In his 1864 book *The Principles of Biology*, Spencer first introduced survival of the fittest with the following passage: "It cannot but happen that those individuals whose functions are most out of equilibrium with the modified aggregate of *external forces*, will be those to die; and that those will survive whose functions happen to be most nearly in equilibrium with the modified aggregate of *external forces*."[25] Spencer's rhetorical inventiveness stretched preexisting beliefs about natural, lawlike explanations for the social world with Darwinian language. Spencer adopted a consequentialist perspective, locating evidence of equilibrium in "the poverty of the incapable, the distresses that come upon the imprudent, the starvation of the idle, and those shoulderings aside of the weak by the strong." But how could we tell who is unfit, incapable, imprudent, idle, or weak? Spencer urged us to look at who was in poverty, distressed, starving, and being shouldered aside. Spencer took comfort in the detached objectivity his "laws of the universe" offered, pointing out, "We have unmistakable proof that throughout all past time, there has been a ceaseless devouring of the weak by the strong."[26]

Spencer did not soft-pedal the brutal implications of survival of the fittest, including the requisite ubiquity of human suffering, pain, and death.[27] But he reframed suffering, pain, and death with new visions of Darwinian adaptation. Recalcitrant individuals had to be molded for adaptation—even if that required human suffering.[28] What's more, pain and suffering could expose the unfit who were in conflict with civilizing forces. As Spencer describes it: "For the more civilized, dread of a long, monotonous criminal discipline may suffice; but for the less civilized there must be inflictions of bodily pain and death. Thus, we hold, not only that a social condition which generates a harsh form of government, also generates harsh retributions; but also, that in such a social condition, harsh retributions are required."[29] Spencer observed the advance of civilization in the conquest of undeveloped societies in distant parts of the globe. Closer to home, Spencer disdained social welfare and charity programs because he wanted the poor to be faced with enough unhappiness that they would reform themselves. After describing the lazy loungers and drunken idlers swarming London, Spencer questioned whether it was natural that "happiness should be the lot of such" or if unhappiness and misery "is a normal result of their misconduct."[30] Spencer was unforgiving, but he took the long view. He conceded that the poor, distressed, starving, and weak would be stuck "in shallows and in miseries" but those immediate and short-term challenges should not distract from the collective pursuit of equilibrium and progress: The misery of the less worthy was symbolic of "a large, far-seeing benevolence."[31] For the fit, misery was temporary, after which "a higher moral nature" will limit "the multiplication of the inferior" and ensure the proliferation of the superior.[32] Spencer affirmed an evolutionary apparatus that organized, sorted, and stratified human beings according to who conformed to the rules of evolution, and in so doing, evolutionary progress became a political sense-making touchstone pointing to an alternative source of social order in opposition to the equality, inclusion, and shared human progress often associated with liberal democracy.[33]

And yet, for all his Darwinian associations, Spencer was not a working scientist. He was a philosopher, a polymath, a phrenologist, and a biological idealist; his normative proclamations were synthetic constructs devoid of scientific evidence.[34] Both his biological work and his account of human evolution did not mesh with Darwin's.[35] Darwin privileged natural selection of random mutations; however, Spencer's syncretic application produced a multicausal theory conflating random mutations with "functionally produced modifications."[36] Nonetheless, Spencer's limitations did little to thwart his capacity to influence public conversations, because his realist rhetorical interventions were never confined to a scientific, technical sphere. What's more, shining a light on the differences between Darwin and Spencer can lend insight into the value of adopting a rhetorical approach when rhetors use scientific appeals to blur the spheres of argument.

Repurposing the language of Darwinian evolutionary theory, Spencer suggested that within a generation, structural changes in species can result from changes in habits.[37] But Spencer's biological and socioeconomic conflation is decidedly un-Darwinian. For example, Spencer believed that Irish immigrants to America could reflect Darwinian adaptation within a generation of immigrating through functionally acquired adaptations, allowing Irish immigrants to shed their "Celtic aspect" and become Americanized.[38] As Longaker argues, that conflation aligned Spencer's survival of the fittest with "the worst of eugenics-based racism, bourgeois elitism, and starve-the-poor social darwinism."[39] By positioning progress in alignment with nature's generative principles, Spencer blurred the boundaries between *science* and *scientism*.[40] More specifically, Spencer's textual persona aligns with a "priestly ethos" that has long been attractive to scientists, as well as a range of nonscientific philosophers, economists, and politicians keen on leveraging scientism for rhetorical impact. Lessl locates the origins of this priestly ethos in the capacity to portray scientists as "mediators of a reality inaccessible to all others."[41] Notice how important it is for Spencer to appear to be an objective scientist debating the finer points of political and economic theory, just like astronomers debate the cosmos. But also notice how Spencer's appeals to natural, divine, and scientific progress reflect a "double life" that, accordingly to Lessl, "references a body of technical knowledge developed through careful scientific study" while also symbolizing a "cluster of intangible meanings at once aesthetic, emotive, affective, rhetorical, and ideological, all moving in relation to ideals of progress."[42] Rather than demarcating the boundaries of science, Spencer focuses on maintaining just enough ambiguity and misdirection to maintain the look of objective scientific imperatives even as he induces individuals into an audience characterized by technical expertise.[43] Accordingly, Thomas Goodnight drew a distinction between a "technical sphere," or specialized arena where experts exchange ideas, and a "public sphere," where information is mediated to broader communities, often beyond where scientists and other experts usually operate.[44] Lessl describes the rhetorical impact of blurring the technical and the public spheres: Expertise can float from the technical to the public, allowing a rhetor like Spencer to offer up knowledge claims "no longer constrained by the same sense of professional etiquette." Further, Lessl points out that this process includes both "the relaxing of standards that are needed to get difficult ideas across to lay audiences" and the enhanced ability to mediate "competing purposes" whenever science meets public policy.[45]

Lessl and Goodnight help us understand how Spencer's textual persona exploits the mythic potency of technical expertise to advance scientific and economic policy arguments. Lessl and Goodnight also help focus attention on the fact that the rhetorical and affective creations that sustained Spencer's influence did not come from the technical sphere alone.[46] To be sure, Spencer's public discourse is replete with facts, statistics, and data. But facts, stats, and data serve to illustrate an argument, not logically demonstrate it.[47] To understand why that distinction is important, recall Spencer's life mission: Spencer sought to protect the evolutionary gains civilization had achieved by preventing the demos from influencing political structures.[48] Survival of the fittest helped accomplish that objective by illustrating a preexisting affective modality linking individual adaptations to political institutions.

Spencer argued that individual, long-term contentment could be achieved only by way of functionally produced modifications in accordance with nature.[49] Thus, he set in motion a perspective that would be affirmed through the oligarchic rhetoric of the twentieth century: Humans should be rewarded and punished according to how well they conform to natural law.[50]

A Fundamental Change in the Form of Structure

Spencer's specific influence on the political Right is evinced in these examples and the familiar contemporary associations with a lean, nightwatchman role for the government. There is evidence to support the argument that Spencer thought government should be limited to its most basic functions. Spencer questioned the warrant for extensive legislative action, arguing that "government measures do not remedy the evils they aim at" but instead make "these evils worse" or entail other, even greater evils.[51] Spencer's rhetoric aligned with the formation of liberal democracy for the next century as he established a ratio-like relationship in passages like these between *government: evil* and *private action: efficiency*. As a result, scholars have positioned Spencer on the political Right. Mark Longaker, for example, describes Spencer imaginatively spinning "an approaching libertarian-anarchist utopia where the law resides within each person's emotionally edified breast and where benevolence emerges in every action that respects liberty and exhibits charity."[52] He also describes Spencer's "anarchist-leanings" and "conservatism [that] grew out of a libertarian hope interrupted by pragmatic acknowledgment."[53] Gary Gerstle says Spencer "opposed poor laws, state-funded or directed charity, and government interference" because "he believed that such interventions meddled with the natural laws of the economy."[54] To be fair, Spencer did think public education and charity were impediments to progress. Justification for state actions, based on the public good, were repudiated, including restrictions on alcohol consumption; safety regulations in mines, factories, and shops; mandatory bathrooms in homes; state-funded libraries and museums; and taxpayer-funded health legislation.[55] Echoing today's familiar concerns about the encroaching "Nanny State," Spencer worried that if appeals to the common good provided a rationale for the state to promote health care, then the state would soon end up dictating how much we all must exercise, what we can eat, and in what quantities.[56] Linking public policy to naturalist arguments, Spencer wrote, "Whenever a government oversteps its duty it inevitably retards the process of adaptation." Poor Laws were especially harmful because they "diminish the demands upon" the poor to improve their penurious state, and as a consequence, they remain unevolved.[57] Once the government discharged such unnatural duties, it would be reduced to its proper scope, which Spencer declared was "to guard its subjects against aggression, either individual or national."[58]

However, linking Spencer to the political Right based on his desire to limit political and social interventions into the market is the product of an incomplete reading of Spencer's conception of naturalist rhetoric. I want to build on the extant literature here by emphasizing how the existing scholarly focus on the individualistic, libertarian implications in Spencer's naturalism underemphasizes the concurrent demands that his worldview places on political institutions and social organizations to also orient themselves in accordance with the divine and natural metrics of successful adaptation. Spencer's primary focus was corporate, not individual. "When the autonomous individual did make an occasional appearance in Spencer's writings it was as a biological unity of the human species that was necessarily sacrificed during evolution," Francis writes.[59] Recall how Spencer's evolutionary social theory required the most fit individuals to adopt functionally acquired peculiarities to display their fitness.[60] Notice also how Spencer makes clear that structural changes in a species result from changes of habit necessitated by changed circumstances, an emphasis that positions Spencer away from facile associations with anarcho-libertarianism.[61] For example, in *The Principles of Sociology*, Spencer wrote, "In metamorphoses, then, so far as they are traceable, we discern general truths harmonizing with those disclosed by comparisons of types. With social organisms, as with individual organisms, the structure becomes adapted to the activity. In the one case as in the other, if circumstances entail a fundamental change in the mode of activity, there by-and-by results a fundamental change in the form of structure."[62]

This is a key passage linking Darwinian evolutionary theory to democratic oligarchy. Spencer assumed nothing prompted the structural changes required for evolution and adaptation as well as the state. Further, because successful adaptation, for the individual or the social organism, was by no means guaranteed, Spencer viewed the state as an indispensable but contingent asset for catalyzing progress.[63] Spencer did believe that individuals found ethical and political norms by conforming to nature, but I want to consider the normative and instrumental consequences for an audience drawn into community by Spencer's argument, because Spencer also affirmed laws and institutions that showed evidence of social evolution, including positive state activities aligned with a conception of oligarchic justice as discussed in the previous chapter.[64] Law and legislation should be proactive, as a result. For this reason, scholars should be cautious about aligning Spencer too closely with a laissez-faire or anarchist-libertarian theories of governance, because Spencer supported state engagement in active market interventions. In an 1871 essay titled "Specialized Administration," Spencer wrote: "Within its proper limits governmental action is not simply legitimate but all-important. . . . Not only do I contend that the restraining power of the State over individuals is requisite, but I have contended that it should be exercised much more effectively, and carried out much further, than at present. And the maintenance of this control implies the maintenance of a controlling apparatus."[65] A source of misconception is revealed when scholars misunderstand Spencer's priority on the rights of the autonomous individual. In *The Principles of Ethics*, Spencer considers and then rejects a state that privileges "the lives of each and all . . . alike in length and breadth" and instead, reminds the reader, "We are met by a fact which forbids us thus to put in the foreground the welfares of citizens, individually considered, and requires us to put in the foreground the welfare of the society as a whole. The life of the social organism must as an end, rank above the lives of its units. These two ends are not harmonious at the outset; and though the tendency is towards harmonization of them, they are still partially conflicting."[66] Spencer doubted anything could replace the proactive and positive functions of a strong state, including the voluntary liberalism preferred by the mid-Victorians of his day. The implications for democratic governance were profound. Extending the assumptions of Aristotle and the American framers alike, Spencer thought the size and scope of positive state activities should be determined by the direction of social evolution, not public deliberation.[67] Spencer thought that in the future, social evolution would require ever-specialized developments in political structures. Unlike an anarcho-libertarian, Spencer believed there was no greater threat to social evolution "than the decay of a regulative system before a better one had grown up to replace it."[68]

Developing Governing Structures

Another vivid source of conceptual confusion concerns Spencer's approach to competition. Spencer's evolutionary theory largely ignored the value of individual competition, and instead, focused on developing governing structures, social organisms, and empires capable of corporate action.[69] Spencer assumed that an autonomous individual competition for resources was evidence of a retrograde and anachronistic conceptualization of evolution. Instead, political structures reflected evolutionary progress when they became too complex for ordinary people to understand and influence.[70] Like John Adams and Alexander Hamilton, Spencer thought highly of the public officials who possessed intimate specialized knowledge for regulating complex public affairs.[71] Spencer viewed the modern state as a bastion of skilled and professional administrators who understood the regulations and consequences of their work. Any attempt by the masses to intervene and control government machinery reduced the effectiveness of the institution and retarded progress.[72] Consider the pragmatic impact of linking Spencer's survival of the fittest with a misguided conceptualization of laissez-faire market competition. Ultimately, Spencer was indifferent to competition and ambivalent about state regulations, depending on whether the state and its activities were oriented according to his discrete, Darwinian interpretation of justice.[73] Affirming a consistent rhetorical thread, Spencer did not view government as a villain; instead, he disdained political and economic conditions that empowered the unfit to exert political influence.

Spencer's approach raises complicated questions about the viability of democratic governance. Garver described democracy's leveling potential, in that a healthy democracy can place every citizen on an equal plane.[74] That type of representative democracy posed a significant threat to Spencer's aspirations because the seizure of power by popular participation would retard progress and promote injustice.[75] Popular rule reflected the incompetence and mediocrity of ordinary people.[76] Echoing Aristotle, Spencer thought the masses were incapable of making complex decisions and so progress would be inhibited when more power was placed into the hands of the people. To Spencer, popular control resembled retrograde human origins when unstable and primitive hordes controlled governing apparatuses.[77] Spencer's theory of representative constitutional governance left no room for popular control by the demos to break into the regular functioning of the government.[78] In *The Principles of Sociology*, Spencer warned that the diffusion of political power down to "certain of our lower classes, such as colliers and brickmakers" would evoke "considerable evils" on the social order.[79] Not only were the masses unintelligent but they lacked the ability to express their will; many ordinary people actually took pride in their ignorance, Spencer wrote.[80]

And yet, Spencer thought his evolutionary theory could be assimilated into a representative democracy by establishing a clear distinction between government controlled by the people and government controlled by elites. More specifically, Spencer's hope for the assimilation of natural law by representative government required power to be concentrated apart from ordinary people.[81] This opened a rich site of rhetorical and affective interventions. Because Spencer doubted the intellectual capacities of the masses, he was adamant that reason and deliberation were not to be prioritized in his evolutionary theory of governance. This expanded the role of government to include a variety of noneconomic functions.[82] Rituals and traditions, for example, could appeal to lower classes in such a way as to align their perceived interests with elite rule.[83] The lower classes could also be moved by their "reverence for authority," which would allow a representative government to maintain order.[84] The end result is "an almost passionless consciousness" for the demos and social arrangements that can appear as "natural phenomena to be understood in their causes and effects."[85]

Spencer's rhetoric unites the theoretical assumptions of the ancient Greeks with the oligarchy features of American democracy today. Echoing Aristotle's emphasis on both rational persuasion *and* customs and social structures, Spencer understood social evolution as a complicated process requiring changes in personal habits, political structures, and public arguments.[86] Far beyond the anti-oligarchic honorifics and pufferies proposed by John Adams, Spencer's focus on rituals and traditions for acquiring the symbolic consent of ordinary people proved prescient for understanding the oscillating relationship between the economic and noneconomic in American democracy, especially in the twentieth century, as the oligarchic-oriented turned more directly to social and cultural interventions through astroturfed social movements, philanthropic institutions, think tanks, foundations, evangelical churches, and schools to justify the concentration (and conflation) of economic and political power into the hands of a superior minority.

Nothing and no one—not even the democratic will of the majority—should be able to interfere with the natural inner workings of the economy. Any attempt to intervene would only adulterate it. Spencer's fixed, systematic conception of the economy would soon allow Gilded Age tycoons, for example, to fend off the accusation that they merely want to pay fewer taxes. Spencer's rhetoric aligned with inflexible natural laws that could not be changed; and even if they could, tinkering with these laws would produce calamities for all.[87] Survival of the fittest justified wealth during the industrial age and offered the rich a self-serving bridge across economic *and* political power. Because the rich were the fulfillment of Spencer's natural law, why should they not deploy the resources of the government to defend and enhance their wealth?[88]

Spencer allowed the rich to cloak a cold-hearted and self-serving outlook under the cover of naturalist rhetoric. He also offered a cogent rebuttal to the equality and inclusion assumed to be at the core of liberal democracy. Instead, inequality and exclusion were aligned with the consequentialist outcomes of an ordered and stable governing system. Spencer's naturalist rhetoric sidelined any significant role for the government in ensuring wealth redistribution away from the ruling elite. Likewise, meddlesome regulations and progressive income taxes could only be understood as unnatural and misguided interference. Because everyone competes equally according to the laws of competition, the wealthy display intellectual and social superiority through their material standing. Only the losers turn to the state for help.

Conclusion

Herbert Spencer's influence would not be confined to Victorian England. Instead, Spencer offered a comprehensive explanation for the pronounced economic stratification marking the entire Gilded Age. In the late 1800s and early 1900s, an emerging class of robber barons began circulating Spencer's politico-economic vocabulary.[89] William Graham Sumner described the rich as "a product of natural selection."[90] John D. Rockefeller responded to accusations that his massive accumulation of wealth was unnatural by claiming that the immense value of Standard Oil's possessions was achieved through "the natural law of trade development."[91] Jay Gould rejected policy proposals aimed at regulating the railroads by suggesting they were already regulated by "the laws of supply and demand, production and consumption."[92] Andrew Carnegie—the focus of the next chapter—invoked the "unwritten laws of competition, petition, consolidation, aggregation, supply and demand, and wages and profits" to explain why he and his company had succeeded.[93] Rockefeller, Gould, and Carnegie made clear that their ability to tap into a transcendent set of immutable laws would have allowed them to prosper in whatever they did.[94] But reflecting Spencer's argument, there was a discernible order and structure to human events that could, with enough effort and the right tools, be revealed to all. These were not mere economic theories. They were moral laws that, like any other law of the universe, were "sure, inflexible, ever active, and having no exceptions," according to Spencer.[95]

Nonetheless, the robber barons' oligarchic rhetoric does not fully explain how oligarchy's geometrical conception of justice coexisted with democracy's arithmetic dominance. Recall the math problem Aristotle described: In a representative democracy, minoritarian concentrations of power could always appear stale, self-serving, and greedy. An effective governing rationale could reconcile democracy and oligarchy—without violence and coercion—by gathering the symbolic consent of the masses. To that end, in the next chapter I explore how Andrew Carnegie embodied Herbert Spencer's Darwinian assumptions.

3

Natural Law and the Rhetoric of Andrew Carnegie

BETWEEN THE END OF THE CIVIL WAR AND THE START OF THE GILDED Age, large American corporations justified self-serving political influence by appealing to natural law.[1] Large corporations pushed down wages by reducing employment and supplying fewer goods, forcing prices up.[2] Millions of Americans ended up being paid less than they should have been in a competitive labor market, even while prices shot up. Later in the nineteenth century, the Union Pacific Railroad paid out millions in bribes to American politicians. Leland Stanford sent his allies to Washington, DC, with suitcases of Central Pacific stock to give to politicians and lobbyists, ultimately handing out the equivalent of $13 million in 2020 dollars. Later, John D. Rockefeller's Standard Oil handed out bags of money to Republican William McKinley's political organizers and Pennsylvania legislators.[3] Rockefeller then cut out competitors and controlled the oil supply, all with the US government's approval.[4] As the muckraking journalist Henry Demarest Lloyd described, Rockefeller did "everything with the Pennsylvania legislature, except refine it."[5]

Entrenched corporations in the railroad and telecommunication industries justified what they called "natural monopolies" on the grounds that a single, universal system would benefit everyone—not just B&O and AT&T. Trusts and monopolies were not portrayed as stifling market interference in desperate need of government interventions; they were a natural outcome of the laws of competition, which allowed the best and brightest to serve the greater good. By the end of the nineteenth century, American corporations produced two-thirds of manufactured goods and employed two-thirds of wage earners. Railroads used their monopoly powers to push out smaller competitors, manipulate supply chains, and gouge customers. Increased size and profits produced increased political influence. Increased political influence produced decreased regulation. Local and state regulators could not control large corporations, and the federal government would not because it would harm economic growth.[6]

The economic reality of the first Gilded Age has led some scholars, such as David Nasaw in *Gilded Age Gospels*, to suggest that industrialists in late 1800s "had no interest in government (as long as public institutions kept their hands off corporate affairs and opened their coffers to capitalist enterprises)."[7] But Nasaw is mistaken. Railroad and telecommunication corporations, along with insurance companies, meat packers, and steel makers, did not want free competition in an unfettered market. They relied on a robust and selectively applied government action for land grants for their railroads, subsidies for their new monopolies, and the legal right to extract and bring to market the nation's iron and oil.[8] Changing economic environments and a new industry required railroad companies like B&O Railroad and Central Pacific to work with Congress. To nudge Congress toward their profitable sites of intervention, railroad companies deployed all the available tools, including lobbying, patronage, bribery, and political interventions. Bribing politicians may seem to contradict a core assumption of a free market; instead, such attempts by railroad corporations one-hundred and fifty years ago to enjoin the state on their behalf highlight a valuable oligarchic lesson: There is no idyllic past where the state stayed out of the market. The railroad corporations would not want such an idyllic past even if they could have it. They wanted to maximize profitability by working together to negotiate rights-of-way, eminent domain laws, and favorable labor laws.[9] Likewise, corporate elites were never as naive to the profitable potential of state interventions as has been so often implied by the Right/Left ideological seesaw. Republic Steel, Armour and Company, Swift & Company, and New York Life plied state legislators with huge sums of money, enjoined the state's monopoly on violence to keep workers in line, and manipulated corporate laws in their favor. Mark Twain popularized the phrase "Gilded Age" to describe these years, but historian Vernon Parrington was more accurate when he described the end of the nineteenth century as the "Great Barbecue," as corporate tycoons devoured the nation's resources. A laissez-faire state marked by a "free market" could not satisfy that hunger. Robert Caro writes that industrialists "moved into government," pouring money into political campaigns and politicians.[10] Such relationships may look unethical, even corrupt. But industrial tycoons and robber barons relied on the strong hand of the government to shelter their profits from overseas competition, resolve labor strife, and develop the infrastructure to bring their goods to market efficiently, profitably, and legally.[11]

CHAPTER 3

Gilded Age millionaires justified such state interventions and the consequential power concentrations they produced as the results of fair and open market competition. As Gerstle wrote, "The fittest firms and businessmen had survived because they had bested, then eliminated, their competition. This was evolutionary progress in its purest form. When the politicians, blinded by an ideological logical abhorrence of monopoly and bigness, interfered with the law of aggregation to protect the vanquished from defeat and extinction, they interfered with evolutionary progress."[12]

Even so, appeals to the natural, lawlike concentrations of wealth and power during the Gilded Age had to overcome the arithmetic challenges posed by majoritarian democracy. Andrew Carnegie's 1889 article "The Gospel of Wealth" offers a fruitful opportunity to explore how his rhetorical realism linked the natural laws governing market economies to an accessible and republican hermeneutic.

The natural laws governing the political economy did not remain secret or exclusive to the rich. Anyone could learn them and put them into action. In other words, Andrew Carnegie does not assume the rich are naturally superior to the rest of us. Instead, they are superior, naturally. Such a distinction is appropriate for his historical moment. Carnegie's argument shifts the reader's focus from entrenched railroad and telecommunication corporations to the individual behavior "some men may occupy" by using his own textual persona to reassure readers that everyone can conform to natural law. Carnegie's realism mediates Spencer's elitism, elevating himself as the embodiment of the American Dream, not because he was born superior but because he conformed to natural law—a confirmation process available to all.

The Gospel of Wealth

Born in Scotland and immigrating to the United States when he was twelve years old, Andrew Carnegie became the richest man in America during the early 1900s by building and then selling what became the U.S. Steel Corporation. He then became a generous philanthropist, giving millions away to charities, foundations, libraries, museums, and universities. In a famous 1889 article, "The Gospel of Wealth," Carnegie explained his philanthropy and urged other wealthy Americans to follow his lead. In the article, Carnegie makes the case that rich Americans should use their growing wealth for charitable social purposes when they are alive, rather than giving it to their family or waiting until they die. But to understand oligarchy's genealogical development in America I am not as interested in Carnegie's philanthropic appeals. I am interested in the textual persona Carnegie establishes in "The Gospel of Wealth" and how his underlying first principles would come to permeate the new American century.

"The Gospel of Wealth" affirmed—yet softened—Herbert Spencer's worldview by cloaking the cold implications of economic Darwinism with American optimism. Carnegie did use the phrase "survival of the fittest" to explain why the "laws of competition" ensured fair resource distribution. But Carnegie's personae also reflected a version of the American Dream as he rose from poverty to immense wealth based on his ability to conform to the immutable laws of capital accumulation, not unlike Horatio Alger, Henry Ford, William Buckley, Ayn Rand, and more recently, Charles Koch and Peter Thiel.

In "The Gospel of Wealth," Carnegie uses the word "law" eighteen times to explain material arrangements. Carnegie concedes the law can be cold, but it is "best for the race, because it ensures the survival of the fittest in every department." Carnegie's self-serving outlook lingers beneath the surface as he assumes "men possessed of this particular talent for affairs, under the free play of economic forces, must, of necessity, soon be in receipt of more revenue than can be judiciously expended upon themselves." Carnegie describes "the Law of Accumulation of Wealth, and the Law of Competition" together as the "highest results of human experience, the soil in which society so far has produced the best fruit." His use of capitalization is revealing. The growing stratification of the Gilded Age is justified through proper nouns. These immutable laws make it clear that equality and inclusion are foolish aims. Carnegie concedes the stratified condition of the Gilded Age, "which inevitably gives wealth to the few," and he endorses that condition not as a contradiction of the laws of nature but as an affirmation.[13]

For Carnegie there is only one relevant question: "What is the proper mode of administering wealth after the laws upon which civilization has been founded have thrown it into the hands of the few?" Carnegie offers his reader three options: The rich can leave their wealth to their kin, leave it for the public at the time of their death, or give it away during their life. Carnegie affirms the latter, and he spends the rest of the essay explaining why. He urges the rich to "busy themselves or organizing benefactors from which the masses of their fellows will derive lasting advantage, and thus dignify their own lives." He praises wealthy New Yorkers who benefited the community by funding public institutions, parks, and means of recreation.

Carnegie's natural law rejects any significant role for the government in ensuring fair resource distribution. For both Herbert Spencer and Andrew

Carnegie, market regulation or a progressive income tax can be understood only as unnatural and misguided interference. Carnegie urges his wealthy readers toward philanthropy because the government is too incompetent to make wise use of the wealthy's resources. In an altruistic turn, the superior rich function as "a trustee of the poor; entrusted for a season with a great part of the increased wealth of the community, but administering it for the community far better than it could or would have done for itself." Carnegie concludes, "Thus is the problem of the Rich and the Poor to be solved." Carnegie's influence was not limited to convincing Rockefeller and Morgan to give away their money before they died. Rather, Carnegie's "The Gospel of Wealth" is a compelling oligarchic case study, because his arguments would become reflected in our new models of citizenship, our collective attitudes toward work and wealth, and the shape of our government-market relationships.

The Captain of Industry

While Herbert Spencer was a trust-fund polymath from Derbyshire who hated manual labor and always wore a tux, Andrew Carnegie grew up destitute in Scotland and immigrated to the United States, where, through gumption and grit, he grew to embody the American Dream decades before the term was coined. But as a source of rhetorical invention, Carnegie's biography can also illustrate the inductive consequentialism well suited to the temporal and communal expectations of his historical moment. He became one of the wealthiest men in the world. And thus, his biography became marked by a synthetic embodiment of God's will and Nature's law. He was precocious, industrious, creative, and bold. As a child, Carnegie worked twelve-hour days in a cotton mill and then as a telegraph messenger. As a young man, he figured out how to turn brittle iron ore into flexible steel, displaying the technical acumen demanded for success in the new industrial age. When no one would invest in a manufacturing plant for his bold innovation, he displayed the self-confidence demanded by a hypercompetitive market and invested his own money.

And yet, Carnegie's personal characteristics provide only a partial account of his wealth and power. At the turn of the century, there were many people who were precocious, industrious, creative, and bold who did not become extravagantly wealthy. Further, there were many wealthy and powerful men who were not described as a "captain of industry." But like Rockefeller, Morgan, and Gould, Andrew Carnegie's classification as a captain of industry illustrates the incommensurability of democratic oligarchy during the Gilded Age. American captains of industry laid tracks across the Appalachians and Rockies, prospected for oil in Pennsylvania and west Texas, and transformed iron ore into steel for building massive skyscrapers and durable bridges.[14] As a discursive tool, "captain of industry" helped the American public make sense of the personal characteristics elevating a discrete type of person atop the largest and most influential corporations of the day. Before the Gilded Age, traits like breeding, bloodlines, and bravery in battle justified the conflation of economic and political power against the stale aristocracies of old Europe. Today, the Übermensch of Silicon Valley's tech billionaires justify political influence far beyond their area of technical expertise because their ingenuity, intelligence, and bold entrepreneurship to move fast and break things transcends their narrow technical expertise.[15] In between, Gilded Age captains of industry embodied a set of personal characteristics justifying their position atop an influential but socially unfamiliar institution: the modern American corporation.[16] But there is daylight between immense wealth and the label "captain of industry"; likewise, there is a conceptual difference between wealth and oligarchy. In other words, Carnegie was not rich and powerful because he was hardworking and bold. He also leveraged economic and political power, enjoining the state to gain substantial control over the resources and means of production, crush rivals, control workers, limit regulation and taxes, erect thick tariff walls, and, through grants, corruption, and sometimes both, bring the nation into an advanced industrialized age.

It did not hurt that Carnegie looked like Santa Claus with warm eyes, a round nose, a white beard, and a gentle smile. Plus, Carnegie justified his altruism as a way to maintain social cohesion—an argument Spencer did not value. Spencer's adherence to the Darwinian laws of competition make clear that the rich deserve their wealth, that they earned it all on their own, and that they should feel no pressure to give it away to the unworthy. In contrast, Carnegie describes the problem of his age as "the proper administration of wealth, so that the ties of brotherhood may still bind together the rich and poor in harmonious relationship."[17] Here is where Carnegie's lasting influence on public argument can be felt. He features "the ties of brotherhood" and "harmonious relationship" in the opening sentence of the article for the same reason Charles Koch and Jeff Bezos would need to embody both technical and rhetorical acumen to build their wealth in the next century. Carnegie set the context—"the problem of our age is the proper *administration* of wealth"—to emphasize that scarce resources would no longer define the human condition. Carnegie's premise is stunning because scarcity defined the human condition for one hundred thousand years. But because wealth *administration* is now the problem of the age, Carnegie can unhitch the hunger and deprivation of his day from a lack of food and hitch his argument to improper distribution. Fair resource distribution would become the defining challenge of the twentieth century. Carnegie's focus is rhetorical. The proper administration of wealth is a moral question concerned with reconciling who gets what, how much, and why.

Carnegie drew a line between absolute and relative wealth. Since Carnegie's day, economists have shown how social cohesion depends less on one's absolute wealth (the presence of food and shelter, for example) and more on relative wealth (how your resources compare to your neighbors).[18] Crop yields and rainfall patterns will become less significant for more of us today. The poor in developed nations have flat-screen HD televisions and the poor in developing nations have internet-accessed smartphones. Harmonious relations, to use Carnegie's phrase, would depend on the rhetorical justification for material stratification—not simply the product of rising absolute wealth.

Carnegie's argument informed changing labor relations. For most of human history, landowners and feudal lords extracted effort and loyalty from their workforce by threatening coercion and violence.[19] Carnegie did rely on coercion to control his own workers, but he knew that was risky. The-foreman-in-the-worker's-mind is more influential than the foreman-with-the-bull-whip. Carnegie conceded to the genteel management of labor—that effort and loyalty should come from labor's affective allegiance. "Harmonious relationships" would not matter otherwise. Grandiose philanthropic support for public libraries and free museums represent a wise PR move. But Carnegie goes deeper. He seems to be mindful of the natural friction between capital and labor and even suggests that society will improve as it becomes more stratified. Here, Carnegie extends Herbert Spencer's economic Darwinism by challenging the premise that inequality is bad and the government should be oriented toward redressing it. Instead, inequality is the consequentialist outcome of just economic and political governance.

It Is a Waste of Time to Criticize the Inevitable

Andrew Carnegie's ability to reconcile inequality and harmony had a lasting impact on oligarchic thought. According to Carnegie, inequality is produced by conformity to natural law. In "The Gospel of Wealth"'s opening paragraph, Carnegie describes how the wigwam of the Sioux chief was little different than that of the poorest brave. He contrasts the chief's shared squalor with the "palace of the millionaire and the cottage of the laborer" as evidence of "highly beneficial progress"—progress that is essential for all humans. "Much better this great irregularity than universal squalor," he writes. The only outcome of the preindustrial age was "crude articles at high prices." Both consumers and producers suffered in the old master-and-apprentice relationship. But no longer. Even if you were uncomfortable with this stratification, little could be done to redress the relationship. Carnegie again foreshadows a potent oligarchic argument, writing, "It is a waste of time to criticize the inevitable."

Carnegie's messaging assumed a telic dimension. Humans are on an escalator reaching heights of greater human development that cannot be altered, only temporarily slowed. Natural selection is the foundation. The end result is inevitable and the material wealth of the most fit preordained. There is no "middle ground which some men may occupy"—according to Carnegie—because our manufacturing and commercial concerns "must either go forward or fall behind: to stand still is impossible." Rather than fight against the immutable, Carnegie encourages the reader to "accept and welcome" our "great inequality of environment, the concentration of business, industrial and commercial, in the hands of a few," and to accept the "law of competition between these, as being not only beneficial, but essential for the future progress of the race."

Carnegie's rhetoric saddles the rich with moral responsibility. They have a duty to put their talent into action, and not just by accumulating wealth. The rich are charged with the proper *administration* of wealth by influencing the largest and most important resource allocator: the government. Beyond public libraries and free museums, Carnegie advocates for direct political activity. He does so by asking the reader a simple question: Would you rather have the champions of economic competition or a government bureaucrat manage resource distribution? Carnegie answered his own question in a way that would become an influential sensemaking touchstone for Americans and their government for the rest of the century. Free markets became shackled by government overreach. The needy became undeserving. Organized labor became a bastion of corruption. And government employees became understood through the prism of popular caricatures of postal service and DMV employees like Cliff Claven on *Cheers*, Patty and Selma on *The Simpsons*, Newman on *Seinfeld*, and Ron Swanson on *Parks and Recreation*. These enemies of economic growth stood in sharp contrast to the entrepreneurial corporate courage of Jack Welch,

Carl Icahn, Warren Buffett, and Donald Trump. The primary task of the government was removing its boot from the neck of these patriotic titans to further free enterprise.[20]

The superhuman contributions of the rich are now held up as arguments against progressive taxation and a robust welfare state.[21] If everyone competes according to the laws of competition, why punish the job creators and reward the moochers? Plus, we all benefit when the rich thrive. Regressive tax policy allows the rich to make their contributions to the common good, including investing in industry-supporting research to invent products and cure diseases. Government interference would only stifle that innovation and spread resources to the unworthy. Collective support for the undeserving contradicted natural law, creating paralysis and dependency. As Carnegie wrote, "Those worthy of assistance, except in rare cases, seldom require assistance. The really valuable men of the race never do, except in cases of accident or sudden change." Over the long run, anyway, state efforts could only temporarily retard the natural laws of accumulation from sifting and sorting the deserving from the undeserving. Collective support hurts the rich, because they have to pay for most of the aid. But collective support also hurts the poor, because they develop dependence instead of the initiative and self-esteem coming from hard work.[22]

One might wonder how Carnegie's argument went over with those in need of assistance, especially during a historical moment marked by rising inequality. Although it was provocative to reinterpret charity as malevolence, the rhetorical record makes clear that Carnegie introduced a durable and transcendent argument into public conversations about the form and function of the state. This is not to suggest that a majority of Americans were persuaded by Carnegie's reinterpretation. Recalling Crowley, rhetorical inventiveness is judged not in this way.[23] Instead, Carnegie enlivened an argument within a discrete temporal and communal context, making available an argument that questioned existing assumptions and creating the discursive conditions for an alternative to circulate, even if it was kept at arm's length. Carnegie invented an argument that—for the rich and the non-rich alike—challenged the assumptions that charity was good and inequality was bad. Carnegie did so by weaving together two new rhetorical baskets: In one, Carnegie placed inequality, the iron laws of competition, and unrestrained capital accumulation; in the other, Carnegie placed equality, central planning, and wealth redistribution. The first basket was woven together by natural, immutable, scientific thread. The second by unnatural, subjective, and flimsy thread.

Accessible Meritocracy

Carnegie assured the ultra-rich that their increased political influence was justified by their ability to improve the lives of all. With power comes responsibility, and so Carnegie showed the ultra-rich how to sidestep accusations of self-serving greed by emphasizing their capacity to vouchsafe the interests of all, an argument propped up by appeals to rising living standards, rising tides, and remnantism—a philosophy based on the idea that a saving elite was responsible for governing society by combatting the unnatural and flawed aspirations of the masses.[24] Robert Asen has detailed how such arguments come from the assumption that the achievements of the rich offer a vantage point above the rest allowing them to look out for the interests of the country and the people that have not done as well in the struggle for resources.[25] Who better to vouchsafe the interests of all than those who can display their fitness on the only scorecard that matters: massive capital accumulation? Would you rather have your local DMV worker set tax laws or the proven champions of economic competition?

The ruling elite surely appreciated the endorsement of their transcendent superiority. The proof of their economic *and* moral worth was in the pudding.[26] Wealth was the scorekeeper, and they were winning. New vocabularies emerged in oscillation with this immutable endorsement as an elite transcendent superiority formed the foundation of oligarchy's argumentative structure. Aligning with an abundance of historical and empirical research, Carnegie advances the belief that the wealthy's transcendent superiority ought to allow disproportionate influence on the political process. In like manner, across the rhetorical record, transcendent superiority emerges as a principal discursive feature of inequality regimes.[27] Recall how Plato, Aristotle, Hamilton, and Adams each believed the rich were superior. But as appeals to bloodlines and "good birth" faded from public conversations, an accessible meritocracy reemerged, reflected in Carnegie's alignment of power hierarchies with individual traits.[28] The elite ranks of political, military, and religious rule were assumed to be populated by the most industrious, innovative, and brilliant, and conversely, the less-than-elite were stigmatized based on their inability or unwillingness to access power hierarchies by displaying proper behavior. Rather than appealing to breeding or bloodlines, Carnegie's oligarchic power concentrations were justified because the affluent bridged the immutable laws governing the natural world to a set of fixed, external, and scientific laws governing the social, political, and economic world. The implied warrant hinges on the public's belief in the assumption that the rich conform to these natural laws better than the rest of us.[29] But as Carnegie's realism reveals, these laws did not remain secret or exclusive to the rich. Anyone could learn them and put them into action.

A benevolent consequence of concentrating power in the hands of the transcendently superior is that all will benefit, rich and poor alike. As a result, appeals to the "common good" emerged as an eloquent and cogent warrant linking the transcendent influence of the affluent to the assumption that the lives of all Americans will be better off when we concede political influence to the rich.[30] The harsh judgment cast on ordinary Americans was mediated by the illusion of accessibility: The corridors of power were no longer determined by birth, and every American had within themselves the potential to conform to the natural law and elevate their station. As Carnegie's biography illustrated, accessible meritocracy represents a significant rhetorical advancement in oligarchic argument, especially for the development of a unique American identity that could draw sharper distinctions between the bloodlines and old money of aristocratic Europe. Carnegie's rhetoric pushed back against John Adams. America was, indeed, exceptional.

Letting the Needy Fail

Carnegie's appeal to natural law offered several distinct rhetorical advantages. Elite power is always susceptible to the potential threat of democratic revolt. This is a damning indictment as the policy preferences of the rich dovetail with the material interests of the ruling class. Of course, the rich affirm a free market if a free market is making them really rich. Carnegie's natural law allows the ultra-rich to remain above this self-serving and partisan fray. By affirming an objective, assumed, and almost uncontestable view of the economy, elites can sidestep self-serving accusations and partisan loyalty. Instead, oligarchs look like sober and objective pursuers of natural and timeless truths. Shifting the explanation for their own elite status to an immutable and amorphous system of laws mediates majoritarian democracy's revolutionary potential by reinterpreting power concentrations as immutable as the laws of gravity.

Carnegie's natural law opened the door of success, but that does not mean everyone will walk through.[31] Rather than ensure equality of outcomes, the state has the duty to close the doors of opportunity to the unworthy and deploy its legal, coercive, and symbolic tools to maintain a maldistribution of resources. A state oriented toward opening doors for all by redistributing resources downward or lifting the floor of opportunity upward is not only unnatural but unjust. Oligarchic justice requires the state to protect the resources of the wealthy against the tyranny of the democratic hoards and defend and enhance existing material relationships.

Carnegie's natural law produces a general distrust of the state as a bastion of losers whose collective solidarity is merely a crutch for individual incompetence. Carnegie warned against giving charity to the homeless because those worthy of assistance seldom required it. That worry is then reflected in the morally hazardous redistribution of welfare, unemployment and disability insurance, and affirmative action policies. As hard as it is, the state must walk by the homeless beggar. Precisely because it is hard, convincing language is needed. Natural law serves this important rhetorical function.

Natural law saps the state's ability to deploy resources toward the interests of the non-elite, including decreased political support for antitrust acts and monopoly-busting policies of their day, and later, gutting legal protections for unions, minimum wage laws, and environmental safeguards. State support mechanisms are portrayed as unnatural, dependency-inducing millstones dragging everyone down. Savvy rhetors avoid connecting the dots, but the logical implications of an immutable market do seep out in public arguments, including references to "letting the needy fail" and letting the destitute fall by the wayside, to be purged and cleansed from the system.[32] State efforts to redistribute wealth are foolish and misguided in the long run, and because state support mechanisms are unnatural, their efforts are mere balms on the destitute's wounds. Conversely, the ultra-rich pose no threat.[33] The rich invested their resources in innovation, factory expansion, and public goods, libraries, and parks. In turn, the public have nothing to fear from concentrated wealth in the hands of the rich. The real fear is the masses of the uneducated and ignorant. Elites are refashioned as a besieged minority holding back the barbarians at the gate. Natural law confirms a conditional loyalty to the state, predicated not on equality, inclusion, or majoritarian democracy but on the state's orientation toward affirming the hierarchies those laws produce.

Ruthless Profit Maximization

During the first Gilded Age, many Americans wondered why the robber barons were so greedy. Could they not pay a little more so their workers could upgrade their cottages if not to mansions, then at least to decent apartments? Could they not create working conditions that were both safe and profitable? Carnegie could still be really rich, enjoying the fruits of his tenacity and innovation. But how much did he need?[34]

Consequentialism justifies concentrations of power, but it does not offer the rich inner peace. Carnegie may be rich now, but he has no guarantee that another player—better aligned with the natural laws of competition—will not soon eat him alive.[35] If natural law describes the rules of competition, then refusing to push the legal and ethical boundaries would put Carnegie at an unacceptable disadvantage.[36] And disadvantage does not just refer to an inability to buy $260 swim trunks or an entire house just for your art collection. If transcendent worth is evinced by profitability, then *disadvantage* is a comprehensive threat to identity—not just the bank account. Fluid loyalties and baffling incongruities are explained away as the rich are expected to take ruthless advantage as a Darwinian expression of self-preservation.

Today, one may wonder why a company like Microsoft or Boeing would need to farm out essential but low-skilled work like buffing the floors or cleaning the break room to independent contractors. Those jobs once functioned as promotional opportunities for the upwardly mobile who lacked advanced degrees or technical experience. But now Microsoft and Boeing must prioritize short-term profitability, and GE must scratch and claw for every offshore tax haven it can find. Natural law demands it. If Microsoft did not take such ruthless measures as Apple did, Microsoft would be at a competitive disadvantage and not long for this world. If Apple did not take advantage of tax shelters, Microsoft would put Apple at a competitive disadvantage, and thus make it less fit to survive the rigors of the competition.[37] It is a jungle out there.

Conclusion

At the start of the twentieth century, Carnegie's natural law emerged as a potent rhetorical touchstone. Its rhetorical residue could be found in the justification for American imperial expansions in the Philippines and Puerto Rico, and then later in elite responses to populist anger during the Progressive era, in the Hoover administration's aloof responses to the boom-and-bust of the 1920s, and even in the American eugenics movement. But this is not to suggest a total and complete rhetorical conquest. Family farmers, laborers, and small business owners were less willing to link the affluent's economic success to political influence, and their protestations and political activism fueled a number of anti-oligarchic laws, first at the state and local level, and then nationwide.[38] Recall that the Sherman Antitrust Act was passed in 1890 in an attempt to reign in oligarchic policy, and in 1914, the Clayton Antitrust Act continued the trend by outlawing price-fixing, monopolies, and anti-competitive acquisitions and mergers.[39] By the late 1920s, economic and political upheaval pushed the public policies drawn from Spencer's discursive reservoir to the margins. The images of schoolchildren and World War I veterans digging for food in the trash prompted many Americans to question the link between oligarchic power concentrations and the common good.[40] Instead, the American public largely blamed oligarchic influence, especially in the banking sector, for the collapse of 1929 and the Great Depression that followed.

Joseph Schumpeter, Karl Polanyi, and most importantly, John Maynard Keynes circulated an alternative. Direct government intervention on behalf of the masses drew widespread support, including support for labor unions, a robust safety net, and trade tariffs designed to stimulate economic growth and protect citizens during economic downturns.[41] Keynes also laid bare how harmful Carnegie's economic approach was for most people. Instead, Keynes's focus on equal opportunity allowed the federal government to emerge as an anchor point for solidifying the interventionist efforts of other political, legal, cultural, and religious institutions. Politically, FDR and the New Deal developed an economic spirit and related programs that reshaped American expectations about the duties and responsibilities of government. The New Deal implemented price controls instead of unfettered markets in many industries, it developed a welfare state as a necessary safety net, it protected organized labor, and it helped government spending limit destructive recessions, and government investment in health care, education, and public pensions improved life for many Americans. FDR won four presidential elections, Harry Truman carried the torch after he died, and federal spending as a percentage of American economic output nearly doubled between 1948 and 1968.[42] In 1937, the American legal system began to support the constitutionality of the New Deal and later, during the height of what came to be known as the Warren Court, the Supreme Court embraced the role of direct government intervention into the market when it could improve the lives of Americans, and in so doing prioritized equality above liberty as a fundamental constitutional value, as Steven Teles writes.[43] American courts sought to make life easier for ordinary Americans by strengthening protections for organized labor and bolstering banking insurance regulations. The Great Depression also revealed to many American Christians how institutions can inhibit the central message of the Christian gospel.[44] The emergence of liberal theological applications expanded the purpose of the church beyond saving individual souls to also include a focus on the redemption of sinful institutions, including those woven into our political system.[45] Liberation theology reoriented many religious denominations toward the interests of the poor and oppressed. Influenced by the politics in the churches of the Global South, many American Christian churches pursued a theology based on what Jon Sobrino called "the preferential option for the poor."[46]

But it was not only the American middle and working classes who understood the value of the New Deal and the Keynesian welfare state. After the Great Depression, America's corporate elite realized that it was safer to give ordinary Americans a political voice, legal protection to organize, and a safety net than risk losing control of the entire edifice.[47] As a result, legal, fiscal, and social systems aimed at reducing inequality were widely accepted by Democrats and Republicans alike. As Piketty wrote: "This transformation of politics depended not only on mobilizing (broadly) social-democratic coalitions but also on the involvement of civil society (including unions, activists, media, and intellectuals) and on a sweeping transformation of the dominant ideology, which throughout the long nineteenth century had been shaped by a quasi-religious theology of markets, inequality, and private property."[48] Few Americans worried that FDR and Keynes were adulterating natural law because FDR and Keynes were making life less difficult. The natural, transcendent superiority pushed by Spencer and Carnegie seemed stale, self-serving, and unconvincing. The ultra-rich wanted what most Americans did not. Oligarchy needed a new argument—or at least an old argument told in a new way.

4

The Road to Oligarchy and the Rhetoric of Friedrich Hayek

DURING THE 1930S AND 1940S, THE ULTRA-RICH WERE BLAMED FOR causing the Great Depression, and the country responded by embracing the New Deal and the Keynesian welfare state.[1] Worse for the ultra-rich, their own personal narrative was disputed. Many of the ultra-rich assumed that because economic stratification was produced by fair competition, they deserved both economic wealth and political power. John Maynard Keynes told them otherwise. And yet, there is little evidence that their marginalization prompted serious introspection, reflexivity, or humility. The oligarchy-oriented remained confident that Keynesianism would fail in the long term—even if it redistributed wealth and power to the less fit in the short term—because handing out scarce resources to the unproductive, unnatural, and mediocre contradicted the laws of nature. Oligarchs did not just lament FDR and Keynes. They began to pour their immense resources into organizations that would return the nation to the "principles upon which our government was formulated," according to a spokesperson for the new American Liberty League.[2] In the 1930s, J. Howard Pew of Sun Oil and Alfred Sloan of GM put their words into action by funding it.[3] In the 1940s, Leonard Read gathered funding from corporate titans running Montgomery Ward, B. F. Goodrich Tire, US Steel, Sears Roebuck, and Westinghouse to fund the Foundation for Economic Education. In the 1950s, Robert Welch founded the John Birch Society for the same nostalgic purpose. Irénée du Pont even suggested the ultra-rich neutralize Keynes by making alliances with the Ku Klux Klan.[4]

The ultra-rich lamented their frustrations with an American public too stupid to understand natural laws and too lazy to hold elected officials accountable.[5] Ordinary Americans could not be trusted to understand their

CHAPTER 4

fears, and due to the popular interventions of the New Deal and the Keynesian welfare state, the market offered no solace. For many ultra-rich Americans, the market was both robust and fragile: in desperate need of protection but paradoxically prone to failure if adulterated by outside forces.[6] Instead of relying on the capriciousness of the masses or the market, a powerful but marginalized cadre of ultra-rich Americans decided to weaken Keynes and strengthen an alternative by focusing their efforts on the upstream formation of public opinion to complement their downstream political and economic aspirations.[7] If the ultra-rich could not trust the market or the masses, they could operationalize oligarchy by making common cause with a new group of brilliant and zealous upstream thought leaders. To this end, some historians trace the discursive origins of neoliberalism to a 1938 colloquium in Paris sponsored by Walter Lippman.[8] There, Ludwig von Mises and Friedrich Hayek—the focus of this chapter—joined other influential thinkers to consolidate a response to Keynesian liberalism. But only one corporate leader, Ernest Mercier, a French industrialist, is listed among the other philosophers, sociologists, journalists, political scientists, and economists who attended. The dearth of corporate influence in 1938 stood in sharp contrast to another meeting of influential thought leaders almost ten years later.

In 1947, Hayek and Mises, along with other intellectual giants, gathered again to plot a response to Keynes. But this time, corporate support for the meeting came from Jasper Crane, an executive at Dow Chemical, Harold Luhnow and the William Volker Fund, Leonard Read, who had held leadership positions in the US Chamber of Commerce and the National Industrial Conference Board, and Alfred Suenson-Taylor and the Bank of England. Not long after, the United Fruit company and U.S. Steel began supporting what emerged from that 1947 meeting: the Mont Pèlerin Society. The International Chamber of Commerce, the National Association of Manufacturers, and the Foundation for Economic Education soon began pouring resources into this new alliance of intellectuals and oligarchs.[9] The alliance reflected a potent combination of the wealthy and well-connected translating their Keynesian dissatisfaction into a flurry of idea-influencing enterprises, including well-funded policy-influencing networks, PACs, and think tanks. A mutually beneficial relationship formed between intellectuals like Mises and Hayek and corporate interests based on protecting the threatened privileges of the ultra-rich.[10]

I want to trace the influence of Friedrich Hayek to this moment. An Austrian philosopher and economist, Hayek began his career with what

Benjamin Friedman described as "pathbreaking theoretical work showing how decentralized markets processed countless bits of information from widely dispersed sources, bringing them collectively to bear on resource allocation and other economic decisions far more efficiently than what any system of centralized planning could achieve."[11] But Hayek was not just a quantoid. He was an exotic and inspiring rhetor whose European sensibility, World War II experience, training in juridical and political philosophy, and zealous confidence offered him the ethos-enhancing devices so crucial for influencing public argument.[12] Hayek would go on to write two of the most influential books of the century—including *The Road to Serfdom*, which became the bible of the postwar conservative movement.[13] Michael Lee described Hayek as an "essential rhetorical resource because he gave conservatives a way to talk about the public interest by talking about private enterprise."[14] Ronald Reagan was an early fan of Hayek, echoing his language in his letters and speeches.[15] It was *The Road to Serfdom* that turned Reagan into a "sincere right-winger."[16] Reagan would later elevate individualism as the defining character in the American drama over and above any reference to the community.[17] Hayek's influence on Margaret Thatcher is evinced in her emphasis on the autonomous individual, Piketty argued, and in her famous belief that "there is no such thing as society."[18] Jones and Mukherjee note an extraction of the individual from the social in Thatcher's public utterances, reflecting Hayek's outlook, including the depoliticization and privatization of difference and the transformation of social identifications and solidarities that were once public into a private sphere of consumption.[19] More recently, Lee positioned Hayek at the core of modern conservative thought, highlighting how libertarian Tea Party activists mined Hayek's work after the 2008 economic crash and how conservative media personalities like Rush Limbaugh and Glenn Beck "jostled with one another over who had been his earliest champion."[20]

But first, Hayek made a name for himself by offering the ultra-rich a rebuttal to the Keynesian welfare state. Public argument shifts when rhetors can influence both symbolic forms and cultivate a new climate of thought.[21] Acknowledging that dual function is needed to understand Hayek's influence, because he never succeeded in totally debunking the Keynesian welfare state. But Hayek did offer an attractive alternative.

Like Herbert Spencer and Andrew Carnegie, the economy was understood by Hayek to be governed by "autonomous laws" that could be discovered by employing the right tools.[22] Economists were best equipped for such discovery because they were like scientists, plying their esoteric branch of knowledge but with the autonomous laws of the political economy as their subject. And not only economists: Perspicacity could also be evidenced through *business expertise*—an affirming qualification for the ultra-rich.[23] Reflections of transcendent superiority are evidenced here in the link between worth, wealth, and merit. For example, Hayek exuded confidence in his ability to understand deep elements of the human condition. More specifically, Hayek was suspicious of Keynes's equality-orientation because it contradicted human nature. Hayek knew some people were better than others. But he worried, with the USSR as a foil, that "a network of small, complicated rules" set by authority figures would keep "the most original minds and most energetic characters" from rising "above the crowd."[24]

In so doing, Hayek adopted the priestly persona observed also in Herbert Spencer. He was a realist—a neutral arbiter of objective economic and political analysis describing the laws of the natural world like a physicist describes gravity. To that end, Friedrich Hayek's argument in *The Road to Serfdom* functions as a compelling illustration of oligarchy's development in the twentieth century.

The Road to Serfdom

The Road to Serfdom (1944) earned Friedrich Hayek fame, influence, and embarrassment. He worried the global phenomenon of what he called his "pamphlet" overshadowed his life of "strictly scientific work."[25] But he came to terms with its success later in life because he understood the impact his short book had on global conversations about political economy.

Hayek began *The Road to Serfdom* with a dedication to the "socialists of all parties." His argument was not subtle. Because socialism led to slavery, and socialism permeated every political party, the entire western world was under threat. Consider Hayek's "road" metaphor in the book title. The road was a metaphor for an impersonal, abstract, objective, and telic force. Hayek essentialized a complicated political economy: We travel down either the road to serfdom or the road to freedom. He saw history progressing in the direction of totalitarianism, and he wrote his book to warn Western democracies against the central planning that accelerated us toward that end.[26] "There is no other possibility than either the order governed by the impersonal discipline of the market or that directed by the will of a few individuals," Hayek wrote.[27] For Hayek, the competitive system was the only way to achieve economic justice—the only way someone born poor can reach great wealth solely by their own efforts. Notice the link between the road metaphor and natural law: Hayek warned readers to get off the road to serfdom and the unnatural orientation toward equality and, instead, to return to the road marked by competition and free enterprise.

Hayek's reader could feel his genuine concern for the fate of western democracy. His context explains some of the urgency. Hayek wrote *The Road to Serfdom* between 1940 and 1943, in the ashes of World War II. His outlook was gloomy because he thought so many countries had already begun down the road that begins with socialism and ends with serfdom and slavery. His context also informs his foils. He linked the road to serfdom and Stalin's Russia. He linked the road to freedom—what he calls "the abandoned road"—to two hundred years of English ideas paving the way for western democracy around the world, including the spread of liberalism and democracy, capitalism and individualism, free trade and peace.[28] "Bondage and misery" await, but the road to serfdom was made initially attractive through appeals to *equality*.

The rhetorical struggle over *equality* emerged as an important fault line. Keynesianism rejected Spencer's natural law, accepted state interventions into the economy, and gathered consent by promising to orient such efforts toward *equality*. But Hayek assumed a state oriented toward equality was bound to fail. In this way, Hayek reflected a cogent rebuttal to Keynes by arguing that appeals to any ethic beyond self-interest was a ruse designed to fleece the wealthy of their hard-earned resources.[29] Inequality is not to be avoided. Rather, inequality consequentially reflects the victors in the competitive economic struggle. According to their conformation to natural and immutable economic laws, the ultra-rich maintain justification to exert influence far beyond the economic sphere. As a result, the ultra-rich are justified in maintaining their wealth and in offering economic and moral prescriptions for the rest to follow—a trend that continues to this day.[30]

Inequality is inevitable, Hayek assumed—even desirable. He wrote: "To give different people the same objective opportunities is not to give them the same subjective chance. It cannot be denied that the Rule of Law produces economic inequality—all that can be claimed for it is that this inequality is not designed to affect particular people in a particular way."[31] But Hayek conceded equality's immediate appeal for majoritarian democracy. He knew his road metaphor must resonate in a climate marked by progressive social movements improving the lives of ordinary people and overwhelming state-action defeating Hitler. "Socialistic trends of the preceding period [were] a necessary outcome," Hayek conceded. However, he worried the passion for equality would crowd out the passion for freedom.[32] By putting equality and freedom on separate roads, Hayek foreshadowed the argumentative parameters marking public conversations today. Equality is unnatural, and thus, so is socialism. Human action is ill-equipped for orienting a complex political economy toward freedom. Any attempt to do so would fail, he wrote: "The indisputable fact that the limits of our powers of imagination make it impossible to include in our scale of values more than a sector of the needs of the whole society, and that, since, strictly speaking, scales of value can exist only in individual minds, nothing but partial scales of values exist—scales which are inevitably different and often inconsistent with each other."[33] We can orient our family farm in the direction of freedom, or even our own factory, but we cannot imagine a political economy where equality does anything more than stifle individual freedom.

Failure would "be laid bare" as his opponent's "collectivist creed" would "inevitably destroy itself."[34] Collectivism was incompatible with the "indisputable fact" that values and morals are best determined by individuals, and any attempt by the collective to make these judgments would fail.[35] Keynesianism was a source of corruption, and "rolling forward the clock of progress" meant moving in the direction of "individual initiative and individual freedom and family responsibility in our society."[36] Hayek tried to intervene before we were enslaved. And he remained hopeful. Serfdom and slavery were not inevitable. Otherwise, Hayek said, "there was no point in writing" his book. "If people realize in time where their efforts may lead," we can get off the road to serfdom and back on the abandoned road leading to freedom and liberty.[37]

Hayek's road metaphor offered several distinct rhetorical advantages. Recall how Foucault described "the market" appearing as a natural and spontaneous mechanism governing the biopolitical dimensions of modern life in the previous century.[38] Coupled with Spencer and Carnegie, Hayek's road metaphor advanced the biopolitical genealogy of the market by portraying the political economy as unaffected by human involvement. Conceptualizing the economy in this way brought relief to the ultra-rich being blamed for causing the Great Depression. In response to public skepticism after 1929, the ultra-rich could now appeal to the road to freedom. Further, they could link their policy preferences to a new generation of anticommunist freedom fighters defending American free enterprise. Rockefeller, Morgan, and the du Ponts could look less greedy and more scientific by using Hayek to reposition themselves against the pursuit of their own selfish interests.[39] The rich were rich for a simple reason: They conformed to the natural, objective laws of capital accumulation. The poor did not. There is very little rhetorical space left to consider structural and systemic explanations for wealth and poverty, such as lead paint, trust funds, inherited wealth, and decrepit schools. Notice how Hayek contrasts the road to serfdom with a road to freedom by positioning success as the result of the "ability and enterprise of the people concerned."[40] Hayek narrows ability and enterprise to a specific set of personal qualities, including independence, self-reliance, the willingness to bear risks, the readiness to back one's own conviction against a majority, the willingness to engage in voluntary cooperation with one's neighbors, individual initiative and local responsibility, respect for custom and tradition, and a healthy suspicion of power and authority.[41] Hayek knows most people do not have these traits. He also knows stories like Andrew Carnegie's—in which a "man who starts poor" reaches great heights—will be uncommon. But that is the point. Great heights are not for everyone.

Hayek affirmed the belief that anyone willing to conform to the objective standards of natural law can become successful in America. Hayek said the signs of impending doom on the road to serfdom were obvious to anyone who had the motivation to see them. He wrote, "One need not be a prophet to be aware of impending dangers. An accidental combination of experience and interest will often reveal events to one man under aspects which few yet see."[42] We succeed or fail based on our own efforts. The ultra-rich were merely doing what anyone could do. In Hayek's terms, the rich have gathered the "experience and interest" that others have not. Those unwilling to notice and act on the objective truths must be either unintentionally naive or willfully ignorant.

True Visionary

Hayek's road metaphor aligned with a shifting intellectual climate, as the study of political economy dropped the first half of its label to assume a more objective, empirical, and apolitical scholarly identity. The discipline of economics offers a rich case study for an entire academic discipline foreclosing the role of the state. The result was enhanced prestige from their focus on mathematical and scientific legitimacy, but that decision came with a cost: namely, the assumption that economics was not only more important than politics but altogether disparate.[43]

After the 1930s, the entire study of economics as a scholarly discipline became aligned with the study of rational economic actors, competitive markets, and individual self-interest designed to produce optimal market conditions for everyone. As Hanan wrote, "The axiomatic assumption of homo economicus—the belief that when provided with the correct sociopolitical conditions, rational economic decision-making is an innate human faculty"—now defined the ontology of modern economic policy.[44] The state is expected to maintain a level playing field so that rational economic actors can compete to maximize profits and accumulate resources. A potent material-discursive touchstone is reflected in this disciplinary turn—a new framework by which "The Economy," and, to a lesser extent, "The Market," informed the rhetorical dimensions of daily life for so many.

The emergence of a discrete, affective economy functions within a biopolitical form of rational economic persuasion that could materially alter one's body—quickly, smoothly, and efficiently.[45] For example, Milton Friedman wrote a preface to *The Road to Serfdom* in 1994 that articulated the bridge between Hayek's aspirations and achievements: Friedman said Hayek's book had "become a true classic: essential reading for everyone who is seriously interested in politics in the broadest and least partisan sense, a book whose central message is timeless, applicable to a wide variety of concrete situations." Ultimately, Hayek's textual persona was read as a neutral arbiter of objective, economic, and political analysis describing the laws of the natural world like a physicist describes gravity. As evidence, consider how George H.W. Bush described Hayek when he honored him with a Presidential Medal of Freedom in 1991. Bush said Hayek was a "true visionary" whose work allowed us to see "beyond the horizon" and "foresaw freedom's triumph" by revolutionizing political and economic thought.[46]

Given Hayek's empirical and apolitical persona, it is unsurprising that Hayek is portrayed today as a "conservative" or "libertarian" intellectual force who focused more on economic science and mathematical modeling than politics.[47] Chaput, for example, argues that Hayek endorsed a minimal state in which "government actions are strictly delimited by a few universally agreed upon rules."[48] Corey Robin describes a conservative table where Hayek was seated next to Ayn Rand and Antonin Scalia.[49] Lee links libertarianism, Barry Goldwater, and Hayek. Benjamin Friedman locates the roots of libertarianism in Hayek's *Road to Serfdom*.[50] But Hayek was not a scientist or a conservative, and his influence is not reflected in the conservative construction of a smaller, leaner political economy. Despite his appeals otherwise, Hayek operates upon what Chaïm Perelman would call *probable*—rather than certain—premises.[51] Appeals to the natural, preexisting economy formally paralleled neutral and objective language, but always imperfectly and incompletely—because human interference always adulterates natural economic conditions. Thus, it would be incomplete to conclude Hayek's story by linking his road metaphor to the right side of the ideological axis. Robin argues that although Hayek is assumed to be the leading theoretician of neoliberalism, it is more useful to classify his contribution within "the most genuine political theory of capitalism the right managed to produce."[52] Robin affirms my analysis by illustrating why Hayek did not seek to produce a "shift from government to the individual, as is often claimed by conservatives," as Robin writes. Nor did Hayek seek "a shift from the state to the market, or from society to the atomized individual."[53] The conceptual value of exploring Hayek's *textual persona* is evinced here. Recall that Hayek was embarrassed by the success of *The Road to Serfdom* because it overshadowed his life of "strictly scientific work."[54] I wonder if Hayek was also embarrassed by the success of *The Road to Serfdom* for another reason: Hayek's road was very unHayekian.[55]

Repoliticize and Recentralize the State

During the second half of his life, Hayek contradicted much of what he wrote in *The Road to Serfdom*, including the "strictly scientific" approach that he said mollified his embarrassment. In 1972, for instance, Hayek's *The Limits of Growth* unhitched political economic research from the "pretense of knowledge" and the methods of the physical sciences because political economic knowledge was always too limited to make scientific propositions.[56] Instead, he conceded, pattern prediction was the best hope for his discipline—a hope that looked inferior in the age of science and computer simulation but was nonetheless a more accurate and humbler epistemology.[57] Hayek would also show himself to be more like Keynes and Polanyi than the metaphor of the road permitted: They each agreed the market could not care for itself.[58] Plus, Hayek had intimate experiences with competent government.[59] The Keynesian welfare state was on the way to saving liberal capitalism in America by weakening communism and socialism as attractive alternatives. A lean federal government would not stand up well against Hitler's war machine, either. World War II sobered the most zealous free market advocates and reminded many how important a powerful, state-run military apparatus could be in promoting the security of a society and its markets. And as it turns out, central planning in America did not lead to serfdom.

An exploration beyond *The Road to Serfdom* offers the chance to extend the scholarly literature. For example, Lee details a Hayekian political philosophy "infused with a predictable skepticism toward concentrating power" and an effort to "protect the public from state violence."[60] Lee also cites Bruce Caldwell, a Hayek biographer, who would align Hayek with the classical liberal inclination to define a "private sphere of individual activity, to grant the state a monopoly on coercion, and then to limit the coercive powers of the state to those instances where it is itself preventing coercion."[61] There is ample evidence from Hayek's early work, especially *The Road to Serfdom*, to affirm his position on the political Right. Consider how the topos of Hayekian *competition* contradicts the aspirations of his wealthy funders, for example. Hayek pursued a "competitive system . . . where it depends solely on him and not on the favors of the mighty, and where nobody can prevent a man from attempting to achieve this result."[62] But also recall that corporate elites like Carnegie, Rockefeller, Morgan, and du Pont did not want to compete on a level playing field with threatening upstarts, and they did not want to compete without state protection. They wanted to be insulated from the competition of a free market. They wanted to control the state—to enjoin it on their behalf. Rather than depoliticize and decentralize, they sought to repoliticize and recentralize the enormous resources of the state to protect and maximize their interests. It is possible corporate elites sincerely aspired to a Hayekian anti-statism, but they were able to detach this principled belief from their pragmatic behavior because they were making so much money after World War II.[63] Even more broadly, Hayek's textual persona does not align with how the modern political economy developed in the twentieth century.

In *The Birth of Biopolitics*, Foucault highlights the need to draw a clear distinction between lean government/free market neoliberalism and the law-and-economic tradition of ordoliberalism. A complex modern economy requires regulation, Foucault writes, which carves out necessary space for "institutions and rules of law exist[ing] in reciprocal conditioning relationship with the economy."[64] Jamie Peck traces the consensus among conservative intellectuals and their ultra-rich supporters in their shared understanding that the minimalist paeans to a nightwatchman state were unworkable in a modern economy.[65] Hayek illuminates the discursive source for this incongruity. Later in life, when Hayek moved from the University of Chicago to Freiburg, his most important scholarly works reflected the law-and-economic tradition of ordoliberalism detailed by Foucault, much more so than the free market/lean government neoliberal tradition he so often carries the torch for.[66]

Appropriate Legal System

Hayek rejected the image of an autonomous nation-state ambling along until it came to a fork in the road.[67] Hayek maintained no loyalty to representative democracy.[68] Hayek admitted he had "no intention of making a fetish of democracy."[69] Instead, Hayek wrote: "Democracy is essentially a means, a utilitarian device for safeguarding internal peace and individual freedom. As such it is by no means infallible or certain. Nor must we forget that there has often been much more cultural and spiritual freedom under an autocratic rule than under some democracies—and it is at least conceivable that under the government of a very homogeneous and doctrinaire majority democratic government might be as oppressive as the worst dictatorship."[70] Reflecting the ambivalent approach to representative democracy detailed previously, Hayek understood social and economic stability required the public's consent. But like Aristotle, Hayek assumed democracy did not contain any inherent value over an autocracy or aristocracy.[71] Democracy was a means to an end, and there were other means. As a result, Hayek's enduring position on the political Right should be reconsidered. Looking closely at a range of representative discourse reveals a complicated affinity for the state, including stark departures from conservative orthodoxy, especially his support for nationalized health care.[72] Hayek admitted, "The question whether the state should or should not 'act' or 'interfere' poses an altogether false alternative."[73] Instead, Hayek acknowledged the importance of government, writing: "The functioning of a competition not only requires adequate organization of certain institutions like money, markets, and channels of information—some of which can never be adequately provided by private enterprise—but it depends, above all, on the existence of an *appropriate legal system*, a legal system designed both to preserve competition and to make it operate as beneficially as possible."[74] I put *appropriate legal system* in italics to emphasize how Hayek's use of that phrase will shed light on an important point of intervention for oligarchic thought over the next century.

More than an economist, Hayek was a legal scholar focused on developing statecraft, law, and legislation to defend the market against representative democracy. Hayek had no real interest in liberating markets. He wanted to institutionalize the rule of law.[75] Hayek affirmed the need for "an authority capable of enforcing [the] rules."[76] Hayek described the "self-regulating" forces of the economy in an inaugural lecture upon his return to Europe, but he did not pivot to a shrunken state after that. To the contrary, he followed with an argument for a "framework" for the economy.[77]

CHAPTER 4

After World War II, Hayek began to use the law as an aggressive tool to build—not just protect—a legal and statecraft framework for the market.[78] Such efforts were never limited to the negative, rolled back, demolition-minded aspirations associated with the icons of the political Right. Hayek conceded as much when he diverged from the road metaphor by describing the political economy variously as clouds, crystals, a leaf, a switchboard, and a garden—each requiring political cultivation and care.[79] Consequently, the economist should not assume the duties of a "craftsman shaping his handiwork." Instead, the economist should assume the duties of a gardener "cultivating growth by providing the appropriate environment."[80]

Hayek's affinity for violence also highlights some of the lingering incongruities in his status on the Right. Recall that Lee argues Hayek "remade libertarian-conservatism as a humanitarian impulse to protect the public from state violence."[81] And yet: Hayek displays an affinity for state-sanctioned violence against the unfit, especially to protect oligarchic profit from the mob tyranny of representative democracy.[82] Hayek's support for violent suppression of protesters in Europe and violent dictators in Latin America is well documented.[83] In 1961, Hayek sent a copy of *The Constitution of Liberty* to Portuguese strongman Antonio Salazar with a note expressing the hope that his book would help Salazar "design a constitution which is proof against the abuses of democracy."[84] Hayek justified his relationship with Augusto Pinochet in Chile by admitting he would "prefer a liberal dictator to a democratic government lacking liberalism" and that "it is possible for a dictator to govern in a liberal way"—while qualifying that this should be only a "temporary transitional arrangement."[85] Aristotle, Spencer, and Carnegie would have concurred.

All the Docile and Gullible

Tolerance for violence is not unique to Hayek. Structural forms of oppression and violence have long appealed to a fantasy of the common good.[86] But an oligarchic governing philosophy oriented toward protecting and enhancing the wealth of the rich and maximizing pain and suffering for the rest points to a pressing contradiction. Because most people are undeserving, the logical next step is an aversion to equality, social justice, democracy, and even peace. The irony is noteworthy. One might assume that freedom from state interference would also mean freedom from state violence, but the rhetorical record shows that professed supporters of liberty, freedom, and a lean state can be surprisingly comfortable with state-sanctioned surveillance, coercion, and violence, including armed suppression of dissenters and protesters, advanced military technologies in local communities, and mass incarceration for minor law violations.[87] The rationale for crushing Civil Rights protesters, striking workers, debt-burdened students, and democracy-minded activists is derived from such cynicism. Violence serves an indispensable instrumental and symbolic function. Oligarchic discourse justifies sacrificing those who come up short according to the yardstick of material stratification. Although the ubiquity of violence seems incongruous, it is reconciled by the assumption that the ability to deploy force is consequentially evinced through existing hierarchies of wealth and power. The person with the most money and biggest guns deserves to exercise their prerogative, in other words. They would not have it otherwise.

Although scarred by World War II, Hayek focused more on FDR and Keynes than Hitler or Stalin. Totalitarian coercion did not worry Hayek, especially later in life, as much as what we would describe today as affective and biopolitical control. Hayek worked hard to develop the language of spontaneous order, economic freedom, and the corruption of big government to better inform an intellectual class that would then—in a top-down fashion—be able to go out and influence the masses.[88] Hayek doubted whether the demos could rationally deliberate about the finer points of the political economy. Hayek's affinity for law and institutions came from the assumption that such rules could provide a framework for individuals to act on their own volition.[89]

Hayek described the "impersonal discipline of the market" as the more promising alternative to totalitarian authoritarianism.[90] Impersonal discipline is an operative phrase, revealing a consistent thread informing the capacity of the ordinary citizen to consciously deliberate toward effective self-governance. Hayek was not suspicious of central government; he was suspicious of majoritarian representative democracy derived from public deliberation.[91] Hayek was skeptical of the people's demands for equality, inclusion, and social justice because he thought most were docile and gullible.[92] He thought most people were willing to submit to uninspiring work and "to do the bidding of others" because their underdevelopment scared them away from the "responsibilities of economic life."[93] Hayek worried elected officials in a representative democracy would reflect the public's ignorance, "covering the surface of society with a network of small complicated rules, minute and uniform," that would sap the energy and creativity of the most fit.[94] To Hayek, legislators were all "fallible men" who lacked the necessary capacity to imagine and centrally plan a complicated, global economy.⁹⁵ The road to serfdom was marked by opportunistic politicians, Hayek wrote: "Able to obtain the support of all the docile and gullible, who have no strong convictions of their own but are prepared to accept a ready-made system of values if it is only drummed into their ears sufficiently loudly and frequently. It will be those whose vague and imperfectly formed ideas are easily swayed and whose passions and emotions are readily aroused who will thus swell the ranks of the totalitarian party."⁹⁶ During the postwar democratic expansion, Hayek pointed to clear and obvious foils to support his democratic cynicism, especially in the global south as decolonization efforts conflicted with the ruling elites' desires. Only elite transnational alliances could circumscribe these democratic trends.⁹⁷ Hayek was suspicious of central planning, organized labor, and representative democracy.⁹⁸ Because the public was so gullible, there was no guarantee western democracy would conform to natural laws—at least in time to save capitalism. Slobodian explained Hayek's focus on transnational legal institutions as a mechanism for elites to "protect the world market against governments."⁹⁹ If the political economy were an ideological seesaw, and Hayek sat on the Right, a word like "protecting" could inform lean government/free market neoliberalism. But I worry such passive and referential language contradicts Hayek's aspirations. Hayek went much further. Hayek desired a state that slammed the doors of opportunity on the unworthy—a state that deployed its legal, coercive, and symbolic tools to maintain a maldistribution of resources.¹⁰⁰ Consequently, the charge upon the state diverges from the stale conservative associations with protecting the market.

This Way Lies Charlatanism and Worse

In December 1974, in his acceptance speech for the Nobel Prize in Economic Sciences Hayek highlighted the incongruity between his most influential public argument and how American democracy actually works. Hayek's speech was unconventional because it was an argument against the very award that he was giving the speech to accept. Like other "sciences of man," Hayek claimed economics "looks superficially like the most scientific procedure [but] is often the most unscientific." Economists are posers, exhibiting the "propensity to imitate as closely as possible the procedures of the brilliantly successful physical sciences" but always failing, and thus "lead[ing] to outright error." Economists are not physical scientists, Hayek argued. Their study of the market "depends on the actions of many individuals" whose "circumstances will determine the outcome of a process" and "will hardly very be fully known or measurable." Physical sciences can explain and predict "based on laws which accounted for the observed phenomena as a function of comparatively few variables." The market is too complex for that set of tools. Economists struggle to test their predictions like scientists because they face "special difficulties about testing proposed explanations" when they apply their "theories to any particular situation in the real world."

Hayek zeroed in on *competition* as an illustration of the economist's plight. Economists making scientific predictions about competition struggle because they "have to deal with structures of essential complexity," which only produce predictable results with a sample size large enough to account for all the variables. But that was a fool's errand. Hayek warned of the "danger in the exuberant feeling of every growing power which the advance of the physical sciences has engendered and which tempts man to try . . . to subject not only our natural but also our human environment to the control of a human will." Hayek cited "some ball game" as an illustration. If you knew all the variables you could predict a game's outcome, including each player's ability, strength, speed, and mental capacity. Gamblers in Las Vegas's sportsbooks make a lot of money this way. But are they scientists? Hayek would say no. Basketball is not a science because you "are not able to ascertain those facts and in consequences the results of the game will be outside the range of the scientifically predictable."

Writing in 1974, Hayek conceded the possibility that "with the help of modern computers it should be easy enough to insert these data into the appropriate blanks of the theoretical formulae and to derive a prediction." Recall that Hayek was speaking during a decade when the pretense of knowledge based on the modeling capacities of modern computers elevated public confidence in a certain and knowable future to new heights.[101] And yet, for Hayek, the modern computer failed to mediate the economist's scientific illegitimacy because he or she could never ascertain all the necessary variables. To assume otherwise betrayed the arrogance of the economists Hayek himself had a hand in promoting. Far too many, he said decades after publishing *The Road to Serfdom*, "happily proceed on the fiction that the factors which can be measured are the only ones that are relevant," leading to testable propositions based solely on the subjective whims of the economist choosing the variables. As a result, economists have produced "deplorable effects." Hayek concludes his opening paragraph by conceding his discipline has "indeed at the moment little cause for pride: as a profession we have made a mess of things." Hayek's low regard for the public is reflected as he linked the economist's scientific ruse to his discipline's growing prestige.

Do not forget that he is giving this address to the Alfred Nobel committee who has just awarded him the Nobel Prize. The Nobel Committee's Memorial Prize in Economic Sciences is itself an example of how far Hayek's ruse penetrated public argument—a reflection of the public's "uncritical acceptance of assertions which have the *appearance* of being scientific," Hayek emphasized. He went on: "Yet the confidence in the unlimited power of science is only too often based on a false belief that the scientific method consists in the application of a ready-made technique, or in imitating the form rather than the substance of scientific procedure, as if one needed only to follow some cooking recipes to solve all social problems." Hayek's textual persona shines through as he illuminates the "conflict between the present mood the public expects science to achieve in satisfaction of popular hopes and what is really in its power." Even if "the true scientists should recognize the limitations of what they do in the field of human affairs, so long as the public expects more there will always be some who will pretend, and perhaps honestly believe, that they can do more to meet popular demands than is really in their power." Remember that Hayek did not think highly of most people. He closed the thought, "It is often difficult enough for the expert, and certainly in many instances impossible for the layman, to distinguish between legitimate and illegitimate claims advanced in the name of science."[102]

Hayek applied his critique to a range of foils across the political spectrum and within his own discipline. He faulted "impetuous younger members of our profession" who "are not always prepared to accept" scientific limitations. By 1974, he had found a clear foil in the mathematization of economics, including the extensive forecasting and modeling of the economy represented by the University of Chicago school of economics. He also blamed President Lyndon Johnson's liberal technocrats who, assuming government should play a proactive role in creating economic opportunity, built an administrative empire on the scientific assumptions Hayek decried. The Kennedy and Johnson administrations, full of postwar triumphalism, thought they could pull the fiscal and monetary levers from the executive branch in a way that would calibrate government interventions to ensure sustained economic growth with scientific precision.[103] "This way lies charlatanism and worse," Hayek warned.

Conclusion

For Friedrich Hayek and his intellectual allies, democratic cynicism justified minoritarian power concentration. The incongruity between *The Road* to *Serfdom* and his Nobel speech belies any principled, consistent loyalty to democratic first principles. The masses were not worthy of such loyalty. Concentrated power was the only north star. Such democratic cynicism was affirmed during the middle of the twentieth century as the American public continued to reject Hayek's outlook and the policies it produced. During the 1950s and 1960s, the Keynesian welfare state enjoyed broad support among the middle and working classes, in large part because of the impact its policies had on their lives, but many corporate leaders also affirmed the postwar economic order because it sparked such massive economic growth.[104] It seemed, at least in this moment, the American public was not ready to embrace the oligarchic orientation championed by Spencer, Carnegie, and Hayek. Instead, the country responded to the Great Depression by embracing an equality orientation propping up the New Deal, the Keynesian welfare state, and in the 1950s the legal rationale of the Earl Warren Court.

Warren's rationale aligned with the larger ubiquity of the equality orientation and its public policy impact during the middle of the twentieth century. Even conservatives affirmed this Keynesian outlook on the state/market relationship.[105] After the Great Depression, America's ruling elite thought it wiser to give ordinary Americans a political voice, legal protection to organize, and a safety net than risk losing control of the entire edifice.[106] But if the equality orientation justified broad support for progressive taxation, regulation, and organized labor, where would it end?

Echoing Spencer's and Hayek's slippery slope fears, many ultra-rich Americans worried that the logic of FDR, Keynes—and now Earl Warren—could one day urge massive wealth redistribution in an effort to align with their equality orientation. But their concerns were rejected by the American public in the face of the Great Depression and World War II as hollow, self-serving, and impractical. The influential University of Chicago economist and law professor Richard Posner put it well: Those troubled by the New Deal and Great Society "didn't have the vocabulary or conceptual system" with which to weaken the existing Keynesian thought structures or propose an attractive alternative.[107]

The ultra-rich seethed. Adolph Coors, Irénée and Pierre du Pont, Jasper Crane, and John D. Rockefeller were marginalized, blamed for the economic collapse of 1929, and unable to pull the levers of power in their favor. They felt betrayed, feckless, angry, and more cynical than ever.[108] As a response, the ultra-rich poured their resources into the courts rather than wasting their efforts on a skeptical American public and their elected representatives.

5

Judicial Oligarchy and the Rhetoric of James J. Kilpatrick

JAMES MADISON, ALEXANDER HAMILTON, THOMAS JEFFERSON, AND the framers of the US Constitution designed the American judicial system to be insulated from majoritarian influence. Compared to the executive and legislative branches, judicial review is supposed to be counter-majoritarian so the courts can constrain democratic energy and protect the rights of minorities.[1] But the court's counter-majoritarian structure also allows wealthy elites to orient the law toward oligarchic ends. The Lochner era provides a fitting example. In 1905, the Supreme Court intervened in *Lochner v. New York* to void a state law limiting the number of hours a bakery employee could work. The Court grounded its ruling in the due process clause of the Fourteenth Amendment.[2] Between the *Lochner* ruling in 1905 and the Court's affirmation of the New Deal in 1937, the Supreme Court struck down almost two hundred worker and social welfare regulations, including laws outlawing monopolies and child labor, protections for minimum wage, and restrictions on banking, railroad, and insurance corporations.[3] Legal historians and journalists, as a result, tend to position the Lochner era on the political Right, describing the Court during the first three decades of the twentieth century as conservative, laissez-faire, and oriented toward economic liberty.[4] By connecting laissez-faire jurisprudence to the Constitution, the Court codified into law the view that "government is best which governs least." Lochner's legal interpretation was well aligned with a larger political and economic logic oriented toward natural order and divine law so that a deregulated and unadulterated political-economic system will, in the long run, work to the good.[5]

To be sure, the Lochner Court affirms public understanding of conservative jurisprudence. But the Lochner era also provides an entry point for exploring how legal discourse lights up the tensions and incongruities in our public conversations about the American political economy. For example, "government is best which governs least" overlooks the fact that in the *Lochner* ruling, the judicial branch of federal government intervened to strike down legislation passed by New York state. Further, describing the Court's legal philosophy as "laissez-faire" neglects to account for the essential role the federal government was playing in the modernizing, industrial economy of the early twentieth century.[6] Robber barons and industrial tycoons understood better than anyone that the government and its courts did not just negate policy; the state also provided the framework by which the market economy functioned. A Supreme Court oriented toward economic liberty and laissez-faire deregulation in public conversations drew attention away from the Court's capacity to concentrate economic and political power through legal support for international treaties, corporate relocations, military actions based on the desires of transnational corporations, and breaking down trade barriers.[7] Since the end of the Civil War, railroad and energy corporations had been leveraging every source of influence from their immense instrumental and symbolic resources to erect insurmountable barriers to entry, pressure state legislators, recruit and fund sympathetic politicians, and punish states that regulated their corporations or industries by withdrawing investment capital and halting new construction.[8] William Magnuson highlighted the specific political interventions of the Union Pacific railroad, who "regularly interfered in the doings of state legislatures, striking down unfavorable bills and defeating candidates who might champion them."[9]

But starting in 1937, a new judicial doctrine began to supplant Lochner's oligarchic orientation by elevating equality over liberty.[10] Soon after, legal and popular support for New Deal–era legislation was codified, including regulation of industry, progressive taxation, and support for organized labor—each highlighting how limited oligarchic influence became in mid-century, postwar America.[11] Ultra-rich corporate tycoons, once dominant, were now rendered feckless. In their eyes, the Supreme Court looked to be contradicting the self-referential, natural, and divine power concentrations necessary for a functioning modern democracy. FDR's New Deal encouraged many Americans to start expecting things from the state, to believe the state owed them something beyond the protection of a few basic rights, and to assume it was the responsibility of the state to eliminate suffering and adversity.[12] Further, they thought the redistributive policies of the New Deal were bringing the country to the brink of collapse, expanding

CHAPTER 5

expectations of citizenship to the undeserving, and upsetting the natural order needed to keep a lid on mob rule. A Supreme Court that was once an ally had turned into an enemy.

The American public disagreed. According to Phillips-Fein, after the Lochner era and the Great Depression, support for FDR's New Deal and John Maynard Keynes's government fiscal interventions grew as Friedrich Hayek's reputation declined concomitantly.[13] Many Americans acknowledged that government spending counterbalanced economic downturns, and a robust welfare state offered protection to needy Americans. From the margins, ultra-rich Americans like Adolph Coors, Irénée and Pierre du Pont, and John D. Rockefeller searched for a rhetorical response that could not be dismissed by the American public as outdated, impractical, or greedy.

Their fears that the Supreme Court was being transformed into a source of unjust, unconstitutional, and unnatural resource distribution were amplified in October 1953 when Governor Earl Warren of California was sworn in as chief justice.[14] Soon after, the Warren Court sparked what became known as a "rights revolution," granting criminal defendants the right to an attorney, non-Christians freedom from prayer in public schools, and the poor new protections for their welfare benefits.[15] Coupled with renewed rights for non-Christians, criminals, and the poor, the Warren Court's *Brown v. Board of Education* ruling in 1954 added racial equality to the growing list of perceived oligarchic threats.

To its critics, the *Brown* ruling misinterpreted the Constitution and violated state and federal separation by intervening in the state and local community's right to oversee their schools. More worrisome for the ultra-rich, the Warren Court was overextending the judiciary's power and ruling unconstitutionally based on the discretionary and partisan whims of the liberal justices now dominating the bench.[16] Reversing *Lochner*, the Court was engaging in a version of judicial activism running counter to the natural order. *Brown*, in particular, looked like an unnatural intervention on behalf of a justifiably marginalized minority causing the legal destruction of a valuable site of adversity-testing: segregated public schools. If wealth and power were outward signs of virtue, then Warren's rights revolution, the Court's prioritizing equality over liberty, and expanding rights for criminals, the poor, and racial minorities represented the unconstitutional intervention of a corrupt federal government. *Brown* was judicial activism at its worst: activist judges pandering to the public, increasing the size and scope of the government, hastening the pace of change, and producing a dependent American citizenry ripe for totalitarian conquest.[17]

JAMES J. KILPATRICK

Many scholars have suggested that postwar conservatism, for the rest of the twentieth century, should be understood as a direct reaction to *Brown*. Barry Goldwater used *Brown* backlash to redefine postwar conservatism against Eisenhower moderates, Rockefeller Republicans, and the Chamber of Commerce's tolerance for the New Deal and Great Society. Nixon's Southern strategy and Ronald Reagan's dog-whistling revanchism followed after.[18] And yet, the alliance of *Brown* reactionaries with postwar conservatism was not inevitable. One can imagine a plausible counterfactual history in which southern segregationists were sidelined and the *Brown* ruling was interpreted in alignment with the core principles of conservatism, including the protections of equal rights spelled out in the Declaration of Independence, the "common defense and general welfare clause" in the US Constitution, and the essential role of quality public education in distinguishing American meritocratic exceptionalism from the welfare states of western Europe. One can also imagine a potent political coalition marked by the alliance of moderate Eisenhower Republicans from the North and newly enfranchised Black voters from the South receptive to conservatism's appeals to stability, order, and religious tradition. Between the 1954 *Brown* ruling and Barry Goldwater's nomination in 1964, the political context was ripe for just such a coalition. Party affiliations and political labels were less calcified than they are today. Nationwide, public support for the southern Civil Rights protestors swung inexorably after *Brown*, and Black Americans soon became a major political force in the South.[19] A harmonious, multiracial coalition could have constituted a community by affirming the structure of constitutional interpretation undergirding Keynesian regulation and organized labor, as well as concede to desegregated schools and the regulatory burden of the Civil Rights Movement's demands for fair employment, wages, housing, and public accommodations.[20] Such a coalition would have altered the course of American political and economic history.

But it was not to be. Postwar conservatism expelled Republican moderates from the Northeast and neglected Black religious conservatives from the South in favor of a motley community of crony capitalists, religious fundamentalists, and southern racists. The religious and racist influence on postwar conservatism has been well covered, including the impact of Jerry Falwell, Pat Robertson, William F. Buckley, Russell Kirk, George Wallace, and Bull Connor.[21] What's been lacking is a rigorous exploration of the ultra-rich, who saw in *Brown* a chance to return to a Lochner era marked by judicial oligarchy. The rhetoric of James J. Kilpatrick represents an opportunity to fill in this gap.

CHAPTER 5

Towering Questions of Constitutional Governance

In 1958, Virginia governor J. Lindsay Almond created the **Virginia Commission on Constitutional Government** to defend states' rights in the wake of the *Brown v. Board of Education* ruling.[22] The commission attracted the leading gentlemen-intellectuals of the Virginia establishment, including journalists, lawyers, and politicians. David J. Mays, a respected attorney and Pulitzer Prize–winning author, would lead the commission, but it was his vice president, James Kilpatrick, who deserves close examination. Kilpatrick was appointed the leader of the commission's publication department. He was a polished debater and an incisive editorialist with valuable political connections.[23] Further, he was not a fulminating redneck bigot. He was among a small group of competent, erudite, and palatable southern conservatives opposing Warren and *Brown*. Described as the embodiment of sophisticated jurisprudence, Kilpatrick did not look like a racist demagogue, but he also was not reflexively egalitarian either.[24]

Kilpatrick was raised in Oklahoma, graduated high school two years early to study journalism at the University of Missouri, and moved to Virginia to assume an influential editorial position at the *Richmond News Dealer*. Although a midwestern transplant, Kilpatrick embodied Virginia gentility, defending the concentration of political and economic power into the hands of a small group of white leaders but without relying on the virulent racism of the John Birch Society or the Virginia Citizens' Council.[25] Kilpatrick balanced gentility, sophistication, and legal acumen with fire-breathing editorials supporting interposition, massive resistance, and the existential defense of the southern way of life against the intrusions of the Warren Court.[26]

Historian William Hustwit described Kilpatrick's reaction to the *Brown* decision as a marriage between segregationist thought and political and intellectual conservatism. Hustwit also called Kilpatrick the "dean of conservatism" and detailed his influence on conservative thought leaders like William F. Buckley, Barry Goldwater, Frank Chodorov, and Frank Meyer (Buckley hired Kilpatrick to write for the *National Review* and Barry Goldwater hired him onto his 1964 presidential election team).[27] "While Kilpatrick certainly was not the singular mastermind behind the postwar South's transformation into a two-party, Republican- dominated region," Hustwit writes, "he was a pioneering authority who used his considerable standing on the Right and his moderated racial language to bring Dixie into alignment with the realities of the post-civil rights world."[28] Many of Kilpatrick's post-*Brown* arguments reemerged in Richard Nixon's Southern strategy, including the primacy of states' rights, limited government, fiscal conservatism, and an emphasis on law and order, but without direct reference to interposition, racial segregation, and virulent bigotry.[29] Later, Kilpatrick's rhetoric would appear in Ronald Reagan's stated hostility toward the federal government, deference to free enterprise, and respect for traditional institutions, values, and private property.

Kilpatrick began his rise as an unyielding and openly defiant segregationist, and his anti-Black racism informs his emergence as an influential conservative voice. Although scholars and journalists tend to highlight the stylistic differences between James Kilpatrick and southern racists like Bull Connor, George Wallace and Jim Clark, his substantive, pragmatic political efforts were applauded by white supremacists in the South.[30] Kilpatrick was a racist, and he was affectively repulsed by the prospect of white Virginian school children being forced to attend public school with Black children. But his public support for racial segregation was unoriginal. As Hustwit wrote, "Since basically every successful public figure in the South was a segregationist in the 1950s and 1960s, little may be gleaned by concentrating only on segregation."[31] Further, his racism alone cannot explain his durability. Over his decades as an influential conservative rhetor, Kilpatrick was not limited by his appeals to states' rights racial segregation and even complicated questions about the federal and state educational policy. If Kilpatrick and his Virginia Commission on Constitutional Government (VCCG) would have remained in their racist lane—publishing books and pamphlets calling for massive resistance, interposition, and segregation—they would not be worth our attention. But Kilpatrick expanded his argumentative scope and target audience, beyond southern racists worried about Black and white children sitting together in the school lunchroom, taking aim at the entire structure of constitutional interpretation undergirding mid-century American liberal democracy.[32]

Kilpatrick's public reaction to *Brown* was sober, clinical, and academic. He promised his *News Dealer* readers that he would "resist this judgment of the court . . . quietly, honorably, lawfully," but with the "strength of a tradition that has resisted tyranny before."[33] His commission was focused on a "matter of law, not sociology," as it sought to set aside the emotion evoked by *Brown* and move onto the realist terrain of constitutional legal rationale. While conceding that much of the commission's messaging would examine the crisis *Brown* caused, its work would not be defined as "a problem of race relations . . . but as a transcendent question of constitutional law."[34]

CHAPTER 5

Kilpatrick charged the Warren Court with misinterpreting the Constitution and ignoring the long-established principles of constitutional law.[35] Kilpatrick understood that "states' rights" as a defense of limited government would repulse many outside the South.[36] "Our concern is constitutional government, especially the relationship of the Federal and State governments," Kilpatrick wrote.[37] His commission was not at war with the Supreme Court or the federal government. Instead, he sought to recalibrate the relationship between the powers of the state and the powers of the federal government.[38] It worked. His publications department at the VCCG authored rebuttals to *Brown* that resonated with audiences all over the country, including policy makers and legislators in Washington, DC, and Columbus, Ohio, lawyers and bar associations in Texas and Wyoming, Chambers of Commerce in Maryland, and high school history students in Virginia.

Kilpatrick tied together his wide net by focusing on reeducating the American public on the betrayal of the Warren Court and the foundation of strict constitutional constructivism upon which sound legal and political machinations rest.[39] The commission focused its initial rhetorical efforts on *Brown*'s constitutional legitimacy, as if the ruling was a sterile legal matter for detached intellectuals to debate. The constitutional question raised by Brown would be unaffected if the phrase "segregated schools" was exchanged for "rent control" or "liquor laws" or "gambling." *Brown*'s desegregation mandate unconstitutionally crossed the boundary between federal and state powers that impacted racial relations in the South only indirectly and after-the-fact. The commission conceded the Fourteenth Amendment's equal protection clause stretched Virginia's constitutional responsibilities to include educating Black Virginians. They could attend school, just as they could own property, enter into contracts, sue and be sued. But the Fourteenth Amendment did not say whether those schools had to be integrated. Such a mandate was beyond the boundary drawn by the Constitution and the Fourteenth Amendment. "As long as some schooling is available to Negro children, even if its separate, most States fulfill their constitutional duties of providing an education [this would not violate the Fourteenth Amendment]," the commission wrote.[40] The constitutional error of *Brown* was comparable to Prince Edward County influencing the federal interest rates or Virginia writing Atlantic City's gambling laws.

Kilpatrick described interposition not "as an idea that had to be planted" by his suasory efforts but "an idea that grew like dandelions and crab grass."[41] In the Jim Crow South, appeals to the Constitution's "plain meaning," states' rights, and interposition resonated with southern racists needing legal cover for segregation, as well as evangelical Christians receptive to the relationship between biblical literalism and constitutional literalism (and oligarchic corporate elites who hoped returning to eighteenth century legal interpretations would produce eighteenth-century tax and regulations policies). But Kilpatrick also understood he may have limited rhetorical appeal if he could not connect strict constitutionalism to postwar conservative arguments beyond the American south. To expand his reach, Kilpatrick needed to provide a sound republican legal framework diverting legal authority from a perverse and partisan group of Supreme Court justices.[42] His preferred discursive tool for attacking the constitutional structure of Warren and *Brown* was strict constitutionalism.

Strict Constitutionalism

As a source of rhetorical invention, strict constitutionalism emerged as an important symbolic resource for meeting Kilpatrick's immediate goal and also affecting conservative legal rhetoric for the long term.[43] Strict constitutionalism is a compelling, coherent, and parsimonious legal philosophy and interpretive methodology defined by emphasizing the words of the Constitution as the framers meant them when they were written. Strict constitutionalism aligns with a rhetoric of realism because its exclusive focus on the Constitution's plain meaning—without consideration of historical changes, social and cultural context, or political consequences—privileges a common sense, individualistic judicial philosophy.[44] In comparison to Warren's equality orientation, strict constitutionalism looked value-neutral, objective, durable, and accessible to the public. Oligarchic elites also saw strict constitutionalism as a way not only to avoid taxes and unfavorable regulation but also to refute the entire legal basis for Keynesian equality—without looking fickle and self-serving.[45]

Strict constitutionalism offered a rhetorical foothold to align mid-century critiques of Keynesian equality, oligarchic fears, and the emerging critique of the form and function of "big government" liberalism fomenting in the work of Friedrich Hayek, Ayn Rand, and soon after, Milton Friedman.[46] Strict constitutionalism couched its critique in the separation of powers enumerated in the US Constitution, in which order is guaranteed and personal freedoms protected by dividing power horizontally (between the branches of the federal government) and vertically (between federal, state, and local governments).[47] For example, strict constitutionalism offered Kilpatrick the inventional opportunity to affirm a conservative outlook on the separation of federal and state authority. Kilpatrick and his commission highlighted the "spirit of self-government, of *local* self-government" as the "vital force in shaping our democracy from its inception."[48] The Constitution was produced in a context marked by the rejection of "centralized government with no distribution of powers" and the framers crafted the sacred document so that "they should never suffer such grievances from a government of their own construction."[49] States' rights and local control—that the states are "left free to govern themselves"—is a vital "part of the strength of the Union."[50] Kilpatrick zeroed in on "the problem of fixing boundaries" and the Warren Court's error in "determining the line at which rights end, and powers begin."[51] The line-crossing metaphor assumed martial significance for many southerners. *Brown* extended an argumentative thread marked by the illegal and unconstitutional boundary-crossing initiated first by Lincoln, Grant, and Sherman, and now FDR, Keynes, and Warren. Kilpatrick's boundary metaphor also resonated with a postwar conservatism lionizing the spirit of local government to beat back New Deal and Great Society encroachments. *Brown* looked to be taking federal encroachment into the sacred space of the community's local schools. Postwar conservatism extended the line-crossing metaphor to decry the Civil Rights bills of the 1960s, affirmative action policies, and labor protections because they each, like *Brown*, represented federal encroachment by illegally crossing a constitutional boundary.[52]

With the Constitution as a sacred touchstone, the Warren Court justices could be portrayed as unconstitutional judicial activists, legislating from the bench. Since 1937, conservatives had been worrying about liberal judges doing just that, as judges overruled the decisions of the elected branches of government and used vague appeals to "equality" to arrive at their preferred partisan rulings.[53] Without restraint, conservatives feared that the operationalized equality in the Warren Court illustrated the turn to an American constitutional system where both the demands of the numerical majority and the elite legal opinions of the Warren Court would produce mob rule and moral disaster. In contrast, strict constitutionalism offered a realist interpretation diverting legal authority from the elite priesthood using legal exclusivity to maintain control.[54]

Strict constitutionalism put distance between legal thinkers like Kilpatrick and demagogic reactionaries like Bull Connor and George Wallace, especially for Americans outside the South. In contrast, Kilpatrick and his commission looked like they had a legal, historical, and sober disagreement with Warren and *Brown*. Kilpatrick was not a hateful racist; he was worried about constitutional misinterpretation and bureaucratic overreach, it seemed. To that end, Kilpatrick claimed to take issue with the process by which *Brown* was decided, less so the outcome. *Brown* erred by "amending the Fourteenth Amendment in a way not countenanced by the Constitution," Kilpatrick argued, avoiding the racial implications.

And yet, scratch the surface of Kilpatrick's conservatism and a glaring set of incongruities appear. Kilpatrick was selective in which traditional institutions his conservatism venerated, which framers his conservatism promoted, and when. He was selective in choosing which individual rights were valorized and to which individuals those rights belonged to. Kilpatrick said he sought a government that obeyed the "unmistakable voice of the people," but he drew sharp boundaries around who counted as "the people."[55] Kilpatrick may have venerated the US Constitution, but he took issue with the powers the Constitution vested in the Supreme Court. Kilpatrick venerated Jefferson and Madison, but less so Alexander Hamilton and John Adams. Further, Kilpatrick focused on the writings of Jefferson and Madison during the last two decades of the eighteenth century, but he neglected the federalism embodied in Thomas Jefferson's presidency and the rejection of interposition in James Madison's later years. (Kilpatrick conceded his selectivity, writing, "I will take Mr. Madison when he was closest to the Constitution; you can take him as an old man in 1830."[56])

Beyond these nineteenth-century incongruities, Kilpatrick's legal rationale sits uncomfortably next to the core principles of conservatism. Interposition was a radical response to the lawful ruling of an esteemed branch of the government empowered by the Constitution. Although the Fourteenth Amendment did not mandate desegregation, the decrepit conditions of racially segregated schools in the Jim Crow South surely raised misgivings about Kilpatrick's loyalty to meritocracy and equality of opportunity. The historical, legal, and rhetorical inconsistencies of conservative legal jurisprudence have been highlighted by scholars and journalists like Erwin Chemerinsky, Emily Bazelon, Jeffrey Toobin, Corey Robin, and David A. Kaplan. Hustwit summed these critiques well when he described that Kilpatrick's "historical and legal thinking often seemed to rely more on rhetorical appeal than logical thought" and his view of "law and politics suffered from a serious deficiency as a result and made him sound hypocritical."[57]

Amplifying the legal inconsistencies in supposedly constitutionalist rulings is meant to sweep the legs from underneath strict constitutionalism and constitutional originalism. Ultimately, a close observer is left with the feeling that Kilpatrick's legal thinking is a fallacy, a ruse, a rhetorical shield without a legitimate analytical framework. Or worse, as Chemerinsky wrote of originalism, "just the rhetoric conservative judges use to make it seem that they are not imposing their own values, when they are doing exactly that."[58]

Once understood as merely rhetorical, rather than historical or legal, conservative jurisprudence, from Kilpatrick to Scalia, can be dismissed as hypocritical and self-serving. If it is all just a rhetorical shield, originalism can then be straw-manned as a danger to democracy because it threatens "advances in equality," according to Chemerinsky, making "life poorer, harder, and more insecure for all but a few."[59] But from Kilpatrick to the Roberts Court, that charge contains no exigence in a world ordered by natural law.

A Higher Power

Although Kilpatrick was not devout, he believed in divine, natural, and strict power hierarchies. Kilpatrick was raised to believe in "the natural order of mankind."[60] He placed a premium on the "natural orders of the world" and he worried *Brown*, Martin Luther King Jr., and the Civil Rights Movement represented futile efforts to "repeal not only the laws of men, but the laws of God." "The good Lord did not create men to be equal," Kilpatrick said.[61] Kilpatrick idealized a natural aristocracy marked by the rule of the most intelligent, able, and competitive individuals evincing their capacity to rule through superior energy, ambition, and merit.[62] His segregationism came from his concern with conceding political power "to a race of people unqualified to administer them."[63]

On November 26, 1960, Kilpatrick displayed his naturalism in a televised debate with Martin Luther King Jr. on an NBC program called *The Nation's Future*. Shortly before it aired, SNCC activists gathered around the television, excited to watch King humiliate Kilpatrick in front of a national television audience. Instead, Kilpatrick delivered to King what Hustwit called "an intellectual beating."[64] Stunned SNCC activists admitted King's lofty attempts to link the Civil Rights Movement to natural rights were no match for Kilpatrick's realist appeals to natural order. King's appeals to the natural rights of all humans relies on a bogus premise, Kilpatrick argued; men were not equal—just look around. Kilpatrick drew from Plato to link natural aristocracies with the need for elite rule to control people's thoughts and contain wayward democratic impulses. Kilpatrick drew from Edmund Burke to suggest democratic order was best maintained through deference to natural inequities.[65] Kilpatrick's belief in a natural and divine Chain of Being offered the clearest repudiation of the liberal worldview espoused by

King.⁶⁶ Natural law was not subject to the will of the masses, no matter the enthusiasm or courage of the Civil Rights protestors. By tilting political and economic power in the direction of popular opinion, Kilpatrick saw in a multiracial southern democracy the disorder that Edmund Burke saw in Revolutionary France.

Kilpatrick also affirmed natural order by drawing on Thomas Jefferson. Like Plato and Edmund Burke, Jefferson believed people should accept their born status and the rule of their superiors. While King and his liberal allies used Jefferson's Declaration of Independence to highlight a constitutional basis for equality, Kilpatrick emphasized Jefferson's distinction between being "born equal by their creator" and the inequality of heights allowed for by differences in initiative and ambition.⁶⁷ To Kilpatrick, King's efforts represented larger government efforts to aid the inferior and deprive Black Americans of the chance to show their unique merit, virtue, and ambition.⁶⁸ Drawing from the Gospel of Luke, Kilpatrick worried the Warren Court "leveled off the high and shining places and filled up the valleys of individual inadequacies, and replaced initiative with contrived security and liberty with the opiate, poppy-seed controls of the transcendent state."⁶⁹ The Warren Court embraced "a dull and plainless mediocrity, in which the shiftless and incompetent are rewarded, and the industrious and thrifty are penalized."⁷⁰ Men may be born equal, but the Warren Court's demands for equality pointed to stagnation. Affirmative Action programs, in particular, elevated the less qualified over more talented candidates. Instead, Kilpatrick idealized the purifying capacities of individual initiative, rather than the sloppy entitlement of government assistance programs.⁷¹

Kilpatrick and the commission also relied on Thomas Jefferson to compare resistance to *Brown* to the framers' resistance to the British. "When Thomas Jefferson conceived of the Declaration of Independence, he understood that he could not appeal to the law, for the laws of colonial America were written by, and supportive of, the imperial rule of the British Crown," wrote a commission pamphlet.⁷² Instead, the pamphlet continued, "Jefferson therefore devised an argument that appealed to a higher power, a higher set of principles, and a higher rule of law. These 'endowments' which he referred to, were guaranteed by a Creator to all humans. These endowments, which include the rights to life, liberty, and the pursuit of happiness—were guaranteed by the social contract that is implicitly part of the fabric that joins us."⁷³ Because Jefferson was not bound by man's law, neither was Kilpatrick's commission. Worse, neither King George nor the Warren Court were merely contradicting "the law." They violated "human nature itself," including "its most sacred rights of life and liberty in the persons of a distant people who never offended him, captivating and carrying them into slavery."[74]

The greater the temporal distance from its source, the greater the potential for legal interpretation to be corrupted. Rather than rely on the "somewhat less gifted draftsmen of the Fourteenth Amendment" or on the partisan discretion of the Warren Court, Kilpatrick grounded his legal rationale in the "unalterable facts of history and long-established principles of law."[75] Kilpatrick transcended both the Warren Court specifically, and the Supreme Court broadly, by positioning *Brown* in contradiction to "English Common Law."[76] *Brown* was another example of the "many firmly established doctrines of Anglo-American jurisprudence coming under attack of late."[77] The cover of one VCCG pamphlet featured a reference to Judges 21:25: "In those days there was no king in Israel: Every man did that which was right in his own eyes." By linking Warren's partisan activism to the lawlessness and disorder of the years between *Brown* and *Roe*, Kilpatrick affirmed conservative concerns that mob rule reigned from college campus to the highest court in the land. Civil Rights protests, campus activists, and anti-war demonstrators applauded the Warren Court's expansion of individual rights. Kilpatrick and his VCCG commission responded by emphasizing the inevitable descent from expanding the rights of the inferior to mob rule and totalitarianism.[78]

With Jefferson's Higher Power as a rhetorical reservoir, Kilpatrick could argue that the Constitution offered a legal remedy for the states to intercede and interpose "against a palatable and dangerous violation of the Constitution."[79] In the 1780s, the states formed a compact to create the Union on the condition that the US Constitution protected each states' legal right to maintain their essential sovereignty, Kilpatrick argued. The states maintained the right and duty to protect their citizens against the tyranny of a centralized, overreaching federal government. After a hundred years and a bloody civil war, the states never gave up the power to hold rulings like *Brown* null and void. As evidence, the commission suggested that the student of constitutional government would be wise to orient their philosophy in relation to the "'The Kentucky-Virginia Resolutions,'" which used the 1789 Sedition Act as a foil to show the potential contradiction between what is legal and what is constitutional. Kilpatrick responded to the overreach of *Brown* by affirming Madison and Jefferson's argument validating the states' rights to defend their citizens against tyrannical rulings.[80] "Jefferson and Madison prophesied a time when the Federal government might usurp powers granted to it," Kilpatrick wrote. "And in such an emergency, these great men asserted, the States may declare their inherent right—inherent in the nature of our Union—to judge for themselves not merely of the infraction, but 'of the mode and measure of redress.'"[81]

For Kilpatrick and the commission, a ruling like *Brown* was both legal and unconstitutional. The commission aligns with a larger discursive formation untethered to the law, the Constitution, or even democratic governance. Because natural law transcends human law, the commission established firm legal footing to defy the Warren Court. The connections to *Brown* were not subtle. Like the Sedition Act, the *Brown* ruling was a "palpable and dangerous violation of the Constitution." Warren's Court may have made desegregation *legal*, but that did not make it *constitutional*. States had a duty to combat such betrayals.

Plain Meaning

The constitutional basis for anti-Black racism was never shrouded in complicated legal theory. Nor was the historical basis of strict constitutionalism. To that end, Kilpatrick and the VCCG presciently citing Article V's "plain meaning" to highlight the state's role in affirming such an amendment.[82] VCCG's original charter included the directive to "develop and promulgate information concerning the dual system of government, federal and state, established under the Constitution of the United States and those of the several states."[83] The commission focused attention on strict constitutionalism's essential question: "What did the words and phrases mean, as applied to a particular situation, *to the framers who drafted the Amendment and to the States that ratified it?*"[84] Desegregated schools were not on the framers' minds when they ratified the Constitution. Instead, the commission wrote, "the plain meaning of Article V was, and is, that the States alone have the power to amend their compact."[85] Kilpatrick urged focusing "on the words in the minds of the parties at the time the instrument was agreed to" would promote a "permanent" and "necessarily fixed" constitutional interpretation.[86] Drawing his legal interpretations from "the minds of the parties" allowed Kilpatrick to then argue "that it was never the intention of those who framed the Fourteenth Amendment to prohibit to the States the power to operate racially segregated schools."[87] "If the meaning and intent can be established on this basis, the search is done," Kilpatrick wrote.[88]

Brown erred by "amending the Fourteenth Amendment in a way not countenanced by the Constitution," Kilpatrick argued. Warren "ruled by fiat

CHAPTER 5

and not by amendment of the Constitution under Article V," and in so doing, Warren "effectively sieved from the States a substantial portion of their remaining political power."[89] Without the support of the framers, Kilpatrick portrayed the Warren Court and its supporters as deviant partisan activists. More than a bad opinion, *Brown* was "a revolutionary act by a judicial junta which simply seized power, and thus far, has managed to get away with its act of usurpation."[90] The commission circulated the visual image of a Constitution under attack, including a popular commission pamphlet showing a vice crushing the Constitution on the cover (the Heritage Foundation and the Federalist Society adopted similar images in the 1970s and 1980s).

James Kilpatrick assumed unique insight on the intent of the framers. But as a realist, he argued that everyone could access the plain meaning of the Constitution. Kilpatrick operationalized an accessible natural law in the racism of the Jim Crow South, affirming a racial hierarchy of white over Black. White elites in Virginia displayed their fitness to rule through cultural and economic superiority. Property was a symbolic expression of where one should be positioned on the power hierarchy. "The right to own, and possess, and manage property is vital to the freedom of Americans," Kilpatrick wrote in the *National Review*.[91] During the Civil Rights Movement of the 1960s, Kilpatrick used the lunch counter protests to illustrate what he saw as a contradiction of plainly visible natural order. During the summer of 1963, Kilpatrick wrote, "the owner of a neighborhood drug store, or dress shop, or soda fountain . . . has a right to choose his customers as he sees fit . . . and even when it may be exercised wrongly, as some believe, it is entitled to full protection of our law."[92] Beyond property, Kilpatrick pointed to generalized Black inferiority to affirm natural racial hierarchies. After describing Black inferiority, Kilpatrick supported his claim by telling a collaborator, "I don't see how any person who weighs the evidence objectively could come to any other conclusion."[93] Compared to white western culture, Kilpatrick equated Black rule with incivility: "The mud hut ought not to be equated with Monticello, nor jungle rule with Periclean Athens."[94] Likewise, Black family dysfunction reflected their larger menace to social order when granted too much power. Kilpatrick referenced venereal diseases, marital infidelity, and family breakdown as obvious, visible, and concrete evidence—just like the words of the framers.[95]

The aesthetic dimensions of Kilpatrick's textual persona affirmed his legal realism. Before Tucker Carlson and Sean Hannity, Kilpatrick created an emotive persona turning strict constitutionalism into an attractive public performance based on "common sense" reasoning.[96] Kilpatrick united naturalism and realism, translating legal support for racial discrimination into a folky, accessible grammar aligned with individual liberty, distrust of the federal government, and faith in authority and traditional institutions. Kilpatrick also looked good on television. Although balding with glasses, Kilpatrick had bright eyes, a warm smile, and impeccable charm that coupled well with his visible passion and sparkling erudition. Kilpatrick was nimble enough to spar on popular television programs and in syndicated newspaper columns—soberly, thoughtfully, and rationally. But no one questioned his devotion to upholding "the ideology of the Old South and the Lost Cause," a colleague wrote.[97] With the enthusiasm of an insecure outsider trying to break into an exclusive but well-defended conclave, Kilpatrick combined decorum, social style, and legal acumen with a full-throated defense of a worldview thought by his target audience to be under attack by arrogant outsiders.[98]

The passage of two landmark Civil Rights bills in the 1960s allowed Kilpatrick to update his messaging for a national audience. Up through the 1960s, Kilpatrick argued that liberty required the "inferior to submit to their masters."[99] But because racial discrimination effectively ended in the 1960s, Kilpatrick said he looked forward to seeing Black Americans demonstrating their equality. They no longer had any excuses.[100] However, venereal diseases, marital infidelity, and family breakdown continued, which Kilpatrick cited as evidence of Black Americans' inability to conform to the expectations of natural order. Instead, Black Americans now assumed total responsibility for their personal failures.[101]

As blatant racial bigotry fell out of fashion, Kilpatrick deftly translated naturalist appeals into an updated conservative vocabulary. Kilpatrick did so by expanding the rationale for inferiority to apply to the poor of all races.[102] Kilpatrick carved out rhetorical space for exceptional Black Americans who did not look to the government for handouts or blame racism for their struggles but instead assumed "the old middle-class precepts of industry and thrift and self-reliance."[103] In 1965, Kilpatrick praised Booker T. Washington as a role model because he displayed "the industriousness of a superior man"—regardless of race.[104] Kilpatrick linked the natural human hierarchy to effective democratic governance, in that the upkeep of the nation required those endowed with natural superiority to rule.[105]

According to Kilpatrick, Earl Warren and Martin Luther King invented rights for criminals, racial minorities, and the poor with no basis in natural law. Kilpatrick then used natural law to defend himself against accusations of callous and cruel public policy. Instead, he emphasized the accessible exclusivity of the top echelons of power hierarchies. Rather than rely on the discretion of federal justices or EEOC bureaucrats, the market determines human worth. In 1759, Adam Smith argued that the market can play a critical role in elevating "marginal men" to deserving heights, including Quakers, Jews, and Unitarians.[106] Two-hundred years later, Kilpatrick applied the same market-based metric to the marginal men of his day, including racial minorities and the poor, as long as the government refrained from adulterating the field of competition.

Consequentialism proved useful for Kilpatrick's post-racial, color-blind appeals. If any individual, Black or white, could evince their conformity to natural law, live up to "western values of maturity and achievement," and "develop the talent that commands respect in the market place," they deserved their reward, Kilpatrick wrote.[107] In 1977, Kilpatrick used the ascendancy of Hank Aaron, Reggie Jackson, Rod Carew, and other Black baseball players as an illustration. Although Kilpatrick said he preferred white baseball stars, "in the competitive marketplace, Black players have proven their skills."[108]

The Process Must Be Honored

Kilpatrick and his commission were willing to support racial integration—as long as the order came from a constitutional amendment. Kilpatrick did not want to look like a dogmatic revolutionary or racist zealot. He was a sophisticated polemicist and a genteel Virginian. Kilpatrick said he would concede to an American public seeking national racial integration, but the process must be honored: "The Constitution expressly sets up its own procedures for amendment, slow or cumbersome though they may be."[109] The Warren Court did not have that mandate. The commission wrote that if the original meaning of the Constitution, "however determined, is to be abandoned, then it must be by consent of the parties and the instrument must be formally amended."[110] In a pamphlet titled "On the Fixing of Boundary Lines," the commission wrote: "The court's power is judicial, not legislative; there is nothing in the constitution affirming racially integrated schools . . . to do otherwise is to usurp the amendatory power that constitutionally is vested in three-fourths of the States alone."[111]

The amendment process put a lid on the numerical advantages of the inferior masses. "In matters of taste and intelligence," Kilpatrick wrote, "public opinion is often worth next to nothing."[112] The implications of such arrogance are insightful for reconciling Kilpatrick's incongruities. Kilpatrick maintained only selective loyalty to the decisions of Congress elected by a representative democracy, but with the prospect of a national constitutional amendment as a solution, Kilpatrick and his allies could look like conservatives defending tradition, order, and stability in the mold of Edmund Burke. Because democratic governance is complex, deference should be given to the institutions and processes that have emerged and survived. Change was inevitable, Kilpatrick understood, but when it came, it needed to come "slowly and in moderation."[113] Further, in the jungle, might makes right, and in a liberal democracy, might makes constitutional amendments and enough money to influence elections.

In turn, *Brown* seemed like an impractical, idealistic, and unenforceable overreach. In a prophetic argument, the commission linked Warren to the federal government's growth since 1787 as a "needless increase in bureaucracy" and a mechanism by those government bureaucrats to "puff up their jobs or those who think that they can best run all the people's affairs."[114] A bloated and distant federal bureaucracy could never respond well to the local needs of the people, and even well-intended efforts to implement equality through affirmative action policies ended up constraining individual liberty and sapping the competitiveness and vitality of the free market. Kilpatrick could then align with a less-ideological dimension of postwar conservatism resonating with moderate, northeastern, Chamber of Commerce Republicans. Further, America's descent into totalitarianism could be marked by the centralization of power into federal bureaucracies, evinced by the public's acceptance of Warren's *Brown* ruling, the passage of the Civil Rights acts, and then popular support for LBJ's Great Society programs. For Kilpatrick, government agencies like the Department of Health, Education, and Welfare and then later the Equal Employment Opportunity Commission were established on unnatural terrain, promising to lift up the inferior by redistributing the resources of the superior.[115] Kilpatrick went so far as to suggest that government agencies, like the Equal Employment Opportunity Commission, supervising preferential treatment for racial minorities, had "done more to destroy good race relations in the past ten years than the KKK did in a century."[116] Kilpatrick preferred a weak, decentralized confederation of states lacking the institutional strength to cobble together the inferiors to account for their weakness in numbers.

Conventional conservative appeals to small government, fiscal discipline, and local control pose unique challenges for large democracies. But under the guise of accessing the framers' minds and recovering the intent of the plain meaning of their words, Kilpatrick represents oligarchic efforts

CHAPTER 5

to redress the paradox of conservative governance by enervating the institutions best equipped to constrain oligarchy, including the EEOC, the SEC, the IRS, and the EPA. Once enervated, weak points of intervention are opened to those with the resources to unite the political and economic.

Conclusion

The judicial oligarchy reflected in the rhetoric of James Kilpatrick points to a source of unproductive legal and political conversations. From *Brown* to the John Roberts court, liberals have responded to oligarchic jurisprudence by highlighting the self-serving inconsistencies in the legal rulings and public arguments of conservative justices, including Antonin Scalia, Clarence Thomas, and more recently, Neil Gorsuch and Amy Coney Barrett. But judicial oligarchy sidesteps accusations of legal incoherence because there is no loyalty to strict conservatism, legal realism, or constitutional originalism. Nothing trumps the raw exercise of power.

Judicial oligarchy poses a unique threat to liberal democracy because the judicial branch of government demands that every person is equal under the law. But that assumption contradicts the oligarchic logics explored in Kilpatrick's rhetoric. People are not equal, and they should not be treated as such. The next link in the logical chain is clear: The courts can and should be used as a mechanism to affirm natural order and consequentialist power hierarchies.

But judicial oligarchy lights up a unique set of paradoxes for audience constitution, especially in the American south. For a discrete southern identity constituted by a Lost Cause, one may wonder how consequentialism is maintained against a history of public defeats against Federalists like Hamilton and Adams, Union leaders like Lincoln, Grant, and Sherman, and integrationists like Eisenhower, Kennedy, and Johnson. Further, oligarchy's metric for evaluating human worth must have been paradoxical for James Kilpatrick on a personal level. He was a "physically unimpressive and often sickly child who suffered from asthma," according to Hustwit.[117] His father and namesake went broke and deserted the family.[118] When Kilpatrick moved to Virginia, he grew popular in national conservative circles, but he said he always felt like an outsider in the crusty exclusivity of Richmond's social circles and country clubs.[119]

His insecurities inform his capacity to evolve. Kilpatrick was always a shrewd opportunist. As a newspaper editorialist, Kilpatrick adjusted his politics based on the expectations of his superiors.[120] Early on in his career,

Kilpatrick seemed to be "on the liberal side" according to his colleagues, but he "learned quickly which side the bread was buttered on" and adjusted his editorials accordingly.[121] Later in life, he shed the bigotry that defined his rise when he realized racial tolerance would elevate his national profile beyond the South.[122] It worked. Kilpatrick became a rich, famous, and influential public rhetor. The oligarchic metrics for evaluating human worth may have assuaged Kilpatrick's insecurities. Kilpatrick's biography illustrates the broader expectations for the oligarchic oriented: Political and legal coherence is far less valued than the capacity to deploy every available resource to separate oneself from the losers. Critics of a conservative jurisprudence will always struggle when they overlook the oligarchic underpinnings of this worldview. Equal justice under the law may be etched above the Supreme Court's imposing colonnade, but the rhetoric of James Kilpatrick shows the influence of a legal, political, and economic thought system oriented toward inequality, adversity, and strife for all but an elite few.

6

Cultivating Political Power and the Rhetoric of Lewis F. Powell

MAJOR EVOLUTIONS IN LEGAL THOUGHT REQUIRE THE SIMULTANEOUS weakening of existing thought systems and the strengthening of compelling alternatives.[1] And so, tracing the genealogy of American oligarchy in the postwar decades requires understanding both the desire of the ultra-rich to maximize their wealth through political machinations and the existing thought system the ultra-rich sought to replace. The alternative to oligarchy is not hard to locate: Recall that between 1930 and 1980, strong countervailing institutions, including the courts, labor unions, public schools, and social-democratic political coalitions, contained oligarchy's legal, political, and economic ambitions.[2] This chapter explores how the rhetoric of Lewis F. Powell encouraged the ultra-rich to overcome these hurdles by synthesizing corporate and political power. But Powell's exigency is incomprehensible without first exploring the incongruity between his deeply held fears about the future of American liberal democracy and the shared prosperity of his historical moment.

The postwar decades reflected a golden age of American capitalism as the United States erected a wall separating the economic from the political, and strong social institutions—like our courts—contained oligarchy's ambitions. Between 1930 and 1980, American liberal democracy combined active state intervention, well-regulated markets, and expanding civic institutions to keep the ultra-rich relatively marginalized. As Hacker and Pierson argue in *American Amnesia*, this mixed economy limited the boom-and-bust cycles of harsh laissez-faire capitalism while also creating a robust, nonsocialist alternative that increased American prosperity.[3] Oligarchs like Coors, du Pont, and Kilpatrick were thought of by many Americans as selfish cranks confined to the political margins. Oligarchy remained in the wilderness, and without acknowledging the presence of an oligarchic alternative, we cannot understand what Lewis P. Powell, and then Milton Friedman and James Buchanan, would one day overcome. Nor can we understand the collective mechanisms that need to be rediscovered to redress oligarchy's influence on American liberal democracy.

The Fordist-Keynesian Golden Age

After World War II, the legitimacy of the federal government grew as the challenges and accomplishments of global war tied together institutional competence, patriotism, and the defeat of fascism.[4] According to David Harvey, the unprecedented economic growth that marked the decades between 1910 and the 1970s in the United States came from balancing advantages in material resources with the intangible interests of shaping labor subjectivity toward productive and profitable ends.[5] The Fordist–Keynesian compromise that emerged during the twentieth century propped up a complex administrative apparatus that shifted public perceptions of the state and the corporation's duties and responsibilities toward its citizens and employees. Although the US federal government historically displayed a reluctance to "govern too much," a set of unprecedented historic conditions, including massive waves of immigration, the rise of the industrial capitalist, and the effects of the Great Depression, prompted more direct interventions into previous off-limits economic and domestic spheres.[6] During this progressive era, the US federal government sought to shape citizen subjectivity and mediate political threats and class conflicts by creating more administrative functions to enhance the well-being of the population.[7]

The postwar Fordist-Keynesian golden age was marked by an active nation-state emerging as the principal anchor point for institutions of social integration, macroeconomic management, and massive public investment in research and development, transportation infrastructure, and scientific research.[8] The federal government supercharged economic growth and sparked many of the scientific breakthroughs that continue to drive the economy today.[9] Active state interventions, including by the courts and labor unions, counter-balanced elite interests through publicly responsive state institutions, well-regulated markets, and vibrant social movements to serve as a powerful normative voice for nonelites and to function as a core equalizing institution during the postwar decades. For example, during the postwar decades, the United States instituted one of the most steeply progressive taxation systems on earth, inventing and then applying a 90 percent top marginal income tax rate on the highest earners, a 50 percent tax on corporate profits, and an 80 percent tax on large estates. With the revenue, the country built public schools and funded public universities that, even today, are the envy of the world and a rich source for productive employees.[10] As a result, the capacity of the American labor force was at its most productive after World War II when the United States was left with half the world's machines and its most stable workforce. Worker productivity rose 96 percent between 1945 and 1973. Between 1973 and 2011, US economic dominance waned, globalization shifted the nature of the economy, and other nations recovered; despite all this, labor productivity continued to rise another 80 percent.[11]

The Fordist-Keynesian compromise led to decades of economic growth. Labor's subjectivity was shaped toward productive and profitable ends, the welfare state was expanded through the Nixon and Ford administrations, and the internal contradictions of capitalism were mediated.[12] For labor, a robust but informal social contract ensured fair compensation, job stability, and safe working conditions. Large American companies assumed responsibility for the well-being of their employees. GM, Boeing, and General Electric, for instance, believed that a prosperous and satisfied workforce benefited the country, community, and shareholders; strong unions intervened when those conditions slipped.[13] Chrystia Freeland highlighted the "Treaty of Detroit" as a useful illustration: a five-year contract agreed to by the United Auto Workers and the big three auto manufacturers in 1950 that not only offered autoworkers generous pensions and health care but also came to be seen as a representative anecdote for a wider set of social, economic, and political institutions marking the postwar decades of middle-class prosperity, including strong unions and robust wages.[14]

Many Americans understood the source of their newfound and shared prosperity. The economist David George, charting shifts in the public opinion about markets and government, found that during the mid-century the government was seven times more likely to be described favorably than unfavorably.[15] Oligarchic policies were unsuitable for the historical moment. The ultra-rich were understood by many to oppose virtually every major political reform passed in the twentieth century—reforms that many Americans appreciated.[16] Further, oligarchic policies were dismissed not only because they were politically impractical but also because they were clearly self-serving; many knew it was the power elite who advocated for these policies and who would benefit most if they were adopted.[17] Oligarchy was a political loser, connected to the failed candidacy of Barry Goldwater and fringe radicalism of the John Birch Society.

But from the view of the ultra-rich, the postwar decades looked much different. Pierre du Pont, near the end of his life, saw the postwar decades as an indictment on his efforts, but writing to a Liberty League ally, he found comfort in the fact that he was at least able to live through the "golden age" of the early twentieth century—before the era of shared prosperity.[18] Phillips-Fein noted that du Pont and his allies in the Liberty League were a joke—the chairman of the Democratic Party quipped that du Pont's American Liberty League "ought to be called the American Cellophane League" because "first, it's a Du Pont product, and second, you can see right through it."[19] Rather than custodians of the common good, the ultra-rich were blamed for causing the Great Depression. Even when a Republican, Dwight Eisenhower, was finally elected president in 1953, he claimed to represent a "modern Republicanism" defined in opposition to the unpopular, pre–Great Depression economic ideas of the ultra-rich.[20] As Marchand noted in *Creating the Corporate Soul*, the ultra-rich attempted to sell an alternative to the public by showing that their ideas were better prepared to meet the demand of the moment than politicians or labor leaders.[21] But their efforts were generally rejected.

Horrified by the Long Sixties, trolled, attacked, besieged, and motivated by the fear of an oncoming socialist revolution, American corporations began to mobilize.[22] The advertising agency Deutsch & Sons took out a full-page ad in the *New York Times* expressing their concern that for the graduating class of '66 "business has become a dirty word": "Isn't it time to say the things that need to be said about business and industry and the way things really are? Now? Before we lose another generation?"[23] In 1971, the CEO of Pepsi looked at the American landscape and wondered, "The hostile youth had vent their spleen on draft boards and their own colleges. But could anyone doubt that the day was fast approaching when the long-hairs would come for American businessmen?"[24] A corporate report from Black+Decker warned, "The hour is getting late. It is time for the voices of those individuals favoring fiscal responsibility in government and a free business system to be heard."[25]

In this anti-corporate climate, oligarchs turned more directly to the courts. But as the previous chapter illustrated, the courts do not operate in a vacuum. In fact, a complex confluence of social and cultural revolutions, along with macroeconomic shifts, offered oligarchs the chance to first penetrate the courts and then turn to the people.

American companies faced new competition as European and Asian economies came back after the devastation of World War II, and activists like Ralph Nader questioned the moral underpinning of American corporations.[26] Nixon resigned in disgrace, the Ford Pinto exploded, and stagflation sucked the life from the economy. Registered Democrats continued to outnumber registered Republicans during the mid-twentieth century because so many Americans linked New Deal legislation to American global supremacy and their own economic security.[27] During the postwar decades, most Americans agreed the federal government should play a direct, robust role in improving the lives of Americans.[28] Few resonated with the fear that Medicare or The Economic Opportunity Act infringed on their liberty or signaled looming Soviet-style central planning. The undemocratic urgings of elites were kept on the margins.[29] But not for long.

Under Broad Attack

No one articulated the ultra-rich's fears—or their preferred oligarchic remedy—as well as Lewis F. Powell. Powell was an accomplished, Harvard-educated war veteran. Powell was also a model of kindness, integrity, and decency, eventually serving on the Supreme Court as an instrumental figure in Nixon's resignation.[30] Before he joined the Supreme Court, Powell was a prominent lawyer in Virginia, former president of the American Bar Association, and a fierce advocate for big business.[31] At a business conference in 1970, he delivered a keynote address that warned of a "broad and virulent attack" on the American political and economic system by radicals who admired Fidel Castro, Che Guevara, Ho Chi-Minh, and Mao Tse-tung and behaved like "Hitler and his storm troopers."[32]

Powell developed a reputation as a shrewd and effective corporate lawyer for Philip Morris, defending the massive cigarette company against state efforts to regulate the tobacco industry. One of the reasons Powell was such an effective advocate was because he displayed remarkable loyalty to his clients—despite shifts in public opinion.[33] Powell represented Philip Morris with tenacity. Even after the link between cancer and early death was established—even after the federal government declared cigarettes carcinogenic—Powell smoked conspicuously as a public display of loyalty to Philip Morris.

Powell's relationship with Philip Morris is revealing because American tobacco companies had intimate experience with the fears described by Deutsch & Sons, Pepsi, and Black+Decker: The American free enterprise was facing an existential threat *because* the most competent and qualified corporate leaders were shirking their responsibilities. Useful for understanding oligarchy's development is a 1971 "Confidential Memorandum" Powell addressed to the US Chamber of Commerce articulating both the fears of corporate elites in this moment and an appropriate response. In the first paragraph, Powell describes the purpose of the memo as "to identify the problem, and suggest possible avenues of action for further consideration."[34] Powell's "Attack on American Free Enterprise System" puts forth a compelling rationale for ruling elites to cultivate political power in response to the Long Sixties and foreshadowed arguments and public policies for decades to come.

Addressing Eugene Sydnor, Chairman of the US Chamber of Commerce, Powell worried that "business and the enterprise system are in deep trouble, and the hour is late."[35] Powell was motivated by his experience reconciling the state's efforts to influence the tobacco market on behalf of vulnerable American consumers versus the rights of an American corporation to provide a product to consenting adults. But Powell did not mention cigarettes in his memo. Akin to James Kilpatrick cloaking racial segregation in a defense of the US Constitution, Powell, instead of defending tobacco, describes a more ambitious attack on "all American business."[36] "No thoughtful person can question that the American economic system is under broad attack," he writes.[37] The attack came from the radicals of the "liberal to the far left." But more worrisome in this moment was the anti-business coalitions forming among "perfectly respectable elements of society," including religion, higher education, mass media, and the courts.[38] Powell opens by conceding there "always have been critics of the system, whose criticism has been wholesome and constructive so long as the objective was to improve rather than to subvert or destroy."[39] But this is different. Powell writes, "But what now concerns us is quite new in the history of America. We are not dealing with sporadic or isolated attacks from a relatively few extremists or even from the minority socialist cadre. Rather, the assault on the enterprise system is broadly based and consistently pursued. It is gaining momentum and converts."[40]

The problem Powell identifies reflects the fears of the oligarchic: The nation-state has betrayed the ruling elite, producing a disordered and unnatural social hierarchy. His "possible avenues of action" lend insight into the oligarchic aim to use the economic power of the Chamber of Commerce to influence political machinations. Powell emphasizes throughout his memo that he is not merely focused on the economic status of the Chamber. Powell synthesizes the economic and political by aligning with oligarchy's governing logic. After describing "the American economic system" under attack Powell includes a footnote at the bottom of the page that reads, "The American political system of democracy under the rule of law is also under attack, often by the same individuals and organizations who seek to undermine the enterprise system."[41] On the next page, Powell warns of revolutionaries "who would destroy the entire system, both political and economic."[42] He describes the war "against the enterprise system and the values of western society."[43] Later, Powell links "the free enterprise system" with "the strength and prosperity of America and the freedom of our people."[44] And before he concludes the memo, Powell warns, "The threat to the enterprise system is not merely a matter of economics. It also is a threat to individual freedom."[45] Powell detailed disparate social and cultural foils, including campus revolts, environmentalism, and Ralph Nader's consumer advocacy—each lumped together in opposition to the American economic system. Powell wanted to jolt his target audience out of their postwar stupor. He warned the corporate elite who would be reading a memo from the Chamber of Commerce that they had become complacent during the post–World War II era of massive economic growth, and those high-on-the-hog days were over. With the survival of the free enterprise system on the line, Powell writes: "The day is long past when the chief executive officer of a major corporation discharges his responsibility by maintaining a satisfactory growth of profits, with due regard to the corporation's public and social responsibilities. If our system is to survive, top management must be equally concerned with protecting and preserving the system itself. This involves far more than an increased emphasis on 'public relations' or 'governmental affairs'—two areas in which corporations long have invested substantial sums."[46]

Powell's fears are made more urgent because the exclusion of corporate elites from public discourse has left them politically feckless. Under the subheading, "The Neglected Political Arena," Powell writes, "Yet, as every business executive knows, few elements of American society today have as little influence in government as the American businessman, the corporation, or even the millions of corporate stockholders. . . . One does not exaggerate to say that, in terms of political influence with respect to the course of legislation and government action, the American business executive is truly the 'forgotten man.'"[47] Powell argues that the corporate prosperity of the postwar American economy has allowed his primary audience to neglect their political responsibilities. But following the warnings of Hayek's road to serfdom, Powell emphasizes that without a course correction, there is only one telic endpoint: "As the experience of the socialist and totalitarian states demonstrates, the contraction and denial of economic freedom is followed inevitably by governmental restrictions on other cherished rights. It is this message, above all others, that must be carried home to the American people."[48]

Powell also reflects the democratic cynicism of oligarchic rhetoric. Majoritarian democracy is an impediment to natural order. "Politicians reflect what they believe to be majority views of their constituents," Powell writes. In turn, politicians cannot be blamed for "making the judgment that the public has little sympathy for the businessman or his viewpoint."[49] Powell argues that American politicians are not wrong, either. "The average member of the public thinks of 'business' as an impersonal corporate entity, owned by the very rich and managed by over-paid executives," Powell laments.[50] Later, he describes an American public unaware "that the only alternatives to free enterprise are varying degrees of bureaucratic regulation of individual freedom—ranging from that under moderate socialism to the iron heel of the leftist or rightist dictatorship."[51] From Powell's orientation, federal bureaucracies like the Department of Health, Education, and Welfare, will remain attractive to, and supported by, the ignorant masses as long as the champions of free enterprise allow majoritarian political influence to go uncontested.

Powell constructs his audience as voiceless and marginalized victims. He describes business as "the favorite whipping-boy of many politicians for many years."[52] He describes American businessmen and his corporate allies as "forgotten men" who have "little influence in government." And he describes a "chorus" of barbarians at their corporate gates, including the most respectable elements of society on "college campuses, the pulpit, the media, the intellectual and literary journals, the arts and sciences, and politicians."[53] Powell's enemy uses those entry points to destroy "the American system" from the inside. He describes his concern about "bright young men" changing a system they have been taught to distrust by "seeking employment in the centers of the real power and influence in our country," including television news media, government and politics, and writers and teachers. "In many instances," Powell continues, "these 'intellectuals' end up in regulatory agencies or governmental departments with large authority over the business system they do not believe in."[54]

Powell was confident he could defend the value of the free enterprise system on its merits. But he worried about his enemy's ability to operate in the shadows. Anti-American arguments on campus and in the media could not be directly countered until it was too late and the long-hair radicals were

CHAPTER 6

storming the corporate boardrooms.⁵⁵ Powell worried about internal enemies. He wrote, "One of the bewildering paradoxes of our time is the extent to which the enterprise system tolerates, if not participates in, its own destruction."⁵⁶ Recall that this memo was originally written to be a confidential call-to-arms by a corporate lawyer to the leaders of the US Chamber of Commerce. His target audience, Powell made clear, must assume part of the blame for allowing this internal infestation. He became more direct later in the memo, "The enemy is us; we have been too cowardly. The painfully sad truth is that business, including the boards of directors' and the top executives of corporations great and small and business organizations at all levels, often have responded—if at all—by appeasement, ineptitude and ignoring the problem."

Powell's description of appeasement and cowardice against an internal enemy resonated with an audience confident in their ability to defend against a frontal assault. But a Trojan Horse full of campus radicals matriculating through liberal media centers and politics was much more dangerous. Powell quoted Milton Friedman to illustrate his fear: "It is crystal clear that the foundations of our free society are under wide-ranging and powerful attack—not by Communist or any other conspiracy but by misguided individuals parroting one another and unwittingly serving ends they would never intentionally promote."⁵⁷ Powell had seen the enemy, and the enemy is us. "The painfully sad truth is that business, including the boards of directors' and the top executives of corporations great and small and business organizations at all levels, often have responded—if at all—by appeasement, ineptitude and ignoring the problem," Powell writes.⁵⁸ Powell is less worried about the external enemy—the Communists, New Leftists, and other revolutionaries—than about the compromising and appeasing insiders, described as the "perfectly respectable elements of society" on college campuses and churches, in the media, and in elected politics. "One of the bewildering paradoxes of our time," Powell writes, "is the extent to which the enterprise system tolerates, if not participates in, its own destruction."⁵⁹ Powell's target audience has ample supporting material to draw from, including the role corporate elites have played in "provid[ing] the capital which fuels the economic system which has produced the highest standard of living in all history."⁶⁰ But Powell finds such fault with the leaders of the enterprise system because the "top executives of corporations great and small" are best-equipped to defend the moderate, rational, and compelling alternative to socialism. Powell positions his target audience as the embodiment of "effective intellectual and philosophical debate."⁶¹

In contrast, Powell's opposition is marked by "mindless slogans," "political demagoguery," "economic illiteracy," and youthful "fallacies."[62] Part of the reason such fallacies are instilled in the young is because they, on the college campus, are more likely to be swayed by "personally attractive and magnetic" faculty members.[63]

Powell holds up consumer advocate Ralph Nader as a vivid illustration of the paradoxical condition of the free enterprise system. Nader has "become a legend in his own time and idol to millions of Americans" by leading a frontal assault on American business. On the surface, Nader's emotional resonance is understandable given the description of Powell's opposition as mindless and illiterate. But Powell also uses Nader's appeal as an illustration of the beneath-the-surface paradox facing corporate elites. According to oligarchy's consequentialist logic, Ralph Nader should know better. In a footnote beneath his description of Nader, Powell describes Nader's twenty-five-hundred-dollar lecture fee for visiting a college to "denounce America's big corporation in venomous language."[64] Because money is expressive and symbolic—and not merely instrumental—Powell seems perplexed that a person could be as valuable as Nader's lecture fee represents while still expressing such ignorance about the contributions of American corporations. Shortly after, Powell details the contributions of business executives, noting their capacity "to manage, to produce, to sell, to create jobs, to make profits, to improve the standard of living, to be community leaders, to serve on charitable and educational boards, and generally to be good citizens."[65] It is a contradiction to natural law for Nader to attract social and material rewards while also rejecting the orientation his own success reveals.

The Only Alternative

As a corporate lawyer for Philip Morris, Powell worried his client's First Amendment rights were being trampled by news organizations that did not offer them a platform to dispute the science connecting smoking and cancer. He also claimed media reports on the connection were grounded in socialist bias in the media. Powell suggested individual corporations respond by creating an executive vice president position to lead counterattacks on the free enterprise system. Powell suggested corporations spread their marketing budgets beyond advertisements of their specific products and services. Ten percent of a corporation's advertising budget would "be a statesman-like expenditure" supporting the long-term viability of American free enterprise.

By the end of the memo, Powell leaves his reader with two choices:

freedom or totalitarianism. He writes, "There seems to be little awareness that the only alternatives to free enterprise are varying degrees of bureaucratic regulation of individual freedom—ranging from that under moderate socialism to the iron heel of the leftist or rightist dictatorship." He made clear that anyone who differs from his prescriptions must prefer "socialism or some form of statism (communism or fascism)." Vocabulary like this is used to show how Powell shaped the political Right in America, articulating the conservative response to the Long Sixties, and foreshadowing the Reagan Revolution and its lean government and free markets.[66] According to Kurt Andersen's *Evil Geniuses*, the Powell memo "electrified the Right, prompting a new breed of wealthy ultraconservatives to weaponize their philanthropic giving in order to fight a multifront war of influence over American political thought."[67]

But Lewis Powell deserves a close reading here not because he reconciled the contradictions of the political Right. Powell's memo is not conservative. To describe its impact that way only adds to our inartful and inaccurate public conversations. Powell did not encourage his Chamber of Commerce allies to shrink the state. Powell did not urge fiscal discipline. And he did not recommend a renewed respect for traditions or institutions. Powell advised the Chamber of Commerce to cultivate political power and use it "aggressively."[68] He encouraged readers to twist and turn political power in their favor, to use their resources to bridge the economic and political, and to manipulate political mechanisms for economic gain. Under the heading "Possible Role of the Chamber of Commerce," Powell urges his target audience that their strength lies "in the scale of financing available only through joint effort, and in the political power available only through united action and national organizations."[69] Otherwise, the ultra-rich would always be threatened by the radical redistributive policies of angry college students, environmental movements, and consumer legislation. It was not enough to separate the market and the state. Powell wrote that political power "must be used aggressively and with determination—without embarrassment and without the reluctance which has been so characteristic of American business." There should be no hesitation, Powell said, to attack those who "seek destruction of the system." Powell rejected even the "slightest hesitation to press vigorously in all political arenas for support of the enterprise system," and there should be no "reluctance to penalize politically those who oppose it."[70] After all, Powell said, his opponents had found success in direct political action for decades without any worry about losing the moral high ground. Corporate elites needed to stop fighting with one hand behind their back and to quit waiting for "gradual change to be effected through education and information." Powell even suggested his opponents might be a rich tactical source of information. His audience "must learn the lesson, long ago learned by labor and other self-interest groups" that "political power is necessary" and such power "must be assiduously cultivated."

The direct political engagement Powell had in mind went far beyond hiring a VP of public relations or pouring more of the marketing budget into promoting free enterprise. Powell focused on changing the rules and winning the battle of ideas.

Neglected Opportunity in the Courts

The courts should no longer be neglected by his audience, Powell said. Under a section titled "Neglected Opportunity in the Courts" Powell wrote, "American business and the enterprise system have been affected as much by the courts as by the executive and legislative branches of government. Under our constitutional system, especially with an activist-minded Supreme Court, the judiciary may be the most important instrument for social, economic and political change."[71] Powell's reference to an activist-minded Court reflected corporate elite's anger toward the Warren Supreme Court and its efforts to protect labor and minorities. The phrase "activist-minded" court would cement itself into public conversations. Powell's stance on the judiciary illuminated efforts to stop treating American courts as a neutral arbiter of constitutional interpretation—of judges calling balls and strikes. Instead, Powell sought out active, deliberative, and well-funded interventions to train young law students and lawyers in oligarchic legal philosophy, shape law schools in oligarchic directions, and cultivate a bullpen of oligarchic judges that could be called on to defend and maximize elite profitability.

Powell described the media as a valuable site of intervention. The media represent a powerful resource, but worse, Powell's opposition had already realized its potential. Ralph Nader, for example, "has become a legend in his own time and an idol of millions of Americans" thanks "largely to the media."[72] As Powell describes it, "The news stands—at airports, drugstores, and elsewhere—are filled with paperbacks and pamphlets advocating everything from revolution to erotic free love." But, he continues, "One finds almost no attractive, well-written paperbacks or pamphlets on our side." As a remedy, Powell urged his side to support sympathetic academics and shape school textbooks. Powell called for a "steady flow of scholarly articles presented to a broad spectrum of magazines and periodicals—ranging from the popular magazines (Life, Look, Reader's Digest, etc.) to the more intellectual ones (Atlantic, Harper's, Saturday Review, New York, etc.) and to the various professional journals."[73]

Powell argued that higher education could also be a valuable site of intervention. Colleges and universities should adopt a staff of scholars, faculty balance, equal speaking time, interventions in business schools, and surveillance of textbooks to ensure academic freedom and "retain the qualities of openness, fairness, and balance."[74] Powell's specific site of rhetorical intervention resembles James Kilpatrick and the VCCG's efforts to exert political influence by publishing educational textbooks. The resemblance is not coincidental. Powell was the chairman of the Richmond School Board when Kilpatrick was emerging as an influential voice in Virginia's conservative circles.[75]

Powell's messaging was soon picked up and circulated by Roger Ailes, a wunderkind of Richard Nixon and a fierce supporter of Powell. Aggressively surveilling the media and schools for signs of socialist thought was key to maintaining fairness and balance. Powell suggests, "The national television networks should be monitored in the same way that textbooks should be kept under constant surveillance. This applies not merely to so-called educational programs (such as 'Selling of the Pentagon'), but to the daily 'news analysis' which featured the most insidious free enterprise critiques. Whether this criticism results from hostility or economic ignorance, the result is the gradual erosion of confidence in 'business' and free enterprise."[76]

Powell's realism protected him from becoming the caricature of a paranoid, tin-hat wearing conspiracy theorist. Recall that he was nominated to the Supreme Court shortly after he authored this memo. Powell maintains a serious, intellectual textual persona by reflecting familiar appeals to balance and moderation. "Few things are more sanctified in American life than academic freedom," and rather than attack this principle, he suggests that by retaining "the qualities of 'openness,' 'fairness' and 'balance'—which are essential to its intellectual significance—there is a great opportunity for constructive action."[77] Although he recommends a robust surveillance system over education and media, his telos is not limited to turning radical communists into champions of the American free enterprise system. Instead, Powell writes, "If the authors, publishers and users of textbooks know that they will be subjected—honestly, fairly and thoroughly—to review and critique by eminent scholars who believe in the American system, a return to a more rational balance can be expected."[78] Echoing an axiom of his opposition, Powell concedes that the police officer in the mind is more important than the police officer on the street corner.

Powell proposed nothing illegal. He did not advocate for violence, theft, or bribery. A respected lawyer and former president of the American Bar Association, Powell even eschews "the irresponsible tactics" of his opposition.[79] Instead, he sought political interventions beyond electoral politics: well-financed and deliberate intervention into the courts, media, and education. Powell wanted to change the rules, not just the final score.

Powell recommended penetrating education, media, and the courts because he distrusted twentieth-century American liberal democracy. Most Americans were too simple to survive and thrive in opposition to the guidance of corporate elites. Traditional institutions like the schools, media, and courts were no longer working. Worse, it seemed to many middle- and working-class white Americans that the police, the courts, the media, and the universities had turned against them.[80] Once-reliable institutional allies turned into powerful advocates for the opposition. Powell detailed the betrayals of education institutions and the media. But also the courts, by looking out for the poor, suspected criminals, and people of color, were understood as a source of undeserved power concentration for coddling the undeserved and elevating well-connected liberal professionals, like Ralph Nader.[81] Powell wrote his memo shortly after the Supreme Court expanded the constitutional rights of criminals, made it harder for police officers to investigate without warrants, and even took over entire state penal systems.[82] It looked to many Americans like the courts were "weighing in on the side of criminals rather than on that of law-abiding taxpayers," according to Zeitz.[83] In turn, the consent-based majority rule that had once determined fair social arrangements was gone.[84]

Powell's Rhetorical Impact

Gershberg and Illing describe Powell's memo as "one of the most ingenious and influential plans for political communication ever drafted in American history, and it was executed to near perfection in the coming decades."[85] Powell's argument would soon be reflected in the wider governing rationale of the Right, including the messaging of the Federalist Society, the Cato Institute, the Manhattan Institute, and Citizens for a Sound Economy.[86] Industrial heir Richard Mellon Scaife and a young Charles Koch were influenced by Powell's memo, and beer maker Joseph Coors said Powell's memo motivated him to start the Heritage Foundation. The strategies and tactics reflected in Powell's messaging also spread from the corner offices of executives in the Chamber of Commerce and well-funded Washington think tanks to public conversations on Main Street.[87] The shift was rapid and widespread. Some worried the era of postwar shared prosperity was over. Many others were reconsidering whether prosperity should even be shared.

Powell's worldview offered an alternative to the Keynesian orientation toward equality. The macroeconomic turmoil of the moment in which Powell's memo appeared added renewed stress to the American public's faith in Keynesian interventions. Keynesian economists and their political allies were stymied by the concurrent stagnation, inflation, and unemployment they thought they had mastered only a few years before. Inflation would rise if we invested in the public sector to lower unemployment rates, and if the Fed tightened interest rates to limit inflation, even more people would be out of work.[88] Not only were liberal politicians and economists unable to cure stagflation, but cultural and social upheaval confounded democratic unease. The national crime rate increased by 176 percent in the 1960s, and the murder rate doubled between 1963 and 1975.[89]

Powell also sheds light on the oligarchic dimensions of the modern political economy. According to Powell's worldview, the state need not be shrunk to limit the influence of the mindless masses. Rather, the state is charged with evaluating our ability to conform to natural laws, constructing and affirming social arrangements where the most intelligent, hardy, and tenacious individuals can rise above the rest and be rewarded when they do so.[90]

Likewise, Powell illuminates the complicated relationship among oligarchy, neoliberalism, and the political Right. Neoliberalism has been described as ethic, an ideology, a rhetoric, a mentality, a rationale, a logic, an epistemology, a hegemony, a self-justifying symbolic matrix, an imagination, a regime, a political formulation and repertoire of conventions, a fairy tale, an epistemic community, an architecture, a world-historical organization, and a critical art. While neoliberalism's definition is contingent, its impact is acknowledged. Aihwa Ong calls neoliberalism "the number one force of reckoning for different aspects of contemporary living." Perry Anderson says neoliberalism is "the most successful ideology in world history."[91] And Bill Grantham and Toby Miller compare neoliberalism to religion and colonialism because it is "one of the most successful attempts to reshape individuals in human history."[92]

Anthropologist David Harvey offers an accessible entry point when he describes neoliberalism as a theory of political and economic practices designed to free people by freeing trade, regulations, and markets.[93] Harvey wrote this in 2005. For historical and practical reasons Harvey's definition has become widely accepted in intellectual and popular circles since then.[94] Powell's impact on the Federalist Society, Charles Koch, and the Chamber of Commerce has affirmed his alignment with the history of neoliberal thought leaders who have used the term to define themselves against FDR, Keynes, and the political Left. The term was developed in 1947 by a group of business leaders, journalists, and foundational officials, including Hayek and Friedman, to strategize a response to liberal dominance.[95] Initially, the group did not know what to call themselves. But after prolonged debate, they decided to label their efforts "neoliberal" because they thought the term best explained their radical efforts to unhinge the twentieth-century American political economy from the influence of FDR and Keynes.[96] As I will explore in the next chapter, Milton Friedman is credited with orienting the Right in a neoliberal direction, including providing the intellectual fuel to reorient government toward free markets and free people, the depoliticization and privatization of difference, and the transformation of social identifications and solidarities that were once public into a private sphere of consumption.[97]

Powell's memo can be aligned with the core principles of neoliberalism. Equality was foolish. People were not equal. Some were better than others. A more coherent political Right emerged in response to this distinction.[98] Today, the political Right talks about a state oriented toward ensuring the most fit, the most tenacious, the most creative can rise above the mediocre. Any attempt to enforce equality retards the natural economic progression of the market. Further, resources devoted to the less accomplished are wasted, as the needy do not put those resources to use as well as the worthy do. A particular *neoliberal meritocracy* defined itself against equality by drawing from neutral, objective vocabularies based on irreproachable first principles, including appeals to naturalism, consequentialism, and realism. In the end, a neoliberal governing rationale valorizing individualism, personal responsibility, and market supremacy emerged in Ronald Reagan's and Margaret Thatcher's efforts to dismantle Fordist-Keynesian social programs, undermine organized labor, destroy the welfare state, and free corporations to profit unencumbered by government interference.

Consider the demands neoliberalism is said to place upon the state: If the state rejects equality and affirms natural hierarchy, then the main responsibility of the state becomes *getting out of the way* and letting the strong and free compete on a level playing field. But if the state continues to prioritize equality over merit, we all suffer. Powell, Friedman, and the Right's opposition to organized labor, the minimum wage, and progressive taxation is then linked to free markets, free people, and free enterprise. Harvey's seminal definition resonates with this discursive history.

Following Harvey, rhetorical scholars have since cataloged the relationship between neoliberal meritocracy and appeals to free markets, small government, and personal responsibility—comparing those utterances to the other critical concepts, including classical liberalism, conservatism, and libertarianism. We explored how Austrian economists and the Mont Pèlerin Society extended those utterances for the specific historical moment. We noted the impact of neoliberalism as the welfare state was sliced-to-the-bone, industry deregulated, and social services privatized. All social, economic, and political life was organized according to the demands of the market logics—and neoliberalism explained why.[99] As Yascha Mounk puts it, we now live in an "age of responsibility" urging Americans to understand power hierarchies as a result of one's individual ability to be self-sufficient.[100] The age of responsibility turned into an entire ecosystem skeptical of coordinated action, collective solidarity, and government interventions in the market.[101]

Theorizing neoliberalism assumed political urgency for scholars because it offered a cogent explanation for the democratic consent of the welfare state's destruction, organized labor's collapse, and progressive taxation's unpopularity.[102] As a discrete category of analysis, neoliberalism developed into a flashlight we shine on hegemony lurking in the shadows. Across the political and cultural spectrum, neoliberalism hollowed out democratic political culture and depoliticized difference in exchange for privatized, consumptive solutions to collective problems.[103] This line of research is vital to understanding part of Powell's impact on American democracy. But only a part.

In 2009, when David Harvey was asked if the Great Recession would signal the demise of neoliberalism, he responded, "It depends what you mean by neoliberalism."[104] His answer—coming from the person who had such influence on what neoliberalism means—is akin to Harry Truman wondering what the Truman Doctrine meant or George Marshall admitting he didn't know how to distinguish the Marshall Plan. But Harvey's response also points to the opportunities and challenges of using neoliberalism to theorize the political economy.

I paraphrased Harvey's definition earlier, but let's examine it more closely now. Harvey said neoliberalism advanced human well-being by "liberating individual entrepreneurial freedoms and skills within an institutional framework characterized by strong private property rights, free markets and free trade."[105] Neoliberal scholarship affirms the second part of Harvey's definition: strong property rights, free markets, and free trade. You cannot understand the American political economy without understanding the discursive links between merit and freedom in public conversations. And yet most of that research does not reconcile the incongruous relationship between a neoliberal market economy and the "institutional framework" in the first part of Harvey's definition.[106]

Powell's memo does not urge the ultra-rich to pine for meritocracy where the strong and free compete on a level playing field. As a general principle, power is insatiable, and the empowered will deploy every tool at their disposal to keep it.[107] The emphasis on freedom in the second half of Harvey's definition has led us to neglect Powell's focus on deploying a robust and intrusive government to defend and enhance capital accumulation. The confluence of economic and political power shows why we need to be more careful lumping together neoliberal political rationales and public appeals to pruning the state, fiscal discipline, and a lean government.[108] When Harvey said, "It depends what you mean by neoliberalism," he was reminding us that the link between individual merit and freedom does not apply to the ultra-rich. Free trade, free markets, fiscal discipline, and a lean government make for strong talking points on the campaign trail, but they do not guide public policy.[109]

Conclusion

A reader may wonder how a confidential, thirty-one-page memo from a tobacco lawyer full of overwrought fear-mongering and self-serving solutions can exert such influence. In the previous section, I included an abundance of direct quotes from Powell's own pen so as to set up an exploration of the relationship between Powell's banality and his memo's immense rhetorical effect.

It would be misguided to evaluate the effect of Powell's memo based on its ability to move public opinion.[110] Instead, Powell—and then Scaife, Coors, and Koch—offered Americans a compelling vocabulary for comprehending the disorientation of the Long Sixties from a fresh perspective. Understanding rhetorical effect by shifting focus from public opinion to shaping the worldview of an audience can be traced back to the origins of rhetorical studies and Aristotle's seminal definition of rhetoric as the faculty of observing, in any given case, the available means of persuasion.[111] Likewise, sophistic rhetoricians developed the Greek term *doxa* to account for the temporal and communal characteristics that influence the expectations of a rhetor and the acceptance of the message. Crowley suggests doxa "designates current and local beliefs that circulate communally."[112] But "designates" points to a referential description of rhetor and message; a more precise phrasing would need to account for the dynamic resonance and co-creation of the communally circulated belief. More recently, Kenneth Burke—the most influential rhetorical theorist of the last century—urged critics to explore the moral impulses that motivate perception, suggesting that beneath-the-surface dimensions highlight "what to look for and what to look out for."[113] The moral impulse underpinning perceptions is "an engine of rhetoric," according to Brummett.[114] This rhetorical tradition highlights how the influence of Powell's memo is incomprehensible apart from the occasion calling forth his message, the rhetor's relationship to the occasion, and the climate of opinion and current events in which the rhetor operates.[115]

Rhetorical scholars now study effect as a condition of complex forces preceding and producing the message.[116] As Zarefsky put it, rhetoric defines the situation and shapes the context in which events are viewed by the public. By defining the world in a certain way, the rhetor can invite certain reactions and discourage others.[117] Jones and Rowland wrote that the worldview-shaping function is one of the primary ways rhetors influence politics.[118] Crowley described how "potential arguments are thrown up by the circumstances of communal life."[119] Arguments are "always already available"—they need only to be activated or enlivened within a rhetorical encounter. The effect of Powell's memo transcends causality, in other words, and lends insight into a shifting worldview concerning the proper role of the government in a market economy. More recent research in psychology and neurobiology also affirms what rhetoricians have been studying for 2,500 years. Sharot, for example, suggests that understanding how to influence public opinion on issues like gun control and vaccines first requires knowing the target's preestablished notions and motivations. With a strong preexisting motivation to believe something is true, contrary evidence can fall on deaf ears.[120] The rhetorical tradition informs the relationship between the rhetorical effect of Powell's memo and the oligarchic worldview it helped to circulate.

Eschewing a causal examination of public opinion to measure effects is especially vital for understanding the reach of Powell's memo far beyond the leadership of the US Chamber of Commerce. As Crowley argued, people can subscribe to beliefs that have bad consequences for them, including women who cling to patriarchal values, and the millions of middle and working-class Americans who will never become oligarchs but remain staunch supporters of the oligarchic worldview offered by Powell.[121]

Powell diverges from the Keynesian orientation toward equality. His memo also sheds light on the most schizophrenic dimensions of the modern political economy. The state need not be shrunk to align with oligarchy's worldview. Rather, the state is charged with evaluating our ability to conform to natural laws, constructing and affirming social arrangements where the most intelligent, hardy, and tenacious individuals can rise above the rest.

America's corporate elites reacted as Powell would have desired. Fear, anger, and cynicism were directed toward the federal government. Midcentury Keynesian liberalism fell out of favor as a particular community began to affirm Powell's outlook on our social institutions: not as a benefactor but as a threat to freedom.[122] But because democratic oligarchy requires the consent of the middling classes, an exploration of oligarchy must consider how Powell's outlook trickled down from the corporate elite to the ordinary American. In the next chapter, I turn to Milton Friedman to show how he brought the oligarchic orientation described by Powell out of the corporate boardrooms and into the mainstream by developing and circulating some of the most consequential oligarchic arguments of the twentieth century.

7

The Laws of Science and the Rhetoric of Milton Friedman

MILTON FRIEDMAN WAS AN ACCOMPLISHED ECONOMIST, A PROLIFIC scholar, and a Nobel Prize winner. Friedman believed deeply that economic theory should be put to the test, and he did so with profligacy and acclaim, by synthesizing statistical data, historical episodes, and scientific experiments.[1] But Friedman was also persuasive, cunning, and likable. The rare celebrity academic, he had a regular column in *Newsweek* and his own ten-part series on PBS. Friedman would have been an entertaining dinner guest. He was warm and disarming, but he could also be a tenacious intellectual sparring partner. It was wise, an opponent observed, to wait until Friedman left the room before arguing with him.[2] When Friedman began to counsel Ronald Reagan, White House advisors learned not to leave Friedman alone with Reagan, because Friedman was that persuasive. Friedman was known to listen to his opponents with a knowing grin until they stopped talking and he could explain why they were wrong.[3]

Friedman understood the limits of rational argument, especially for achieving the public policies he desired in a majoritarian democracy populated by what he assumed to be apathetic and short-sighted citizens. A consistent theme linking oligarchic rhetors is their shared assumption that our decisions emerge from an unconscious orientation. Thus, to achieve the public policies Friedman and his allies desired, he needed to focus on the foundation of public sense making.[4] Friedman was an idealist, but he was confident implausible public policies would become feasible when his preferred "intellectual climate of opinion" could begin to shape the "unthinking preconditions" and "condition the reflexes" of the demos and their leaders.[5] Friedman predicted that "only a crisis" could produce the changes he desired. Until then, his life's purpose was keeping alive alternatives to

Keynesian policies until "the politically impossible becomes politically inevitable."[6] By the 1970s, Friedman had his crisis.

The Seeds of Its Own Destruction

Friedman extended the prophetic warnings of others by criticizing Keynesian government programs as betrayals of the economic and political principles of true liberalism.[7] Like Hayek, Friedman was confident Keynesianism would fail because it contradicted a familiar set of immutable, natural economic laws. On his PBS series *Free to Choose*, Friedman told his audience that Keynesian central planning has within it "the seeds of its own destruction." Friedman continued, "There is no way in which a system constructed like the present, in my opinion, can avoid creating more and more social problems, and something is going to have to be done."[8] Friedman was sure that because Keynesian central planning contradicted nature, the result would be a "natural human reaction to [resist] the attempt by other people to control your life when you think it's none of their business."[9] Friedman framed Keynesian efforts "to help the poor" as an exercise in power concentration by a new class of government bureaucrats who never met a problem they could not solve with taxpayer dollars and more bureaucracy.[10] For the rest of the century, the ultra-rich and their allies criticized the New Deal and the Great Society using quasi-altruistic and counter-hegemonic arguments: Aid to Families with Dependent Children incentivized fatherless families; unemployment insurance hindered the self-worth of the recipient; Social Security loosened family bonds because adult children did not have to care for their aging parents; and disability insurance encouraged people who could be working to amplify their minor aches and pains.[11] In the end, Friedman worked hard to make it look like Keynesianism was doing the opposite of what it promised to do: It harmed the needy by empowering unnatural bureaucracies and sapped motivation, pride, and self-reliance. And we were all worse off for it. The authenticity of appeals to the common good were questionable. But their public arguments do highlight a deeply held belief that the Keynesian welfare state was misguided, foolish, and unjust—not only because the poor do not deserve the help, as evidenced by their need, but because any attempt to come to their aid would thwart economic progress. Further, this aid would not fulfill the demands of natural order because the needy would not put the aid to use as well as the rich.

Friedman did not merely amplify this pessimism and fear. Friedman was a happy warrior, hopeful that a "strong enough component in our society" will "turn this trend back" and "cut government down to size" so that they can "lay the ground work for a resurgence, a flowering of that diversity which has been the real product of our free society."[12] In his bestselling *Capitalism and Freedom* (1962), Milton Friedman echoed Hayek's elevation of the individual, writing, "To the free man, the country is the collection of individuals who compose it, not something over and above them. . . . He recognizes no national purpose except as it is the consensus of the purposes for which the citizens severally strive."[13] Freedom and liberty were best protected by individuals looking out for their own interests and values, free from external constraints, Friedman said. Freedom depended on understanding the country as a "collection of individuals," he wrote; nothing more than that.[14] There was no national purpose apart from striving for your own interests. Thus, Friedman positioned "freedom as the ultimate goal and the individual as the ultimate entity in society."[15] Consequently, as freedom flourished and we pursued our own interests, private property must be sacrosanct, government's responsibility was limited to defense and preservation of order, and state intervention in the market produced more harm than good—no matter how well intentioned.

On the surface, Milton Friedman's textual persona aligned with the conventional orientation of the political Right in the 1970s and 1980s. Consider the plight of Barry Goldwater as an example. Goldwater tried to assume the mantle of authentic conservatism as the Republican nominee to the presidency in 1964. But Goldwater ended up losing forty-four states, winning only five in the Deep South and his home state of Arizona.[16] Media accounts of Goldwater's defeat were stinging. James Reston wrote in the *New York Times* that Goldwater did not just lose the election; he did irrevocable damage to his larger cause. Goldwater's defeat was understood by many as a crushing and lasting blow to a conservative alternative to New Deal and Great Society interventions.[17] But by 1980, Goldwater's political economic program had reemerged in the candidacy of Ronald Reagan. And as it turns out, Goldwater did not actually lose to LBJ in 1964. George Will would later write, "It just took sixteen years to count the votes."[18] Milton Friedman praised Goldwater as a trailblazer for Reagan, priming the American people not quite ready for Goldwater's zeal in 1964. By 1980, Friedman argued, "the people had come around to wanting to hear what he was saying."[19] And yet, during the sixteen years between Goldwater's crushing loss and Reagan's conservative revolution, Friedman crossed the bridge from accomplished economist to accomplished rhetor—and not because he offered the American public a preordained and inevitable extension of conservatism.

The Magic of the Price System

Milton Friedman's textual persona drew individuals into a new, contingent community under the umbrella of "conservative Republicans" by describing government regulations into the market economy as a contradiction of the laws of science.[20] In this way, Friedman began circulating political economic vocabulary more appropriate for laboratories full of beaker jars and lab coats—a strategy also adopted by Frank Knight, Aaron Director, Gordon Tullock, and other influential rhetors from the University of Chicago's school of economics.[21] Friedman claimed to withhold normative judgments. Instead, he tested falsifiable hypotheses mathematically, developing objective and apolitical propositions. Friedman was not a dogmatic, anti-Nazi freedom fighter. He was a disinterested, post-partisan economic scientist. Even when the public disagreed with his draconian public policies, like selling Yosemite and abolishing the minimum wage, he never lost the appearance of scientific legitimacy. Consider one strange but revealing exchange on Friedman's PBS program *Free to Choose*: Friedman asked the host and moderator Robert McKenzie if he had ever seen a cat that barked. After McKenzie responded, "Not especially, no," Friedman made his outlook clear, describing how "governmental agencies and governmental laws follow their own laws. Just as the physical laws say that cats don't bark, these laws of social science say that when you set up a regulatory agency with power, those powers are going to be used."[22]

While Friedman drew from a familiar discursive aquifer, his scientific textual persona filled in some of the rhetorical gaps left within mid-century economic conservatism.[23] In *Invisible Hands*, Kim Phillips-Fein describes the work of Friedman and the Chicago school of economics as "less political" than Hayek and the Austrian economist strain because Friedman focused more on economic science and mathematical modeling than political theory.[24] Brian Doherty in *Radicals for Capitalism* says Friedman and the Chicago school "tends to be more empirical" than Hayek and the Austrians.[25] And Catherine Chaput describes Friedman's legacy as the establishment of "scientific legitimacy for decades of economic exploration."[26] With these descriptions of Friedman in mind, we can begin to better understand why the political Right was able to link Friedman and the Chicago school's economic science with "conservative" economic policies during the Reagan administration. In contrast to the 1930s and 1940s, many Americans after Reagan began to assume that Republicans were the party of fiscal discipline and balanced budgets, in part because Friedman constructed an affective

CHAPTER 7

modality linking "conservative" economic policies with uncontestable "laws of social science," as he put it.[27]

Friedman knew better than to affirm this link by using rational economic arguments alone. "It's no accident," Friedman said, that "economic freedom promotes human freedom."[28] But an important disjuncture will emerge as Friedman would publicly concede the rhetorical value of linking the laws of science with social harmony while personally disdaining such a pursuit. For example, consider the iconic reference to the yellow No. 2 pencil Friedman offered to viewers of his PBS series: "When you go down to the store and buy this pencil, you are in effect, trading a few minutes of your time for a few seconds of the time of all of those thousands of people. What brought them together and induced them to cooperate to make this pencil? There was no commissar sending out offices, sending out orders from some central office. It was the magic of the price system, the impersonal operation of prices that brought them together, and got them to cooperate to make this pencil so that you could have it for a trifling sum. That is why the operation of the free market is so essential, not only to promote productive efficiency, but, even more, to foster harmony and peace among the peoples of the world."[29] More than a writing instrument, the pencil brought humans together naturally, without central planning. Rather than rely on the imposition or legislation of "philosopher-kings," Friedman was confident the free market could produce "the spontaneous and voluntary cooperation of individual human beings."[30]

While the magic of the price system promised harmony, peace, and cheap pencils, Friedman emphasized that it did not promise equality, social justice, or general public interest. That distinction is at the core of Friedman's original rejection of Keynesianism.[31] Friedman pined for the hierarchy of Edmund Burke, not the equality of Earl Warren. "I am not in favor of egalitarianism," he said.[32] Friedman warned Americans by pointing out that Britain was losing its ablest, best trained, and most vigorous people because their drive for equality was keeping them from using their talents for their own benefit.[33] Equality explains why postwar Britain fell so far behind the United States and Japan in improving the economic conditions of ordinary people.[34]

Consider the relationship between Friedman's magical price system and Hayek's telic road metaphor. Friedman would make the links explicit in his 1994 preface to *The Road to Serfdom*: "Fundamentally, there are only two ways of coordinating the economic activities of millions. One is central direction involving the use of coercion—the technique of the army and of the modern totalitarian state. The other is voluntary cooperation of individuals—the technique of the market place."[35] Friedman's preface is reductive, fallacious, and even naive—especially coming from a Nobel Prize winner in economics. But because its economic axioms are cloaked in scientific legitimacy, any disagreement betrays the opposition's ignorance. Only cranks dispute settled science. Thus, Friedman's opponents deserve pity as much as scorn for their inability to understand how the economy actually works.[36]

What Is Politically Feasible?

Friedman was a brilliant rhetor, but his public propositions did not conform to the basic requirements of the scientific method. In his public arguments, Friedman had the tendency to feature his findings before he had the evidence to affirm them.[37] In his own words, Friedman was an idealist, a dreamer, and a millenarian. On PBS, Friedman said: "I don't apologize for a moment for being millenarian; because I think unless we know where we want to go, the timid steps that we take in that direction will go in the wrong direction. And if we're gonna go in the right direction, we ought to have a view."[38] A *millenarian* is someone within a religious, social, or political movement who believes in the coming transformation of society, in which all things will be changed. By definition, millenarianism cannot be scientific.[39] Scientific inquiry begins with uncertainty. Science risks being wrong. But Friedman could never be proven wrong. Political pressure precluded his propositions from empirical testing. The American public is unlikely to return to the days when children worked the coal mines, companies dumped pollution into rivers with impunity, and we let people starve to death on the streets. Friedman saw this reluctance as weakness. But he also recognized how shrewd the demos could be. Ordinary Americans knew they were too weak and ignorant to survive on their own, but they could leverage their strength in numbers to overwhelm their betters. When Friedman conceded that his global free trade propositions were fantastic, he admitted "on the politics of it, of course, it's not politically feasible because it's only in the *general interest* and in nobody's special interest."[40] But that political hurdle offered Friedman an ever-present rhetorical escape hatch. Friedman's policies affirmed limitless faith in the free market, but when the market fails, it can only be the impurities in the system fouling it up.[41] In a massive democracy, impurities are never hard to find. The "execution" argument is always available when we are unwilling to eliminate the minimum wage or send our children back to the coal mines. The political Right can also fault the demos for our lack of commitment. The public is too stupid and impatient and the media too biased. Even Republican politicians are too quick to sell-out. Economic utopia is always just around the corner if only the demos had the patience.

Friedman's approach resembles a mythic, abstract thought experiment. His propositions sounded like falsifiable scientific hypotheses predicting real outcomes, but the process was always adulterated by human beings who do not behave according to formulas.[42] Nonetheless, Friedman synthesized the language of mathematical calculations and statistical enumerations with his scientific ethos to assume an aura of quantitative authority that, before then, had mainly applied to Keynes, Galbraith, and Polanyi.[43] The rhetorical representations of Friedman's economic positivism advanced Smith's invisible hand, Spencer's survival of the fittest, and Hayek's autonomous laws to an elevated status marked by neutral scientific methods.

That popularity and influence should not distract from the contingency underpinning Friedman's public arguments. Milton Friedman suggested that public opinion about government regulation would change, for instance, if the public knew about the products the Consumer Product Safety Commission kept from coming to market. "It's very easy to see the good results. The bad results are very much harder to see," he said. He continued, "You haven't mentioned the products that aren't there because the extra costs imposed by Consumer Product Safety Commission have prevented them from existing."[44] Friedman's fallacious appeal to ignorance fails a basic requirement of the scientific method because he attempts to disprove a negative. Likewise, Friedman suggested that if we opened our borders, the American public would soon agree with his proposals to gut the welfare system.[45] He also suggested that we would see how superior private and charter schools were compared to public schools once we sold all our public schools and their land and equipment to private owners.[46] Because we will not open our borders or sell all our public schools, his propositions cannot be verified. Notice also Friedman's fantastic solution to racial discrimination. If we relied on his free market principles, rather than Civil Rights legislation, American racism would depress wages for Black workers. Depressed wages reduced production costs for companies employing Black workers. Companies would be incentivized to hire more Black workers, shrinking the labor market, and driving up their wages. Virtue would triumph without government meddling.[47] All Friedman needs to test his proposition is a society of homo *oeconomicus* subjects devoid of racial prejudice.

You might expect a Nobel Prize–winning economics professor to know the difference between empirical science and hypothetical thought experiments. And he did. Friedman admitted legislative efforts to limit the power and scope of government are "doomed to failure."[48] In his book *Free to Choose*, under the subheading "What Is Politically Feasible?" Friedman acknowledged that his "fine dream" had "no chance whatsoever of being enacted at present."[49] It was impossible to reform American health care in accordance with his preferences, for instance, because the American public expected nontaxable medical care provided by their employer. Changing that would result in such a "big political fuss."[50] He disdained Social Security, but he also knew it could not be eliminated overnight. Instead, he sought "to develop a series of policies which enable us to gradually move from where we are to where we want to be. The first and most important step, in my opinion, is to stop moving in the wrong direction."[51]

What describes the rhetorical reconciliation in Friedman's public messaging? How can such a brilliant, accomplished, and influential rhetor flunk a basic epistemological expectation and still wield such enormous influence? For insight, recall the blurred boundaries between *science* and *scientism*.[52] Friedman adopted the priestly persona that nonscientific philosophers, economists, and politicians rely on for rhetorical impact and to portray themselves as having access to insights unavailable to others.[53] Friedman looked like an objective scientist debating the finer points of political and economic theory, and in so doing, affirmed Lessl's conceptualization of the "double life" connecting perceptions of scientific expertise to aesthetic, emotive, affective, rhetorical, and ideological ideations.[54] In other words, the scientific validity of Friedman's messaging was never as important as the *appearance* of validity. Friedman and his Chicago school economists needed to look like well-intentioned intellectuals discussing the finer points of economic theory. They were confident the American public would not know the difference.[55] Friedman's textual persona maintained objective scientific imperatives even as he induces individuals into an audience defined by scientism. Friedman also blurred the technical and public spheres, transcending the public's understanding of the scientific method. To the public, Friedman's realist rhetoric resembled an astronomer describing stars unseen by the naked eye or a sonogram technician looking at a blurring bump on an ultrasound and seeing a healthy boy.[56]

In the end, Friedman's textual persona absorbed and circulated the dispositions, sentiments, and affectations of his scientism, ultimately securing a scientific defense of oligarchic capitalism to replace the Keynesian welfare state. Friedman was untroubled by his quasi-scientific propositions because

CHAPTER 7

he understood how economic rhetoric moves individuals through a dynamic confluence of text and context, argument and affect. Friedman thought only historical events forced people to consider massive structural changes, and it was his job to make sure everyone was ready when those changes arrived.[57]

Keeping Options Available

Friedman understood that his efforts to redress what he saw as the "evils of paternalistic programs" would not be widely accepted by the American public right away.[58] Conceding the uphill battle, Friedman aligned himself with "a small beleaguered minority regarded as eccentrics by the great majority of our fellow intellectuals."[59] But if oligarchy is "the rule of the few," it makes sense why Friedman was comfortable on the intellectual margins, patiently waiting for the right kairotic moment to implement his policies.[60] Near the end, Friedman summarized his life's work by suggesting economists like himself "do not influence the course of events by persuading people that we are right when we make what they regard as radical proposals. Rather, we exert influence by keeping options available when something has to be done at a time of crisis."[61] Binyamin Appelbaum interpreted Friedman's "keeping options available" quote to suggest that Friedman's ideas were akin to a can of beans sitting on the shelf waiting to be eaten.[62] But Friedman is being too humble and Appelbaum too naive. Friedman's policies were not as passive as the beans-on-the-shelf metaphor implies. The conceptual value of understanding Friedman's textual persona is evinced in such incongruous vocabulary. Friedman was a rhetorical pit bull—a full-throated zealot advocating for a stratified political hierarchy constructed in accordance with the laws of science. But he covered that hierarchy in an abstract and neutral vocabulary allowing radical policies like abolishing the minimum wage and repealing the Civil Rights Act to seem sober, objective, and empirical.

Ultimately, Friedman's textual persona is aligned with the Right's lean government and free market, especially his influence on a generation of business and political leaders, including Barry Goldwater, Charles Koch, Margaret Thatcher, Ronald Reagan, George Will, and Paul Ryan.[63] Public conversations affirm that relationship. As a result, a tight, coherent link emerges between Friedman and the Right's conservative political prescriptions.[64] And yet, Friedman's oligarchic rhetoric offers another chance to complicate these connections. Friedman was more pragmatic than his status as a conservative icon implies. His public arguments are littered with the selective applications of his own doctrine, including evolving approaches to antitrust laws, free trade, and Social Security.[65] Friedman expressed concern about corporate power, and he argued one of the federal government's few legitimate functions was restraining corporations to enhance competition. He admitted his ideal "free enterprise" was always restrained by "businessmen [who] whenever [they] have the chance they will, of course, use government to pursue objectives which may or may not be in the interest of the public at large."[66] Or consider Friedman's evolving attitude toward antitrust laws. "When I started in this business," Friedman said, "as a believer in competition, I was a great supporter of antitrust laws. I thought enforcing them was one of the few desirable things that the government could do to promote more competition." But his "views about the antitrust laws have changed greatly over time" because, he said, the government had never enforced them aggressively enough. "I have gradually come to the conclusion that antitrust laws do far more harm than good and that we would be better off if we didn't have them at all, if we could get rid of them."[67] Friedman's antitrust evolution is understandably practical. Politics is the art of the possible; if antitrust enforcements were impossible, we should "get rid of them," as Friedman suggested. But by the same measure, Friedman's antitrust evolution is hopelessly naive, producing a political economy dominated by entrenched corporate monopolies.[68] Friedman and his Chicago school allies also conceded the need for the state to provide "the framework within which business, local-public and private, may effectively be conducted," as Henry C. Simons wrote.[69] Jamie Peck said Friedman "expressly sought to transcend the 'naïve ideology' of laissez-faire, in favor of a 'positive' conception of the state as the guarantor of a competitive order."[70] Chaput noted how Friedman also substituted nineteenth-century laissez-faire for "the goal of competitive order," which obliges the state to ensure market operations "proceed according to the rules of free exchanges."[71]

However, *competition* is an ideographic quagmire, capable of being pulled and tugged in various directions. Peck and Chaput are correct in suggesting that Friedman eschewed a lean, laissez-faire government for a more robust and proactive state. But it does not seem like Friedman wanted the state to function as a guarantor of a competitive order. Instead, he took a selective approach to "the rules of free exchanges." Friedman wanted the state to freeze hierarchies of power according to the historical struggle revealed by one's status in a natural power hierarchy. In his own words, Friedman saw "no justification whatsoever for cutting down all the tall trees in order that there be no tree in the forest that is taller than the other."[72] Friedman cited Alexis de Tocqueville's quote in which he called any human quest for equality "depraved" because it "impels the weak to attempt to lower the powerful to their own level, and reduces men to prefer equality in slavery to inequality with freedom."[73]

Friedman constructed a governmental apparatus oriented toward pronounced and justly constructed hierarchies based on the scientific application of his price system that assumed priority over aspirations toward equality, social justice, and general interest. Low taxes and minimal regulation for the entrenched elites mark an important dimension of Friedman's telos, but we should not confuse that aspiration with facile and conventional links to the Right's lean government and free market. Friedman also sought a state oriented toward inflicting pain and suffering on those unwilling or unable to conform to the laws of science.[74] Friedman understood the democratic contradictions inherent in conservative policies could not be sorted out peacefully. In comparing his economic program to Keynesianism, Friedman wrote, "Fundamental differences in basic values can seldom if ever be resolved at the ballot box; ultimately they can only be decided, though not resolved, by conflict. The religious and civil wars of history are a bloody testament to this judgment."[75] In describing the dangers of government interference in the market, Friedman wrote: "If we continue down this path, there is no doubt where it will end. After all, if it is appropriate for the government to protect us from using dangerous cap guns and bicycles, the logic calls for prohibiting still more dangerous activities such as hang gliding, motorcycling, skiing."[76] Friedman's warnings resonate today in the Right's accusations of an overreaching federal government monitoring the size of our soda cups and water pressure in our toilets. But notice how Friedman goes on to then argue that government interference in the market "occurs at the expense of the kind of healthy development of new, dynamic, adaptive industries that would surely occur if the market were allowed to operate freely." If the laws of science could prevail without government's adulteration, the free market would then fulfill its consequentialist function and "separate out the unsuccessful ventures from the successful ones, discouraging the unsuccessful and encouraging the successful."[77]

American corporate culture would come to reflect Friedman's intellectual promulgation. GE's iconic CEO Jack Welch began a rank-and-yank system that codified "worker insecurity by constantly identifying a quota of doomed losers," wrote Kurt Andersen.[78] This meant that one out of ten GE workers would be fired each year—no matter what. GE called it the "Vitality curve." Other companies adopted similar sacrificial policies cloaked in banal corporate-speak, including IBM's "Personal Business Commitments,"

Motorola's "Individual Dignity Entitlements," and Amazon's "Purposeful Darwinism."[79] In 2012, Mitt Romney admitted that he liked to fire people—as he ran for president of the United States.[80] Accordingly, Friedman encouraged a governing logic that deliberately inflicted painful shocks on the American people. Swallowing this bitter medicine, Friedman argued, would eventually lead to economic vitality and the widespread acceptance of his scientific prescriptions.[81]

Cut It Off

If there is no compelling general interest, and public thought is shaped only by special interest, then Keynesianism and its equality orientation are rendered feckless, and a discrete market economy prevails, rewarding the superior and punishing the inferior. Friedman condoned an unrestrained maximization of personal resource accumulation.

In Friedman's world, no one conceded another's fundamental right to exist. There was no prerogative to respect another's body or belongings. In fact, personal survival often contradicted social order.[82] Self-defense came by increasing one's own resources and decreasing everyone else's. Pronounced hierarchies of power were the a priori condition of human relations: Some were simply stronger, more competent, and more talented than others.[83] The rising tide did not lift all boats in Friedman's world. Nor should it. Because it is a jungle, we expect some carnage.[84] For example, Milton Friedman asked his PBS audience to imagine how the US government could effectively end welfare: "But suppose you were cruel and simply took away the welfare overnight. Cut it off. What would happen? He would find a job. What kind of a job? I don't know. It might not be a very nice job. It might not be a very attractive job. But at some wage, at some level of pay, there will always be a job which he could get for himself. It might be also that he would be driven to rely on some private charity. He might have to get soup kitchen help or the equivalent. Again, I'm not saying that's desirable or nice or a good thing; it isn't, but as a matter of actual fact as to what would happen, there is little doubt that he would find some way to earn a living."[85]

Friedman conceded the man in his scenario may not find a "very nice job." But he would be kept alive without losing his dignity by depending on others. Cruel public policy offered motivation to those unwilling to conform to the scientific laws of economic competition while also lessening the responsibility of those who did.[86] Many Americans distrust state efforts to provide health care or social services today because without skin in the

CHAPTER 7

game, those who rely on public help will abuse the system. Edwin Meese, Ronald Reagan's attorney general, operationalized Friedman's concern in defending Reagan-era cuts to poverty programs, saying, "We've had considerable information that people go to soup kitchens because the food is free and that's easier than paying for it."[87] In the summer of 2021, many states led by Republican governors elected to end unemployment benefits just as the country began to recover from the coronavirus pandemic based on similar fears that the weekly checks were facilitating laziness and sapping gumption. Economist Tyler Cowen justified the scientific laws of competition as the only way to advance the cause of economic liberty and human freedom by requiring more people to fend for themselves. Consequently, the worthy would flourish and everyone else would "fall by the wayside," as Cowen put it.[88] But as an upside, the losers have less to lose in a bargaining relationship. Because their lives are literally worth less, they can leverage their precarity for a stronger bargaining position.[89]

Milton Friedman succeeded in blaming much of the Long Sixties turmoil on Keynesian central planning. Public opinion shifted, the welfare state now seemed to induce dependency, financial regulations gummed up the free movement of capital, and bloated government institutions adulterated the purity of the free market. As Friedman hammered away, public perceptions of welfare changed—especially toward Aid to Families with Dependent Children.[90] Friedman took advantage of the shift, writing in *Why Government Is the Problem*, "The major social problems of the United States—deteriorating education, lawlessness and crime, homelessness, the collapse of family values, the crisis in medical care—have been produced by well-intended actions of government."[91] Virtually all government programs turned to "ashes" in Friedman's words, including the welfare state, public housing, trade unions, public schools, federal aid to education, and affirmative action policies.[92]

Friedman's influence is also evinced in his approach to race and political economy. Friedman ended up on the wrong side of history, just like James Kilpatrick. But his racial policies aligned with a transcendent worldview. In a revealing series of editorials condemning US sanctions on Rhodesia, Friedman linked universal suffrage to minority rule. But Friedman did not mean "minority" in the less-than-half sense. Friedman could count. Friedman meant "minority" in the *justly disempowered* sense. Friedman wrote, "'Majority rule' for Rhodesia today is a euphemism for a Black-minority government, which would almost surely mean both the eviction or exodus of most of the whites and also a drastically lower level of living and opportunity for the masses of Black Rhodesians."[93] Friedman understood discrimination. He suffered from anti-Semitism throughout his career. In fact, he linked his personal experience with anti-Semitism to the anti-bigotry capacities of economic science. And yet, the link between Friedman's worldview and Friedman's racial attitudes is evinced here. Friedman perpetuated white systematic supremacy by generalizing Black negativity in Rhodesia, just like Kilpatrick in Virginia. He assumed Black-majority rule in Rhodesia would lead to "lower levels of living and opportunity" because incompetence, laziness, and corruption function as transcendent traits across Black Rhodesians.[94] Put any of them in charge and Friedman knew what would happen.

Conclusion

Milton Friedman developed a vocabulary appropriate for a social and cultural moment oriented toward the scientific study of capitalism.[95] Friedman drew the American public's attention because he was able to link scientific inquiry with a spirit of anti-communist patriotism. Further, Friedman aligned with a kairotic moment in which technological advancement and mathematical modeling underpinned a rational economic ontology.[96] Friedman wore a suit. Not camouflage fatigues and a beret. Because he was a scientist—not a revolutionary, polemicist, or even a political theorist—Friedman could intervene in upstream cultural and intellectual influence. In Chile, Juan Gabriel Valdes described how Friedman-inspired, University of Chicago–trained economists assumed influential government positions, which allowed them to exercise control over intellectual reproduction in legal, educational, political, and cultural settings.[97] The same process was noticeable closer to home as economic scientists tried to exert public influence through their endowed professorships and think tanks, including the American Enterprise Institute, the Hoover Institution, and the National Bureau of Economic Research.[98]

Scholars of neoliberal economic theory highlight the late 1970s and early 1980s as the moment when Americans began to evaluate everything the government did based on "strictly economic and market terms," as Michel Foucault wrote.[99] Friedman urged a permanent critique of the state, leading us to look suspiciously at government interventions in the market. In *Stormy Weather*, Henry Giroux detailed the suspension of the social contract and a government now sliced to the bone in total genuflection to the free market.[100] As an alternative to Keynesianism, this rolled back version of neoliberalism encouraged the state to remove itself as much as possible so the strong and free could compete. Following Friedman, state interference meant limiting government functions to preserving law and order, enforcing contracts, protecting private property, supervising the issuance of currency, and fostering competitive markets.[101]

To that end, the public arguments of Milton Friedman drew heavily from the past. Each era of government growth represented a stinging betrayal of the US Constitution and the freedom it guaranteed.[102] Accordingly, the Right's policy prescriptions were characterized by a rolled back form of government where social programs were cut, the labor market deregulated, the social contract suspended, environmental protections sacrificed, and those who did not comply disciplined.[103] But it was not enough to merely cut government spending; the cutting needed to be hard, fast, and deep. Any pain from these cuts was merely a sign of impending relief, evidence of a free market emerging from under the thumb of big government. Following Friedman, Grover Norquist recommended reducing government so much that it could be "drowned in a bathtub"—with much more pernicious consequences for those who rely on welfare checks, disability insurance, workers' comp, and SNAP benefits. Charles Koch offered an arbor metaphor, suggesting government be pulled out "at the root," leaving only a clean and more easily tilled field.[104]

Although nostalgic appeals may inform Friedman's efforts to weaken the Keynesian welfare state, they do not fully explain the oligarchic alternative emerging in its place. Despite ubiquitous public messaging deriding Big Government liberalism, we never actually exchanged the Keynesian welfare state for a lean, laissez-faire government.[105] Friedman, and then Ronald Reagan, urged us to evaluate, separate, and dispose of society's undeserved losers based on their inability to conform to natural economic laws, individual accountability, and competition. But that same metric was never applied to the state, especially the positive, proactive, and rolled out efforts of the Reagan administration to concentrate power into the affluent's hands through direct government interventions, subsidies, tax breaks, tariffs, international trade agreements, and military actions.[106] Instead, the state was reoriented toward the interests of a small group of the ultra-rich and away from the interests of ordinary Americans.[107]

Nostalgia cannot function as an autonomous governing logic. Nostalgia maintains no loyalty to the decisions of Congress elected by a representative democracy because naturally produced hierarchies of talent and skills offer the ruling elite unique perspicacity denied to the rest of us.[108] Friedman's realist rhetoric offered him insight on the intent of the Founders and the lessons of our sacred founding documents. Everyone *can* access the original meaning, but it is the ruling elite who have taken advantage of the opportunity. But beneath this ephemeral outlook, a set of challenging shifts began to emerge in the 1980s: Soon after Ronald Reagan's election, economic growth started flowing mainly to the affluent, millions of blue-collar jobs with pensions and reliable health care disappeared, higher education became essential and unaffordable at the same time, anti-monopoly and antitrust enforcement slacked, corporate spending on elections ballooned, political lobbying increased by 1000 percent, and the federal government became more sympathetic to big business, as Kurt Andersen details.[109] More specifically, Reagan's conservative revolution sought to look like a populist, working-class movement, but it ended up making the lives of ordinary Americans much more difficult.[110]

In the 1980s, Reagan's schizo-state—both small and large, lean and bloated, rolled back and rolled out—eluded tidy classification. Descriptions of "fiscal discipline," "competition," and "common good" only muddied the conceptual waters.[111] *Belt-tightening* became a common metaphor during the Reagan era, and allusions to austerity dominated the decisions of the Department of Education and HHS. But the Pentagon's budget grew every year Reagan was in office. Appeals to *competition* were never universal but reserved for explaining the plight of the poor. An oligarchic orientation assumes the game has already been played, the winners proven fit, and there is no longer any need for them to compete. And while appeals to the *common good* still lingered, they were never linked from public argument to public policy within any pragmatic coherence.

Kurt Andersen tries to argue that Americans in the 1980s began to accept the appeals of Friedman and Reagan because it seemed like they "had finally figured out a way to have no losers at all and no fights over deciding who gets how much."[112] But figuring out how to have "no losers at all" contradicts the rhetorical evidence aligning an oligarchic community against equality and toward hierarchy. Instead, the value of tracing oligarchic arguments in this moment is to better understand why we withdrew our support for ordinary Americans in favor of praise and adulation for the ultra-rich. We conceded to more regressive taxation, deregulation, and crony capitalism while also slashing support for the welfare state, education, health care, and organized labor because only the weak needed the latter and only the strong deserved the former. Many Americans suffered as a result, but nature's hierarchy was reaffirmed. We would rather punish the needy, and risk our own well-being in the process, than risk any chance of the losers getting what they do not deserve.[113]

The state need not be shrunk. Rather, the state is charged with evaluating our ability to conform to natural laws, constructing and affirming social arrangements where the most intelligent, hardy, and tenacious individuals can rise above the rest and are rewarded when they do so. The expanded demands of the state are justified by appealing to a unique conception of oligarchic justice. The ultra-rich are convinced an oligarchic state oriented toward their interests fulfills their most compelling expectations of justice. An oligarchic state oriented toward the interests of the ultra-rich aligns with the sincere conviction that economic worth should translate into political potency, effectively breaking down political/economic walls that had been maintained during the postwar decades of shared economic growth.[114]

For the ultra-rich, the self-serving appeal of oligarchy is clear. But the democratic entailments of oligarchy urge a continued exploration of oligarchy's incongruous resonance with ordinary Americans. To that end, I focus in the next chapter on the incongruity between democratic oligarchy and American Christianity.

8

Conjoint Depletion and the Rhetoric of James M. Buchanan

BEFORE HE DIED IN 2013, JAMES McGILL BUCHANAN WAS A DISTINguished fellow of the Cato Institute, a mentor to the Koch Brothers, the president of the Mont Pèlerin Society, and a Nobel Prize winner in Economic Sciences. After the Long Sixties, Buchanan changed public conversations about welfare, organized labor, and the state-market relationship. He cut a wide swatch. He popularized terms like "public choice economics" and "constitutional economics." And he laid the intellectual foundation for the Reagan Revolution, the Koch brothers' political activity, the Tea Party, and Donald Trump's conquest of the modern Republican Party.[1] And yet, Buchanan's influence is often misunderstood. Scholars and journalists describe Buchanan as conservative, neoliberal, libertarian, and pro-market—a "deeply political foot soldier of the right," in Nancy MacLean's words.[2] MacLean also describes Buchanan as the "missing puzzle piece" for understanding the neoliberal Right. According to MacLean, Buchanan provided the intellectual and political force without which the economic policies of the Right would have stayed on the intellectual margins of corporate-funded think tanks and libertarian internet cranks.[3]

On Buchanan's importance, MacLean is correct. But on Buchanan's relationship with the Right, MacLean is mistaken. When we are careful with our definitions and precise with our language, it is clear Buchanan transcends our extant economic categories. If the economy is a seesaw, Buchanan is an aberrant plank splintering off from the two poles. To understand his divergence, consider the emergence of the phrase "conjoint depletion" in relation to Buchanan's worldview.

CHAPTER 8

Conjoint Depletion

Conjoint depletion assumes a cutthroat, negative-sum struggle for resources that grew in resonance after the Long Sixties. It assumes people are like lions carving up an antelope carcass, and your quality of life represents an external cost to mine.[4] Conjoint depletion rejects any normative pole beyond strategic self-interest. It rejects liberal appeals to shared-prosperity-through-coordinated-action.[5] It even rejects homo oeconomicus. Instead, we are *homo mendax*: moochers, liars, and thieves.[6] Civilization depends on a robust symbolic and coercive effort to contain our impulses. Criminals need to be contained by the real or prospective threat of sanction or harm, not granted constitutional rights like the Warren Court. Conjoint depletion, therefore, lends insight into oligarchy's affinity for a robust state—when the elite can control it. The rationale for the state is to contain the natural impulse we all have to lie, cheat, steal, and threaten our way to the accumulation of resources. Only the introduction of a sovereign state propped up by legal rationales and a monopoly on violence can threaten and cajole immoral social actors into the cooperation required for a modern economy.

After the Long Sixties, conjoint depletion filtered into the outlook of many ordinary Americans who began to unite their identity with this cold political rationality. Material wealth became evidence of fitness. Conjoint depletion assured us we have a responsibility to provide for ourselves and no one else.[7] The collective is a ruse. Requesting charity reveals one's own personal failure to live up to one's responsibility. The needy, according to Buchanan, should be "treated as subordinate members of the species, akin to . . . animals who are dependent."[8] Poverty was described as a cleansing process: separating the wheat from the chaff and filtering out the less worthy—each description underpinned by the assumption that one's worth, one's ability to survive, is justly reflected in one's material status.[9] The next link in the logical chain was clear: Those who did not measure up—those unwilling or unable to conform to natural law—must be plagued by a deep character flaw.

Conjoint depletion's implications were on display in its approach to racial equality. Buchanan, describing the challenges facing the Black community after emancipation, suggested that their failure evidenced that "the thirst for freedom, and responsibility, is perhaps not nearly so universal as so many post-Enlightenment philosophers have assumed."[10] Buchanan criticized the elimination of poll taxes and literacy tests because such actions expanded the voting franchise beyond white Americans, and thus produced an enlarged public sector funded by progressive tax policy. Buchanan was quite direct, complaining that federal bills to enhance voting protections in the South would put "colored heels upon white necks" and create "negro supremacy." Buchanan's bigotry was sordid but coherent. His racist worldview was held together by his belief in a negative-sum struggle for scarce resources. Because we are each fighting for individual achievement and self-sufficiency, we can be evaluated and ranked based on our ability to conform to the demands of capital accumulation.[11]

Buchanan personally embodied conjoint depletion. He was clever, sharp-tongued, and utterly confident in his intellectual abilities. He considered himself an Ayn Rand–type hero, destined to exert dominance.[12] His red-faced rages were legendary among his students. When challenged, he would become unrelenting, explosive, and unforgiving.[13] MacLean traces Buchanan's desire for individual dominance back to a lonely childhood. Even as an adult, Buchanan had few friends. At his memorial service, MacLean asked a man who had known Buchanan for thirty years how he had gotten to know him. "Did I?" the man replied.[14]

What does a lonely childhood and few friends have to do with oligarchy and democracy? It is useful to consider Buchanan's personal life as a microcosm of the ideal social hierarchy produced by conjoint depletion. It is lonely at the top. But with Truth on his side, James Buchanan could still attract the best and the brightest to his cause. His influence on the University of Chicago, the University of Virginia, and George Mason University was reflected in their reputations for "no holds barred combat," with Buchanan operating like a corporate titan.[15] He was accountable to no one, and he knew it. He hired whomever he wanted and rejected the normal collective deliberation that often goes with institutional decision-making.[16] He was shocked when colleagues wanted to offer input on faculty hiring and other important administrative matters.

Buchanan's outlook is noticeable in the wreckage he left as he moved through academic departments. He began at the University of Virginia, where his Thomas Jefferson Center for Studies in Political Economy and Social Philosophy was innocuously named to cover its extreme views.[17] Buchanan's militancy made him oblivious to the concerns and relationships needed to survive in an academic institution, and his scholarly enterprise at Virginia soon fell apart.[18] In search of greater autonomy, Buchanan left for Virginia Tech. But he was again shocked when other faculty members, including his department chair, expected him to negotiate and compromise.[19] Wherever Buchanan went, faculty alliances would collapse into enmity, and exasperated chairs and deans tired of the toxicity. Buchanan demanded complete submission. His militancy could not survive within a collective governance structure.[20]

The Long Sixties pushed Buchanan toward militancy, cynicism, and zeal. He developed the term "post-constitutional" to describe how the Long Sixties led the American public from alienation to betrayal. Buchanan said he idealized the period before the social upheaval of the day and the Warren Court fouled it up—a nostalgic moment he referred to as a "constitutional era" where government was weaker, few rules constrained how one could get wealthy, and instead, great restraints were put on the government to provide little more than order and security.[21] The social compact had dissolved and individual dissatisfaction with state-prescribed laws set in.[22] Buchanan was affected by more than Berkeley protests and Watts riots. He also hated the postwar democratic expansion and shared affluence. For a conjoint depleter, wealth and power were scarce resources reserved for a ruling elite, not cheap birdseed to be scattered to every hungry pigeon. Because most people were inferior, affluence and democracy flattened the hierarchy, cheated the laws of competition, and made us all soft.[23] Buchanan worried, "As incomes have increased, and as the stock of wealth has grown, men have increasingly found themselves able to take the 'soft options.'"[24] "Once this stage is reached," Buchanan wrote, "the individual abides by existing law only because he is personally deterred by the probability of detection and subsequent punishment."[25]

Buchanan rejected classical liberalism. Consider for example Ludwig von Mises's famous explanation for why the tailor, with a rational economic outlook, will not go to war with the baker.[26] Mises assumed the tailor did not want to bake his own bread. A positive-sum, mutually beneficial economic system is then produced. Order and productivity are maintained by making war expensive. In turn, classical liberalism's shared social contract will govern relations between the tailor and the baker. Everyone will have peace, prosperity, clothes, and warm bagels. But not if you see the world as a Darwinian struggle for resources. For Buchanan, there are only two reasons the tailor will not go to war with the baker: He might lose, or an external force will make war too painful. Right here, Buchanan carved out a vital role for the state—a role that remains theoretically underdeveloped. The ruling elite are charged with controlling the mechanisms of power to defend and maximize their wealth against the redistributive aims of an expanding demos. Notice how well Buchanan's charge aligns with the definition of oligarchy—the manipulation of political structures by the ruling elite for their own economic gain. Accordingly, Buchanan hated the New Deal, organized labor, the welfare state, and the Civil Rights Movement. But more importantly, Buchanan rejected the conventional chasm separating the political from the economic.

Buchanan faced the familiar arithmetic challenge discussed in previous chapters: There were simply not enough rich people to operationalize oligarchic policies at the ballot box. And yet, before he died in 2013 Buchanan influenced economic conversations like few others. Why would our representative democracy allow such a cynical person with such a cold outlook to shape American economics and politics in such profound ways? How could a viable governing coalition—much less a dominant strand in American politics—resonate with Buchanan's outlook? How did Buchanan overcome the arithmetic challenge? Buchanan seemed to realize that if he wanted to reorient American democracy, and if politics were downstream from culture, he could have an impact by retelling a foundational cultural touchstone: the parable of the Good Samaritan.

The Samaritan's Dilemma

The Good Samaritan parable attempts to answer three questions: Who is God? Who are we? And what describes our relationship? But James Buchanan is uninterested in those questions. Instead, Buchanan finds in the parable a source of "descriptive clarity" to diagnose and cure what ails the United States after the Long Sixties. Buchanan's reinterpretation was dark. He said our efforts to live out the parable's lessons were leading us to "self-destruction."[27] Buchanan sought to show that the ethics of Jesus Christ led to perverse results in a modern, global economy. "We may simply be too compassionate for our own well-being or for that of an orderly and productive free society," Buchanan said.[28] His purpose was to reorient public policy. Buchanan hoped his essay informed "current policy discussion of welfare reform" and, more specifically, warned the reader against "the public and social costs" of mimicking the Good Samaritan.

The Good Samaritan begins in the Gospel of Luke when a lawyer stood up to test Jesus. He asked, "Teacher, what must I do to inherit eternal life?" Wanting the lawyer to answer his own question, Jesus responded, "What is written in the law? What do you read there?"

"You shall love the Lord Your God, and your neighbor as yourself," the lawyer said.

Jesus told him, "Do this, and you will live."

CHAPTER 8

But Luke pressed on, saying the lawyer "wanted to justify himself" by asking Jesus a more complicated question: "And who is my neighbor?"

Jesus's answer became the Good Samaritan parable—a short, challenging story featuring a traveler who is attacked by robbers, stripped, beaten, and left half-dead in a roadside ditch. A priest and then a Levite see the wounded man, but they pass by him on the other side of the road. It was not until a Samaritan, moved by pity, helped the man from the ditch, bandaged his wounds, and brought him to an inn to be restored to health. The labels "priest," "Levite," and "Samaritan" light up the parable's narrative force.

The Good Samaritan is not a story about being nice. Recall its origins in the lawyer's question: Who is my neighbor? For Jesus's listeners, the word "good" would never go before the word "Samaritan." A good Samaritan is an unlikely hero, and the street-crossing priest and Levite are unlikely villains. Scandalously, Jesus pushes the parameters of altruism beyond sect and tribe. The story would be renamed today the Good Terrorist.

For thousands of years, Christians have understood the parable as a lesson in selfless generosity across axes of ethnic, religious, and socioeconomic difference. In the original telling, Jesus urges his audience to be more like the Samaritan. In his retelling, James Buchanan urges his audience to be more like the priest and Levite and to wake up to the deviousness of the wounded man in the ditch. The Gospel of Luke describes a man "going down from Jerusalem to Jericho" who "fell into the hands of robbers." The description is passive, tame, bland. But Buchanan does not view the wounded man as a victim. As he draws out the parable, Buchanan describes people like the wounded man as "predators" and "parasites"—terms he uses twenty-six times in fourteen pages. Buchanan is worried Jesus offers divine permission for too many "to live parasitically off and/or deliberately exploit its producers."[29]

Buchanan shifted the reader's focus from the Samaritan to the wounded man. Buchanan hailed his readers into a constitutive community marked by a punitive conception of responsibility. In the parable, Buchanan constituted a consequentialist reader who would wonder why the traveler was attacked, why the traveler did not defend himself, and why the traveler was on such a dangerous road in the first place. But because his focus is not on a Jericho road, Buchanan's consequentialist reader should also wonder why modern parasites do not just get clean, get sober, and get a job.[30] There is only one reason the traveler ends up in the ditch: *He deserves it*. By focusing on the parasitic impulses of the traveler, Buchanan affirms a larger argumentative strand woven into a range of oligarchic messaging: Anyone deserving of the Samaritan's charity would not be in the ditch in the first place.

Buchanan drew a connection between an unruly, tantrum-throwing child at a candy store and the aid of the welfare state on society's "parasites." For Buchanan, our postwar affluence has turned the state into a weak-willed mother who "can afford candy to bribe misbehaving children."[31] Proper behavior gets nothing but toil. But throw a fit and you get some chocolate. Buchanan is swimming in stereotypes of the undeserving poor. Anyone interested in avoiding hard work? Jesus offers an answer: crawl in a ditch and leverage the altruism of those passing by. Or, birth more children than you can afford, get hooked on drugs, or fake an on-the-job back injury, and then stay home and watch *The Price Is Right* all day.[32]

Buchanan suggests predation may not be conscious. As a consequentialist, he even shows some begrudging appreciation for the parasites' creative ability to exploit the producers. But Buchanan's appreciation for the poor is not central to his constitutive aims. Because "governments do little more than reflect the desires of their citizens," his primary target audience is not the man in the ditch or the welfare queen. It is a person reading a chapter in an edited scholarly monograph called *Altruism, Morality, and Economic Theory*. It is you and me. And, in Buchanan's words, we are "sleeping at the switch."[33]

For his target audience, James Buchanan has good reason to recast the parable in the title of his essay as a *dilemma*: The Samaritan's behavior contradicts natural law. Buchanan expands from the narrow behavior of the Samaritan to indict modern society, suggesting that our larger inability to "maximize utility in the strategic sense" will lead to a society without "an ethic of responsibility, and where no collective action is taken toward laying down jointly preferred codes of conduct."[34] Buchanan uses two illustrations to emphasize the dilemma. In a nod to his reader's experiences, Buchanan cites a grade-grubbing student asking a professor to modify her grade. An obliging instructor gets the student's immediate gratitude. But a cagey instructor will notice the dilemma caused by acquiescence. Grade grubbing will increase in the long run. For Buchanan, this is the dilemma posed by expanding Christian altruism to a global superpower with 250 million people. Grade modification portends social destruction because immediate gratification will increase the number of grade grubbers, and thus "this behavior will increase the number of student complaints generally." For the rational instructor, "utility maximization may require rigid adherence to some sort of no-grade-change rule."[35]

Later in the essay, Buchanan uses the captain of a hijacked airplane to illustrate the strategic courage he sought to promote. Buchanan writes that when an airplane is hijacked by terrorists, "strategic courage exercised by a single captain or crew member may generate spillover benefits to all others who might face hijacking threats. This will occur if the predictions of potential hijackers are modified and if their behavior is adjusted accordingly. This direction of effect can be denied only if all elements of rationality are assumed absent in potential hijackers' choices."[36] Buchanan's strategic courage requires immediate pain: The passengers may die. But a courageous captain is willing to sacrifice his plane to save the lives of future airline passengers. The captain's courage thwarts future hijacking attempts.

If the state represents the captain and the hijackers represent the parasites, then a captain offering welfare is endangering all future airline passengers. But if he holds fast against the immediate threat posed to his life, passengers, and plane, everyone is better off in the long run. For the reader, Buchanan concedes that it hurts to walk past the wounded man in the ditch. Andrew Carnegie, Milton Friedman, and Paul Ryan make similar concessions.[37] Economic rationality requires courage. The grade-grubbing student with the ailing grandmother must be sacrificed for the sake of academic integrity. Without aiding the traveler in the ditch—without changing grades or negotiating with terrorists—people suffer. But suffering is not to be avoided; in contrast, suffering offers valuable lessons about individual responsibility, work ethic, and accountability. Recall Friedman's "cut it off" prescriptions for welfare reform. Suffering is central to the oligarchic orientation: Pain is a motivating force, a refining fire.[38]

A Modern Age as One Without Heroes

After Buchanan's essay, Edward F. McClennen, professor of philosophy at the University of Western Ontario, offered a commentary on the Samaritan's dilemma. McClennen worried Buchanan "misperceives the values of others" and was unwilling to acknowledge how "mutual gains through cooperation" have contributed to our modern affluent society.[39] James Buchanan cannot rebut McClennen's rebuttal. But his essay offers enough insight into how Buchanan would respond if we could. In his mind, Buchanan is clear-eyed about "the values of others" and he rejects "mutual gains through cooperation." Buchanan describes a "modern age as one without heroes. And without heroes to emulate each man 'does his own thing.'"[40] Akin to Kilpatrick's fears, society disorder and mob rule await. As a result, most are unworthy of collective support. And when the unworthy get what they do not deserve, we are all worse off. Look at Berkeley and Watts. Look at Detroit and Newark. Look at the welfare queens and the Warren Court. Look at the Great Society and the New Deal. Each—like the Good Samaritan—contradictions to the natural order.

Buchanan is no champion of majoritarian democracy. He blames the turmoil of the Long Sixties on expanded voting rights, writing, "The effective size of community has become larger over time, and this size factor has been reinforced by a complementary influence. Western societies have been increasingly 'democratized' in the sense that a larger and larger proportion of the potential membership has been effectively enfranchised in the formation of the social environment."[41] Rather than an "increasingly democratized" social environment, Buchanan reflects Aristotle in his preference for concentrating power within a "small and well-defined group of 'leaders' to set patterns of behavior that might then serve as norms for others." Buchanan is no champion of shared affluence either. Buchanan wrote his essay in 1975, near the height of American postwar prosperity. A thriving middle-class had just emerged. Most experienced a dramatic improvement in their standard of living.[42] Shared affluence worried Buchanan as much as Berkeley protests and Watts riots, because shared affluence contradicted conjoint depletion. Buchanan thought most people did not deserve to be affluent.

Scholars have linked Buchanan's diagnosis to conventional economic categories. MacLean links Buchanan with "the stark morality of libertarianism" and Amadae describes "Buchanan's neoliberalism marking a sharp break from classical liberalism."[43] Buchanan's connections to these right-leaning economic assumptions are not without merit, especially his expressed and nostalgic longing for a shrunken state unable to be exploited by the parasites in our ditches. Buchanan looked back fondly on the historical moment before the Warren Court, where "the liberty of the individual" was preserved, government was weak, few rules constrained how rich one could get, and there were great restraints on wealth redistribution.[44] But MacLean is a historian and Amadae is a political scientist, and without more focused attention on the rhetorical representations and affective modalities of James Buchanan, we end up misunderstanding his influence on the American political economy.

Buchanan's textual persona complicates the economic orthodoxy that MacLean and Amadae describe. At times, Buchanan's nostalgia is stale, useless, and cliché. In "The Samaritan's Dilemma," he surveys the landscape and concludes, "There are few if any signs of a return to the behavioral standards of a half-century past."[45] Modern man is a gullible dupe, "incapable of making the choices that are required to prevent his exploitation by predators of his own species, whether the predation be conscious or unconscious."[46] Buchanan worries "short-term utility maximization seems on the ascendancy" and "long-term maximization seems less characteristic of behavior than in periods that are past."[47] The "lower classes" draw Buchanan's ire. He worries their short-term utility maximization will infect the rest of America "on a massive and pervasive scale."[48] Worse, far too many American Samaritans "seem unwilling to behave strategically or to adopt rules of conduct that will achieve the differing outcomes through time."[49] The future looks bleak, Buchanan warns, as "all signs point" toward the "continuing erosion in strategic courage at all levels of decision."[50] We are too weak to walk past the man in the ditch. We lack strategic courage. We are too compassionate.

But there is hope. Buchanan notes that the only "escape from the generalized samaritan's dilemma, in its public form" is the "collective adoption and enforcement of rules that will govern individual situational responses." Here, Buchanan carves out an important role for the state in doing what the demos cannot do on our own. The state is well equipped to mediate our irrational but well-intentioned compassion and shackle the good samaritan's altruistic but misguided intentions.

What does Buchanan's alternative state look like? Conservatism is too stale, classical liberalism is too democratic, and neoliberalism and libertarianism are too fantastical. The best resource for reorienting public policy toward his objective is a strong, robust, and intrusive state. Such a state can collectively do what we cannot do alone, mediating our compassion and orienting our public policy strategically and courageously toward "long-run utility maximization." The state is our collective guilt-release valve, Buchanan writes, "reducing the pressure on the individual to select either an economically or an ethically optimal course of action."[51] Buchanan's state is reoriented away from a sliced-to-the-bone pipe dream. He rejects a lean state in favor of the "collectivity acts" of an external force with the coercive, legal, and symbolic legitimacy to prevent parasitic exploitation. Buchanan describes the results: "If the collectivity acts to impose uniform behavior rules on all potential samaritans, and if these rules are observed to be enforced, the response patterns of potential parasites will be modified. As a result, the whole community of potential samaritans enjoys the benefits."[52] In this passage, Buchanan reveals the distance between his outlook and the stale associations with the Right.[53] Buchanan's "The Samaritan's Dilemma" reveals a reorientation of "government coercion" in favor of the ruling elite. Based on Buchanan's outlook, the state should be a well-armed and alert sentinel riding shotgun for an oligarchic wagon train. The state should not be leaned-up, sliced-to-the-bone, pulled out by the root, or drowned in a bathtub. The state has a robust and specific mandate: Defend and maximize the wealth and power of the ruling elite.

Buchanan can pick a fight with Jesus Christ in an edited economics anthology. Ronald Reagan had to be more sophisticated. But influencing electoral politics was not Buchanan's primary pursuit. Because he knew culture precedes politics, Buchanan first sought to influence the think tanks, the churches, the legal societies, and the economics departments. Like a patient farmer tilling the ground in anticipation of next season's harvest, Buchanan's aim went far beyond short-term political victory. Thirty years later, Nancy Maclean said the essay was "picked up by the right" to show how limited the ethics of Jesus are for a modern global economy.[54] But again MacLean misunderstands rhetoric's constitutive value. Buchanan's essay was not picked up by the right. There was no "right." American men and women were working, and living, and watching television. Maybe older, straight white middle- and upper-class American men would resonate with Buchanan's outlook after the Long Sixties. But the "right"—as a stable community, as MacLean used the term—is incomprehensible until it calls out to us and we respond.[55]

In an effort to better understand how concentrated wealth can exist in a democracy, without blatant coercion, Buchanan offers important insights. Buchanan described an ideal political economy prioritizing a version of liberty in which the state ensures no one has control over anyone else. Likewise, Milton Friedman described an ideal political economy where the "tall trees" tower above and the needy are cut off. Ronald Reagan described an ideal political economy where the state promoted freedom and responsibility by getting out of the way. Charles Koch described an ideal political economy aligned with the fundamental laws of the natural world. They got what they wanted. The welfare state shrunk, along with a progressive tax system to fund it. The state felt no compulsion to prevent suffering, hardship, or discrimination. The "market" is now responsible for handling those challenges.[56]

The state is not a fumbling night watchman promoting freedom and liberty by getting out of the way, and no one is trying to shrink the state to a size that can be drowned in the bathtub. The state is more like a snowplow clearing the way for the ultra-rich to defend and maximize their wealth and power. The state has been given an expanded role, charged with actively intervening into our economic and political lives. The familiar neoliberal description of a lean, sliced-to-the-bone state is not wrong. But it only describes one part of the political economy.

The expanded demands of the state are justified by appealing to a unique conception of oligarchic justice. Buchanan illuminates the warrant connecting an ideal political economy to oligarchic public policies. Because he is confident wealth is acquired through a Darwinian competition, the implications for public policy are logical and self-referential. Not only do the ultra-rich deserve the low tax rates and regulations described by neoliberalism, but they also deserve disproportionate influence in the political mechanisms guiding the state.[57]

Buchanan cloaks oligarchic justice in appeals to liberty, freedom, and free enterprise, but those words tether oligarchic public policies to a pernicious outlook. Oligarchy maintains a dark and cynical launch point. We are all criminals. We are all trying to imprison each other. Being able to do so reflects might and worth. Because we are incapable of consensual agreement, social exchanges of all types must be monitored by threat, punishment, and coercion. Thus, we need an external force to maintain trade relationships. As rational actors unhinged from normative or ethical constraints, we need a robust surveillance state to ensure lawful compliance.[58] The state is charged with maintaining justice by flash-freezing power hierarchies, directly intervening into our economic and political lives, and justifying public policy based on the consequentialist impact policy has on the ultra-rich. The winners are expected to exert dominance, as a reflection and direction of their status. Internal consistency is for the campaign trail and convention platform, not for pragmatic public policy. Recall how suspicious James Buchanan was of the Good Samaritan's wounded traveler. Not only was the traveler a mooch, but he was a weak coward who could not defend himself against his attackers. Anyone worthy of support would not be such an easy mark.

The ubiquitous presence of coercive force is incomprehensible apart from this conception of justice.[59] The state as night watchman may have the same skill set, but he has an expanded purview far beyond basic appeals to law and order, keeping weights and measures, and enforcing sound currency. An engorged federal government can still conform to the political Right's expectations as it watches the welfare state collapse and defunds social programs, but it never conforms to the demands of fiscal discipline or shrinking its scope and function.

James Buchanan can sleep soundly at night if he thinks his wealth and power are justly earned and if he knows the state is oriented toward defending and maximizing justly earned wealth. That much is expected. But the more urgent contribution I hope to make in this chapter concerns how the trickling down of Buchanan's oligarchy from the affluent ruling elite to ordinary Americans is detectable in American public policy, including the oligarchic reorientation of private property, public education, and tax policies.

State-Sanctioned Robbery

Private property is relational.[60] If Jeff Bezos has three adjoining Central Park apartments, the citizens of New York City do not. In turn, private property can physically separate the ruling elites from the unwashed masses and then stratify everyone based on the land's value. Private property is also a scarce resource. In addition to reflecting just power hierarchies, private property allows the rich to maximize their wealth and power. No one is making more land, and everyone has to live somewhere. Controlling land equals controlling wealth. More wealth equals more political influence. More political influence equals greater opportunity to protect and maximize property value. Buchanan's ideal oligarchic state responds by defending and enhancing the property value of the ultra-rich. Oligarchy's influence is all over our collective decisions about where to build expensive high-rise condominiums, for example. Likewise, oligarchy's influence is all over our collective decisions about where to build noisy airports, ominous prisons, and smelly landfills. We too often assume we consent to oligarchic land use because we are swayed by rational appeals to the greater good.[61] The ultra-rich will make better use of the land than slum dwellers. Thus, the state is justified in deploying its legal and coercive monopoly to forcibly extract the undeserving from profitable areas. The ruling elite can then maximize land values. And we are all better off. But that pragmatic impact is also embedded in a rhetorical and affective biopolitic disparaging the lives of the less affluent. Justice is not measured by enhancing the quality of human lives. Justice is achieved when the deserving are rewarded and the undeserving suffer. This distinction is vital for understanding the policy impact of oligarchic justice and where our existing vocabulary falls short.

Consider the story of Roy Child as an example of how Buchanan's conception of justice informs public policy today. An earnest libertarian, Roy Child recommended all private property in America be returned to its original owners.[62] Child was seeking to reconcile the core values of libertarian freedom and the wealth-generating capacity of private property with the sordid history of land-theft, colonization, and genocide in America. His recommendation went nowhere. "Barely a word has been breathed about it from any libertarian publications or institution since," Brian Doherty writes.[63] For good reason. Returning land to its original owners may have affirmed the core values of libertarianism. But his recommendation went nowhere because returning land contradicts oligarchy's demands. Oligarchy does not care who the original property owners are. If you have the land, you deserve the land. Possession is ten-tenths of the oligarchic law. Private property flows to the deserving. That is why the Native Americans no longer possess the land. They do not deserve it. If they did, they would still have it.

Second, consider the incongruity between Buchanan's outlook and support for public education. Education enhances the technical capacity of the educated to generate wealth. The economic benefits of a college degree are well known.[64] An elite education also serves a vital stratification function, pricing out ordinary Americans and allowing the scions of the ultra-rich to develop profitable social networks. Strong, state-subsidized public education in a liberal democracy is designed to emphasize the former and limit the latter. Public education is the stepstool ordinary American students climb on to penetrate the rarified world of the ruling elite. Subsidizing strong public schools through progressive taxation on the ruling elite benefits students and their families who would never have access to such opportunities otherwise. But this rationale also contradicts the core values of oligarchic justice. And so, we can gather more insight about oligarchic public policy by observing how Buchanan talked about public education.

Buchanan's textual persona reflects a worldview that sees public education as wasteful and misguided because it relies on the distribution of resources from the deserving rich to the undeserving ordinary. The threat posed by public education is compounded when lower-income families are educated. Every rhetor examined in this book despised public education; Milton Friedman even complained that progressive taxation of public education allowed parents to have more children than they should.[65] But he also wanted parents to "assume the full burden of education" because he viewed the funding mechanism as a source of liberal corruption, preventing education from stratifying the strong and the weak. Friedman and Buchanan bristled when young people from lower-income families were educated, especially in the liberal arts tradition. They worried that art history and English majors would become *citizens*, not just employees.[66] Public education, from Buchanan's perspective, is a conspiracy against the wealthy. The majority leverages their numerical advantages at the ballot box to pry the funding for public schools from the affluent, ultimately upsetting a powerful symbolic and instrumental site of oligarchic justice. In contrast, Buchanan's oligarchy seeks to reorient public education from liberal arts to STEM majors better prepared for the workforce.

Third, because Buchanan is a consequentialist who believes the ultra-rich deserve their wealth, he also believes the state has no right to take it. Like the rationale for strong public education, redistributive tax policies contradict oligarchic justice. American tax policy is akin to "legalized gangsterism" and "state-sanctioned robbery," according to James Buchanan.[67] Instead of progressive taxation, oligarchy prefers either a flat tax or a consumption tax, allowing the wealthy to pay a smaller proportion of their income in taxes. A shift from progressive to regressive tax policies in America since the 1980s illustrates Buchanan's oligarchic influence on public policy.[68] The regressive shift in tax policy occurred in relation with the American public's acceptance of oligarchic justice. Public attacks on "the government" made progressive tax policies look unpatriotic, undemocratic, and, worse, uncool because only chumps paid all their taxes. Taxes were lumped together with theft, and the public began to support more regressive tax policies—even if most Americans did not stash their money in the Caymans. Gone was the moral imperative to pay taxes.[69] Thus, oligarchs avoid paying all their taxes for the same reasons they exercise violence: because they can.

Conclusion

As he closed his essay, Buchanan predicted that most people would disagree or misunderstand his reinterpretation of the Good Samaritan parable. But he was comfortable with rejection because most people were too stupid to understand his provocation. In fact, public rejection affirmed his central argument. He expected nothing else from the ignorant masses. Buchanan's realist rhetoric is on display as he writes: "If you find yourself in basic agreement with me, my hypothesis is at least partially falsified. Agreement would signal that you are fully aware of the dilemma that I have discussed, and your awareness could be taken as reflective of general awareness in the academic community. On the other hand, and I suspect this is the case, if you find yourself in basic disagreement with me, my hypothesis is at least partially corroborated. Disagreement would signal your failures to recognize the dilemma, along with your implied willingness to submit to further exploitation than we yet have witnessed."[70] Buchanan's paradoxical closing remarks make clear that public dissent did not worry him. The worthy will concur with Buchanan's argument. The rest of us are either too dumb or too complicit in the self-destruction of western civilization.[71] In fact, public dissent would affirm his elitism. Buchanan positions himself as the voice in the wilderness—out of step and set apart from social expectations.[72] Buchanan offers a theological apologia for an individualized, atomized, messianic form of liberation through wealth accumulation. Although he assumes the persona of a prophet without a home, in the end, Buchanan affirms existing power hierarchies, comforts the comfortable, and makes affluence the answer for injustice.

To be sure, college professors like James M. Buchanan worried less about gathering public consent than more public-facing thought leaders. This is not to downplay Buchanan's influence on the way Americans thought and talked about liberal democracy by shaping upstream academic institutions, think tanks, and private foundations. But democratic oligarchy describes the confluence of economic wealth and political power through the acquisition of the public's consent. Further, democratic oligarchy describes the process by which the elite's unpopular and self-serving public policies assume the force of law against the best interests and stated desires of the majority of ordinary people.[73] In the next chapter, I focus on Charles Koch—the Kansas industrialist and billionaire CEO of Koch Industries—because he offers a rich opportunity to explore the tensions and incongruities between American political practice and the desires of American citizens. Of special concern is how Charles Koch gained public consent in the face of democratic oligarchy's daunting arithmetic hurdle. I also consider the impact of Koch's economic-political influence on Kansas and the country, and I tie those findings together with the book's underlying focus on why—without a more precise vocabulary—oligarchs like Charles Koch cannot be described, understood, or held accountable.

9

The Science of Success and the Rhetoric of Charles Koch

DECADES OF EMPIRICAL DATA HIGHLIGHT THE DIVERGENCE BETWEEN the policy preferences of billionaires like Charles Koch and the desires of American citizens. Although a majority of Americans disagree with their policy preferences, the ultra-rich have used their wealth to create favorable policies related to the estate tax, capital gains and personal and corporate income taxes, funding Social Security and health care, the minimum wage, the earned income tax credit, and the imposition of governmental austerity measures during times of economic downturn.[1] That divergence can be reconciled—without gathering the public's consent—through a process called "stealth politics."

When non-elites are kept ignorant, oligarchic political influence is simple. Page, Seawright, and Lacombe develop the term "stealth politics" to explain the limited public engagement of the richest Americans.[2] Most American billionaires do not articulate their policy preferences out loud; instead, most billionaires are active behind-the-scenes, influencing public policy through financial contributions to political candidates and campaigns, hosting lucrative fundraisers, and bundling their wealthy friend's contributions. Page, Seawright, and Lacombe focus on David Koch as an illustrative case study. In 1980, David Koch was the Libertarian Party's nominee for vice president. He ran on a platform that promised to abolish Medicare, Medicaid, and Social Security, end individual and corporate income taxes, and shutter the SEC, EPA, even the FBI and CIA. But David Koch's candidacy attracted 1 percent of the vote, a very public failure that encouraged him and his brother Charles to conclude that stealth politics may be a more effective political strategy in the future.[3] David Koch's candidacy can be understood in relation to the extant literature on wealthy Americans who were confident that they could (and should) leverage their economic wealth for nominal political power, and no one could gather the public consent as well as they could.[4] But David Koch's failure also affirms what happens when they lose. According to Page, Seawright, and Lacombe, David and Charles Koch pivoted to stealth politics, including retreating to the private activities of funding politically oriented foundations and think tanks, providing the infrastructure and logistical support for preferred social movements, astroturfing loose coalitions, and donating billionaires of dollars in dark money to issue-oriented policy-focused causes.

In this chapter, I argue that the rhetorical representations of Charles Koch allow for a more compelling explanation for the divergence between the political aims of the ultra-rich and the desires of ordinary Americans. Stealth politics, in other words, is limited in explaining the influence of oligarchs like Charles Koch, because his political machinations are, frankly, not very stealthy anymore. Many Americans now understand Koch's political aims and the methods he deploys to achieve those aims—thanks to the recent efforts of investigative journalists like Jane Mayer, Christopher Leonard, Kurt Andersen, and Binyamin Appelbaum, historians like Theda Skocpol, and the efforts of Democratic politicians like Barack Obama, Elizabeth Warren, and Bernie Sanders. "The Koch brothers" has become a representative anecdote of American corporate corruption. And while the precise financial impact and the influence on Koch-funded groups like Americans for Prosperity and ALEC may remain opaque, enough Americans understand Koch's political aims and the methods he deploys to seek those aims to defy the term "stealth."[5] More specifically, it is well known that Koch's personal influence rivaled that of the Democratic and Republican parties, and he used the immense resources of the state to achieve such influence and to gather the consent of the public, in Kansas and the rest of the country. And yet, an incongruity remains: Koch's public messaging is limited to cliches about "economic freedom" and the threat of impending socialist doom whenever a Democrat like Barack Obama or Joe Biden wins.[6] But his public messaging contradicts the conceptual integrity of labels like "conservative" and "libertarian."

To generate his enormous wealth and unrivaled political influence, Koch employed the most important profit-generating force in American liberal democracy: the federal government. Charles Koch and Koch Industries are marked by well documented efforts to influence one-party local and state rule and enjoin the state through special favors, benefits, tax breaks, subsidies, corporate incentives, expensive government purchases and contracts, and sympathetic regulation and lax legal accountability. Koch's material wealth and political influence can be traced directly to his family and his company's relationship with the state. This is not to single out Charles Koch as an aberration. But it is especially important to recognize the state's impact on a company so heavily reliant on extractivist methods for profitability and influence. Koch Industries did not make the original product they pulled from the ground, refined, and transported; Koch took advantage of the productive resources of the physical world. Koch also took advantage of the productive resources of the state and its social functions, including a well-trained workforce, the basic research yielding profitable applications, and state-structured property rights and tax laws to encourage and protect the acquisition of the Kochs' competitors, which Koch took advantage of to form his company in the first place.[7] It is also important to recognize that unlike Facebook or Wal-Mart, Koch Industries was always in a uniquely antagonistic relationship with the state (and the people the state represents). Koch Industries imposed a direct net cost on the public, including the company's propensity for oil spills and its contributions to ecological catastrophe resulting from its primary product. Plus, Koch Industries generally does not sell its products directly to customers under the "Koch" brand. You can buy Bounty Towels off the shelf (made by the Koch-owned parent company Georgia Pacific), but you cannot buy Koch brand fertilizer at Home Depot.

Nonetheless, Koch never sought to acquire the public consent by conceding the state's vital contributions to his company's profitability. As a result, Charles Koch was positioned firmly on the political Right in public conversations. Page, Seawright, and Lacombe describe the Kochs as "conservative" and "libertarians."[8] Kurt Andersen describes Charles Koch as a "rich young right-winger."[9] Christopher Leonard distills his 900-page book *Kochland* by describing Koch's core philosophy as one-part "maximizing profits" and one-part "general disdain for the government."[10] Daniel Schulman writes that by his late twenties, "Charles had become a full-throated libertarian evangelist . . . in which the role of government was nearly nonexistent."[11] As the Kochs' influence grew, Schulman writes, "libertarian ideology [was] deeply embedded in Koch's corporate DNA," and "fully embracing the Koch mind-set meant believing in the self-regulating powers of the market and the socialistic evils of big government."[12] Ron Formisano details the Kochs' efforts "to spread the gospel of free enterprise, anti-regulation, and low taxes."[13] In the *Washington Post*, Matea Gold describes the links between the Kochs and their donor networks of the US Chamber of Commerce, the

CHAPTER 9

National Rifle Association, and Americans for Tax Reform as a "coalition of groups that share the brothers' libertarian, free-market perspective."[14]

Koch's own words affirm his position on the Right side of the seesaw. He said he wanted to "pull government out at the root" and he described himself as a "libertarian" in the 1970s and a "conservative" after that.[15] He lined his living room bookshelves with Ludwig von Mises and Friedrich Hayek, and he funded the research and advocacy of Milton Friedman and James M. Buchanan. In 1974, Charles Koch delivered a speech to his Institute for Humane Studies in which he decried "confiscatory taxation, wage and price controls, commodity allocations programs, trade barriers, restrictions on foreign investments, so-called equal opportunity requirements, safety and health regulations, land use controls, licensing laws, outright government ownership of businesses and industries."[16] In 1978, he began describing his political activity as a "movement" that must "destroy the prevalent statist paradigm."[17] Later, he admitted his goal was "not to *reallocate* the burden of government" but to roll it back.[18] Koch assumed the state should prioritize protecting individual liberty and free market capitalism; if done properly, all would benefit, leading to a virtuous and prosperous society. Koch's messaging praised the market as if they were unrelated to the state. All government intervention (which he referred to as "socialistic") created more harm than good, illegitimately encroaching on free enterprise and the liberty of individuals to make money.[19] As he told the Wichita Rotary Club, in Koch's ideal setup, the only role for the government was as a "night watchman" protecting the public from fraud and outside threat.[20]

Market-Based Management

Charles Koch even translated the Right's economic principles into his own vocabulary: Market-Based Management. MBM described Koch's comprehensive, nonnegotiable "blueprint for achieving prosperity and freedom" replete with ten guiding principles posted throughout company headquarters, including on the coffee cups.[21] Charles Koch's 2007 book *The Science of Success* offers a clear distillation of the links between MBM and Koch's incongruity. On the first page, Koch introduces MBM as "the distinctive business and management philosophy that has enabled Koch Industries to become one of the largest and most successful private companies in the world."[22] The rest of the book is an extended argument for MBM and its ability to "enable organizations to succeed long term" and "allow free societies to prosper."[23] Koch uses communism as a foil, describing it as a "system that takes 'from each according to his ability' and redistributes 'to each according to his needs,'" while MBM takes, in contrast, "from each according to his ability, to each according to his contribution."[24] From there, Koch offers a familiar illustration of the rhetorical smokescreen clouding the oligarchic dimensions of American democracy.

First, Koch justifies MBM by blurring the boundaries between science and scientism. Koch seems keen on making sure the reader understands that his credibility is not based on the fact that he inherited a profitable company from his father. Instead, Koch develops a textual persona marked by unique perspicacity into "the discipline of economics, ethics, social philosophy, psychology, sociology, biology, anthropology, management, epistemology and the philosophy of science."[25] Koch establishes his credibility in the preface of the book, writing, "As an engineer, I understood the natural world operated according to fixed laws."[26] He filled *The Science of Success* with epigrams and quotations from his father, Friedrich Hayek, and Michael Polanyi and also Albert Einstein, Frédéric Bastiat, Abraham Maslow, and in the final chapter, Charles Koch himself. Drawing on Koch's engineering background, MBM comprised a set of scientific principles designed to guide every action and every employee in the company.

Second, Koch made clear a connection between the laws dictating what happened in the physical world—laws well understood by physicists, chemists, and engineers—and MBM's assumption that there are similar laws governing affairs in the human world.[27] "Just as living things are more than a collection of molecules," Koch writes, "organizations that combine all these factors become something beyond an ordinary collection of people, activities, and assets."[28] Koch goes on, "MBM works because it is grounded in consistent, valid theory that is fully integrated and applied across every aspect of the organization."[29] At Koch Industries, "decisions should be made using economic and critical thinking, logic and evidence, rather than emotion or gut feeling. We should be explicit about the mental models we are applying and communicate them clearly."[30] Koch was a realist. He repeatedly described MBM as "the Science of Human Action" rooted in the "systematic study of classics in history, economics, philosophy, psychology, and other disciplines [to] reveal certain laws that govern human well-being."[31] But MBM's laws were not limited to the natural or the economic. MBM was not merely a precondition for employment at Koch or an efficient management discourse to make a profit in the energy industry. MBM was a transcendent, scientific set of laws lighting the path toward a virtuous and prosperous life far beyond oil extraction.[32] Because it "integrates theory and practice"—and because "the theory of MBM is rooted in the Science of Human Action"—MBM also informed "lessons learned from the successes and failures of humans to achieve peace, prosperity, and societal progress."[33] MBM's purpose aligned with natural law's rhetorical history: If fixed laws governed the natural world, and Charles Koch conformed to them, he deserved both economic and political influence.

Third, MBM draws on a Darwinian foundation marked by natural power hierarchies. Koch explicitly rejected the Left's equality orientation, writing, "If every person and every part of the earth were equal in every way, there would be much less benefit from the division of labor."[34] Koch's faith in the free market and free enterprise leads to a cruel, but justifiable assessment of the people and companies that cannot compete. In his book's first chapter, Koch explained his company's success as a result of carefully managing "creative destruction" and his ability to run Koch Industries "as a meritocracy, with positions, authorities, and compensation—including that of our shareholders—set according to proven ability and actual contributions."[35] Koch does not shy away from the cold implications of MBM and the natural laws it is based upon. In *The Science of Success*, Koch justifies his need to "shed businesses and assets that are unprofitable or worth more to others" because if Koch did not "drive creative destruction internally . . . creative destruction will drive us out of business."[36] As it applies to his workforce, Koch writes that because lower-ranked employees "put us at a competitive disadvantage," they should not be retained.[37] "Such objectivity is sometimes painful," Koch later conceded, but it is essential to best practices, as long as it is done "objectively" and "with humility and intellectual honesty."[38]

There is a silver lining. Koch accounts for the cruelty of the natural world by highlighting how "even the most disadvantaged individuals have comparative advantages."[39] Koch does not directly name their advantages, but the links to the larger body of oligarchic rhetoric offers some insight into his belief in an incentive structure that separates the deserved from the undeserved. He does, however, draw a clear distinction between producers who "build beneficial relationships and trust with people from all walks of life" and predators who "perpetuate legal or illegal plunder."[40] Koch admitted he had no pity for people who run a business that does not adhere to the market's laws. "Every time I hear of an entrepreneur going out of business I cheer," he said, because their inability to serve the customer justified their extinction.[41] Plus, the laws of nature were not secret or exclusive to the rich. Anyone can learn them and put them into action. The rich just do this better than anyone else. That is why they are rich.

MBM leads to virtue, not merely to profitable oil extraction. MBM is a lifestyle undergirded by the immutable laws of the natural world and informing biology, management, philosophy, sociology, and politics. And yet, describing Koch as a conservative or libertarian explains only one part of his political project. Recall Christopher Leonard's attempt to describe Koch's outlook as a combination of maximizing profit and general disdain for the government. There is abundant evidence for the first part of Leonard's claim. A bold captain of modern industry, Koch combined his engineering expertise, judicious risk-taking, and midwestern gumption to grow Koch Industries into the largest, most profitable private company in the country. If Hayek or Friedman became industrialists, Koch Industries is the business they would have run, constantly pushing the envelope and waging a multifront war against the EPA, DOE, and organized labor. Most importantly, Koch won. He was rich, but he also employed thousands of Americans and devoted millions of dollars to philanthropic causes all over the country. But we know that maximizing profit and government disdain are contradictions. If Charles Koch sought to maximize profit, he would not disdain government; he would use it to defend and enhance his wealth and power. He did. And he has reaped the rewards. The more interesting question is why we have allowed it.

Charles Koch did not want an unregulated free market, and the Kochs did not become the richest family in the country by outperforming their competition on a neutral, free market playing field. And they did not reorient the American political landscape by passively accepting the capriciousness of majoritarian democracy. Charles Koch was too cunning, shrewd, and ruthless to depend on the market or the masses for his wealth. Charles Koch understood the state's importance. Koch was a brilliant engineer and savvy businessman, especially astute at identifying undervalued commodities. Beyond fertilizer and pipe, he also realized how undervalued political power was and how essential it was for the Kochs' long-term profitability.[42] Despite his public praise for Hayek and Friedman, Charles Koch knew how misguided it was to describe the market as "free." Koch admitted that the American economy was not a free enterprise now, and it had not been at least since 1929.[43] The state and the market were inextricably bound. Koch knew there was no ideological seesaw: Instead, there was a tangled web of political economy, marked by a complex confluence of state policy and corporate machinations.[44] Even as Charles Koch linked MBM and freedom he never ran his business like John Galt.

Charles Koch proclaimed to hate the government but understood how rich the government made him. He offered an insightful illustration of his own pragmatism when he compared his policy preferences to the zeal of his true-believing friend Leonard Read: Koch said that if someone put a button in front of Read that, when pushed, would immediately end all illegitimate state actions, all that he thought violated our right to life, liberty, and property, Read would push it. But Koch admitted that he would not. "I mean, if we did away with government tomorrow . . . I'd have to say to Leonard, no, I would not push that button! That approach scared me to death. We'd have mass chaos. I want to go just as fast and as far as we continue to get better results but we must do it in a way that the change demonstrates that people will be better off. I don't see how we'll get far down the road if we take steps that make people worse off."[45]

Koch talked about the market like a libertarian: as if the market was an organic system that could grow like a weed as long as it was left alone.[46] But he did not put much faith in it. Like the robber barons of the 1800s, Koch knew an unfettered market was risky, allowing for new competitors, shifting consumer preferences, and rapid fluctuations. Further, a profitable market needs robust monitoring and protection, and there is no better entity than the state, with its immense symbolic, legal, and coercive resources, to do just that.[47] Koch helped grow and protect the market in his interests through a huge lobbying apparatus, well-funded think tanks, and an astroturf army of political supporters to advocate for a market oriented in his favor.[48]

Charles Koch also does not trust democracy. The masses are capricious and fickle. The invisible hand and later iterations of the "rational economic actor" place too much trust in acquiring the consent of the unpredictable and ignorant democratic hoards. Koch assumed the American public was misinformed, even delusional.[49]

Koch's cynicism was not a hypothetical exercise in right-wing genuflection. In the 1990s, he was burned by the market and the masses. Koch Industries' focus on growth led to irresponsible acquisitions, massive losses, and the very public failures of Purina Mills and Koch Agriculture.[50] The Kochs were also "one of the largest, most flagrant violators of environmental laws in the United States during the 1990s," according to Christopher Leonard.[51] In 1998, Koch Industries was fined $6.9 million—the largest fine of this type in Minnesota's history—by the Minnesota Pollution Control Agency, and the next year in federal court they pled guilty to years of dumping ammonia and leaking oil into the area surrounding their Pine Bend refinery.[52] Leonard also detailed a consistent pattern in which

Koch Industries bilked clients across Kansas, Texas, Oklahoma, North Dakota, and New Mexico. They were eventually caught. At the federal trial, Koch employees one after the other, under oath, described how they were trained to mismeasure oil extraction. The testimony revealed an intentional, top-down, and lucrative pattern of malfeasance, earning Koch Industries $10 million in stolen profit each year. Koch was embarrassed by the fines and scandal. In response, he created a new slogan: "10,000 percent compliance." Every Koch employee would commit to adhering to 100 percent of the law 100 percent of the time. No more million-dollar fines, no more public embarrassment in the *Wichita Eagle*, no more FBI agents interrogating Koch employees at their homes.[53] Of course, "10,000 Percent Compliance" is an empty puffery. Is there a company that would admit to lawbreaking even 1 percent of the time? But beneath the surface, the slogan did signal a significant shift for Koch Industries after the fines and public embarrassment. For my purposes, "10,000 percent compliance" also lends useful insight into the definitional features of oligarchy in action. In response, Koch Industries fully crossed the economic-political bridge deploying their tremendous resources to defend and enhance profitability and, in so doing, unhitching themselves from any sort of conservative or libertarian coherence.

The Kochtopus

Koch deployed every weapon in his arsenal to influence the market to support their interests. Koch Industries leveraged political influence for economic gain, including favorable tax laws, special tax credits and subsidies available to the oil, ethanol, and pipeline business, farm subsidies and targeted tax breaks, and state protection for their industries from foreign competition, extracting profit from a range of federal subsidies, including artificially low grazing fees for their cattle to feed on federal land, to a sweetheart deal selling millions of barrels of oil to fill up the Strategic Petroleum Reserve.[54] They also expanded their efforts to recruit and fund political candidates, to influence the media, and to punish states considering stronger regulation by threatening relocation to more compliant states.[55] Political influence allowed Koch Industries to manipulate the market for their own gain. Koch Industries built one of the biggest, most influential and well-funded lobbying arms in the country. Koch Industries expanded its influence toward favorable tax laws, opening an office on Grand Cayman allowing for one Koch subsidiary to keep its annual tax rate below 4.15 percent between 2010 and

2013.[56] Charles Koch did not worry about jail time when those tax documents were revealed because he was not breaking the law.[57]

Once Charles Koch felt satisfied with his ability to mediate legislative threats, he turned his attention to the judiciary—an institution less affected by political donations or traditional lobbying efforts and thus ripe for creative interventions. In the 1990s, Koch began to reorient the American justice system.[58] Koch-funded nonprofit groups graded state judges on how well they ruled according to their criteria. Low-scoring judges were embarrassed publicly, especially in conservative states like Oklahoma and Kansas. Koch then offered a remedy: company-sponsored seminars at beachfront locals and mountain ski resorts coupled with free lectures on the free market and American prosperity.[59] Koch felt no need to bribe judges because he could pack *The Road to Serfdom* within a ski retreat.

The Kochs expanded their political influence through a multipronged constellation of Super-PACs, think tanks, industry trade groups, research institutes, endowed chairs at colleges and universities, nonprofit foundations, and nonpartisan philanthropic activities. Koch's political operation expanded as he increased his wealth, earning the nickname "Kochtopus" to describe the tentacled political operations of Koch Industries.

Koch sidestepped accusations of opportunistic greed by portraying his philanthropy with the Cato Institute, the Heritage Foundation, and ALEC as nonpartisan and disinterested. Brian Doherty affirmed these efforts, arguing that anyone supporting libertarianism "out of pecuniary interests is a fool."[60] The fact that most libertarian think tank funding comes from corporate elites like Charles Koch is immaterial, Doherty goes on to suggest. Instead, funders like the Kochs are "following a personal interest in these ideas not seeking quick advantage."[61] If you believe Doherty, then I know a deposed Nigerian prince that would like your email address.

As Jane Mayer points out, it is not a coincidence that Koch's political efforts dovetail seamlessly with his economic interest.[62] There was no need for Charles Koch to spend millions bribing American judges, because he secured their allegiance earlier in the pipeline as they were educated in law schools and academies to rule in his interests before they reached the bench. Koch had little need to monitor religious leaders, because their pulpits and podcasts already aligned his material interests with divine order and natural law. And Koch had nothing to fear of American democracy, because his material interests were aligned with patriotic appeals to celebrate his own success. Ordinary working- and middle-class Americans aspired to be Charles Koch, not to take from him.

The Kansas Experiment

For anyone curious about what Koch's oligarchic aspirations looked like applied to an entire state, Sam Brownback's "Kansas Experiment" offers an answer. After serving fifteen years as a US senator, Samuel Dale Brownback was elected governor in 2010 by promising to "turn Kansas into a bulwark against Barack Obama's Big Government liberalism."[63] A self-described "farmboy from Parker, Kansas," Brownback had the experience, reputation, and connections to put such campaign promises into action.

In 2011, Brownback began implementing an economic-political program aligned with the Right's touchstones. He first marginalized moderate Republicans who wilted in the hyperpartisan, Tea Party–inspired moment. He drew inspiration from his favorite columnist George Will, who Brownback praised as a "strong conservative thinker." And he drew direct counsel from Stephen Moore of the Heritage Foundation and Arthur Laffer of the American Legislative Exchange Council. Brownback even brought Laffer out to Kansas and paid him $75,000 to educate the Kansas legislature on how to promote economic growth by cutting taxes.[64] Brownback then pushed through the deepest personal income tax cuts in American history.[65] He eliminated Kansas's top income tax bracket, lowered the top tax rate on wages, salaries, and investment income by almost 29 percent, and instituted a complete income tax exemption for limited liability companies. This LLC exemption was called the crown jewel of Brownback's plan because it allowed 330,000 independent business owners to avoid almost all state income tax.[66] The political Right in Kansas praised Brownback's legislative victories and looked forward to his plan for a flat tax and a repeal of the estate tax. The Cato Institute gave Brownback an "A" for signing "into law one of the most impressive tax reforms of any state in recent years."[67] Grover Norquist of Americans for Tax Reform described Brownback's Kansas as the model for Republican governance.[68]

During his first term, Brownback could walk the halls of the Topeka capital confident he was also supported by the intellectual ghosts of Friedrich Hayek and Milton Friedman. Friedman promoted tax cuts with a zeal that transcended economic policy. Tax cuts, even when they cause short-term fiscal pain, should be prioritized because they would force profligate leaders of both parties to be chastened, and then gaps in the budget would have to be closed by cutting funding for social programs.[69] Tax cuts took on a moral appeal, motivating fiscal discipline and stewardship. If you do not buy the ice cream at the grocery store, you do not have to see it in your freezer. Likewise, if tax cuts blew a hole in the budget there would be no money to waste on social programs for the inferior. Brownback and his allies conceded the perverse attraction of budget deficits. Brownback promised to "keep pruning state government any place that we can."[70] His plan to eventually eliminate corporate and personal taxes was described as a "march to zero." Representative Owen Donohoe affirmed Brownback's budget deficits as the "greatest thing that's ever happened to Kansas" because lost revenue would "force us to be more efficient."[71]

Still, Brownback was moving into uncharted territory. Cutting taxes to inflict fiscal pain had been tried in Chile and Iraq but never in America's heartland. Brownback mediated the mystery by drawing from a familiar aquifer. Brownback promised that his budget would "restore fiscal sanity to government" and his tax cuts would allow "Kansas families and businesses to keep more of their hard-earned money" because "they know how to spend it more effectively than government does."[72] Descriptions of his untested and complicated tax laws—and their impact on the nonwage income of LLCs, S corporations, and pass-through businesses—were simplified for public consumption: Kansas's job creators and family farmers would keep more of their income, businesses would reinvest and expand, and more jobs and more revenue would go to hardworking Kansans.

The farmboy from Parker drew legitimacy by connecting his efforts to the "normative science" of free market economics established by University of Chicago faculty and affirmed by their Nobel Prizes. He described his efforts as a "real live experiment" in supply-side tax policy, as he sought to "turn Kansas into an incubator for innovation and entrepreneurial success."[73] On MSNBC's *Morning Joe*, Brownback sounded like a scientist: neutral, objective, willing to follow the data. He said, "On taxes you need to get your overall rates down and you need to get your social manipulation out, in my estimation, to create growth. And you know we'll see how it works. We will have a real-life experiment right next to some other states that haven't lowered taxes.... You'll get a chance to see how this impacts a particular experimental area, and I think Kansas is gonna do well."[74]

Brownback latched onto the scientific legitimacy of supply-side economic theory. First developed in the late 1970s and popularized in public conversations in the 1980s, supply-side emerged as an ideograph connecting economic growth to tax cuts and deregulation.[75] Originally a term of derision, a group of conservative senators led by Jack Kemp in the 1970s repurposed "supply-sider" to describe efforts to combat the Keynesian welfare state.[76] The Laffer Curve also added intellectual legitimacy to supply-side efforts to cut taxes and regulation, claiming a theoretical relationship between government revenue and tax rates. Because tax cuts spark economic growth, lower taxes on the job-creators brings in more revenue than raising funds by taxing job-creators. The rich loved it. But supply-siders also included appeals to the common good. As you cut taxes and regulations, the ultra-rich made more and kept more, and then hired more and spent more. In an op-ed for the *Wall Street Journal*, Brownback wrote that because most Kansans worked for small businesses, "giving these companies more money to reinvest in their businesses [would] enable them to hire more people and invest in needed equipment."[77]

The Truth Caucus

In 2004, Thomas Frank wrote a book called *What's the Matter with Kansas?* His premise—that something was the matter with Kansas—grew out of the pernicious policy implications facilitated by economic, political, and religious alliances. He detailed why the ultra-rich were willing to put up with bouts of silliness, like evangelical crusades against teaching evolution in public schools because the political power the alliances offered made wealthy Kansans richer than ever.[78] Brownback's supply-side governance reflected a logical outcome of Frank's argument. Economic growth was a given—almost preordained by the natural and scientific laws governing the market. Brownback's Republican allies created a "Truth Caucus" to support Brownback's economic rationale.[79] Tax cuts and a leaner state would offer industrious Kansans the chance to grow their businesses. Economic growth would then incentivize the wealthy to keep making what Frank described as "superhuman contributions to society."[80] Everyone else would be incentivized to sink or swim depending on their own ability. Each Kansan would get what they deserved. The only question was how much the Kansas economy would grow.[81]

But a familiar challenge would soon emerge as Brownback began to test his Kansas Experiment. The link between economic science and physical science is limited because unlike subatomic particles, Kansans make economic decisions based on endogenous factors.[82] Also, the ultra-rich benefiting from tax cuts and deregulation do not pour all their new wealth back into the local economy. They also stash it in Grand Cayman.

Kenneth Burke taught that words generate motive.[83] He did not teach that words *name* motive. Rather, our words come first, and our motives follow. Burke's distinction is subtle but vital for understanding what ultimately

CHAPTER 9

happened to Kansas and why we struggle for the words to describe motive, wealth, and political power. Given the limited options available, most journalists had no other vocabulary to describe Brownback in Kansas. A Republican farmboy governor funded by the Koch brothers' think tanks, touting supply-side economic theories, dining with former Reagan administration officials, governing a deep red-state marked by anti-Obama animus and Tea Party fervor: Where else could Brownback sit than on the Right side of the seesaw?

Brownback's goals and policies were described in local and national outlets as if they were informed by "supply-side economic theory" and "conservative economics."[84] Dan Balz of the *Washington Post* wrote that if Brownback failed, he would become an "object lesson in the limits of conservative governance in a conservative state." But if he succeeded, his "victory will be seen as an endorsement of the Kansas experiment in supply-side economics."[85] Justin Miller of the *American Prospect* described Brownback's efforts to turn the Sunflower State into a petri dish for radical conservative economics.[86] When PBS's economics correspondent, Paul Solman, visited Kansas for a national story on the *NewsHour*, he justified his program's focus on a state with only 3 million people by describing Brownback's efforts as a microcosm of larger economic debates that were raging for decades.[87] Solman suggested that Kansas could be used to explore what happens when the Right side of the seesaw can put its promises into policy. Furthering the petri dish analogy, Solman wanted to use Kansas to explore in vivid detail the public debates between Hayek and Keynes, Friedman and Polanyi, Elizabeth Warren and Paul Ryan—right there in Topeka, Kansas.

For journalists like Balz, Miller, and Solman, phrases like "Conservative governance" and "supply-side economics" were handy and familiar. By that standard, Brownback failed. His economic policies produced one of the worst-performing state economies in the country.[88] Brownback assumed cutting corporate taxes would encourage corporations to invest more in the state, increase job creation, and grow tax revenue. They did not. His tax policies prompted tax evasion, not job creation. Brownback blew a hole in the state budget. State revenue plunged, falling $713 million from 2013 to 2014.[89] To plug the hole, Brownback drew down the state's reserve fund. He also increased borrowing—adding $1.3 billion to the state's debt.[90] Moody's downgraded the state's bond rating. Brownback was unfazed. Rather than moderate his ambitions, he called for an increase in regressive taxation disproportionately hitting the middle and working classes. Brownback suggested the state pay for roads and schools affected by declining revenue by raising sales and cigarette taxes, rather than rolling back taxes on the wealthy and corporations. But reflecting how his political fortunes had turned in five short years, his flat tax proposal garnered just three votes in the Kansas state Senate. By 2016, Brownback was the least-popular governor in the country, according to a Morning Consult poll, with 26 percent approval rating—even worse than Chris Christie, the New Jersey governor suffering through his Bridgegate scandal.[91]

Brownback was so confident when he began his experiment. How did he respond to the fiscal disaster? Did he wonder about his economic plan's scientific assumptions? Did he wonder about Milton Friedman's influence? What about Laffer's famous supply-side napkin? Wasn't that in the Smithsonian?[92]

We should not be surprised Brownback failed in Kansas. While the depth of his cuts were unprecedented, his ambitions were not. If Brownback's efforts were described as an experiment, we already knew the results.[93] Tax cuts do not boost economic growth. Improving infrastructure, education, and developing specific policies to encourage rural development, entrepreneurship, and a diversified economic base were better suited for fulfilling his promises.[94] What's more, we could have predicted Brownback's policies would clash with the demands of majoritarian democracy. Americans do not like paying taxes, but do we like what taxes pay for. Most Americans support government spending on infrastructure, education, public transportation, foreign aid, and aid to farmers.[95] Even Republican voters—when asked directly about policies like Brownback's—do not support cuts to Medicare, education, and health care.[96] Historically, the public outrage sparked by more moderate supply-side implementation, including state deregulation, free markets, and privatization, is so great that politicians either lose public support (Paul Ryan), moderate their ambitions (Ronald Reagan), or get ousted in a public coup (Chile). Kansas was no exception. Kansans liked the *idea* of cutting taxes. They resonated with conservative appeals to fiscal discipline and family farmers, but they also liked well-funded schools, roads, and hospitals. As expected, Kansas's economic reality clashed with the economic ambitions of conservative governance.

Although he died in 2006, Milton Friedman may have applauded Brownback's efforts, but he would have anticipated his struggles. "On the politics of it, of course it's not politically feasible," Friedman said.[97] Friedman could have also prepared Brownback for some pain.[98] Majoritarian democracy is a hurdle; repealing the earned income tax credit, defunding special education, and raising sales tax on Bud Light would have allowed for massive corporate tax cuts and fiscal discipline. But Kansans would not allow it.

Don't Let Anybody Tell You Any Different

And yet, Brownback's inability to fulfill his ambitions explains why the supply-side has yet to be relegated to economic theory's dustbin. Democracy's constraints offered Brownback a rhetorical escape hatch.[99] Like an embarrassed offensive coordinator, blaming a shutout on a rookie quarterback, unfulfilled promises can be blamed on the execution. The Kansas Experiment affirms limitless faith in the free market, and when the market fails, it can only be the impurities in the system fouling it up. In America's sprawling democracy, impurities are easy to locate, and the "execution" argument is always available when we are unwilling to eliminate the minimum wage or send our children to the coal mines.

Brownback and his allies explained their failures by blaming the people for a lack of a commitment. Kansans were too cowardly it seemed. The public was too stupid and impatient, and the media too biased. Even Republican politicians were too quick to sell out. Economic utopia was just around the corner, if only Kansans had the patience. PBS correspondent Paul Solman asked Brownback ally and state representative Ty Masterson what lessons the nation could learn from the Kansas Experiment. Masterson conceded Brownback's promises were not met. But not because of a flaw in the economic model. Masterson accused his Republican allies of selling out too quickly, allowing more moderate Kansas Republicans to also give in to the demands of the uninformed masses. Masterson also blamed the media for misreporting the economic reality. Masterson lumped his opponents together to suggest the real cause of Kansas's economic woes was the crash of oil, gas, and farm prices—underemphasized by the liberal media—rather than any failure on the part of Brownback's policies. To Masterson, Kansas voters were not hardy enough. They were unwilling to put up with the temporary pain caused by tax cuts so they could not wait for the coming economic growth. Masterson deployed a medical metaphor, comparing lean-government tax cuts to a bariatric surgery that would have allowed Kansans to trim down from "being morbidly obese, [to] just simply overweight."[100] Masterson implied that if only Kansans had enough grit to push through the pain of economic dieting the state would soon enjoy economic fitness. Likewise, Sam Brownback would foreshadow a recurring theme when he said in a 2014 reelection ad, "The sun is shining in Kansas and don't let anybody tell you any different."[101] It seemed blind ignorance was required to reconcile reality and ambitions.

In 2014, days after Brownback squeaked out reelection, budget analysts reported Kansas would be $1 billion short of revenue estimates in the next two years. Brownback conceded the temporary economic challenges but justified his $280 million proposed budget cuts by comparing his plight to Ronald Reagan's; he cut taxes in 1981 and was punished in the 1982 midterms. Undaunted, Brownback conceded, "There was difficulty, but it also then led to, I believe, 20 years of good growth in the country. Income tax policy does take time, but the data is all very clear about the impact of higher income taxes versus lower income taxes."[102] Brownback's description is correct, regarding data's clarity. He is wrong about the economic impact.[103]

The rhetorical escape hatch emerged also when Brownback's former allies began to ditch him. Soaring spending—caused by democracy, by embarrassed Kansans who did not want their schools to end the year early—gave Brownback's allies cover. Analysts from Koch-funded ALEC blamed Kansas's failure on the inability to reduce spending (as if more cuts to special education could have made up for the $500 million in corporate tax cuts). The Kansas state director of Americans for Prosperity affirmed this excuse, blaming the failure on "soaring government spending."[104] Brownback failed, according to this logic, because he did not repeal itemized deductions and the earned income credit or implement the scheduled sales tax reduction.[105] The Kansas tax reform plan "was never fully implemented," wrote Jonathan Williams, vice president of ALEC's Center for State Fiscal Reform, "making any honest judgment of the original plan's success or failure impossible."[106] Ty Masterson lamented, "I wish I could've had a stronger influence on my colleagues and have trimmed the growth of government even further." He continued, "We were still anticipating more growth, and we didn't keep the government in check in the out-years."[107]

The conclusion that Brownback failed in Kansas rests on the assumption that conservative economic principles were being tested. But for understanding what happened to Kansas, "Conservative governance" and "supply-side economics" are inadequate, inaccurate, and unhelpful. Brownback talked like a conservative, but he governed like an oligarch. And journalists like Solman, Balz, and Miller ended up like drunks looking for their car keys under the streetlight: They described the wrong experiment because they found the wrong words.

Conservative economics did not fail in Kansas because conservatism was not being tested. Brownback was cruel but not conservative. He slashed government support for the middle and working classes. The budgets for public schools and state universities were cut. Brownback and his allies proposed delaying payments to teacher's pension funds and reducing the base aid per-pupil for Kansas public school districts.[108] Brownback decided to cut taxes when he entered office rather than restore the school funding that was cut during the Great Recession, straining the budget of urban and rural schools the most. Two districts even had to end the school year early.[109] Brownback cut aid for Medicaid recipients and funding for public roads. Without revenue and unwilling to repeal tax cuts, Brownback took almost $100 million from the state's highway fund and cut the state's contribution to the employee retirement system by $40 million.[110] Kansas drained its financial reserves and stopped making deposits into its employee pension funds. Brownback allowed the Kansas health care system to nearly collapse due to intransigence and dogmatism: He privatized state Medicaid services and refused essentially free money from Obama's expansion of Medicaid for low-income Kansans. Several rural hospitals almost closed.

A fiscal conservative would have balanced the budget. Brownback blew up the budget, borrowed to fill it, accumulated massive debt on the borrowing, which added more debt, tore through the state's savings, got his state's credit downgraded, and then stuck his head in the sand. He never seriously tried to shrink the size of the state government. If Brownback did value fiscal discipline, there was an obvious remedy. He could have restored the tax cuts and then decreased spending. Brownback loved the state-budget-as-a-family metaphor, and he could have put that metaphor into action. When the family budget is tight, someone picks up an extra shift or a second job to increase revenue. Or, the family cuts back on traveling or eating out to decrease spending. In Kansas, Brownback could have repealed his tax cuts to increase revenue or cut energy subsidies to decrease spending. He did neither. If I can extend the family/budget metaphor, Brownback turned off the home's HVAC and water, and then made the kids get their haircuts at the cosmetology training school. Kansans ended up saving a few bucks on haircuts, but essential state functions were neglected, and the kids were embarrassed to leave the house.

Rural hospitals were defunded in Fort Scott, and underfunded public schools in Kansas City had to end the year early. But wealthy Kansans appreciated Brownback's governance. The business profit exemption was widely manipulated, functioning as a legal tax haven for millionaires in Kansas.[111] According to a team of researchers, Brownback's tax policy fueled more tax evasion than job creation.[112] Brownback's exemption allowed wealthy

Kansans to create limited liability companies, draw the minimum salary required by law, and then receive the rest of their income untaxed.[113] The University of Kansas basketball and football coaches did this. Head basketball coach Bill Self took advantage by taking only $230,000 of his $3 million salary in income, and then—because he was an independent contractor—drew the additional $2.75 million for "professional services rendered." Kansas Athletics wrote a $2.75 million check to *BCLT II, LLC*, owned by Bill Self, so that he could avoid paying $126,500 in taxes to the state of Kansas. Coach Self's setup illustrates the foolishness of Brownback's promises. Even the most die-hard Jayhawks fan knew Coach Self did not own the KU hoops team or use the $126,500 he saved to hire more power forwards.[114]

One wealthy lawyer told a *Kansas City Star* reporter that he and his partners were each saving about $10,000 a year under Brownback's new tax plan (while the taxes of administrative staff and paralegals did not change). "I'm making out like a bandit, and it's completely unfair," he boasted, before telling the reporter about his plans to use the savings to vacation in Cancún.[115]

While the state reeled, the ruling class of Kansas grew wealthier. By leveraging Brownback's economic idealism, rich lawyers bronzed themselves on Mexican beaches, and the only people who suffered were the Kansans who relied on public roads and public schools.

Conclusion

Eventually, Brownback was booted from public office and Kansas began to recover. But I hope this case study affirms Kenneth Burke's foundational premise: public words matter, especially inaccurate public words. The disaster that became Kansas reflects larger linguistic deficiencies. And if we cannot understand what we cannot name, we have no chance to marginalize future Sam Brownbacks.

Sam Brownback never had to worry about staying true to conservative economics because he was not a conservative. Milton Friedman did not worry about libertarian purity because he was not a libertarian. Charles Koch did not have to respond to accusations of neoliberalism because he was not a neoliberal. Kenneth Burke showed how our *selection* of public words inevitably forces us to *deflect* a set of words and the reality they help create.[116] When we are describing Kansas as "conservative" or "supply-side," we are not describing how the rich use wealth to defend wealth; we are not describing how the ruling elite use of political power to defend and maximize profitability in

CHAPTER 9

undemocratic ways; and we are not describing an alternative allowing more Americans to live full, productive, viable lives if we cannot name the force preventing that noble mission. Put more simply, when we select "conservative" or "neoliberal" to describe Kansas, we are deflecting the more accurate and useful word: oligarchy.

10

Class Consciousness and the Rhetoric of Tucker Carlson

DURING THE 1990S AND 2000S, TUCKER CARLSON DEVELOPED A REPUtation as a dynamic and thoughtful conservative intellectual, championing conventional Republican positions during the George W. Bush administration, including fiscal responsibility and preemptive military action against terrorists. However, Carlson was a shape-shifter, not wed to policy or party. Stylistically, Carlson excelled on TV and online. He knew how to get noticed and stay relevant. Although he was positioned on the political Right in public conversations, he was never anchored to conventional conservatism. His public messaging contained nostalgic genuflections—the "disposition to preserve" of Edmund Burke—but those appeals were undeveloped and unconvincing.[1] Instead, a close analysis of Tucker Carlson's messaging can illuminate oligarchy's structural coherence in the twenty-first century.

Traitor to His Class

Carlson was a populist champion of the forgotten American struggling against an elite cabal. He was a traitor to his class, spewing disrepute on social institutions and constituting an audience marked by institutional betrayal, cynicism, and, ultimately, a democratic apathy well-suited to democratic oligarchy in a moment of political upheaval. In January 2016, Carlson wrote an article for *Politico* in which he predicted Trump's nomination and election. Carlson decided to reprint the article in *The Long Slide*—a compilation of thirty years of Carlson's essays. In the 2021 book, Carlson prefaced the reprint by writing: "By the beginning of 2016, it seemed obvious that Trump could win the nomination and be president. I wanted to predict that in print before it happened, so I wrote this in a single sitting, banging away on my iPad in my kitchen in Washington, reading passages aloud to my wife, who because she's a nice person nodded in agreement."[2] Carlson conceded that although most of the people he knew "in Washington were baffled and enraged by Donald Trump," the movement Trump led "always made sense."[3] Carlson explained Trump's appeal with a hard truth for his DC beltway community: "He exists because you failed."[4] Under the heading "Washington Really Is Corrupt," Carlson described the Trump movement as a reaction "against the stupidity and obtuseness of American politics, a status quo that clearly couldn't continue."[5] Under the heading "Truth Is Not Only a Defense, It's Thrilling," Carlson addressed his reader directly, asking, "When was the last time you stopped yourself from saying something you believed to be true for fear of being punished or criticized for saying it? If you live in America, it probably hasn't been long."[6] If Carlson's question resonated, then Trump's emergence was not at all baffling. Trump's brash and refreshing ability to highlight the malevolence and hypocrisy of DC political insiders is "not just a talking point about political correctness," Carlson wrote. "Trump is the ideal candidate to fight Washington corruption not simply because he opposes it, but because he has personally participated in it. He's not just a reformer; like most effective populists, he's a whistle-blower, a traitor to his class."[7] After then comparing Trump to Teddy Roosevelt, Carlson concluded, "Anyone can peer through the window in envy. It takes a real man to throw furniture through it from the inside."[8]

Carlson's explanation for Trump's emergence implicitly reflects his own evolution. In 1999, while writing for the *Weekly Standard*, Carlson appeared on C-SPAN and discussed the viability of Patrick Buchanan, the populist commentator and fringe Republican presidential candidate. Carlson said he agreed with Buchanan on certain issues, but he took issue with Buchanan's conspiratorial reaction whenever criticized for adopting unconventional positions. Mimicking Buchanan's reaction, Carlson said, "The tiny cabal that controls American politics doesn't like me because I speak truth to power . . . that I offend the plutocracy, that I am a wanted man by the inside-the-beltway people." Carlson went on to say he worried that in "every sense [Buchanan] cast himself as a victim, a sort of Karen Silkwood of politics, someone who is so truthful they are being hunted down by the conspiracy that runs Washington."[9] Carlson's portrayal of Buchanan lends insight into why, early in his career, Carlson was thought to be a serious and clever conservative with regular gigs on CNN and C-SPAN.[10]

In 2009, Tucker Carlson delivered a prophetic speech to the Conservative

Political Action Committee. Republicans were becoming the "party of stupid," and Carlson had the credibility to level the accusation.[11] Carlson warned his audience their media organizations will "fail if they don't put accuracy first." He conceded, "I'm as conservative as anyone in this room; I'm in the process of stockpiling weapons and moving to Idaho so I don't take a second seat to anyone in this room ideologically." But he went on, "If you create a news organization whose primary objective is to create inaccurate news you will fail. The *New York Times* is a liberal paper, but it is also . . . a paper that actually cares about accuracy," he said. "Conservatives need to build institutions that mirror those institutions. . . . That's the truth."[12] Shortly after, he started the *Daily Caller*, a serious conservative magazine designed to fulfill Carlson's charge at CPAC—to not just carry water for Republican positions but, in Carlson's words, to "explain what your government is doing."[13] What happened next informs the Right's evolution from the Party of Reagan to the Party of Trump. The *Daily Caller* ended up wielding limited political influence. It has since evolved to reflect the same survivalist strategies as the GOP: The *Daily Caller* now combines fringe conservative conspiracy theories with internet click bait, including links to the ten hottest Syrian refugees.[14]

In 2015, Carlson emerged as an influential figure on *Fox News* and a bestselling author by offering withering social commentary well suited for a GOP audience in the age of Trump. For Carlson, the evolution paid off. Fox paid him $6 million a year. His 2018 book, *Ship of Fools: How a Selfish Ruling Class Is Bringing America to the Brink of Revolution*, was a number-one *New York Times* bestseller, and his 2021 memoir, *The Long Slide*, was an instant bestseller. When the *New York Times* devoted a three-part series to Carlson's influence on American life, they described him as "Fox's most influential employee" and a "potential candidate for president." Carlson's evolution paid off for Fox as well. *Tucker Carlson Tonight* was the most successful show in the history of cable news, reliably drawing more than three million viewers a night. His television show drew the largest audience of any show on television during the end of Trump's presidency, and in every year between 2018 and 2022 his program brought Fox more ad revenue than any other show.[15]

Carlson was a furniture thrower. His television program, for example, was unlike *Meet the Press* or *Firing Line*. While Carlson once featured guests, his program evolved so that as he spent more time on his opening monologues, talking directly to viewers, his ratings and influence grew.[16] During the Trump era, the interlocutors faded away. No oppositional voice joined him on set. Carlson did not argue with an opponent or grapple with counterarguments from an alternative perspective. Akin to Jon Stewart, John Oliver, Rachel Maddow, and Sean Hannity, Carlson opened his program with a diatribe delivered to the viewer directly. *Tucker Carlson Tonight* was an aptly named one-man show. He laid out his argument, often involving a grand conspiracy of the ruling elite, a social issue reflecting larger rot, or a hypocritical politician. Carlson then exposited, mocking the foil, often with a poor impression or a disgusted facial expression. *Can you believe how absurd this is?*

And yet, Carlson was more than an angry internet troll. His rhetorical potency affirmed and extended the rhetoric of the fringe communities he was said to represent, including fascists, far-right populists, and white Christian nationalists.[17] According to Jason Stanley, fascism tends to reject Enlightenment rationality in exchange for waving banners of "nationalism in front of middle- and working-class white people to funnel the state's spoils into the hands of oligarchs."[18] According to Nathan Crick, fascist rhetorical strategies emerge when people willingly embrace "irrational principles to justify preserving or expanding the unearned privileges of an inherited social hierarchy, culminating in a general attitude of contempt for everything outside one's social group."[19] Ultimately, fascism promises to reestablish threatened privilege and restore the marginalized to the top of the hierarchy where they belong. To be sure, by appealing to a naturalist form of transcendent justice, Carlson defended unequal power concentrations.[20] Carlson also affirmed fascism's telic end point. But his appeals to naturalism, realism, and consequentialism cannot be reduced to fascist appeals to false premises, violent insults, and exaggerated bluster.[21] Carlson featured the accumulation of evidence uncovering a divine, objective, and causal link between *getting* and *deserving*. Unlike the bluster and passion of fascism, Carlson's rhetoric pursued justice according to natural appeals to deservedness and merit, and in the process, Carlson's textual persona hovered above the emotional subjectivity so central to fascist power concentration.

It's the Central Theme of the Show

After Trump's electoral defeat in November 2020, a clip from Carlson's TV program went viral in which Carlson summarized the central purpose of his show. "After four years, this may be the single most open-minded show on television," he said.[22] His show's open-mindedness was reflected in his coverage of election fraud, Silicon Valley conspiracies, and even UFO segments because, as Carlson put it, "there is evidence that UFOs are real and everyone lies about it."[23] Carlson went on, justifying his unconventional editorial choices by defining his program's purpose in opposition to the established authorities: "And we don't care who mocks it. The louder the Yale political science department and staff of the *Atlantic* magazine scream 'conspiracy theory!' the more interested we tend to be. That is usually a sign you are over the target. A lot of people with impressive sounding credentials in this country are frauds. They have no idea what they're doing. They're children posing as authorities, and when they're caught, they lie, and then they blame you for it. We see that every day. It's the central theme of the show and it will continue to be."[24] Roderick Hart and Johanna Hartelius show why this form is perfect for modern American politics.[25] The authority and simplicity, the need for a hot take, and the unrepresentative sample drawn out to explain it all. Carlson's realism was even better for virality. His rants were like extended YouTube clips: snarky, mic drops unencumbered by nuance, complexity, or modesty—perfect for an American audience always online.[26] Carlson appeared to float above political deliberation, never landing to engage in argument or dialogue. Who could respond? It was just him at his desk ranting to the camera.

And yet, Tucker Carlson was not the political Right's only class traitor. American conservatism is marked by a history of "class passing" because that persona allows the rhetor inventive opportunities to fuse together economic, political, and cultural interests in the defense of the ruling elite.[27] But usually, the result is a *rhetoric of classlessness* that, according to Ralph Miliband, cloaks the political defense of elite economic interests in "ideological clothing suitable for political competition in the age of 'mass politics.'" Miliband went on to suggest that "one of the special functions of conservative political parties is to provide that necessary clothing."[28] Conservative thought leaders tend to explicitly reject class consciousness as inappropriate for an American democracy devoid of class envy, including Thomas Jefferson's American exceptionalism and Alexis de Tocqueville's "equality of condition" to Mitt Romney and Marco Rubio today.[29] Conservative classlessness is nostalgic for the historical moment before the corruption of FDR and the New Deal, when social relations aligned with a Jeffersonian vision of a classless, agrarian America defined against the relics of European aristocracy.[30] Classlessness pointed to the political dominance of the middle-class majority containing the emergence—and even the existence—of a ruling class.

But the classlessness of Jefferson, Tocqueville, Rubio, and Romney contradicts the reality of American democracy. The ultra-rich in America function as an observable, differentiated, and coherent social group marked by incommensurate definitive boundaries. In America, a small number of people own a disproportionate share of material wealth, and their income is derived mainly from that ownership and by commanding the most important sectors of the economy. Public conversations are often marked by references to "the working-class" or "the middle-class," but the ultra-rich maintain the features of a coherent class identity, distinct and specific social formations united by a combination of characteristics affecting its members in opposition to members of other classes.[31] Ultimately, class consciousness allows the ultra-rich to maximize their economic status by leveraging relationships with the state.[32]

Into this incongruity Carlson offered a unique extension of conservatism by highlighting the class consciousness of the American elite and describing their machinations as so conspiratorial, so far-reaching, and so paralyzing that the only appropriate response for his constituted audience was apathy and cynicism. According to a *New York Times* analysis, Carlson invoked the phrase "ruling class" in more than eight hundred shows.[33] Carlson's discursive associations with falling birthrates, urban crime, and immigrant invasions aligned with the populist rhetoric of Father Coughlin, Patrick J. Buchanan, and Donald Trump. But to attribute the cause of American descendancy so explicitly, so directly, to a "ruling class" of pro-war, pro-China, anti-American, Democratic *and* Republican elites, including Big Tech and normally untouchable corporate executives, was unprecedented. The first rule of class warfare: You do not talk about class warfare.

A Better Time

As he concludes *The Long Slide*, Carlson describes how reading over his thirty years in journalism has made him "realize how much has changed, and forever. The world his book describes is mostly gone."[34] If a conservative is someone who seeks to conserve, then it would be wise to consider what discrete features of the past Tucker Carlson looks fondly upon. His messaging fit a larger pattern characterized by institutional betrayal dating back to FDR's New Deal—at least. His book titles are revealing: *Ship of Fools* and *The Long Slide* reflect an outlook marked by the decline of American exceptionalism and the corruption of the institutions integral to American supremacy. Carlson's nostalgic rhetoric conforms with conservatism: Just as Milton Friedman was worried about the government protecting us from cap guns and bicycles, Carlson lamented that his children were born in a moment when "there were no more go-karts on city streets."[35] Carlson wrote fondly about spending "many happy afternoons eating crab cakes in the main dining room" of an exclusive restaurant in Washington, DC, listening to his waiter tell him sex jokes. Carlson made few attempts to disguise his class status; unlike Mitt Romney in 2012 exchanging his limo for a Chevy on the way to presidential campaign rallies, Carlson's persona exhibits no shame in the privilege allowing him to dine on crab cakes and drink lunchtime martinis on a weekday. "You could do that then in Washington," Carlson wrote. "It was normal for men to take a couple of hours in the middle of the day, have a drink, and swap stories. A better time."[36]

But how normal was it? Normal for whom? And who is the "you" enjoying the lunchtime crab cakes? Apart from any empirical reality, Carlson brazenly constitutes an audience that once dined next to him. But no longer. Carlson's audience has been betrayed. Betrayal implies a temporal evolution from a position of power and privilege to a regressive historical moment when Carlson's audience can no longer rely on the meritocratic foundations of Western civilization and its Great Chain of Being. Betrayal is the defining condition for "a country that no longer makes any pretense of being a meritocracy," Carlson wrote in *The Long Slide*.[37] As Carlson's lunchtime crab cake anecdote illustrates, he attracts a discrete audience through second-person pronouns standard for populist rhetoric: "You" and "Yours" have been let down by the elites entrusted to care for you and yours.

Carlson's betrayed audience is defined against a clear and vivid foil. In *The Long Slide*, Carlson wrote: "If you live in an affluent ZIP code, it's hard to see a downside to mass low-wage immigration. Your kids don't go to public school. You don't take the bus or use the emergency room for health care. No immigrant is competing for your job. (The day Hondurans start getting hired as green energy lobbyists is the day my neighbors become nativists.) Plus, you get cheap servants, and get to feel welcoming and virtuous while paying them less per hour than your kids make at a summer job on Nantucket. It's all good."[38] But it is not "all good." Carlson's audience is not living in an affluent ZIP code, with cheap servants and summer jobs on Nantucket. In contrast, Carlson's audience is hailed as defenders of conservative values—a "you" marked by a concern for "Western civilization and democracy and families, and the ferocious assault on all three of those things by the leaders of our global institutions."[39] Carlson positions his own neighbors beyond the discursive parameters of his audience—revealing much about his textual persona's paradoxical relationship within the class-conscious hierarchy he established. His neighbors' ignorance was enhanced by their isolation; in contrast, Carlson urges an audience unfamiliar with the dire state of the country—including the need to hire armed bodyguards if they criticize Joe Biden—to simply "ask around" and they will be educated on the reality of life in America today. Carlson's arc of the moral universe is short and it bends toward collapse.

Elite corruption and incompetence saturated his messaging. His fear reflected a problem facing the entire Western civilization, "a symptom of deeper rot" caused by the people in charge retreating into a fantasy and demanding we all join them. Carlson was worried about homelessness, drug use, and filth in American cities. He relished the chance to expose climate-change crusaders he considered hypocritical, like Hillary Clinton, Leonardo DiCaprio, and Bill Nye the Science Guy.[40] Carlson was worried "something awful is happening to men in America" as "our leaders pledge to create more opportunities for women and girls."[41] He worried men were becoming less male, as sperm counts across the West plummeted, down almost 60 percent since the 1970s, according to Carlson.[42] In 2021, Carlson began capitalizing on his audience's fears with a synergistic promotional video for *Fox Nation*, his network's nascent streaming service. With the "total collapse of testosterone levels in American men," Carlson touted a remedy from a company called "Joovv" promising to revive underperforming testicles by shining a red light on them.[43] There was little scientific evidence for Carlson's concerns about declining levels of testosterone in American men, but the issue aligned with Carlson's larger critique: Even the most intimate dimensions of his audience's identity were under threat.

In an article reprinted in *The Long Slide*, Carlson featured Joel Suprise as a revealing touchstone. In Appleton, Wisconsin, Suprise made the world's most advanced potato cannons, and he attracted Carlson's attention because he "taught me that not all geniuses work at hedge funds. Some of them you'll find sitting in the garage drunk on beer at two in the morning, turning out works of art on homemade lathes."[44] Carlson portrayed Joel Suprise as a representative anecdote for the institutional betrayal felt most acutely by American men. "There used to be a lot of men in America like Joel Suprise, guys who could fix and create complicated things with their hands. That's not a romantic view of the past; it's true. Guys like Joel Suprise built the American economy. When manufacturing died, a lot of them drifted off into semipermanent uselessness, getting by on disability payments. Some OD'd on fentanyl. I caught Joel at the last moment in our history before video games and porn gave restless men an easy way to burn energy late at night."[45]

Washington, DC, was portrayed as the epicenter of conspiratorial corruption. Carlson once described New Hampshire senator Bob Smith as "the least cynical man in Washington" in a profile reprinted in *The Long Slide*. "Needless to say," Carlson continued, "Smith didn't last long."[46] The city's economy was tied to the federal budget, and DC was the wealthiest metro region in the country. Unlike Omaha and Akron, Washington, DC, was insulated from the real world by the federal government. Political figures leveraged the relationship to enrich themselves and their allies. In *Ship of Fools*, Carlson writes, "The District of Columbia and its surrounding suburbs are now the wealthiest metro region in the country. Washington's job market is effectively bulletproof. Political figures cycle in and out of government, from lobbying to finance to contracting and back, growing richer at every turn. In Washington, prosperity is all but guaranteed. To the rest of the country, this looks like corruption, because, essentially, it is. But if you live there, it's all upside."[47]

In 1980, Milton Friedman stood in front of the massive Department of Health, Education and Welfare building to decry the growth of the federal government "into a veritable empire."[48] Likewise, DC is the foil to define Carlson's audience against. In *The Long Slide*, Carlson shares his disdain for the physical architecture of Washington, DC, describing it as "a city that hasn't constructed a graceful public building in fifty years," prompting Carlson to "wonder about our own empire."[49] Carlson's textual persona is reflected in how he positions himself *in* Washington, DC, but not *of* it. Carlson is a traitor to his class. He knew DC's seedy underbelly, but he spoke for "the rest of the country" in a way few others could. Carlson revealed the truths only an insider would know, but he had the fortitude to betray the ruling elite and spread the word.

Carlson painted with such a broad brush that threats to "the rest of the country" included a bipartisan roster of villains. Carlson's attacks on Big Tech expanded the parameters of the ruling elite as social and cultural evolutions demanded. William Buckley did not attack George Pake like Carlson attacked Mark Zuckerberg. Zuckerberg represented both an out-of-touch elite—a thirty-four-year-old worth $72 billion who, according to Carlson, was "completely cut off from reality"—and a threat to democracy, telling us what "political opinions you're allowed to hold" even though no one voted for him.[50] Carlson stretches the conspiratorial reach from DC to Silicon Valley and back. Carlson describes the "tech oligarchs join[ing] forces to censor their political opponents." And if his audience assumed as much, Carlson says, "You weren't being paranoid to worry about this. You were absolutely right."[51]

CHAPTER 10

The media was a monolithic bloc that once held government accountable but is now indistinguishable from the powerful people it covers.[52] In the introduction to *The Long Slide*, Carlson writes, "Censorship is now the rule in popular media; news outlets openly censor ideas they don't like, and encourage others to do the same. Journalism has been utterly corrupted."[53] As evidence, Carlson highlighted his own iconoclastic textual persona, noting later in the same introduction: "If small-minded partisans had been in charge, I never could have stayed in the business. As this point, people with my opinions can't. They've been driven from traditional journalism. That's what I thought about as I reread the pieces that follow. Not only were they written a long time ago, but many of them couldn't be written today. Enjoy the time capsule."[54] On his TV show, Carlson asked his audience to imagine journalists Hunter Thompson, Mike Wallace, or Geraldo Rivera calling Trump after dinner or dancing to Cher at a Clinton party on Martha's Vineyard. On May 4, 2019, Carlson synthesized media complicity with undemocratic technological dominance in a revealing monologue: "Remarkably, our media think that's great. Journalists are supposed to defend free speech. But when corporate America issues an order, they reflexively obey. Listen to them celebrate Mark Zuckerberg and sell you out completely."[55] Carlson follows with an edited clip of "media" fawning over Zuckerberg and his disarming promises to democratize everything.

Tucker Carlson urged you to feel like a wise insider floating above partisan squabbles. Watch Carlson and you feel knowledgeable, without being soiled by the muck of "politics." You knew enough already. You did not need to look twice because the world was not that complex. Carlson offered the appearance of political wisdom without the hard work. He drew together an audience that sounded and felt informed. His audience could discuss Benghazi, email servers, Hunter Biden, and Eastern European politics for days. Carlson's audience was not stupid. Or lazy. No one who knew that much about Burisma or bleached emails could be accused of apathy.

Carlson drew together an audience that had it all figured out from watching forty-four minutes of TV each night; no need to attend city council meetings, read the local newspaper, or seriously consider an opponent's argument. His audience was marked by ironic distance—by observation, not participation. Ironic distance from the catastrophe is the source of pure pleasure. Better cynical insulation than being lumped together as part of it. If the government is incompetent, politicians corrupt, and the ruling elite sold-out, the hard work of acquiring political wisdom, and acting on it, is a waste of time. Who is elected does not matter. Carlson constituted an audience that voted with their middle fingers.

The Tyranny of Woke Capital

Carlson also found fault with conservatism's sacred cows far beyond government bureaucrats and the liberal media. On foreign policy, he wrote: "Pretty much every major foreign policy decision in recent years has been a disaster. Yet elite enthusiasm for nation building and pointless wars continues unabated. Our leaders still seem more committed to liberating Syrian towns from some armed group or other than to fixing rotting suburbs in Akron. Our leaders seem less interested than ever in the country they actually govern."[56] Carlson offered a fresh takedown of conservativism's friendly links to corporate America. On a May 2019 episode of *Tucker Carlson Tonight*, Carlson warned viewers, "The tyranny of 'woke' capital is real, and it is terrifying. Just because they're selling you products, doesn't mean it's not a dictatorship."[57] In *The Long Slide*, he praised Josh Hawley, then a first-term Republican senator from Missouri, as "one of the rare anti-corporate voices in a party that has long taken its direction from the Chamber of Commerce."[58] Carlson also blamed corporations for upending traditional gender relationships. He faulted Disney and Netflix for being so keen on expanding their labor pool, lowering wages, and increasing profits they engaged in a "grotesque scam" to oppress women—even to the point of supporting abortion rights to shrink, or even disappear, the family, leaving "women free to devote their lives to the company—reliable little worker bees."[59] Carlson was unafraid to point out how the American tax code grants preferential treatment to capital income over labor income.[60] In *Ship of Fools*, he asks: "Why do we tax capital at half the rate of labor? That might be the first one. Why is it fair that some inherited-money loser living off the interest from an investment portfolio he didn't create pays half the taxes per dollar that you do? You get up every morning to go to work. He stays home, smokes weed, and watches online porn. You get hit twice as hard on April 15. He's being rewarded, while you're being punished. Is he twice as necessary as you are? Does he contribute twice as much to America?"[61]

The second-person pronoun lends insight into Carlson's idealized audience: *You* get up in the morning and go to work, but *they* stay home and watch porn, and as a result, *you* pay more in taxes because your efforts are undervalued. In alignment with the economic populism of the post–Great Recession, Carlson reinvents Reagan and Friedman's welfare queen in the "inherited money-loser." But more than a conventional mid-century conservative critique, Carlson messaging resembles an instrumentalist Marxist critique of the capitalist state.[62] Carlson highlighted the class consciousness of his villains, pointing out how the rich and well-connected use the state to dominate the rest of society, ultimately constituting a lazy, immoral, and ignorant ruling class rigging the game against his audience. In Carlson's world, the natural order has been perverted and consequentialism has gone awry as the inferior populate the elite ranks. Worse, without recognizing the elite's class consciousness, no one could be held accountable for corruption and malevolence. In *Ship of Fools*, he writes: "In a healthy society, decades of obvious failures by elites would force a change of ideas or a change of leadership. Neither has happened. The same class of lawmakers, journalists, and business chieftains holds power, despite their dismal record. America now has not only one of the least impressive ruling classes in history, but also the least self-aware. They have no idea how bad they are."[63]

The Least Impressive Ruling Classes in History

Carlson titled his 2018 book *Ship of Fools* as a riff on a reference from Plato's *The Republic*, but his indictment was far more cynical than foolish.[64] Carlson described a ship of devils. The cover of his book featured carnivalesque, oversized drawings of the ruling elite in a ship heading toward the cliffs. Maxine Waters, Jeff Bezos, Hillary Clinton, Mark Zuckerberg, Nancy Pelosi, Mitch McConnell, Lindsey Graham, and Bill Kristol were guiding us over the edge, each representing the book's subtitle: the selfish ruling class bringing America to the brink of revolution. Notice the Republicans in the ship of fools: McConnell, Graham, and Kristol. Unlike Limbaugh or Hannity, Carlson was not a partisan hack. His loyalty is to his audience, not the Republican Party. In *The Long Slide*, Carlson derides the George W. Bush presidency, noting that "for eight years, there was a born-again in the White House. How'd that work out for Christians, here and in Iraq?"[65] On his TV program, Carlson felt comfortable criticizing Trump, asking, "Where is the White House?" as tech moguls like Mark Zuckerberg make our country "unfree."[66] He felt comfortable criticizing Republican leadership, too, complaining, "Republicans in Congress don't care about the territorial integrity of the country they run."[67] He praised Elizabeth Warren for her "economic patriotism."[68]

In August 2021, Carlson moved his entire television production from New York City to Hungary, filming a week of shows portraying Prime Minister

Viktor Orbán as an authentic conservative and Budapest as "a kind of capital" for western civilization under threat.[69] In contrast to Minneapolis and Portland, Carlson showed his audience footage of clean, well-lit Budapest streets. "Notice as you watch," Carlson narrated, "that you don't see tent cities of drug addicts living in the parks; there isn't garbage and human waste littering the sidewalks; people don't get beheaded at intersections; BLM is not allowed to torch entire neighborhoods in Budapest."[70]

Carlson's liberal critics accused him of working as a PR proxy for an eastern European fascist.[71] Carlson conceded how unusual it was to feature "a small country in the middle of central Europe with no navy, no nuclear weapons, and a GDP smaller than New York state."[72] Given its size, Carlson said, "you wouldn't think leaders in Washington would pay a lot of attention to Hungary but they do, obsessively." But here is where Carlson's unusual decision to film his TV show from Hungary comes into focus. Carlson justified his decision because America's ruling elite are obsessed with Orbán and Hungary. By "rejecting the tenets of neoliberalism, Victor Orbán has personally offended them and enraged them," Carlson said. Carlson seemed to draw rhetorical energy from the angst Orbán aroused in Washington, DC, elites. Carlson described with glee how liberals were "so triggered" by what Orbán described as "Hungarian conservative Christian Judeo-Christian democratic thinking."[73]

The *New York Times* wrote that Carlson visited Hungary and featured Orbán "to frame his own arguments about an American civilization under attack by alien forces."[74] But more than fawning over a fascist, his visit to Budapest offered Carlson an opportunity to enhance his own textual persona, defined against the ruling elite. Carlson focused, for instance, on Hungary's strict immigration policies. He reassured his audience that they already knew why Orbán's immigration policies could not be implemented in the United States: "The answer, as you know, is because our leaders don't want to have it. They benefit from the chaos and the pain of illegal immigration when the rule of law collapses; they become more powerful [and] that's why we have open borders."[75] Carlson did not use Hungary as a foil for democracy. In his introduction, Carlson notes how "Orbán has been vilified [and] left-wing NGOs have denounced him as a fascist a destroyer of democracy."[76] Orbán, like Carlson, represented the class traitor defending traditional, pro-family Judeo-Christians against the authoritarianism of the left. Ultimately, Carlson uses Hungary to affirm a regime in which the ultra-rich rule *through* democratic institutions—not in opposition to them.[77] Carlson's focus on the weaknesses, incompetence, and corruption of "our leaders"—in the United States and eastern Europe—obscured the fact that bureaucracies like the federal government, the media, and higher education are often the mechanisms best suited to mediate the power concentrations of unrestrained economic and political power.[78] To assume that Carlson's cynicism and distrust provides the antidote to fascist authoritarianism is potent propaganda but weak political theory.[79]

The oligarchic antidote requires active democratic participation. Carlson says it is not worth it. Carlson pours gasoline on an already burning political fire. If you are already disaffected by Iraq, the Great Recession, and a warming planet, if you are already cynical toward politics and the ruling elite, it matters less which particular ruling elite leads the flim-flam. Politics are the sour grapes from Aesop's fables, and Carlson's audience is urged to walk away content with knowing the grapes would not be sweet anyway. If they are all corrupt, what difference does it make? Ultimately, the prophecy is fulfilled, and we get the oligarchy we thought we had the whole time.[80]

Confirm the Preexisting Biases

For close observers of American democracy, maybe the most galling extension of oligarchy is the near-total disappearance of subtlety on the part of oligarchic rhetors like Carlson. Consider the incongruity of people like Carlson voicing the disaffections of long-haul truck drivers from Akron and pig farmers from Asheville. That Carlson speaks for the disaffected is more than ironic. It is strategic. Carlson *was* the ruling elite. The space between Carlson, DiCaprio, Clinton, and Zuckerberg was thin compared to the space between Carlson and his imagined audience: the disgruntled, "real" American betrayed by the coastal secular elites. NewsCorp paid Carlson $6 million a year. He was raised in San Francisco and Southern California. His father was a news anchor in Los Angeles and ambassador to the Seychelles; his stepmother was heir to the Swanson frozen food empire. Carlson attended private high school and college, and he lived in La Jolla. Yet he guards the gates keeping the elite barbarians out.

Consider how Carlson attacks Bill Nye the Science Guy. Carlson complains that Nye has no background in climate research or the natural sciences. On his TV program, Carlson said of Bill Nye: "He had no numbers at all. He had no facts whatsoever. For a science guy, there was no science, just a lot of yelling. . . . He is back with another warning about the planet. He is Bill Nye, the falsely named science guy."[81] As Carlson writes in *Ship of Fools*, Nye does not need numbers or facts because when his primary task is to "confirm the preexisting biases of people making more than one hundred thousand dollars a year, facts only get in the way."[82] But the irony escaped Carlson.

It seems personal credibility, a characteristic political theorists long thought was important for potency, is irrelevant now. Carlson did not adopt a working-class aesthetic to mediate the incongruity between his wealth and his imagined audience. Carlson functioned as a vivid example of his own critique. He was the Ruling Class fleecing you. He was the justification for democratic indifference. They were all hypocrites. And that does not undercut their worldview. It illustrates it. "We are all crooks!" they shout. Even us. Carlson tells his audience, "You think your ruling elite are so great? Look at me. I am one of them. And I am a complete phony."

Further, the state is not incompetent. And I do not just mean the ability to make the trains run on time. I mean the ability to concentrate power and wealth. Oligarchs know this better than anyone. This is what may separate Tucker Carlson from Jon Stewart, John Oliver, and Rachel Maddow. Consider how well the import-export bank and the US tax code funnels wealth and power to the wealthy and powerful.[83] But Carlson focuses our attention on the clowns in the parade, not the thieves working the back of the grandstand. We focus on the Kellyanne Conways and Anthony Scaramuccis. Not Andrew Wheeler, the former coal lobbyist who ran the EPA, or David Bernhardt, the former oil and gas lobbyist who ran the Department of Interior, and Leonard Leo of the Federalist Society who guided Trump's Supreme Court nominees.

Carlson's Class Consciousness

The ultra-rich have always sought to capitalize on economies of scale, to concentrate and centralize capital, and to influence policy toward their interests by adopting, implementing, and enforcing preferential public policies through political machinations.[84] The historical record shows the ultra-rich have no qualms about meeting their oligarchic aims by stifling innovation, underinvesting in long-term research and production, gouging consumers, bottling up supply chains, and destroying the environment.[85] But during the golden age of liberal democracy, oligarchic power concentrations were diffused by responsive and representative social institutions, near-universal suffrage, fair elections, free speech, and an independent judiciary. Democratic political engagement made it possible for non-elites to agitate, mobilize, and organize for their interests, especially to influence the state to redistribute income and services away from the ultra-rich.[86] After the Great Depression and World War II, the state was compelled to implement social policies, economic reforms, and institutional changes that conceded the demands of ordinary, non-elite Americans. The state intervened to show that entrenched poverty and massive economic inequality were not caused by God's will or Nature's Laws.[87] As a result, democratic participation forced the state to maintain less bias toward the ultra-rich, and lapses of impartiality were thought to be aberrations from the fundamental nature of liberal democracy.[88]

But beginning in 1980, democratic accountability mechanisms began to break down, and social cynicism began to resonate in a democracy distrustful of its leaders and the institutions they represent.[89] Enter Tucker Carlson. Carlson's audience is distrustful of the leaders and institutions conforming with his rhetorical representations. But without trusted leadership, there is no social solidarity or mutual obligation.[90] In Carlson's oligarchic state, the apparatus of state power is decentralized, restricted in its range of actions, and unable to act against the interests of the ultra-rich. Carlson constitutes an audience conditioned to believe we are on our own, responsible for no one but ourselves and our tribe. Aligning with what Ralph Miliband described as "the second face of power," Carlson's cynicism hails an audience comfortable with social norms, institutional practices, and political machinations limiting the scope of democratic participation to the banal and innocuous. There is a reason Carlson features testosterone, porn, and Bill Nye, and not the import/export bank, tax subsidies, or the Kochs' lobbying.[91]

Once Carlson's audience is hailed by democratic disengagement, cynicism, and apathy, a logical consequence is the development of a class consciousness defined by limited access to state power and ignorance of their unique capacity to do anything about it.[92] The Joel Suprises of the Upper Midwest are left marginalized and disempowered—either through the coercion described by James Buchanan or the genteel hegemony of Carlson's red-light remedies for underperforming testicles. Without democratic engagement and collective solidarity, the only threat Carlson's servile underclass poses to the ruling elite is confined to replacing the production of the world's most advanced potato cannons for drinking beer and watching porn.

Carlson's audience was marked by institutional cynicism because the US government was so incompetent and corrupt. To illustrate, Carlson had many targets. His daily TV production meeting required his writers to track down concrete and appalling instances of government incompetence and corruption. Not hard to do. Two million people work for the federal government, including plenty of morons. We have a four trillion-dollar federal budget, which leads to millions of wasted dollars. But about government competence, Carlson is wrong. The US government is the most successful mass democracy in human history. No institution has elevated the opportunity for more people to live rich, full, viable, safe, and productive lives. No institution has turned its historical and geographic advantages into the Genome project, the Internet, the international space station, the National Weather Service, strong public education, taxation with representation, the Social Security administration, national highways, food safety guidelines, and air traffic control.[93] Carlson's messaging shrouds such competence.

About government corruption, Carlson is also wrong. Transparency International publishes a Corruption Perception Index each year, and the United States has been in the Top 20 least-corrupt countries for all but two of the last twenty-three years.[94] But Carlson was not an outlier: A Gallup poll found 75 percent of Americans said corruption was "widespread" in our government.[95] Like Carlson, they are also wrong. "No other country has done so well at containing corruption while leaving so many of its people convinced it has done poorly," according to Charles Homans.[96] Homans notes that most healthy democracies do not think they are as corrupt as most Americans think their own country is.

Carlson's textual persona reconciles the incongruity. Incompetence and corruption are charges made compelling by Carlson as long as his audience stays focused on the morons and waste—and not on the government employee from the Energy Department who organized the first successful cleanup of a nuclear weapons factory, or the government employee at the Federal Trade Commission who built the Do Not Call Registry, or the government employee at the National Institutes of Health who pioneered immunotherapy, or the 2020 election volunteers in Atlanta who gave up their weekend to recount ballots during a global pandemic.[97]

The incompetence and corruption described by Carlson reflects a flawed premise. Institutions contain enormous potential: They can consolidate wealth and power in authoritarian, oligarchic directions, or they can unleash the benevolence of community, markets, science, and technology to enhance the opportunity for more people to live less difficult lives.[98] In the United States, strong federal and local government, strong public schools, strong safety nets, strong courts, and strong labor unions once walled off the political and the economic, allowing a market economy to contain its most greedy impulses and facilitate the coordinated action needed for liberal democracy. Our countervailing institutions operationalized collective public action to prevent oligarchy. Through cultivated bonds of community, a collective subject urged the democratic machinery to fulfill its promises.[99] Institutional strength is obvious for the ruling elite because they are aware of the value of enjoining the state to concentrate wealth and power. Carlson does not want everyone else to realize it.

Conclusion

The policy impact of ceding political control to the ultra-rich should surprise no one. For most of the twentieth century, public policy was justified based on its impact on ordinary Americans. Had FDR ceded political influence to the du Ponts, the policy implications would be the same as Trump letting Fred Smith write our tax laws or Charles Koch enforce emissions regulations. Our oligarchic state reflects a massive divergence from the liberal democracy that transformed a thinly populated upstart of a country into the most successful and wealthiest democracy in human history.

Successfully justifying public policy based on the interests of the rich is unprecedented. But the oligarchic conquest of American democracy reflects a slow, incremental process. The ultra-rich have long sought to orient public policy in their interests, and ordinary Americans have long sought the alternative. The oligarchic conquest of liberal democracy is not a story of oligarchic rhetors like Tucker Carlson conquering American hearts and minds by brute rhetorical force, ultimately propelling Trump into the White House and Carlson into our living rooms. Rather, democratic oligarchy stokes an alternative, keeping it alive on the fringes of the political Right until social conditions make the alternative attractive to enough Americans. The economy and social crises of the Long Sixties prompted many Americans to reconsider the core assumptions of liberal democracy, especially the value of justifying policy based on its impact on ordinary Americans. When they did, Tucker Carlson was ready.

Conclusion

The Oligarchy We Deserve

IN 1941, LOUIS D. BRANDEIS WARNED, "WE CAN HAVE DEMOCRACY IN this country, or we can have great concentrated wealth in the hands of a few, but we can't have both." Brandeis's warning has become an intuitive, patriotic, and inspiring part of the American progressive narrative. If concentrated wealth comes from malfeasance, corruption, or untoward political influence, we expect democracy to course correct. Indeed, American democracy can be dangerous for those who pursue unjust political influence because our democracy contains revolutionary potential threatening those invested in upholding unjust power hierarchies.[1] In *Undoing the Demos*, Wendy Brown says that because it is "the only political form permitting us to all share in the powers by which we are governed," democracy maintains the potential for power to be wielded on "behalf of the many, rather than the few."[2] Between 1930 and 1980, American liberal democracy did just that. But between 1980 and 2020, oligarchic trends highlighted the contingent capacity of American liberal democracy for political and economic disjuncture among the state and ordinary Americans.[3] The oligarchic dimensions of American liberal democracy force us to concede that democracy's potentiality is not always realized.[4] The steady ascent of democracy is as much a narrative of retraction and contraction as of forward progress and expansion.[5] As it turns out, wealth can be concentrated into the hands of a few, and a tiny fraction of the ultra-rich can reorient the political economy toward their interests. In fact, the acquisition and concentration of elite wealth can be embedded in our democratic system.[6] Since 1980, the highest income tax bracket was cut in half, minimum wage has not kept up with inflation, loopholes in the tax code were passed into law to protect the ultra-rich and their inherited wealth, the repeal of Glass-Steagall eliminated federal oversight of investment banking, and the Supreme Court's *Citizens United* decision opened up the floodgates for the wealthy to influence campaigns and elections.[7] As a result, political shifts allowed the ultra-rich to tear down the wall separating the economic from the political. Rather than seek to further the public interest, the rules of the game have been perversely optimized to benefit the entrenched interests of the ultra-rich.[8]

As evidence of democratic oligarchy's stunning rhetorical conquest, a recent trove of empirical evidence has highlighted the fact that economic elites have a far greater chance of influencing policy in their interests than ordinary Americans. "Not only do ordinary citizens not have uniquely substantial power over policy decisions," Gilens and Page write, "they have little or no independent influence on policy at all."[9] The preferences of ordinary Americans, they continue, "appear to have only a minuscule, near-zero, statistically non-significant impact upon public policy."[10] In *Billionaires and Stealth Politics*, Page, Seawright and Lacombe affirm the influence of the ultra-rich, noting that "when one statistically takes account of what affluent Americans and organized interest groups want from government, the average American's wishes appear to have virtually *no* influence on policy making at all."[11] While their inquiry focused on affluent multimillionaires, the next logical link in the chain is clear: If multimillionaires have more influence on policy than ordinary Americans do, then billionaires likely have even more.[12]

What's more, the preferences of affluent Americans set public policy even when their preferences contradict the desires of most people. Public arguments during the Trump presidency were marked by this concern, but the empirical data affirmed these peculiar implications long before 2016. Multimillionaires and billionaires tend to devote their tremendous resources toward policies that sharply diverge from those that benefit ordinary Americans, including shifting federal income tax rates into regressive payroll taxes, repealing the estate tax, reducing capital gains and personal and corporate income taxes, opposing carbon taxes, giving preferential treatment to capital income over labor income, cutting Social Security benefits, championing austerity measures aimed at reducing entitlement programs, obliterating unions and workers' rights, fighting against efforts to raise the minimum wage, dismantling health insurance, and supporting self-serving immigration policies. In each case, economic elites actively support public policy in their interests.[13]

As an example of affluent Americans enriching themselves through political means, consider the link between the lack of market competition and licensing.[14] Lawyers, dentists, and doctors enjoy inflated incomes because of occupational licensing, for example. Licensing does ensure quality care, protect customers, and limit ambulance chasing and quacks selling snake oil.[15] But licensing is also a wonderful example of *rent-extraction*.[16] Licensing laws allow the government to influence the market by restricting the supply of doctors, dentists, and lawyers and inflating demand for their services. Medical doctors and their associations deploy the strong arm of the government to limit competition, restricting the number of available positions at medical schools and residencies, the number of foreign-trained doctors, and the role of nurses. Likewise, lawyers rely on the American Bar Association and its support from the government to manipulate the market. Dentists rely on legal restrictions limiting what dental hygienists can do to make sure they are protected from cheaper competition. Thomas Philippon described such efforts as a perfect way for wealthy lawyers, dentists, and doctors to protect rents because threatening upstarts are excluded from competition.[17]

Large corporations in the financial, pharmaceutical, software, and entertainment industries rely on the government for monopoly rent extraction.[18] For major pharmaceutical companies like GlaxoSmithKline, the government protects drug patents to prevent the release of less expensive generics. The US government played a vital role in getting Apple into Asian markets during the 1980s. And as global competition increases for companies like Apple, they rely on the US government to implement and support intellectual property laws all over the world. As Mariana Mazzucato writes, "The added protection created for Apple by local and federal authorities continues to provide this form of subsidy, which allows the company to continue innovating."[19] Energy subsidies, access to public lands, government contracts and permits, and favorable tax laws determine which extractive industries thrive.[20] Intellectual property laws and federal R&D determine which technology companies thrive. Google and Apple spend more money on lawyers litigating and acquiring patents than on R&D. Patent protections also determine which drug makers thrive. Occupational licensing determines which health care companies thrive. Franchise fees determine which cable operators and internet providers thrive. Even car dealers, hospitals, and funeral homes thrive or wilt based on government regulations shielding them from competition.[21] But most ordinary Americans must face the cold rationalities of the market alone. Home health care aids, along with retail and food service workers, cannot enjoin the government like the affluent can. As a result, ordinary Americans earn much less than their government-protected counterparts, and they remain in the middle of international pay rankings, far below American doctors, lawyers, and dentists, who earn much more than their peers outside the United States.[22]

The pragmatic impact of oligarchic policy can begin to make plain that democratic oligarchy is terrible for (almost) everyone. Between 1970 and 2020, income gains almost exclusively went to the ultra-rich.[23] As a way to limit threats, incumbent drug, finance, and energy companies deploy an army of lawyers and lobbyists to acquire competitors before they reach the market.[24] Industry leaders and entrenched corporations are less threatened by new competition. Fewer upstart competitors threaten market share because higher barriers of entry keep them out.[25] Entrenched incumbents leverage their political power to limit competition and lobby politicians to protect their rents.[26] As a result, capital markets in the United States are now less competitive than in Europe.[27]

The ultra-rich have manipulated political processes to enrich and entrench themselves and concurrently created a less dynamic, less productive American economy. Ordinary Americans end up paying higher prices for inferior goods and services, with fewer high-quality options. Customers are paying higher prices for fewer choices, including broadband internet access, hearing aids, and prescription drugs. Worker pay has been dampened and freedom to change jobs restricted. Philippon even put a dollar figure on the lack of fair competition, suggesting that American households lose more than $5,000 a year because of lower wages and higher prices.

The results are bleak but not surprising. Because we have allowed the wealthy to control politics, they have reoriented the state in their interests, and they justify their efforts by assuming all of us would do the same if we could. Ruling elites deploy their resources to influence candidates and campaigns in their interest; those policies make them even richer. The ruling elite then have more potential to influence politics in favorable directions. Economic power through political manipulations has become self-sustaining.[28]

The lack of competition is harming the economy's dynamism and vitality. In his 2019 book *The Great Reversal*, Philippon described in rich, empirical detail a less innovative and competitive American economy marked by a sustained decline in entry and exit rates of factories, stores, and firms.[29] Fewer new American businesses are starting in this century compared to last, and existing businesses have slowed their pace of hiring.[30] Corporations are also investing less in new equipment and buildings. But because the economy is less dynamic, large corporations can buy up smaller competitors before they can bring threatening products to market.[31] "Large corporations are often able to increase profits not by providing better products than their rivals but instead by being so big that they exercise power over workers and consumers," David Leonhardt writes.[32] Philippon concedes that we do not know exactly why our economy is less dynamic. It could be that all the innovative ideas are gone. Or it could be that "declining competition and rising barriers to entry have allowed incumbents to rest on their laurels."[33] As a result, wealth is now the result of distorting markets, restricting free and fair competition, and using political influence to entrench advantages. In other words, *politics* is making life harder for most Americans and easier for the ultra-rich. Our political system entrenches the elite and slows American productivity, growth, and dynamism.

Although oligarchy is not unique to the United States, no other advanced industrial country is experiencing its impact to the same degree.[34] Consider Philippon's description of oligarchy's impact on American citizens: "Most U.S. domestic markets have become less competitive, and U.S. firms charge excessive prices to U.S. consumers. Excess profits are used to pay out dividends and to buy back shares, not to hire and invest. At the same time, barriers to entry have increased, and antitrust enforcement has weakened. These trends in the U.S. were not exported to Europe, and, in a stunning reversal of history, many European markets (airlines, cell phones, and internet providers, among others) are now more competitive and cheaper than their American counterparts."

Wealth and power now work together. The ruling elite have more potential to influence politics in favorable conditions. Acquiring wealth through political machinations has become a self-reinforcing process.[35] A vicious cycle begins and, like a snowball going down a hill, economic power gathers force from political power gathering force from economic power. Ultimately, although Brandeis's warning was intuitive, patriotic, and inspiring, it was also inaccurate. We can have democracy and great concentrations of wealth; we can have a political economy marked by the ultra-rich manipulating the government to defend and enhance their material wealth; we can have a democratic oligarchy.

American Oligarchy

For the ultra-rich, the capacity to use the state to pursue personal interest is a shameless consequence of conforming to natural law. Economic turmoil, military interventions, and the global pandemic caused by COVID-19 are understood to be opportunities for the deserved to capitalize on state interventions into the economy.[36] For example, George Packer pointed out how Kelly Loeffler, then a Republican senator from Georgia, capitalized on her position and became even richer by selling off her stocks shortly after she received insider information not yet available to the general public in an eye-opening private briefing about the threat of the oncoming COVID-19 pandemic.[37] Democratic oligarchy mediates any shame that may arise from Loeffler's ethically compromised position: Loeffler deserves the privileged information from the private briefing because she was a US senator; she was a senator because she was rich; and she was rich because she deserved to be. You would do the same if you could.

Like its approach to the market, democratic oligarchy demands a selective allegiance to majoritarian democracy. Since the Trump presidency, public argument and opinion polls reflect deep concerns about the continued viability of representative democracy in America. More specifically, the political Right in America expresses hostility, not just to democratic principles like maximizing equality and universal participation but also increasingly to the word "democracy" itself, Robert Draper argues.[38] But productive dialogue remains elusive without discerning the influence of democratic oligarchy. For example, Evan Osnos argues that Mitch McConnell bothered "less and less with the gestures of democracy" as the influential senator from Kentucky reshaped America's courts according to his conservative outlook. Osnos points to McConnell halting Merrick Garland's Supreme Court nomination process as an example. For shattering democratic norms, McConnell's opponents hoped he would be punished by Kentucky voters. He was not. McConnell suffered no political cost because Kentucky voters are constituted by an alternative moral framework prioritizing the raw exercise of power over all else. Like Kelly Loeffler, McConnell did what he did because he could. Any gesture toward democratic deliberation and argumentative consistency justifying his actions during Garland's nomination disappeared after Ruth Bader Ginsburg died before the 2016 election and McConnell rushed to fill the seat. He articulated democratic oligarchy's alternative moral framework when, in 2019, he was speaking to a roomful of supporters in Kentucky and was asked if roles were reversed and he had the chance to fill a Court vacancy with a Republican nominee, he told the crowd, "Oh, we'll fill it." The room responded with hearty laughter.[39]

Concerns about the viability of majoritarian democracy are also evident in public conversations about state legislatures, including reporting from North Carolina and Wisconsin detailing the breakdown of liberal democracy. GOP officials in North Carolina "offer a glimpse of democracy shorn of liberal constraints" as they "exploited the power of the legislature" in 2015 to concentrate power within their party, according to Gershberg and Illing.[40] In Wisconsin, countermajoritarian machinations allowed conservative lawmakers to disregard the interests of half the voters in an evenly split state and, instead, gain iron-clad control of political power in the State Supreme Court, State Senate, and Wisconsin State Assembly. Countermajoritarian influence came to a head in Wisconsin after the Supreme Court's *Dobbs* ruling limiting the constitutional right to an abortion. The state legislature was able to decide what to do about such a fraught and unsettled public policy without considering the interests of the majority of citizens. In North Carolina and Wisconsin, countermajoritarian influence in these examples reflects a version of democracy unhinged from an ethics of prudence and forbearance.[41] But like Mitch McConnell in Kentucky, state legislators in Wisconsin and North Carolina did not suffer any consequences from breaking democratic norms because enough people in each state simply did not prioritize an ethics of prudence and forbearance. Democratic oligarchy illuminates a source of rhetorical invention that can explain why.

Finally, Donald Trump's perspective on the form and function of the state remains incomprehensible apart from democratic oligarchy. Democracy is an inventional resource for Trump, offering support for him and his policies when he wins elections and evidence of fraud and corruption when he does not. For Trump and his supporters, defeat contradicts the natural order. This is why Trump never admits defeat and also why he was never held to account for espousing an obviously false, self-serving, and childish reaction to any competition he enters. In 2012, Trump claimed political bias kept *The Apprentice* from winning an Emmy. In 2016, Trump claimed fraud explained his loss to Ted Cruz in the Iowa caucuses; and then later, he anticipated fraud would explain his loss to Hillary Clinton in the general election. Trump's fears disappeared after he won. In 2020, after losing to Joe Biden, Trump claimed he actually "won in a landslide" and he rage tweeted about "Massive Voter Fraud in the 2020 Presidential Election Scam," alleging that voting machines fraudulently stole the election. "We have an election that was stolen from us. It was a landslide election, and everyone knows it, especially the other side," he said on January 6, 2021, in a video to supporters.[42] He was not alone. On Twitter and in public speeches, his allies reflected a similar democratic appeal. Kevin McCarthy said, "President Trump won this election. So everyone who's listening, do not be quiet. Do not be silent about this."[43] Mike Pence said, "I'll make you this promise; we're going to keep fighting until every legal vote is counted!"[44] But notice what is left out of these arguments: Trump and his allies never justify power concentration based on Trump's individual qualities alone. He never admits, for example, that he lost but Trump should be president anyway. Trump never repudiates his allegiance to democracy; his concern is with its corruption. There is no other way to explain how the superior could lose.

The state is charged with intervening on behalf of the superior and restoring order and justice, just as it is charged with intervening in the market when necessary. Notice how Trump's claims of democratic injustice have sparked renewed forms of civic participation to ensure the state is reoriented accordingly. Such efforts complicate expressed concerns about the decline of democracy in public argument. Robert Draper, of the *New York Times Magazine*, interviewed an Arizonian voicing concerns about democracy while attending a candidate forum hosted by the "Republican Women of the Hills." Trump's false claims about invalidating ballots motivated another Arizonian to greet every voter outside the voting center at the Cottonwood Bible Church with ballpoint pens he bought with his own money. "I know they were passing out the felt-tip pens last election and not all the votes counted," the man said, referring to the disproved claim that election workers in Maricopa County sought to invalidate Republican ballots in 2020 by forcing voters to use Sharpies. "I just wanted to do my part," the man told Draper.[45] Draper also described three senior citizens who, after taking inspiration from the specious documentary *2000 Mules* featuring disproven claims about fraudulently stuffed ballot boxes, brought their folding chairs to monitor their county's voting box in a grocery parking lot.[46] Concerned Trump supporters also ran for parliamentarian positions in local and county elections and secretary of state positions all over the country, in what can charitably be described as an effort to ensure injustice does not prevail again—like they believe it did in 2020.[47] Trump and his supporters never relinquished democracy as their source of rhetorical invention.

Consider antithetical examples, like the Oath Keepers' efforts to attack the US Capitol on January 6, former national security advisor Michael Flynn calling for the imposition of martial law after the election, and the six men in Michigan, inspired by the boogaloo movement on the Internet, who plotted to kidnap Michigan governor Gretchen Whitmer.[48] Each reflected larger historical patterns in which democracy is an impediment to justice. In his public messaging, Trump toed the line, but he never crossed it. Gershberg and Illing note that after Trump beat Hillary Clinton in 2016, his victory speech was filled with gracious platitudes affirming liberal-democratic norms, including passages praising Hillary Clinton for "serving her country well" and promises to "reach out to all who didn't vote for him."[49] In the video Trump tweeted out on January 6, 2021, after the US Capitol was attacked by his supporters, Trump repeated stale election fraud concerns. But he also said, "You have to go home now; we have to have peace. We have to have law and order."[50] Evan Osnos interviewed several Trump supporters at the Capitol that day, showing the vexed relationship between political violence and political rhetoric. Osnos quoted a man in a MAGA hat who, surveying the damage, told him, "They sent a message. That's enough." He turned to walk away and added, "Of course, if we come back, it will be with a militia."[51] Osnos asked another supporter if the violence at the Capitol was an example of taking things too far. She responded, "Whose house is this? This is the house of 'We the People.' If you do a bad job, your boss tells you about it." She nodded toward the Senate, where the elected officials had already evacuated to safety: "We're not happy with the job you've done." She drew a distinction between the scene in front of her and the domain of enemies she called "Antifa and BLM," who, she said, have "no true aim except destruction and anarchy."[52]

Redressing Democratic Oligarchy

Although my primary aim has been theorizing the rhetorical representations and affective modalities conducive to democratic oligarchy's emergence, I would like to consider as I close some pragmatic steps for redressing these oligarchic trends. Because democratic oligarchy represents an economic challenge, scholars and journalists have proposed a set of ambitious, macroeconomic interventions, such as breaking up the banks, tech monopolies, airlines, financial services and telecommunication companies, and pharmaceutical industries. Anti-oligarchic interventions could also pursue new antitrust policies, empower more workers to bargain collectively, raise the minimum wage, expand health care, restrict licensing, and modify corporate governance structures.[53]

Those interested in redressing the oligarchic trends in American liberal democracy must also focus on the upstream interventions influencing the downstream political efforts. More specifically, before the banks can be broken up, the concentration of political power among an oligarchic class must be broken up, including efforts to reduce the influence of ultra-rich donations in political campaigns, increase voter representation in non-elite demographics, tighten lobbying laws, and reduce the democratic unrepresentativeness of the US Senate, the two major political parties, and the presidential election.[54] American liberal democracy protects minority rights, including those of billionaires. In turn, efforts to restrict the oligarchic influence of the ultra-rich cannot infringe on Fred Smith and Charles Koch's First Amendment rights. However, efforts to reduce the affluent's ability to exert boundary control are more conceivable. Exchanging gerrymandered political districts for independent and bipartisan election commissions and implementing open primary and ranked choice voting could diffuse the potency of ultra-rich donations in local and state elections. Increased voter turnout during off-year election cycles could be expanded through access to mail-in voting and automatic voter registration. Page, Seawright, and Lacombe also highlight the federal government's unique administrative units, like the Federal Election Commission and the Security and Exchange Commission, as mechanisms that can make the stealth politics of oligarchs less stealthy.[55] Instead of trying to redress oligarchic influence at the state level, legislatively or judicially, enhanced transparency requirements administered by the Federal Election Commission may spark more public efforts to organize, agitate, and mobilize in a way that encourages the ultra-rich to refrain from oligarchic practices because they could be punished by their customers. Without violating the First Amendment, enhanced transparency through political disclosure requirements could force oligarchs to publicly justify their political involvement.

Pragmatic political interventions must be built atop a reconceptualized representation of the nation-state. Public argument must reflect the potentiality of the federal government to respond to the interests of ordinary Americans against the interests of the oligarchic class by emphasizing the multiple logics of the state. Michael Lewis popularized this reconceptualization in his bestselling book *The Fifth Risk*. American democracy is replete with what Barrow calls "islands of administrative expertise" capable of administering social programs functioning through a weak institutional design but still capable of leveraging the state's unique capacity to raise tax revenue and redistribute resources against the interests of oligarchic forces, including programs such as Social Security, Pell Grants, and Medicaid.

In the end, we have the oligarchy we deserve. Government decides policy. Markets do not exist in a vacuum. Oligarchic policies are terrible for almost everyone, but the ultra-rich influence public policy more than ordinary Americans because we have allowed it. We have allowed it because we so often equate wealth and general mastery. We have adopted a worldview linking oligarchic wealth and advanced human development and knowledge with the capacity to control political and economic systems. Indeed, material wealth can be evidence of advanced skills and abilities. But material wealth can also evince the antithesis. Wealth can distort reality, judgment, and character, rending otherwise ordinary people unfit for making wise decisions and influencing public policy.

But the ultra-rich do not rule by fiat. The arguments and policies detailed here are the result of the ultra-rich struggling successfully against a democratic system hostile to their desires.[56] From that perspective, oligarchy policies reflect a stunning rhetorical conquest because oligarchic policies are achieved by persuading individuals who do not share their class origins or enjoy their material rewards.

And yet, the history of American liberal democracy offers hope. Democratic oligarchy is not inevitable. In the mid-twentieth century, Americans exerted the political will to reject public policies oriented toward the ruling elite. We raised taxes on the rich, protected labor, closed tax loopholes, and used the additional revenue to improve the safety net, education, and health care.[57] A democratic feedback loop resulted. Strong institutions enhanced collective engagement to reorient the state away from the interests of the elite. Middle- and working-class Americans used the legal and political potential to redress these allocation differences. We could do all this because the democratic arithmetic was on our side. It still is. And with the arithmetic on our side, we can do it again. But because we cannot contest what we cannot name, it is my hope that democratic oligarchy can emerge in public conversations to describe an American political economy the ultra-rich would prefer remains unnamed.

Acknowledgments

FOR THEIR SUPPORT, GENEROSITY, AND WISE COUNSEL, I WANT TO ACknowledge and thank Bill Whitaker, Joshua Hanan, Kevin Musgrave, Heather Canary, Brian Spitzberg, Alec Baker, George Dionosopolous, Kara Bauer, Allie Doherty, David Schlueter, Blair Browning, Aaron Zimmerman, Andrew Armond, Rachel Toomes, Steve Taylor, Robert Asen, John Lucaites, Andrew Ishak, Matthew Schreiner, and Barry Brummett.

This book is an outgrowth of being in a community of smart and supportive people at San Diego State University, Baylor University, the National Communication Association, and the Rhetoric Society of America. The feedback I received from the conference submission and the manuscript review process improved this book immensely. I cannot name my reviewers, but I am indebted to those in my community who are willing to selflessly (and anonymously) share their erudition and insight with me. I can acknowledge and thank Dan Waterman, Joanna Jacobs, and Penelope Cray and the reviewers and editorial board at the University of Alabama Press for the thoughtful guidance, robust feedback, and unwavering faith in the project.

My parents, Dale and Karen Winslow, and my siblings, Karmelle and Ben, continue to provide an abundance of love, wisdom, and guidance. Finally, to my wife, Addie, and my children, William, Benjamin, and Owen: thank you for your support, inspiration, and boundless joy.

Appendix

Theorizing Democratic Oligarchy

Rhetorical criticism can take seriously the oligarchic dimensions of American democracy. Democracy and oligarchy are tensional, sustained through political systems, laws and policies, and forms of life ordered by structural contradictions buried inside their symbolic resources, lines of argument, and discursive forms.[1] Democracy and oligarchy operate simultaneously as entailments and contradictions, because democracy, as a functional form of collective self-government, must concede governing power to the elites. But tensions emerge whenever a direct democracy expands beyond a small community and begins to grapple with who is best suited to represent the people. Engels described the tensions that result when political leaders begin to live *off politics* rather than *for politics*, because power's hubristic and arrogant pull urges elites to focus on their interests and become unresponsive toward those they govern.[2] Tensions and contradictions offer the critic rare moments of insight via discursive analysis of reconciliation.[3] In turn, the methodological approach I take reflects a synthesis of three branches of rhetorical studies: ideological criticism, public address, and economic rhetoric.

Kenneth Burke sets the course for this methodological program through what he calls "the charting of human motives."[4] Although incongruity is the law of the universe, symbol-using humans are equipped to manage incongruity without coercion and violence through discursive reconciliation.[5] As Burke writes, "We must name the friendly and unfriendly functions and relationships in such a way that we are able to do something about them. In naming them, we form our characters, since the names embody attitudes; and implicit in the attitudes there are cues of behaviors."[6] Lingering incongruities force us to "symbolically erect a higher synthesis" of conceptual imagery well-suited for the most complicated and pressing incongruities, especially those related to big questions concerning power, politics, and resources.[7]

Rather than avoiding the minefield, rhetors seek out incongruities therein, exploiting them as sources of rhetorical invention. According to Burke, influential rhetors, including speakers, writers, poets, philosophers, and scientists, act in the code of the names by which they simplify and interpret reality. Rhetors name, and as they do, they shape social relations, prepare people to respond for or against the world, and instruct *how* you "should be for or against" the world.[8] The rhetor's symbolism builds the mental equipment by which an audience drawn into community by discourse is equipped to make sense of the world and reconcile incongruity.[9] Naming allows abstractions like class, authority, and freedom to function discursively as the "concrete symbol deputized for an abstraction," according to Burke.[10] Burke describes the poet's linguistic selectivity as being akin to affecting a man with a tic who "squints and jerks when some words are spoken, and other wise not."[11] We interpret the historical situation and adapt to it through organized systems of meaning called "frames of acceptance."[12] Frames of acceptance urge us to accept some interpretations and reject others. In this way, frames of acceptance "prepare us for combat and draw the lines of a battle."[13] Burke cites Karl Marx, who developed a frame designed to accept the inevitability of class conflict.[14] In a similar manner, Ayn Rand's Objectivism functioned as a frame for accepting the suspicion of centralized authority and William Buckley's mid-century conservatism functioned as a frame for viewing government and freedom in an incommensurate relationship.[15]

The critic is expected to disclose the symbolic organization of the tic by finding the class of words that provides it.[16] Rhetorical scholars have built on Burke's critical formulations. McGee, for example, encourages critics to study discursive usage patterns to understand how communities use rhetorical discourse.[17] Lee showed that because rhetoric precedes action, the critic can find fodder for examination like an archeologist uses a shovel: through unearthing political language, including popular narratives, dominant lines of argument, and the god and devil terms characterizing the historical moment.[18] Discourse is the communally specific collection of rhetorical resources through which symbolic diversity can yield potency and flexibility. Shared symbol systems hold communities together, teaching communities how to talk and think.[19] The critic pays attention to words because words reveal attitudes, how the rhetor sees the world, and most importantly for my focus on economic-political rhetors, "how he imagines the relationship between speaker and audience," as Engels wrote.[20] For the critic, for whom words are equipment, the goal is to build out rhetorical theory through an inductive process of analyzing and cataloging symbolic resources.[21]

Burke is again useful for describing how public vocabularies do not exert influence in a vacuum but instead through "the dialectic interaction of mental and material factors."[22] Burke describes how rhetors "can even coach the language, deliberately inventing new abstractions" as a resource to be "cashed in on" by a rhetor.[23] Burke points out that if the community's doxa is marked by a belief that it is wrong to murder a friend, then a poet can "cash in on" this symbolic influence, as Shakespeare did in depicting relations between Brutus and Caesar in *Julius Caesar*.[24] Burke also notes the emergence of a "bureaucratization of sterile cleanliness emerging just as the desire for birth control gained favor."[25] Beyond conceptualizations of rational symbolic instrumentalism, the links among social systems, customs, and democratic governance highlight the role of biopolitical influence in democratic oligarchy.[26]

Accordingly, to theorize democratic oligarchy requires mapping the formal principles of oligarchic governing logics onto American democracy to explore how public consent is gathered and maintained. I use the term "formal" on purpose. Burke developed *form* to explain how audiences are influenced through sensibilities, as well as word choice.[27] James Aune built on Burke's form by describing the resulting impact as a "material force" that creates an appetite in the minds of the audience.[28] Aune links language, form, and materiality when he writes that "when one hears the first clause of the antithesis, one feels compelled to complete the figure with the second clause."[29] Consider the sound that functions to situate, evoke, and persuade when we turn on our computers or the unique audio blast that accompanies the beginning of an HBO television program.[30] We involuntarily jump to our feet when we witness an incredible feat of athleticism because we are physiologically oriented toward affective responses that are shaped through experience.[31] Affect, language, and cognition are inseparable.[32] A phrase like "Support the ____" may be filled in with a word like "troops" for many Americans but less so for Costa Ricans, perhaps, who do not maintain a standing army. "Support the ____" could also be filled with a word like "union" or "Seahawks" depending on one's worldview. Expanding our critical focus to include language and ideology, and also making room for the more open-ended and instinctual orientations influencing our political economic activity, offers a more nuanced and coherent explanation for the modern American political economy.[33] More specifically, an exploration of democratic oligarchy cannot be limited to human beings, their cultural representations, or political structures.[34] At the same time, moving beyond theoretical abstraction also requires exploring how affect is symbolically constructed and discursively maintained.[35] Joshua Gunn articulates the critical nuance required when he concedes "social, political, and cultural influence today is not necessarily by the mouth or pen of a particular person." But because sense making is influenced by subtle vocabularies and unconscious structures, scholars of rhetoric are well-equipped to theorize the influential potential of economic rhetoric through discourse analysis.[36]

Burke describes the "critical formulations" enabling the rhetorician to access an analytic set of tools for reassembling what the rhetor has taken apart. The result, according to Burke, is the disclosing of the content of a symbol so as to disclose its function—a very consequentialist approach to criticism that I will develop in the next chapter.[37] Burke urges the critic to begin with the end in mind, orienting their critical tools toward inductive theory building and the elucidation of the symbol's pragmatic political function.

Since the 1970s, rhetorical scholars have applied their tools to economic issues first, exploring how rational deliberations allow economic actors to make decisions based on thoughtful assessments of evidence.[38] Rhetorical criticism is well-suited to exploring the symbolic and discursive influence of economic discourse, revealing how economic policy uses public messaging to flatten our economic ontology.[39] The ontology of democratic oligarchy, especially the state's positive but undertheorized interventions, relies on a modality that can be discursively tracked through symbolic and discursive appeals.[40] Given this approach, the telos of economic rhetoric was to access an economic reality marked by coherent internal logic.[41] Deirdre McCloskey and the Project on the Rhetoric of Inquiry (POROI) evinces rhetoric's epistemic instrumentalism by attributing the conquest of modern economics in the West to effective rhetorical representations.[42] McCloskey argues that the rhetoric of economists and policymakers contains the key to understanding how economic decisions are made.

However, because the world is not organized by an all-powerful, top-down instrumentalism, rhetorical potency must be understood as constituted discourse.[43] Modern rhetoricians have, as a result, shifted the critical focus from referential to constituted analysis. But the urgency of this shift is magnified for critics interested in economic rhetoric because the subjectivities urged by governing logics—like democratic oligarchy—transcend the rational deliberation of political and economic argument.

And so, my approach is also informed by ideological rhetorical scholars, who in the last forty years have explored how ideas and language construct a false consciousness according to the reality of the rulers who espouse it.[44] Modern economic rhetoric, therefore, focuses on how consciousness is reabsorbed into the material world to align with affective realities, an assumption that has inspired a tradition of ideological criticism focused on the ideological relationship between language and capitalism. The approach of scholars like Michael McGee, James Aune, and Dana Cloud assumes that many Americans are not critical consumers of economic discourse and policy, and because such consumption guides behaviors—at the supermarket and the voting booth—economic rhetoric research can explore how habits are shaped beyond rational thought and so enlighten the public out of their false consciousness.

And yet, without accounting for deeper structures of feeling, consciousness-raising efforts can lead to a dead end, because ideological criticism of economic rhetoric too often assumes that audience energy and action hinge on the strength of the argument.[45] Chaput points out "a futility in this consciousness raising" as "one belief system gives way to another ad infinitum, preventing the actuality of a nonideological worldview. Even as we learn to see things differently, our practices resist adjusting to that knowledge, doing so inconsistently and at a snail's pace."[46] Melissa Gregg reminds us that there are "visceral forces beneath, alongside, or generally other than conscious knowing" that serve to drive us toward movement, toward thought and extension. David Fleming reminds us that rhetoric can operate "independent of and prior to human agency" and thus, at times, is "insusceptible to reason" and "*outside* of our control." Diane Davis warns against focusing on individual reason as the origin of public argument and instead develops the term "rhetoricity" to describe how political and economic thought can "precede and exceed symbolic intervention." Cintron describes how language can formally resonate through "storehouses" of energy that exert influence independent of its "sign-nature."[47] In *Ambient Rhetorics*, Rickert highlights how environments unconsciously prime our dispositions. Longaker suggests that "once the environment changes" and people adapt accordingly, then "social organisms will evolve."[48] Likewise, the most influential economic rhetors seem to have understood how misguided it was to assume that symbolic interventions alone would shape public argument. Milton Friedman understood that public opinion changes when people instinctively embrace policy changes already circulating in public conversations—a task that can be initiated and accelerated by enterprising economic rhetors.[49] Hayek believed that our individual opinions about the political economy are not the result of logical processes but represent the "conscious residue of a larger unconscious ordering process."[50] Our environment can prime our outlook—often unconsciously.[51] In other words, rather than focusing only on someone like Fred Smith and his oratorical abilities, we must explore how oligarchic rhetoric can influence a political reality, shape an environment, narrow a definition, and plead a cause.

But where to look and what to look for? Michael Lee's work on mining the canon of conservatism offers a path to follow. He analyzes a set of conservative texts that "acquired long lives as each was transported from its original context" and in the process were made ripe for rhetorical analysis.[52] Canonical texts offer instruction on *how* to take a position: forming identity construction based on ideology, logic, and style.[53] Political language is essential to the public performance of identity, and so conservatives mined the canon for lessons on lean government and individual freedom.[54] But "the canon" is not a metaphysical end point because "the canon" is contingent and fluid; some texts fall out of favor while others are rediscovered based not only on the demands of the moment but on their ability to function as potent sites of rhetorical invention. Lee illustrated the contingency of the canon when he noted that after the 2008 Great Recession, libertarian Tea Party activists mined Hayek's *The Road to Serfdom* and prominent conservative media personalities like Glenn Beck and Rush Limbaugh tussled over who loved Hayek first.[55]

The standards of methodological rigor in rhetorical studies are met by offering the reader an abundance of discursive evidence. As Kenneth Burke writes, analytical findings cease to be tenuous and dubious "only when backed with internal evidence" that meets standards of plausibility.[56] Accordingly, the critic looks for patterns, not inflective and fleeting arguments, based on frequency, durability, and formal coherence. Burke urges the critic to analyze the rhetor's "modes of summing up," which manifest patterns corresponding to the rhetor's motive.[57]

Beyond words, the critic needs to pay attention to the rhetor's personal story. Engels notes that ethos is "integral to persuasion" and that it is vital for rhetorical critics to consider the public discourse in relation to the rhetor's broader biography.[58] The oligarchic rhetors are marked by shared traits: They are highly accomplished, arrogant, and passionate true believers. Their public arguments betray these traits. But additionally, the aesthetic dimensions of public presentation will be considered. Aesthetic style is a critical tool that can be employed to uncover ethos, by way of analyzing clothing, trapping, and grooming.[59] Style combines logical appeals with an emotional defense of a discrete political identity. More specifically, the oligarchic rhetors under examination can be organized stylistically by what Lessl calls a priestly ethos, including the unique ability to mediate realities that are inaccessible to others, containing essentially religious properties, and to receive and interpret sacred signs.[60]

And yet, I do not assume a provocative rhetor, argument, or concept is imposed on an audience through a single text capable of moving the audience to a particular predefined and inevitable outcome. Nor am I exploring the featured rhetors merely because I find their pragmatic political influence distasteful. Instead, in the preceding, I position these rhetors and their arguments in relation to larger cultural vocabularies made accessible by observing their material, historical, and empirical effects.[61] I then work backward to build theory by analyzing the rhetorical provocations and affective circularities reconciling the paradoxical dimensions of American democracy.[62]

I feature a discrete rhetor in each chapter, but I draw a distinction between a biographical or historical account of a flesh-and-blood human being and what I call a "textual persona."[63] This approach affirms a basic understanding of text and textuality across the humanities. While *text* implies a written or spoken document, rhetoricians tend to use the term "text" to explain how a public figure can be "read off," in Brummett's words, to illuminate sources of symbolic action within specific cultural moments.[64] In the previous chapters, there is a human presence saturating a text, and each rhetor performs and constructs a role, but always in dynamic interaction with an audience and a context.[65] Each rhetor, in other words, may appear to be donning a mask, like a stage actor, but in reality, their ability to exert agentic force is always mediated by a complex confluence of cultural dynamics and audience constitutive capacities. Organizing each chapter as an exploration of a textual persona will also prevent me from, in Michel Foucault's words, fetishizing "the author."[66] Instead, I position the rhetor and his arguments as nodes through which discourse is co-constituted in a contingent and dynamic way.

Emphasizing the textual persona will also highlight the critic's role in establishing the textual parameters of an object of inquiry.[67] I concede disagreements between some of the extant literature in economic rhetoric and my forthcoming analysis. I will note these disagreements in an effort to highlight how our existing critical vocabulary may be limiting our analytic capacities. I will also note disagreements in how rhetors are positioned along our ideological axis, how terms like "free market" and "small government" are leading to imprecise analysis, and where I think the criteria for empirical and scientific economic research is muddled.[68] In so doing, what I hope to show is that the public arguments and affective modalities of the most influential voices in political economy reflect democratic oligarchy as an underexplored yet politically urgent governing rationale. To put it another way, the extant literature on economic rhetoric reflects a bias toward preexisting conceptualizations of political economy, including conservatism, libertarianism, and neoliberalism. I want to introduce my own bias to the scholarly conversation: Democratic oligarchy reflects an important gap. And so, I set out to detail the discursive origins and pragmatic effects of democratic oligarchy and present that evidence to the reader in an effort to thicken the rhetorical landscape.

Notes

PREFACE

1. Chrystia Freeland, *Plutocrats: The Rise of the New Global Super-rich and the Fall of Everyone Else* (New York: Penguin Press, 2012), Kindle Location 149; Thomas Piketty, *Capital and Ideology* (Cambridge, MA: Belknap/Harvard University Press, 2020), Kindle Location 596.

2. Barry Brummett, "Rhetorical Theory as Heuristic and Moral: A Pedagogical Justification," *Communication Education* 33, no. 2 (1984): 97–107; Karlyn Kohrs Campbell, "Rhetorical Criticism 2009: A Study in Method," in *The Handbook of Rhetoric and Public Address*, ed. Shawn. J. Parry-Giles and J. Michael Hogan, 101 (Hoboken, NJ: Wiley-Blackwell, 2010); Thomas B. Farrell, "Practicing the Arts of Rhetoric: Tradition and Invention," *Philosophy & Rhetoric* 24, no. 3 (1991): 183–212.

3. Zac Gershberg and Sean Illing, *The Paradox of Democracy: Free Speech, Open Media, and Perilous Persuasion* (Chicago: University of Chicago Press, 2022), 270.

4. Robert Hariman, "Norms of the Rhetorical Theory," *Quarterly Journal of Speech* 80, no. 3 (1994): 329–32; Steven Pinker, *Enlightenment Now: The Case for Reason, Science, Humanism, and Progress* (New York: Viking, 2018); 83; Mary E. Stuckey, "American Elections and the Rhetoric of Political Change: Hyperbole, Anger, and Hope in U.S. Politics," *Rhetoric & Public Affairs* 20, no. 4 (2017): 667–94.

5. Jeremy Engels, *The Politics of Resentment: A Genealogy* (University Park: Pennsylvania State University Press, 2015), 118; Mark Garrett Longaker, *Rhetorical Style and the Bourgeois Virtue: Capitalism and Civil Society in the British Enlightenment* (University Park: Pennsylvania State University Press, 2015), 11.

INTRODUCTION

1. Jim Tankersley, "A Broken Promise on Taxes," *Daily* (podcast), *New York Times*, November 19, 2019, hosted by Michael Barbaro, produced by Rachel Quester and Jonathan Wolfe, and edited by Lisa Chow.

2. Tankersley, "A Broken Promise on Taxes."

3. Tankersley, "A Broken Promise on Taxes."

4. Tankersley, "A Broken Promise on Taxes."

NOTES

5. Jim Tankersley, Peter Eavis, and Ben Casselman, "How FedEx Cut Its Tax Bill to $0," November 17, 2019. Fred Smith and FedEx were not alone. As George Packer wrote, "His major legislative accomplishment, one of the largest tax cuts in history, sent hundreds of billions of dollars to corporations and the rich" ("We Are Living in a Failed State," June 2020, *Atlantic*).

6. Catherine Chaput, *Market Affect and the Rhetoric of Political Economic Debates* (Columbia: University of South Carolina Press, 2019), 18, 53; Joshua Hanan and Jeffrey St. Onge, "Beyond the Dialectic Between Wall Street and Main Street: A Materialist Analysis of *The Big Short*," *Advances in the History of Rhetoric* 21, no. 2 (2018): 166.

7. David Zarefsky, "Presidential Rhetoric and the Power of Definition," *Presidential Studies Quarterly* 34, no. 4 (2004): 610.

8. Diane Davis, *Inessential Solidarity: Rhetoric and Foreigner Relations* (Pittsburgh: University of Pittsburgh Press, 2010), 361.

9. Jeffrey A. Winters and Benjamin I. Page, "Oligarchy in the United States?" *Perspectives on Politics* 7, no. 4 (2009): 732.

10. S. M. Amadae, *Prisoners of Reason: Game Theory and Neoliberal Political Economy* (Cambridge: Cambridge University Press, 2016), 180.

11. Freeland, *Plutocrats*, Kindle Location 150.

12. Rhetorical scholars have also deployed oligarchy as a conceptual tool for explaining American democracy. Jeremy Engels detailed how "oligarchic elites employ the politics of resentment" in their quest for corporate rule (Engels, *The Politics of Resentment*, 11). Ralph Cintron affirmed the symbiotic relationship between democracy and oligarchy, dispelling the assumption that the governing systems are discrete and instead positioning oligarchy "at the dead center of democracy"; see Ralph Cintron, *Democracy as Fetish* (University Park: Pennsylvania University Press, 2020), 11–12, 45.

13. Clyde W. Barrow, *Critical Theories of the State: Marxist, Neo-Marxist, Post-Marxist* (Madison: University of Wisconsin Press, 1993), 13, 24–27; Ralph Miliband, *The State in Capitalist Society* (Pontypool, Wales: Merlin Press, 1969/2009), 193. And yet, in detailing these concrete practices, I need to be careful not to conceptualize the state as a monolithic, essential, and overdetermined force (Barrow, *Critical Theories of the State*, 76, 156). The immense political influence of the affluent, and their specific ability to deploy the state to make money, can produce a narrow, totalizing view of American democracy. A state totally dominated by elites implies a lack of autonomy for the state to act against a discrete capitalist class in the interests of ordinary Americans. Often reflected in Marxist theory, Holloway and Picciotto detail the limitations of theorizing the state as a singular mechanism for the interests of capital: the result is too often a deterministic and reductionist approach to theorizing the state; see John Holloway and Sol Picciotto, "Introduction: Toward a Materialist Theory of the State," in *State and Capital: A Marxist Debate*, ed. John Holloway and Sol Picciotto (Austin: University of Texas Press, 1978), 1; see also Miliband, *The State in Capitalist Society*, 6. Overlooked in this approach is the history of non-elites using the state to push back against the interest of the ultra-rich.

14. Barrow, *Critical Theories of the State*, 25.

15. Barrow, *Critical Theories of the State*, 17; Miliband, *The State in Capitalist Society*, 34–40.

16. Barrow, *Critical Theories of the State*, 22. This is not to suggest that oligarchy is unique to the United States. Hierarchical societies marked by centralized leadership and political inequality have always produced material inequality. From stateless primitive societies to advanced industrial economies, the primary function of social stratification has always been the redistribution and mobilization of goods and resources upward toward elites; see Timothy K. Earle and Jonathan E. Ericson, "Exchange Systems in Archaeological Perspective," in *Exchange Systems in Prehistory*, ed. Timothy K. Earle and Jonathan E. Ericson (New York: Academic Press, 1977), 10; Timothy K. Earle, "A Reappraisal of Redistribution: Complex Hawaiian Chiefdoms," in *Exchange Systems in Prehistory*, ed. Timothy K. Earle and Jonathan E. Ericson (New York: Academic Press, 1977), 213. The elite stratum in chiefdoms and primitive states were removed from production and thus depended on the mobilization of goods and services upward from the labor of nonelite populations to finance the administrative capacities of hierarchical societies in primitive economies. Centralized hierarchies, dependent on upward resource distribution, defined the archaic states of "Egypt and Babylonia, the householding activities of a medieval manor and African *kraal*, the distribution of meat in a band society, and the mobilization of goods through annual ceremonial collections in primitive Hawaiian societies," wrote Earle ("A Reappraisal," 214; 225). American democracy is not anomalous in its capacity to use centralized leadership to redistribute wealth upward.

17. Miliband, *The State in Capitalist Society*, 13.

18. Barrow, *Critical Theories of the State*, 18; Miliband, *The State in Capitalist Society*, 35.

19. Barrow, *Critical Theories of the State*, 23.

20. Miliband, *The State in Capitalist Society*, 34.

21. Corey Robin, *The Reactionary Mind: Conservatism from Edmund Burke to Donald Trump*, 2nd ed. (Oxford: Oxford University Press, 2018), 73. For more on the braiding together of economic, cultural, social, and political power, see Jamie Peck, *Constructions of Neoliberal Reason* (Oxford: Oxford University Press, 2010), 51; Thomas Philippon, *The Great Reversal: How America Gave Up on Free Markets* (Cambridge, MA: Harvard University Press, 2019), Kindle Location 2885; Ganesh Sitaraman, *The Crisis of the Middle-Class Constitution: Why Economic Inequality Threatens Our Republic* (New York: Vintage, 2017), 234; and Jeffrey A. Winters, *Oligarchy* (New York: Cambridge University Press, 2018), xiii.

22. Consider as an illustration Donald Trump's political reach, even before 2016. Trump illustrates why the amount of income separating the rich from the wealthy, or the wealthy from the oligarchic, is less relevant than the political influence wealth can leverage. Before his presidency, Trump exerted tremendous political influence. He even boasted during his 2016 campaign that his wealth ensured politicians always called him back. "That's why I give," he said. But he went bankrupt six times. And according to a *New York Times* investigation, between 1985 and 1995 Trump lost $1.17 billion. Tax records also show that Trump lost more money than almost any other American during these years—double the nearest taxpayer (Russ Buettner and Susanne Craig, "Decade in the Red: Trump Tax Figures Show

Over $1 Billion in Business Losses," *New York Times*, May 8, 2019). Almost every American had more *income* than Trump during these years, but that did not limit his oligarchic capacities. For decades, Trump used the state as a transaction tool for economic gain. As Corey Robin detailed, before he was president, Trump saw money as an instrument of state power and state power as a vehicle to make more money (Robin, *The Reactionary Mind*, 260). Some of these mechanisms positioned Trump on the conventional political Right, including efforts to relax regulations of corporations and reduce spending on social safety net programs to justify cuts to corporate and high-end income taxes; see Benjamin I. Page, Jason Seawright, and Matthew J. Lacombe, *Billionaires and Stealth Politics* (Chicago: University of Chicago Press, 2019), 1–2; Matthew Stewart, *The 9.9 Percent: The New Aristocracy That Is Entrenching Inequality and Warping Our Culture* (New York: Simon & Schuster, 2021), 259. But Trump's oligarchic orientation also demanded ideological flexibility so as to reject the conventional assumptions of the political Right whenever profit maximization demanded it.

23. Miliband, *The State in Capitalist Society*, 3; Thomas Piketty and Steven Rendall, *A Brief History of Equality* (Cambridge, MA: Belknap/Harvard University Press, 2022); see also David Marchese, "Thomas Piketty Thinks America Is Primed for Wealth Redistribution," *New York Times Magazine*, April 10, 2022, 39.

24. Christopher Leonard, *Kochland: The Secret History of Koch Industries and Corporate Power in America* (New York: Simon & Schuster, 2019), Kindle Location 1537.

25. See Barrow, *Critical Theories of the State*, 30–44.

26. See Miliband on the ruse—and the reality—of corporate elites and their aversion to formal political power (*The State*, 41–42).

27. In 2016, Donald Trump did not appeal to his own self-interest, and it was hard to find ordinary Americans voicing support for concentrating power and wealth into the ultra-rich's hands. Trump did not campaign on the premise that wealth and power should naturally gravitate to him; see Steve Fraser and Gary Gerstle, eds., *Ruling America: A History of Wealth and Power in a Democracy* (Cambridge, MA: Harvard University Press, 2005), Kindle Location 189. Journalists covering Trump's surprise victory in 2016 failed to find West Virginians in red "Make America Great Again" hats supporting Trump because they wanted Trump and his family to profit. That Putin and Trump would publicly reject self-interested rationales points to a historical aberration. The material abundance of Russian tsars and English kings was once justified because it was assumed that serfs and farmers appreciated living under their ruler's warm glow (Robin, *The Reactionary Mind*, 52). Not anymore. Elites attempting to cross the economic-political chasm now justify their entrance into formal positions of power apart from their own material abundance. For this reason, I do not consider tyrannical dictators or kleptocracy feudal lords as oligarchs (Winters, *Oligarchy*, 36). In a democratic oligarchy, the state is not just a nightwatchman the rich must avoid. The state is a cudgel for entrenched elites to beat back competitors and maximize profits—legally, consensually, and peacefully.

28. Barrow, *Critical Theories of the State*, 31, 101.

29. Barrow, *Critical Theories of the State*, 42–43; Jamie Lowe, "With 'Stealth Politics,' Billionaires Make Sure Their Money Talks," *New York Times Magazine*, April 10, 2022, 27; Miliband, *The State in Capitalist Society*, 57.

30. Eugene Garver, *Aristotle's Politics: Living Well and Living Together* (Chicago: University of Chicago Press, 2011), 117–18, and 223.

31. Cintron, *Democracy as Fetish*, 11–12, 24, 48. I need to juxtapose Cintron's perspective on oligarchy and democracy with the conceptualization Wendy Brown offers in her book *In the Ruins of Neoliberalism*. On first page of the first chapter, Brown contrasts democracy with oligarchy by suggesting that "democracy signifies political arrangements through which a people rules itself"; Wendy Brown, *In the Ruins of Neoliberalism: The Rise of Antidemocratic Politics in the West* (New York; Chichester, West Sussex: Columbia University Press, 2019, 23. But following Cintron, I will concede that democracy, by definition, requires that the people rule, but transcend the dichotomy Brown seems to set up here by showing how democracy and oligarchy can coexist when the demos consent to the rule of the oligarchic ruling elite.

32. Public conversations are replete with references to right/left axis and see-saw metaphors. Influential thought leaders like Thomas Frank, Evan Osnos, Ezra Klein, Binyamin Appelbaum, Ron Formisano, and Kim Phillips-Fein have relied on descriptions of American democracy that draw a neat and tidy separation between conservative Republicans on the Right and liberal progressives on the Left based on the amount of government intervention into the market. Thomas Frank describes George W. Bush's economic creed, the opinion pages of the *Washington Post*, and the research papers of the Cato Institute as the "holy trinity of deregulation, privatizations, and free trade"; Thomas Frank, *Pity the Billionaire: The Hard-Times Swindle and the Unlikely Comeback of the Right* (New York: Metropolitan Books, 2012), 27. Evan Osnos describes the ideological orthodoxy of Republicans in DC, after being trained by wealthy conservatives as low taxes and small government"; Evan Osnos, *Wildland: The Making of America's Fury* (New York: Farrar, Straus, and Giroux, 2021), 173. Ezra Klein describes a united Republican Party defined "by mistrust of the federal government, opposition to redistribution, and faith in state and local rule"; Ezra Klein, *Why We're Polarized* (New York: Simon & Schuster, 2020), Kindle Location 624. Benjamin Appelbaum in his book *The Economists' Hour* describes "economic conservatives" as those who felt "profoundly threatened by the expansion of government" in the Long Sixties; Binyamin Appelbaum, *The Economists' Hour: False Prophets, Free Markets, and the Fracture of Society* (New York: Little, Brown, 2019), Kindle Location 246. In *Invisible Hands*, Kim Phillips-Fein describes the conservative businessmen that were the subject of her study as those who "celebrated the market with enthusiasm"; Kim Phillips-Fein, *Invisible Hands: The Businessmen's Crusade Against the New Deal* (New York: Norton, 2010), Kindle Location 6643. Ronald Reagan alumni now influencing the Trump administration were described in a *Politico* article as "united by undying affection for each other and for laissez-faire economics"; Ben Schreckinger, "Reagan's Supply-Side Warriors Blaze Comeback Under Trump," *Politico*, April 22, 2019. And Ron Formisano, in *American Oligarchy*, describes the Kochs' "campaign to spread the gospel of free enterprise, anti-regulation, and low taxes"; Ron Formisano, *American Oligarchy: The Permanent Political Class*. Urbana, IL: University of Illinois Press, 2017.

33. George Will, *The Conservative Sensibility* (New York. Hachette, 2019), xvii.

34. Will, *The Conservative Sensibility*, xxiv.

35. Will, *The Conservative Sensibility*, 20.

36. Michael J. Lee, *Creating Conservatism: Postwar Words that Made an American Movement* (East Lansing: Michigan State University Press, 2014), 11, 68.

37. Paul Elliot Johnson, *I The People: The Rhetoric of Conservative Populism in the United States* (Tuscaloosa: University of Alabama Press, 2022), 16; Margaret Somers, *Genealogies of Citizenship: Markets, Stateless, and the Right to Have Rights* (Cambridge, UK: Cambridge University Press, 2008), 55.

38. Megan Foley, "From Infantile Citizens to Infantile Institutions: The Metaphoric Transformation of Political Economy in the 2008 Housing Market Crisis," *Quarterly Journal of Speech* 98 (2012): 389.

39. Johnson, *I The People*, 17.

40. Johnson, *I The People*, 5; Lee, *Creating Conservatism*, 6.

41. Johnson, *I The People*, 26–27.

42. Osnos, *Wildland*, 140.

43. Engels, *The Politics of Resentment*, 131; Johnson, *I The People*, 26.

44. Michel Foucault, *The Birth of Biopolitics*, trans. Graham Burchell (New York: Picador, 2008), 3, 131; see also Giorgio Agamben, *Homo Sacer: Sovereign Power and Bare Life*, trans. Daniel Heller-Rozen (Palo Alto, CA: Stanford University Press, 1998); Wendy Brown, *Undoing the Demos: Neoliberalism's Stealth Revolution* (Brooklyn: Zone, 2015), 61; Henry A. Giroux, *Stormy Weather: Katrina and the Politics of Disposability* (Boulder, CO: Paradigm, 2006), 28. Like Aristotle and Piketty, Robin focuses on symbolic consent, writing, "The masses must be able to locate themselves symbolically in the ruling class or be provided the real opportunities to become faux aristocrats in the family, the factory, and the field" (*The Reactionary Mind*, 30).

45. Miliband, *The State in Capitalist Society*, 191.

46. Miliband, *The State in Capitalist Society*, 135–36.

47. Barrow, *Critical Theories of the State*, 122. For further reading, see Antonio Gramsci, who in the 1930s began to describe ideological power as a result of alliances between intellectuals and elite-dominated institutions (Antonio Gramsci, *Selections from the Prison Notebooks of Antonio Gramsci*, ed. and trans. Quintin Hoare and Geoffrey Nowell Smith (New York: International Publishers, 1971); see also Miliband, *The State in Capitalist Society*, 131.

48. Gabriel Zucman and Gus Wezerek, "This Is Tax Evasion, Plain and Simple," *New York Times*, 2021.

49. David Kocieniewski, "At G.E. on Tax Day, Billions of Reasons to Smile," *New York Times*, September 23, 2015.

50. Emmanuel Saez and Gabriel Zucman, *The Triumph of Injustice: How the Rich Dodge Taxes and How to Make Them Pay* (New York: W. W. Norton, 2019), Kindle Location 1337.

51. Saez and Zucman, *The Triumph of Injustice*, Kindle Location 1337–1340.

52. Leonard, *Kochland*, Location 6689, 8282.

53. Saez and Zucman, *The Triumph of Injustice*, Kindle Location 1340.

54. Alex Carey, *Taking the Risk Out of Democracy: Corporate Propaganda Versus Freedom and Liberty* (Urbana: University of Illinois Press, 1995), 27; Brian Doherty,

Radicals for Capitalism: A Freewheeling History of the Modern American Libertarian Movement (New York: PublicAffairs, 2007), 407, 449; Miliband, *The State in Capitalist Society*, 41; Phillips-Fein, *Invisible Hands*, Kindle Location 3881.

55. For more on delusional voters, see Leonard, *Kochland*, Location 5965; Fraser and Gerstle, *Ruling America*, Location 1539. I concede that democratic oligarchy wades onto the terrain of conspiracy theory, but I want to emphasize that if we are precise with our definitions, conspiracies can include the outlandishness of tin-hats and QAnon but also the empirical and the falsifiable. For more, see Eric J. Oliver and Thomas Wood, "Conspiracy Theories of the Paranoid Styles(s) of Mass Opinion," *American Journal of Political Science* 58, no. 4 (2014): 952–66; Charles J. Stewart, Craig Allen Smith, and Robert E. Denton, *Persuasion and Social Movements*, 6th ed. (Long Grove, IL: Waveland Press, 2014), 285.

56. Compared to their European counterparts, American corporations devote more resources to such efforts (Philippon, *The Great Reversal*, Kindle Location 2731). In 2018, Marianne Bertrand led a study for the National Bureau of Economic Research that explained why. American companies devote more resources to political campaign contributions and lobbying than do their European counterparts because they have more political influence than their European counterparts. Bertrand put it well: "At the intersection between the political and the economic spheres lies the lobbying industry. Trillions of dollars of public policy intervention, government procurement, and budgetary items are constantly thoroughly scrutinized, advocated, or opposed by representatives of special interests"; Marianne Bertrand, Matilde Bombardini, and Francesco Trebbi, "Is It Whom You Know or What You Know? An Empirical Assessment of the Lobbying Process," *American Economic Review* 104, no. 12 (2014): 3885–3920. See also Marianne Bertrand, Matilde Bombardini, Raymond Fisman, and Francesco Trebbi, "Tax-Exempt Lobbying: Corporate Philanthropy as a Tool for Political Influence," *American Economic Review* 110, no. 7 (2020): 2065–2102. Gehl and Porter highlight the pharmaceutical industry's efforts to reveal lobbying's return-on-investment. Between the late 1990s and 2017, drugmakers spent $740 million to limit opioid regulations. "Pharma's efforts succeeded," Gehl and Porter conclude, "as revenue soared, and 200,000 Americans overdosed on opioids and died"; Katherine M. Gehl and Michael E. Porter, "Fixing U.S. Politics," *Harvard Business Review*, July–August 2020.

57. Philippon, *The Great Reversal*, Kindle Location 2965 and 2866.

58. Miliband, *The State in Capitalist Society*, 123.

59. Barrow, *Critical Theories of the State*, 26; Holloway and Picciotto, "Introduction," 3. I use the label "American liberal democracy" in relation to the extant literature theorizing the role of the state in advanced capitalist economies. At a fundamental level, the United States government is a sovereign political territory maintained, governed, and administered by a state apparatus marked by judicial, ideological, and political subsystems working together administratively to coordinate its executive authority. It may be helpful to begin by identifying what the state is not. Miliband described the state as a "special institution" because, unlike Koch Industries or Apple computers, the state maintains unique and discrete capacities, including social investments, such as building airports and highways, and outlays taking the form of social consumption, such as education, health care, and housing

NOTES

(Barrow, *Critical Theories of the State*, 106). The state also maintains unique capacities to centralize institutional coherence through maintaining a monopoly on professional, discipline violence, propped up by the unique ability to generate revenue through tax collection, which taken together comprise a set of meaningful analytic concepts that distinguish the state from Koch Industries or Apple computers (Barrow, *Critical Theories of the State*, 132; Miliband, *The State in Capitalist Society*, 5). Additionally, the state regularly intervenes in civil society through the development of normative and cultural values related to social life, family, education, and religion (Barrow, *Critical Theories of the State*, 6–7, 82). Of specific interest to my inquiry is the relationship between the state and the market. Panitch argues that one of the greatest misconceptions of our era is that the state has recently retreated from capitalist market relationships; see Leo Panitch, "Forward: Reading *The State in Capitalist Society*," in *The State in Capitalist Society*, Ralph Miliband (Pontypool, Wales: Merlin Press, 1969/2009), ix. From there, it is important to acknowledge that state intervention was present at the birth of social stratification from the beginning. In various forms, the state has always been involved in the constitution and reproduction of economic relationships (Barrow, *Critical Theories of the State*, 54; Miliband, *The State in Capitalist Society*, 9). Stewart has pointed out that at the most basic level, the creation of economic wealth requires the combination of individual talent and efforts with networks of cooperation across society (Stewart, *The 9.9 Percent*, 140–41).

60. Robin, *The Reactionary Mind*, 59–60; Appelbaum, *The Economists' Hour*, Kindle Location 166; Christopher Ellis and James A. Stimson, *Ideology in America* (Cambridge: Cambridge University Press, 2012), 3; Milton Friedman, *Capitalism and Freedom* (Chicago: University of Chicago Press, 1962), 19; Hanan, "The Oikos as Economic Rhetoric."

61. Even when scholars have deployed oligarchy as a conceptual tool, the nation-state remains ill-conceived. Engels, for example, linked the era of neoliberalism with limited and unregulated government. To be sure, Engels offers a compelling account of the biopolitical construction of oligarchic-oriented citizens based on the assumption that most people are unfit to govern and, thus, must defer to their bettors for political and economic guidance. But democratic oligarchy extends the implications of this biopolitical subjectivity by problematizing Engels's consequences. Engels points to personal political acquiescence and a new art of neoliberal government modeled on the market; unfortunately, Engels misses the anti-competitive telos of the elites who shape American democracy (Engels, *The Politics of Resentment*, 131). Cintron affirms the symbiotic relationship among democracy and oligarchy, dispelling the assumption that the governing systems are discrete and, instead, positions oligarchy "at the dead center of democracy" (Cintron, *Democracy as Fetish*, 11–12, 45). But Cintron stretches oligarchy too far so that its discrete explanatory power is diluted. For example, Cintron uses oligarchy to describe general power concentrations so that oligarchy describes elites who "represent collective interests" and every political today as oligarchic because they filter out who can be elected to office (Cintron, *Democracy as Fetish*, 49, 52).

62. Hanan and St. Onge, "Beyond the Dialectic," 174.

63. Robert W. McChesney, *Rich Media, Poor Democracy: Communication Politics*

NOTES

in Dubious Times (Urbana: University of Illinois Press, 1999), 6; Bradford Vivian, "Neoliberal Epideictic: Rhetorical Form and Commemorative Politics on September 11, 2002," *Quarterly Journal of Speech* 92, no. 1 (2006): 8; Mahuya Pal and Patrice M. Buzzanell, "Breaking the Myth of Indian Call Centers: A Postcolonial Analysis of Resistance," *Communication Monographs* 80, no. 2 (2013): 216; Helene A. Shugart, "Consuming Citizen: Neoliberating the Obese Body," *Communication, Culture & Critique* 3, no. 1 (2010): 112.

64. Stewart, *The 9.9 Percent*, 154–55.

65. Pinker, *Enlightenment Now*, 364.

66. Kenneth Burke, *Grammar of Motives* (Berkeley: University of California Press, 1945/1969), 58. See also Vincent Mosco, *The Political Economy of Communication* (Los Angeles: Sage, 2009), 49.

67. Jennifer Mercieca, *Demagogue for President: The Rhetorical Genius of Donald Trump* (College Station: Texas A&M University Press, 2019), 13.

68. Gunn, *Political Perversion*, Kindle Location 102.

69. Lee, *Creating Conservatism*, 149.

70. Gunn, *Political Perversion*, Kindle Location 1769.

71. Fredric Jameson, *The Political Unconscious: Narrative as a Socially Symbolic Act* (Ithaca, NY: Cornell University Press, 1971), 60–83.

CHAPTER I

1. Gershberg and Illing, *The Paradox of Democracy*, 2.

2. Gershberg and Illing, *The Paradox of Democracy*, 6.

3. In her analysis of demagoguery's resonance, Patricia Roberts-Miller concedes that more and better rational persuasion alone may not enlighten the working class to the possibility that their own political allies are not coming to their aid, especially if their (supposed) allies engaged in outsourcing jobs, cutting health benefits, and weakening organized labor. Benjamin Friedman's exploration of the relationship between religion and economics is premised on similar skepticism about the influential potential of instrumental and rational persuasion. Friedman notes the "increasing tendency of large numbers of lower- and even middle-income Americans to vote, in national elections and often at the state and local levels too, in ways that run counter to their individual economic interest." He asks: "Why do so many Americans who have only the remotest prospect of ever making their way into the top income tax bracket nonetheless favor keeping the tax rate on top-bracket incomes low? More startling yet, why do so many Americans who have no chance whatever of inheriting money from a taxable estate passionately advocate abolishing 'death taxes'?" Part of the answer, according to Friedman, is that many Americans are "unaware of how religious ideas shape our economic thinking." By "religious ideas" Friedman does not limit his focus to the cycle of ritual observances or attending church each Sunday morning. He includes a focus on the "inner belief structure that forms an essential part of people's view of the world in which they live." Benjamin Friedman notes how scientific theory emerges from the scientist's worldview. Likewise with painters, poets, and philosophers whose work follows from a worldview that underlies it. There is no reason political economic thinking is any different; see Roberts-Miller, *Rhetoric and Demagoguery*, 185; Benjamin

NOTES

Friedman, *Religion and the Rise of Capitalism* (Knopf, 2021), Kindle location 71; 6905; 7700).

4. Thomas Frank, *What's the Matter with Kansas? How Conservatives Won the Heart of America* (New York: Metro, 2004), 6.

5. Frank, *Pity the Billionaire*, 3.

6. Frank, *What's the Matter with Kansas?* 76.

7. Frank, *Pity the Billionaire*, 154–55.

8. Frank, *Pity the Billionaire*, 12.

9. Frank, *Pity the Billionaire*, 95, 110, 166–67.

10. Engels, *The Politics of Resentment*, 23.

11. Cintron, *Democracy as Fetish*, 53.

12. Johnson, *I The People*, 122; Osnos, *Wildland*, 139.

13. Johnson, *I The People*, 141.

14. Johnson, *I The People*, 150. To be sure, Johnson acknowledges the hybrid forces influencing the Tea Party from the grassroots up and the Koch brothers down. I use their language describing the ideological potency of the Tea Party and conservative elites in Kansas to illustrate false consciousness as a discursive explanation of an incongruous political economy.

15. Sharon Crowley, *Toward a Civil Discourse: Rhetoric and Fundamentalism* (Pittsburgh: University of Pittsburgh Press, 2006), 47–48; Gershberg and Illing, *The Paradox of Democracy*, 34.

16. Piketty, *Capital and Ideology*, 711.

17. Michel Foucault, *Discipline and Punish: The Birth of the Prison*, trans. A. Sheridan (London: Tavistock, 1977); see also Barbara Herrnstein Smith, *Belief and Resistance: Dynamics of Contemporary Intellectual Controversy* (Cambridge, MA: Harvard University Press, 1997, xix); and Crowley, *Toward a Civil Discourse*, x.

18. Cintron, *Democracy as Fetish*, 58; Johnson, *I The People*, 141; Sides et al., *Campaigns*, 45.

19. Cintron, *Democracy as Fetish*, 39.

20. Cintron, *Democracy as Fetish*, 39.

21. Engels, *The Politics of Resentment*, 136; Gershberg and Illing, *The Paradox of Democracy*, 2, 211. Giorgio Agamben in *State of Exception* details the history of American presidents prioritizing order and stability over equal representation of the voice of the people. Abraham Lincoln wrote that although he was unsure "whether it was strictly legal or not," he openly justified concentrating power in violation of the constitution when "the very existence of the union and the juridical order were at stake." During World War I, President Woodrow Wilson followed Lincoln's lead, finding it necessary to assume broad power, including complete control over the administration of the country, by amplifying exceptions for the sake of order. In 1933, Agamben argues, Franklin D. Roosevelt also assumed extraordinary powers to cope with the Great Depression, showing how unequal power concentration can stretch from war to economic crisis; see Giorgio Agamben, *State of Exception*, trans. Kevin Attell (Chicago: University of Chicago Press, 2005), 20–21.

22. Aristotle, *The Politics*, 1996, III, viii 1279b, 35–39.

23. Aristotle, *Politics*, [1288b] [10].

24. Aristotle, *Politics*, [1288b] [10]

25. Ron Chernow, *Alexander Hamilton* (New York: Penguin, 2005), 476.

26. Chernow, *Alexander Hamilton*, 627.

27. Adams to Jefferson, July 13, 1813, and December 16, 1816; cited in Joseph J. Ellis, *American Dialogue: The Founders and Us* (New York: Knopf, 2018), 76.

28. Adams to Jefferson, November 13, 1815; cited in Ellis, *American Dialogue*, 77.

29. Adams to Jefferson, June 14, 1813, *AJL*, 2:330, 346–47, 461, cited in Ellis, *American Dialogue*, 76.

30. Adams to Jefferson, July 9, 1813, *AJL*, 2:351–52, cited in Ellis, *American Dialogue*, 81.

31. Adams to Jefferson, December 6, 1787, cited in Ellis, *American Dialogue*, 89.

32. Ellis, *American Dialogue*, 78.

33. Chernow, *Alexander Hamilton*, 518. Echoing the framers, Alexis de Tocqueville writes in *Democracy in America* that the human quest for equality was "depraved" because it "impels the weak to attempt to lower the powerful to their own level, and reduces men to prefer equality in slavery to inequality with freedom." More recently, Walter Lippman doubted the capacity of ordinary Americans to live up to the demands of democratic politics because the average person could never know enough to offer intelligent contributions to complicated political conversations; see Gershberg and Illing, *The Paradox of Democracy*, 8–9.

34. Jedediah Purdy, *Two Cheers for Politics: Why Democracy Is Flawed, Frightening, and Our Best Hope* (Basic, 2022).

35. Gershberg and Illing, *The Paradox of Democracy*, 35. For example, American history is marked by minoritarian influence turning (initially) unpopular public policy and laws into widely beneficial outcomes, including Alexander Hamilton's financial system, the Supreme Court's rulings on school desegregation, NASA's Apollo space missions, and the 2008 American Recovery and Reinvestment Act (Chernow, *Alexander Hamilton*, 298, 305); Ibram X. Kendi, *How to Be an Antiracist* (New York: One World, 2019), 208.

36. Chernow, *Alexander Hamilton*, 521.

37. Eugene Garver describes Aristotle's focus on how rulers were selected in *The Politics* as an exercise in reconciling the "systematic divergence between people's interests and their political preferences." Corey Robin notes a consistent need in the work of Thomas Hobbes, Friedrich Nietzsche, Edmund Burke, and Samuel Johnson to justify "why the lower orders should not be allowed to exercise their independent will, why they should not be allowed to govern themselves or the polity." Like Aristotle, Edmund Burke refused to concede to all men "power, authority, and direction . . . in the management of the state"; see Eugene Garver, *Aristotle's Politics: Living Well and Living Together* (Chicago: University of Chicago Press, 2011), 117–18, and 223; Robin, *The Reactionary Mind*, 7–8, 145; Friedrich Nietzsche, *Thus Spake Zarathustra*, trans. Walter Kaufmann (New York: Vintage, 1966), 27, 149; Edmund Burke, *Reflections on the Revolution in France*, ed. J. C. D. Clark (Stanford, CA: Stanford University Press, 2001), 217–18.

38. Aristotle, *The Politics*, 1996, III, viii 1279b, 35–39.

39. Piketty, *Capital and Ideology*, 710. Aristotle's interest in persuasive public argument is irrelevant when governing logics are based on violence and coercion.

NOTES

"Once the poor man become a subject and not simply an object, it became necessary to 'own' him by other means and specifically in the realms of discourse and merit," Piketty writes; see also Anand Giridharadas, *Winners Take All: The Elite Charade of Changing the World* (New York: Vintage, 2018), Location 547.

40. Hamilton, Federalist #22, fn80, cited in Chernow, *Alexander Hamilton*, 261.

41. Thomas Piketty details the dominance of elite transcendent superiority as a principal discursive feature of inequality regimes across the historical record (Piketty, *Capital and Ideology*, 710). Edward Said also traces the origins of orientalism to the sincere belief in the cognitive, intellectual, and civilizing superiority of western colonizers—not just brute military strength. In the eighteenth and nineteenth centuries, justifications for American and British colonialism deployed meritocratic appeals, related first to the general superiority of the white race and then to their more evolved cognitive superiority that is better suited for the civilized western world. Susan Neiman finds that meritocracy appeals justified inequality in Nazi Germany. Isabel Wilkerson finds similar appeals justifying white supremacy in the American south in the twentieth century; see Edward W. Said, *Orientalism* (New York: Pantheon, 1978). See also Ben Carrington, *Race, Sport, and Politics: The Sporting Black Diaspora* (New York: Sage, 2010); Susan Neiman, *Learning from the Germans: Race and the Memory of Evil* (New York: Farrar, Straus and Giroux, 2019); and Isabel Wilkerson, *The Warmth of Other Sons: The Epic Story of America's Great Migration* (New York: Vintage, 2011).

42. Freeland, *Plutocrats*, Kindle Location 239; Formisano, *American Oligarchy*, 9; Kristof and WuDunn, *A Path Appears*, 10; Sitaraman, *The Crisis of the Middle-Class Constitution*, 234–39; Saez and Zucman, *The Triumph of Injustice*, Kindle Location 1041.

43. Plato, cited in Gershberg and Illing, *The Paradox of Democracy*, 8.

44. Chernow, *Alexander Hamilton*, 234.

45. Chernow, *Alexander Hamilton*, 265.

46. Chernow, *Alexander Hamilton*, 387.

47. Madison, cited in Chernow, *Alexander Hamilton*, 252.

48. Chernow, *Alexander Hamilton*, 252.

49. Edmund Burke, "Reflections on the Revolution in France," in *Works*, 368–69.

50. Kendi, *How to Be an Antiracist*, 155–56, 205.

51. Adams to Jefferson, October 9, 1787, cited in Ellis, *American Dialogue*, 97.

52. Chernow, *Alexander Hamilton*, 387.

53. Adams, *Works*, 4:380, cited in Ellis, *American Dialogue*, 87.

54. Adams, *Works*, 4:585, cited in Ellis, *American Dialogue*, 88.

55. Ellis, *American Dialogue*, 94–95.

56. Ellis, *American Dialogue*, 94.

57. Ellis, *American Dialogue*, 95.

58. Ellis, *American Dialogue*, 99, 114.

59. Ellis, *American Dialogue*, 87.

60. Ellis, *American Dialogue*, 95–96.

61. Chernow, *Alexander Hamilton*, 628.

62. Adams to John Pope, April 4, 1818, cited in Ellis, *American Dialogue*, 91.

63. Chernow, *Alexander Hamilton*, 628.

64. Barrow, *Critical Theories of the State*, 130.
65. Barrow, *Critical Theories of the State*, 100.
66. Miliband, *The State in Capitalist Society*, 4; Stewart, *The 9.9 Percent*, 245, 274.
67. Barrow, *Critical Theories of the State*, 87.
68. Joshua Zeitz, *Building the Great Society: Inside Lyndon Johnson's White House* (New York: Penguin, 2018), Kindle Location 218.
69. Barrow, *Critical Theories of the State*, 134.
70. Barrow, *Critical Theories of the State*, 135; David Rothkopf, *American Resistance: The Inside Story of How the Deep State Saved the Nation* (New York: PublicAffairs, 2022).
71. Miliband, *The State in Capitalist Society*, 100, 104.
72. Barrow, *Critical Theories of the State*, 130.
73. Engels, *The Politics of Resentment*, 8.
74. Engels, *The Politics of Resentment*, 10.
75. Gershberg and Illing, *The Paradox of Democracy*, 259.
76. Robert Putnam has detailed how the size and scope of the federal government oscillates in relation to public attitudes about the effectiveness of the government. One could find support for the folk theory of democracy in this argument, as the preferences of ordinary citizens are being carried out by their elected leaders; see Robert D. Putnam, *The Upswing: How America Came Together a Century Ago and How We Can Do It Again* (New York: Simon & Schuster, 2020), 318; see also Gershberg and Illing, *The Paradox of Democracy*, 2.
77. Cintron, *Democracy as Fetish*, 35.
78. Engels, *The Politics of Resentment*, 131.
79. Bradley Jones and Roopali Mukherjee, "From California to Michigan: Race, Rationality, and Neoliberal Governmentality," *Communication & Critical/Cultural Studies* 7, no. 4 (2010): 402.
80. Engels, *The Politics of Resentment*, 6.
81. Engels, *The Politics of Resentment*, 4. George Packer's reporting added texture to Engels's resentment. Packer describes the end of the Trump presidency as a time of mystery and confusion regarding how to respond to COVID-19, producing a population of citizens living in "a failed state" (Packer, "We Are Living in a Failed State," 2020).
82. Crowley, *Toward a Civil Discourse*, 47–48.
83. Amadae, *Prisoners of Reason*, 248; Gershberg and Illing, *The Paradox of Democracy*, 262; Lee, *Creating Conservatism*, 89; Ken Binmore, *Natural Justice* (Oxford: Oxford University Press, 2005).
84. Ibram Kendi illustrates the contingency of justice in the story of a slave named Sambo who disclosed to his master a plot for a slave revolt. When his master wanted to thank him with a reward, Sambo refused. The master asked why, and Sambo said his betrayal was "but an act of justice" and he was sufficiently rewarded "in the act" (Kendi, *How to Be an Antiracist*, 145).
85. Osnos, *Wildland*, 407.
86. See Cintron, *Democracy as Fetish*, 50.
87. Garver, *Aristotle's Politics*, 13.

NOTES

88. Garver, *Aristotle's Politics*, 14. For insight into the link between Aristotle and affect, see Gregg, *The Affect Theory Reader*, Kindle Location 4454.

89. Nicholas Buccola, *The Fire Is Upon Us: James Baldwin, William F. Buckley Jr., and the Debate Over Race in America* (Princeton, NJ: Princeton University Press, 2019).

90. Burke, *Attitudes Toward History*, 292.

91. Andrea Wulf, *The Invention of Nature: Alexander von Humboldt's New World* (New York: Vintage, 2015), 234.

92. Robin, *The Reactionary Mind*, 254.

93. Burke, *Rhetoric of Motives*, 155.

94. Frances Fitzgerald, *The Evangelicals: The Struggle to Shape America* (New York: Simon & Schuster, 2017), Kindle location 9382.

95. Luke Winslow, *American Catastrophe* (Columbus: Ohio State University Press, 2020), 38.

96. Jonathan Haidt, *The Righteous Mind: Why Good People Are Divided by Politics and Religion* (New York: Vintage, 2012), 72.

97. Haidt, *The Righteous*, 195.

98. On the history of elites tactically using populist rhetoric, see Jeffrey Hart, *The Making of the Conservative Mind: National Review and Its Times* (Wilmington, DE: ISI Books, 2005), 8, 140.

99. Vox, *Existential Threats*.

100. Frank, *Pity the Billionaire*, 3; James Hay, Stuart Hall, and Lawrence Grossberg, "Interview with Stuart Hall," *Communication & Critical/Cultural Studies* 10, no. 1 (2013); Phillips-Fein, *Invisible Hands*, Location 2064.

101. Gershberg and Illing, *The Paradox of Democracy*, 219.

102. Johnson, *I The People*, 3.

103. Donald Trump repeated some variation of "I'm the president and you're not" many times throughout his presidency. For several examples, see Michael Scherer, "Can President Trump Handle the Truth?," *Time*, April 3, 2017; Lesley Stahl, "President Trump on Christine Blasey Ford, His Relationships with Vladimir Putin and Kim Jong Un and More," *60 Minutes*, October 15, 2018, CBS; and CNN, "Trump Flips Out on Reporter: 'I'm the President of the United States!,'" November 26, 2020, YouTube (website).

104. Richard Nixon, "Transcript of David Frost's Interview with Richard Nixon," 1977.

105. Chernow, *Alexander Hamilton*, 633.

106. Kendi, *How to Be an Antiracist*, 17–18.

107. Ibram X. Kendi, *Stamped from the Beginning: The Definitive History of Racist Ideas in America* (New York: Nation Books, 2016), 147.

108. Charles W. Mills, *The Racial Contract* (Ithaca: Cornell University Press, 1997), 4.

109. Burke, *Attitudes Toward History*, 292.

110. Mills, *Racial Contract*, 64.

111. See Johnson, *I The People*, 139; Packer, "We Are Living in a Failed State," 2020.

112. Frank, *Pity the Billionaire*, 67.

113. Frank, *Pity the Billionaire*, 67; Kevin Musgrave, *Persons of the Market: Conservatism, Corporate Personhood, and Economic Theology* (East Lansing: Michigan State University Press, 2022); Quinn Slobodian, *Globalists: The End of Empire and the Birth of Neoliberalism* (Cambridge, MA: Harvard University Press, 2018), Kindle Location 1709.

114. Burns, *Goddess of the Market*, 251; Lee, *Creating Conservatism*, 87; Osnos, *Wildland*, 169.

115. Democratic oligarchy's temporal distinctiveness clarifies how scholars have conceptualized the form and function of the state. Both Paul Johnson and Thomas Frank argued that conservatives opposed the American Recovery and Reinvestment Act and the Bush-era TARP recovery plans (See Frank, *Pity the Billionaire*, 49; Johnson, *I The People*, 133). Because they prioritized fiscal restraints, influential conservatives like the Koch brothers channeled their opposition to such robust state interventions into support for the Tea Party protests in 2010. Concerns about "moral hazard" also motivated conservatives to oppose the bailouts on the grounds that the state should not be bailing out the unsound and profligate, as Rick Santelli gave voice to so persuasively. But the conceptual daylight between the fiscal restraint of conservatism and the flexible pragmatism of democratic oligarchy shines through as influential oligarchs, like the Koch brothers, quickly dropped their opposition to the government bailouts when they realized how much their investment portfolios would suffer without them. As Jane Mayer wrote, "the Kochs' personal interest in protecting their portfolio trumped their free-market principles"; Jane Mayer, *Dark Money: The Hidden History of the Billionaires behind the Rise of the Radical Right* (New York: Doubleday, 2016), 21.

116. Frank, *Pity the Billionaire*, 39.

CHAPTER 2

1. Charles Darwin, *On the Origin of Species by Means of Natural Selection* (London: John Murray, 1859), 58; see also Wulf, *The Invention of Nature*, 87, 234.

2. B. Friedman, *Religion*, 612.

3. B. Friedman, *Religion*, 736, 6204, 5842.

4. B. Friedman, *Religion*, 6907.

5. B. Friedman, *Religion*, 6187.

6. B. Friedman, *Religion*, 7995.

7. B. Friedman, *Religion*, 6204.

8. Mark Francis, *Herbert Spencer and the Invention of Modern Life* (Ithaca, NY: Cornell University Press, 2007), 247, 285; Longaker, *Rhetorical Style and the Bourgeois Virtue*, 102.

9. Francis, *Herbert Spence and the Invention of Modern Life r*, 312.

10. Francis, *Herbert Spencer and the Invention of Modern Life*, 8.

11. B. Friedman, *Religion*, 5842.

12. Michel Foucault, *Security, Territory, Population: Lectures at the College De France, 1977–1978*, trans. Graham Burchell (New York: Picador, 2007), 31; see also Chaput, *Market Affect and the Rhetoric of Political Economic Debates*, 148.

13. Chaput, *Market Affect and the Rhetoric of Political Economic Debates*, 53.

14. B. Friedman, *Religion*, 6905.

NOTES

15. Garver, *Aristotle's Politics*, 223.
16. B. Friedman, *Religion*, 4430.
17. Roberts-Miller, *Rhetoric and Demagoguery*, 28–29.
18. Longaker referred to Spencer's 1862 book *First Principles of a New System of Philosophy* as a "scientifico-philosophic evolutionary theory" articulating a "law to account for development" in societies and biological organisms alike (Longaker, *Rhetorical Style and the Bourgeois Virtue*, 110). But at the same time, Spencer synthetized this education with the appropriate references to the influence of "the Almighty" and the "Divine will" by which all creation moves in accordance (Spencer, *Proper Sphere of Government*, 187; see also Longaker, *Rhetorical Style and the Bourgeois Virtue*, 105).
19. Francis, *Herbert Spencer and the Invention of Modern Life*, 9; Longaker, *Rhetorical Style and the Bourgeois Virtue*, 105.
20. David Duncan, *The Life and Letters of Herbert Spencer* (London: Methuen, 1908), 80–81.
21. Duncan, *Life and Letters of Herbert Spencer*, 125.
22. Duncan, *Life and Letters of Herbert Spencer*, 209.
23. Francis, *Herbert Spencer and the Invention of Modern Life*, 248; 261
24. Lester F. Ward, "Herbert Spencer's Autobiography," *Science* 19, no. 493 (1904): 873–79 (accessed February 4, 2020), 897.
25. Spencer, *The Principles of Biology*, vol. I (1864), part 3: The Evolution of Life, Ch. 7: Indirect Equilibration.
26. J. D. Y. Peel, *Herbert Spencer: The Evolution of a Sociologist* (New York: Basic, 1971), 100; Spencer, vol. I, part 3, ch. 2, General Aspects of the Special-Creation-Hypothesis; also see Fraser and Gerstle, *Ruling America*, Location 1443.
27. Francis, *Herbert Spencer and the Invention of Modern Life*, 13.
28. Herbert Spencer, *Essays: Scientific, Political and Speculative* (England: Williams and Norgate, 1891), 34. See also Francis, *Herbert Spencer and the Invention of Modern Life*, 254; Longaker, *Rhetorical Style and the Bourgeois Virtue*, 113.
29. Spencer, *Essays*, 168.
30. Spencer, *The Man "versus" the State*, 302–3.
31. Spencer, *Social Statics*, 1851, part III, ch. 25: Poor-Laws.
32. Spencer, *The Principles of Biology*, vol. II (1867), part 6: Laws of Multiplication, Ch. 8: Human Population in the Future.
33. Chaput, *Market Affect and the Rhetoric of Political Economic Debates*, 93, 177; Richard Weaver, *The Ethics of Rhetoric* (South Bend, IN: Regnery/Gateway, 1953), 212–15; see also Lessl, *Rhetorical Darwinism*, 16–36. Cintron also showed how equality, for the progressive left, functions as an ethos or ethic that can, at a maximum, become a "set of laws with the capacity to forcefully restrain" (13). Likewise, appeals to the *natural* allow policy to be ranked according to how well it aligns with the preestablished telos of the state. God-terms like these "fix the scale."
34. Francis, *Herbert Spencer and the Invention of Modern Life*, 247, 300, 303, 330.
35. Francis, *Herbert Spencer and the Invention of Modern Life*, 2.
36. Herbert Spencer, *The Complete Works of Herbert Spencer: Essays, Scientific, Political, and Speculative*, Volume 1, 405–6; See also: Longaker, *Rhetorical Style and the Bourgeois Virtue*, 114.

NOTES

37. Spencer, *The Principles of Biology, Vol. I*, part 2. chapter 7: Heredity, 310; see also Longaker, *Rhetorical Style and the Bourgeois Virtue*, 114.

38. Spencer makes clear the difference between scientific Darwinism and social Darwinism in a passage on heredity from *The Principles of Biology*. Spencer writes, "But the best examples of inherited modifications produced by modifications of function, occur in mankind. To no other cause can be ascribed the rapid metamorphoses undergone by the British races when placed in new conditions. In the United States the descendants of the immigrant Irish lose their Celtic and become Americanized. This cannot be ascribed to mixture, since the feeling with which Irish are regarded by Americans prevents any considerable amount of intermarriage. Equally marked is the case of the immigrant Germans who, though they keep very much apart, rapidly assume the prevailing type. To say that "spontaneous variation" increased by natural selection, can have produced this effect, is going too far. Peoples so numerous cannot have been supplanted in the course of two or three generations by varieties springing from them. Hence the implication is that physical and social conditions have wrought modifications of function and structure, which offspring have inherited and increased"; see *The Complete Works of Herbert Spencer; The Principles of Biology - Vol. I*, part 2, chapter 7: Heredity, 310.

39. Longaker, *Rhetorical Style and the Bourgeois Virtue*, 115.

40. Lessl, *Rhetorical Darwinism*, 23. Lessl also pointed to Huxley as an example of "carefully managing the symbolic expansion of evolutionary science into evolutionism" so as to avoid drawing attention "to the unscientific bases" of his arguments (xxiii).

41. Lessl, *Rhetorical Darwinism*, 16.

42. Lessl, *Rhetorical Darwinism*, xi.

43. Lessl, *Rhetorical Darwinism*, 246.

44. G. Thomas Goodnight, "The Personal, Technical, and Public Spheres of Argument: A Speculative Inquiry into the Art of Public Deliberation," *Argumentation & Advocacy* 48 (2012): 198–210.

45. Lessl, *Rhetorical Darwinism*, 22.

46. To emphasize the systematic and generalizable dimensions, Lessl offered a similar description of Huxley's ability to transverse the technical and the public in *Rhetorical Darwinism* (42).

47. Roberts-Miller, *Rhetoric and Demagoguery*, 24. Lessl details a similar disjuncture in his analysis of the Miller-Urey experiment appeared to *demonstrate* the natural generation of amino acids where the "one vital condition necessary for the origin of life" but upon closer inspection "did not *demonstrate* that life can or did evolve from nonlife," but instead skirted the methodological standards of technical sphere by offering up an explanation for how life "could begin" leaving "more sufficient and immediate ones that still remain unknown (244–45). Roberts-Miller highlights the rhetorical advantage of effectively blurring the technical and public spheres in an unlikely place: the demagogic appeal of Donald Trump. Roberts-Miller identifies an important and pragmatic implication when an audience is constituted by methodological standards outside the technical sphere. For years, Trump changed his positions and said things that were "clearly untrue,"

according to Roberts-Miller. And yet, millions of Americans perceived Trump to be more honest and authentic than Hillary Clinton or Joe Biden. Roberts-Miller explains why: Trump supporters perceived shifting positions, the absence of forethought, and even contradictions and falsehoods as a refreshing and reassuring "lack of calculation" that humanizes the rhetor, vaults authenticity over accuracy, and blurs the existence of an objective reality, with the rhetor being truthful to his or her own views (Roberts-Miller, *Rhetoric and Demagoguery*, 186).

48. Francis, *Herbert Spencer and the Invention of Modern Life*, 312.
49. Francis, *Herbert Spencer and the Invention of Modern Life*, 248.
50. Paul Krugman, "Trump's Big Libertarian Experiment," *New York Times*, January 11, 2019; Nancy MacLean, *Democracy in Chains: The Deep History of the Radical Right's Stealth Plan for America* (New York: Penguin, 2017), 213; Mayer, *Dark Money*, 315, 360.
51. Spencer "Over-regulation" (July 1853 *Westminster Review*).
52. Longaker, *Rhetorical Style and the Bourgeois Virtue*, 108.
53. Longaker, *Rhetorical Style and the Bourgeois Virtue*, 118.
54. Fraser and Gerstle, *Ruling America*, Location 1458.
55. Spencer, *The Principles of Sociology*, 584.
56. Francis, *Herbert Spencer and the Invention of Modern Life*, 268.
57. Spencer, *Social Statics*, 149.
58. Spencer, "Over-regulation" (July 1853 *Westminster Review*).
59. Francis, *Herbert Spencer and the Invention of Modern Life*, 258.
60. Spencer, *The Complete Works of Herbert Spencer: Essays; Scientific, Political, and Speculative*, 405–6.
61. Longaker, *Rhetorical Style and the Bourgeois Virtue*, 114.
62. Spencer, *The Principles of Sociology*, 587.
63. Longaker, *Rhetorical Style and the Bourgeois Virtue*, 117.
64. Spencer, *The Complete Works of Herbert Spencer*, 439.
65. Spencer, *The Complete Works of Herbert Spencer*, 418; see also Francis, *Herbert Spencer and the Invention of Modern Life*, 322.
66. Spencer, *The Principle of Ethics*, 133–34.
67. Francis, *Herbert Spencer and the Invention of Modern Life*, 303.
68. Spencer, *The Principle of Ethics*, xiv.
69. Francis, *Herbert Spencer and the Invention of Modern Life*, 296.
70. Francis, *Herbert Spencer and the Invention of Modern Life*, 304.
71. Francis, *Herbert Spencer and the Invention of Modern Life*, 316.
72. Francis, *Herbert Spencer and the Invention of Modern Life*, 339.
73. Spencer even expressed enthusiasm for despots and monarchs who dispensed coercion and even tortured their own citizens, as long as their actions furthered evolutionary justice (Spencer, *The Study of Sociology*, 277; see also Francis, *Herbert Spencer and the Invention of Modern Life*, 282–83).
74. Garver, *Aristotle's Politics*, 50.
75. Francis, *Herbert Spencer and the Invention of Modern Life*, 325
76. Francis, *Herbert Spencer and the Invention of Modern Life*, 321.
77. Francis, *Herbert Spencer and the Invention of Modern Life*, 304.
78. Francis, *Herbert Spencer and the Invention of Modern Life*, 298. Spencer

NOTES

illuminates an assumption reflected in the forthcoming conservative movement, specifically the deep-seated fear of upending "natural social hierarchies." Michael Lee, for example, notes how George Nash assumed "social traditions should guide the creation of moral politics and feared that factions guided by 'reason' would create hell on earth by attempting to upend natural social hierarchies" (Lee, *Creating Conservatism*, 11).

79. Spencer, *The Principles of Sociology*, 230.

80. To refute a more representative theory of government, in which "a number of citizens, deeply interested in good government are endowed with political power," Spencer wrote, "several considerable classes of electors have little or no *will* in the matter. Not a few of those on the register pique themselves on taking no part in politics—claim credit for having the sense not to meddle with things which they say do not concern them. Many others there are whose interest in the choice of a member of Parliament is so slight, that they do not think it worth while to vote. A notable proportion, too, shopkeepers especially, care so little about the result, that their votes are determined by their wishes to please their chief patrons or to avoid offending them. In the minds of a yet larger class, small sums of money, or even *ad libitum* supplies of beer, outweigh any desires they have to use their political powers independently" (Spencer, *Essays*, 292–93).

81. Francis, *Herbert Spencer and the Invention of Modern Life*, 299.

82. Francis, *Herbert Spencer and the Invention of Modern Life*, 278.

83. Francis, *Herbert Spencer and the Invention of Modern Life*, 317–19, 334.

84. Longaker, *Rhetorical Style and the Bourgeois Virtue*, 108.

85. Spencer, *The Principles of Sociology*, 232.

86. Longaker, *Rhetorical Style and the Bourgeois Virtue*, 100.

87. Fraser and Gerstle, *Ruling America*, Location 1590.

88. Fraser and Gerstle, *Ruling America*, Location 1413.

89. Fraser and Gerstle, *Ruling America*, Location 1441.

90. William Graham Sumner, cited in Phillips-Fein, *Invisible Hands*, Location 781; see also Gerstle, *Ruling America*, Location 110.

91. John D. Rockefeller, cited in Fraser and Gerstle, *Ruling America*, Location 1462.

92. Jay Gould, cited in Fraser and Gerstle, *Ruling America*, Location 1462.

93. Andrew Carnegie, cited in Fraser and Gerstle, *Ruling America*, Location 1462.

94. Fraser and Gerstle, *Ruling America*, Location 110; Jackson Lears, *Something for Nothing: Luck in America* (New York: Viking, 2003), 3; Phillips-Fein, *Invisible Hands*, Location 781. Natural law bridges economic accomplishment to transcendent superiority evidenced in social, cultural, and political arenas. And this bridge is not limited to Gilded Age robber barons. North Korea's Kim Jong-Il shot eleven holes-in-one at the 7,700-yard championship course in Pyongyang during *his first round of golf*, according to state media. NFL great Nate Newton dominated his sport during his play days, and so, after he was arrested, he explained his lofty aims during his second career as a major drug dealer by saying, "I couldn't see myself not being the biggest dope man."

95. Spencer, cited in Fraser and Gerstle, *Ruling America*, Kindle Location 1443.

NOTES

CHAPTER 3

1. B. Friedman, *Religion and the Rise of Capitalism*, Kindle Location 6157; 6253; Eric Posner, "You Deserve a Bigger Paycheck: Here's How You Might Get It," *New York Times*, September 23, 2021; Stewart, *The 9.9 Percent*, 157.

2. William Magnuson, *For Profit: A History of Corporations* (New York: Basic, 2022), Kindle Location: 1,639.

3. Magnuson, *For Profit*, Kindle Location: 2964; 4669.

4. Leonard, *Kochland*, Kindle Location 374.

5. Henry Demarest Lloyd, "The Story of a Great Monopoly," *Atlantic*, March 1881. Para. 11; see also Adam Winkler, *We the Corporations: How American Businesses Won Their Civil Rights* (New York: Liveright, 2018), Kindle Location 171; Adam Cohen, *Supreme Inequality: The Supreme Court's Fifty-Year Battle for a More Unjust America* (New York: Penguin, 2020), Kindle Location 2581.

6. Appelbaum, *The Economists' Hour*, Location 2186; Eli Cook, *The Pricing of Progress: Economic Indicators and the Capitalization of American Life* (Cambridge, MA: Harvard University Press, 2017), 232; Formisano, *American Oligarchy*, 207; Leonard, *Kochland*, Location 1554; Roland Marchand, *Creating the Corporate Soul* (Berkeley: University of California Press, 1996), 74.

7. David Nasaw, "Gilded Age Gospels," in *Ruling America*, ed. Fraser and Gerstle (Cambridge, MA: Harvard University Press, 2005), Kindle Location 203.

8. Robert Caro, *Master of the Senate: The Years of Lyndon Johnson III* (New York: Vintage, 2009), 28.

9. Magnuson, *For Profit*, Kindle Location: 2200; Winkler, *We the Corporations*, 123, see also 197.

10. Caro, *Master of the Senate*, 28.

11. Fraser and Gerstle, *Ruling America*, Location 1341.

12. Fraser and Gerstle, *Ruling America*, Location 1612.

13. Andrew Carnegie, "The Gospel of Wealth" (New York: Carnegie Corporation of New York, 2017, first published in 1889); see also Fraser and Gerstle, *Ruling America*, Location 1423.

14. Ellis, *American Dialogue*, 99; Winkler, *We the Corporations*, 122.

15. Margaret O'Mara, *The Code: Silicon Valley and the Remaking of America* (New York: Penguin, 2019), 4.

16. Magnuson, *For Profit*, Kindle Location: 2200.

17. Carnegie, "Gospel of Wealth," 90.

18. Robert H. Frank, *Success and Luck: Good Fortune and the Myth of Meritocracy* (Princeton, NJ: Princeton University Press, 2016); See also Ezra Klein, "Robert Frank's Radical Idea," *Vox*, May 26, 2020.

19. Piketty, *Capitalism and Ideology*.

20. Brown, *Undoing the Demos*, 166.

21. Winters, *Oligarchy*, 227.

22. James Garfield, cited in Fraser and Gerstle, *Ruling America*, Location 1590.

23. Crowley, *Toward a Civil Discourse*, 47; see also Amos Kiewe and David W. Houck, "Introduction," in *The Effects of Rhetoric and the Rhetoric of Effects*, ed. Amos Kiewe and David W. Houck (Columbia: University of South Carolina Press, 2015), 4; Zarefsky, "Presidential Rhetoric and the Power of Definition," 610.

24. Buccola, *The Fire*, 16; Steven M. Teles, *The Rise of the Conservative Legal Movement: The Battle for Control of the Law* (Princeton, NJ: Princeton University Press, 2012), 93.

25. Robert Asen, "Neoliberalism, the Public Sphere," *Quarterly Journal of Speech* 103, no. 4 (2007): 7–8.

26. Mayer, *Dark Money*, 78; Phillips-Fein, *Invisible Hands*, Kindle Location, 317, 536.

27. Piketty, *Capital and Ideology*, 710.

28. Piketty, *Capital and Ideology*, 711.

29. As Robert Hariman wrote, once a rhetor can claim to have discovered "the vectors of power in a field of material forces," there is no need to debase yourself with trying to understand social or political practices (*Political Style*; see also Aune, *Selling the Free Market*, 30).

30. Piketty, *Capital and Ideology*, Location 1243.

31. Greg Lukianoff and Jonathan Haidt, *The Coddling of the American Mind: How Good Intentions and Bad Ideas Are Setting up a Generation for Failure* (New York: Penguin: 2018), 221.

32. Blinder, *After the Music Stopped*, 353; MacLean, *Democracy in Chains*, 212; Friedman, *Free to Choose*, vol. 10; Mayer, *Dark Money*, 232.

33. Fraser and Gerstle, *Ruling America*, Location 1478.

34. Giridharadas, *Winners Take All*, Location 2590; also see Desmond, "Why Work," September 16, 2018; Charles Duhigg and David Kocieniewski, "How Apple Sidesteps Billions in Taxes," *New York Times*, April 28, 2012.

35. See Miliband, *The State in Capitalist Society*, 129; Stewart, *The 9.9 Percent*, 145.

36. Leonard, *Kochland*, Location 6689.

37. O'Mara, *The Code*, 199.

38. Formisano, *American Oligarchy*, 207. See also Appelbaum, *The Economists' Hour*, Location 2186; Philippon, *The Great Reversal*, Kindle Location 2466; David Nasaw, "Gilded Age Gospels," in *Ruling America*, ed. Fraser and Gerstle, Location 203, Location 242.

39. Appelbaum, *The Economists' Hour*, Location 2186; Philippon, *The Great Reversal*, Kindle Location 2466.

40. T. J. Jackson Lears, *Something for Nothing: Luck in America* (New York: Viking, 2003), 150.

41. Joshua S. Hanan, "Home Is Where the Capital Is: The Culture of Real Estate in an Era of Control Societies," *Communication & Critical/Cultural Studies* 7, no. 2 (June 2010): 181; Jamie Peck and Adam Tickell, "Neoliberalizing Space," *Antipode* 34 (2002): 380–404.

42. Appelbaum, *The Economists' Hour*, Location 178.

43. Teles, *The Rise of the Conservative Legal*, 44.

44. Randall Balmer, *Mine Eyes Have Seen the Glory* (New York: Oxford University Press, 1993), 189.

45. The theological/political conflation of mainline Protestant and Catholic churches during the middle of the twentieth century can be hard to picture during the Trump presidency. But even the larger alliance between American Christians

and the Right is more recent than we often acknowledge. The thought leaders of the Right recommended, for decades, that conservative Republicans infiltrate American churches with their message. And for decades they failed, miserably. American Christians didn't want to hear it. What Phillips-Fein described as "halfhearted gestures toward mobilizing Christians for conservative politics" failed because they "had no organic basis in any church community" (Phillips-Fein, *Invisible Hands*, Location 4087). During the middle decades of the twentieth century, American churches were unwilling to align with what would become a powerful conservative religious-political alliance.

46. Sandra L. Barnes, *Live Long and Prosper: How Black Megachurches Address HIV/Aids and Poverty in the Age of Prosperity Theology* (New York: Fordham University Press, 2013), 95.

47. Freeland, *Plutocrats*, Kindle Location 284; see also Jacob S. Hacker and Paul Pierson, *American Amnesia: How the War on Government Led Us to Forget What Made America Prosper* (New York: Simon & Schuster, 2016); MacLean, *Democracy in Chains*, 46, 52; Marchand, *Creating the Corporate Soul*, 239; Phillips-Fein, *Invisible Hands*, Location 1099; 2745; Jeffrey St. Onge, "Neoliberalism as Common Sense in Barack Obama's Health Care Rhetoric," *Rhetoric Society Quarterly* 47 (2017): 297–98.

48. Piketty, *Capital and Ideology*, 763.

CHAPTER 4

1. Appelbaum, *The Economists' Hour*, Location 170; Mayer, *Dark Money*, 78; Phillips-Fein, *Invisible Hands*, Location 151, 536, 580.

2. Phillips-Fein, *Invisible Hands*, Location 286.

3. Doherty, *Radicals for Capitalism*, 61.

4. Phillips-Fein, *Invisible Hands*, Location 279.

5. Doherty, *Radicals for Capitalism*, 449.

6. Phillips-Fein, *Invisible Hands*, Location 752.

7. MacLean, *Democracy in Chains*, xxv; Teles, *The Rise of the Conservative Legal Movement*, 14; see also Rebecca Gill, "The Evolution of Organizational Archetypes: From the American to the Entrepreneurial Dream," *Communication Monographs* 80, no. 3 (September 2013): 332–33.

8. Slobodian, *Globalists*, Kindle Location 125, 1137.

9. Slobodian, *Globalists*, Kindle Location 2467.

10. Slobodian, *Globalists*, Kindle Location 2839.

11. B. Friedman, *Religion*, 7210

12. James Arnt Aune, *Selling the Free Market: The Rhetoric of Economic Correctness* (New York: Guilford Press, 2001), 166; Chaput, *Market Affect and the Rhetoric of Political Economic Debates*, 86

13. Lee, *Creating Conservatism*, 81.

14. Lee, *Creating Conservatism*, 82.

15. Lee, *Creating Conservatism*, 90.

16. Kurt Andersen, *Evil Geniuses: The Unmaking of America: A Recent History* (New York: Random House, 2020), Location 1767.

17. Asen, "Neoliberalism, the Public Sphere," 9; John M. Jones and Robert C.

NOTES

Rowland, "Redefining the Proper Role of Government: Ultimate Definition in Reagan's First Inaugural," *Rhetoric & Public Affairs* 18 (2015): 706.

18. Piketty, *Capital and Ideology*, 707.

19. Jones and Mukherjee, "From California to Michigan," 407; see also Amanda Nell Edgar, "Commenting Straight from the Underground: N.W.A., Police Brutality, and YouTube as a Space for Neoliberal Resistance," *Southern Communication Journal* 81, no. 4 (September 2016): 225; Yascha Mounk, *The Age of Responsibility: Luck, Choice, and the Welfare State* (Cambridge, MA: Harvard University Press, 2017); Will, *The Conservative Sensibility*, xxix.

20. Lee, *Creating Conservatism*, 103–4.

21. Chaput, *Market Affect and the Rhetoric of Political Economic Debates*, 125.

22. Slobodian, *Globalists*, Kindle Location 1212.

23. Slobodian, *Globalists*, Kindle Location 1216, 1224.

24. See F. A. Hayek, *The Road to Serfdom: Text and Documents; The Definitive Edition (The Collected Works of F. A. Hayek, Volume 2)* (Chicago: University of Chicago Press, 2009), Kindle Location 1295.

25. Hayek, *The Road to Serfdom*, Kindle Location 1509.

26. Lee, *Creating Conservatism*, 88.

27. Hayek, *The Road to Serfdom*, Kindle Location 4996. As I will show shortly, Hayek ultimately rejected this essentialist approach to the political economy, but in another example of textual persona diverging from nuanced political economic theorizing, notice how this either/or perspective lingered; see Appelbaum, *The Economists' Hour*, Location 1701; David Harvey, *A Brief History of Neoliberalism* (Oxford: Oxford University Press, 2005), 43; Sitaraman, *The Crisis of the Middle-Class Constitution*, 218; Mayer, *Dark Money*, 81–87.

28. Hayek, *The Road to Serfdom*, Kindle Location 1822.

29. Hay, Hall, and Grossberg, "Interview with Stuart Hall," 19; Phillips-Fein, *Invisible Hands*, Location 1304 and Location 1290.

30. Phillips-Fein, *Invisible Hands*, Location 1304.

31. Hayek, *The Road to Serfdom*, Location 2874.

32. Hayek, *The Road to Serfdom*, Kindle Location 134.

33. Hayek, *The Road to Serfdom*, Kindle Location 2545.

34. Hayek, *The Road to Serfdom*, Kindle Location 2042, and Location 2690.

35. Hayek, *The Road to Serfdom*, Kindle Location 102.

36. Not limited to the *Road to Serfdom*, Hayek's telic confidence was embedded in his life's work; see Friedrich von Hayek, *The Constitution of Liberty*, ed. Ronald Hamowy (Chicago: University of Chicago Press, 2011), 44; see also Aune, *Selling the Free Market*, 9; Phillips-Fein, *Invisible Hands*, Location 4134.

37. Hayek, *The Road to Serfdom*, Kindle Location 1574. See also Lee, *Creating Conservatism*, 79.

38. Foucault, *Security, Territory, Population*, 31.

39. Lee, *Creating Conservatism*, 91.

40. Hayek, *The Road to Serfdom*, Kindle Location 3279.

41. Hayek, *The Road to Serfdom*, Kindle Location 5354 and Location 5385.

42. Hayek, *The Road to Serfdom*, Kindle Location 57.

43. Mosco, *The Political Economy*, 21–23.

NOTES

44. Hanan, "The Oikos as Economic Rhetoric," 2018.

45. Chaput, *Market Affect and the Rhetoric of Political Economic Debates*, 20.

46. George H.W. Bush, "Remarks on Presenting the Presidential Medal of Freedom Awards," November 18, 1991.

47. For example, see Friedman, in Hayek's *Road to Serfdom* introduction: Kindle Location 6178; see also Phillips-Fein, *Invisible Hands*, Location 1024; Doherty, *Radicals for Capitalism*, 18.

48. Chaput, *Market Affect and the Rhetoric of Political Economic Debates*, 87–88.

49. Robin, *The Reactionary Mind*, 29.

50. B. Friedman, *Religion*, 7310.

51. Chaïm Perelman, *Realm of Rhetoric* (South Bend, IN: University of Notre Dame Press, 1982); see also Aune, *Selling the Free Market*, 83.

52. Robin, *The Reactionary Mind*, 133.

53. Robin, *The Reactionary Mind*, 133.

54. Hayek, *The Road to Serfdom*, Kindle Location 1509.

55. Hayek, *The Road to Serfdom*, Kindle Location 1509.

56. Friedrich A. Hayek, "The Pretense of Knowledge," in *New Studies in Philosophy, Politics, Economics, and the History of Ideas*, ed. F. A. Hayek (Chicago: University of Chicago Press, 1978); see also Slobodian, *Globalists*, Kindle Location 4521.

57. Pattern prediction was the best alternative his discipline could aim for because his discipline could "ascertain only some, but not all, the particular circumstances which determine the outcome of a given process." Hayek concedes that his calls for intellectual "humility" would look inferior "compared with the precise predictions we have learnt to expect in the physical sciences" and he admits that "pattern predictions is a second best with which one does not like to have to be content; see Friedrich von Hayek, "Friedrich von Hayek Prize Lecture," December 11, 1974. Nobel Prize (website); see also Slobodian, *Globalists*, Kindle Location 89.

58. Slobodian, *Globalists*, Kindle Location 89.

59. Likewise, the personal biographies of Mises and Hayek reveal positive experiences with community support and competent government. Mises lived in a rent-controlled apartment in New York City for much of his adult life (Slobodian, *Globalists*, Kindle Location 2155). Ayn Rand leaned on the collective support of her immigrant community when she first came to the United States (Aune, *Selling the Free Market*, 76). Milton Friedman attended Rutgers on a scholarship paid for by the state of New Jersey. Friedman describes how the New Deal benefited him: "Ironically, the New Deal was a lifesaver for us personally," Friedman writes. "The new government programs created a boom market for economists, especially in Washington. Absent the New Deal, it is far from clear that we could have gotten jobs as economists" (Appelbaum, *The Economists' Hour*, Location 379). Pragmatism would remain a defining feature of the Right. Ronald Reagan admitted his childhood subsidence came "through the largesse of the New Deal"; see Jill Lepore, *These Truths: A History of the United States* (New York: W. W. Norton, 2018), Kindle Location 11, 856.

60. Lee, *Creating Conservatism*, 83, 107.

61. Lee, *Creating Conservatism*, 87. See Bruce Caldwell, *Hayek's Challenge: An Intellectual Biography of F. A. Hayek* (Chicago: University of Chicago Press), 101, 338. See Hayek, *The Constitution of Liberty*, 205; *The Road to Serfdom*, 81, 90–91.

62. Hayek, *The Road to Serfdom*, Kindle Location 3289.
63. Teles, *The Rise of the Conservative Legal Movement*, 58.
64. Foucault, *The Birth of Biopolitics*, 167.
65. Peck, *Constructions of Neoliberal Reason*, 52–54.
66. Slobodian, *Globalists*, Kindle Location 280.
67. Slobodian, *Globalists*, Kindle Location 4688.

68. Naomi Klein, *The Shock Doctrine: The Rise of Disaster Capitalism* (Picador: New York: 2007), 8; Slobodian, *Globalists*, Kindle Location 5584; Juan Gabriel Valdes, *Pinochet's Economists: The Chicago School in Chile* (Cambridge: Cambridge University Press, 1995).

69. Hayek, *The Road to Serfdom*, Kindle Location 2693.
70. Hayek, *The Road to Serfdom*, Kindle Location 2693.
71. Slobodian, *Globalists*, Kindle Location 896.
72. Peck, *Constructions of Neoliberal Reason*, 52; B. Friedman, *Religion*, 7217.
73. Hayek, *The Road to Serfdom*, 21, 89.
74. Hayek, *The Road to Serfdom*, Kindle Location 2196.
75. Chaput, *Market Affect and the Rhetoric of Political Economic Debates*, 105.
76. Slobodian, *Globalists*, Kindle Location 2395.
77. Hayek, "The Pretense of Knowledge"; Slobodian, *Globalists*, Kindle Location 184.
78. Slobodian, *Globalists*, Kindle Location 2826.
79. Slobodian, *Globalists*, Kindle Location 4688, 5079, 4533.
80. Hayek, "Friedrich von Hayek Prize Lecture."
81. Lee, *Creating Conservatism*, 107.
82. See Klein, *The Shock Doctrine*; MacLean, *Democracy in Chains*, 110; Amadae, *Prisoners of Reason*, 177; Phillips-Fein, *Invisible Hands*, Location 4267.
83. Klein, *The Shock Doctrine*, 8; Slobodian, *Globalists*, Kindle Location 888 and 5584; Valdes, *Pinochet's Economists*.

84. Robin, *The Reactionary Mind*, 164; Karin Fischer, "The Influence of Neoliberals in Chile Before, During, and After Pinochet," in *The Road from Mont Pèlerin: The Making of the Neoliberal Thought Collective*, ed. Philip Mirowski and Dieter Plehwe (Cambridge, MA: Harvard University Press, 2009), 327.

85. Bruce Caldwell and Leonidas Montes, "Friedrich Hayek and His Visits to Chile," *Review of Austrian Economics* 28, no. 3 (2015): 261–309; see also Slobodian, *Globalists*, Kindle Location 5584.

86. Gunn, *Political Perversion*, Kindle Location 1909.
87. Amadae, *Prisoners of Reason*, 180; MacLean, *Democracy in Chains*, 107. 2345.

88. Chaput, *Market Affect and the Rhetoric of Political Economic Debates*, 101; see also Appelbaum, *The Economists' Hour*, Location 230; Robert J. Neubauer, "Dialogue, Monologue, or Something in Between? Neoliberal Think Tanks in the Americas," *International Journal of Communication* 6 (2012): 2179; Alice O'Connor, "Financing the Counterrevolution," in *Rightward Bound: Making America Conservative in the 1970s*, ed. Bruce Schulman and Julian Zelizer (Cambridge, MA: Harvard University Press, 2008), 152.

89. Chaput, *Market Affect and the Rhetoric of Political Economic Debates*, 106.
90. Hayek, *The Road to Serfdom*, Kindle Location 4996.

NOTES

91. Chaput, *Market Affect and the Rhetoric of Political Economic Debates*, 100.

92. Hayek, *The Constitution of Liberty*, 81–84; see also Doherty, *Radicals for Capitalism*, 546; Slobodian, *Globalists*, Kindle Location 5678.

93. Hayek, *The Constitution of Liberty*, 186–89.

94. Hayek, *The Road to Serfdom*, Kindle Location 1295.

95. Hayek, *The Road to Serfdom*, Kindle Location 2774; see also Slobodian, *Globalists*, Kindle Location 4521.

96. Hayek, *The Road to Serfdom*, Kindle Location 3886.

97. Slobodian, *Globalists*, Kindle Location 5274.

98. Hayek, *The Road to Serfdom*, Kindle Location 4996.

99. Slobodian, *Globalists*, Kindle Location 5069.

100. Most public rhetors, like Reagan and Thatcher, avoided highlighting the logical implications of Hayek's argument in favor of appeals to the common good. But a number of popular thought leaders linked to the political Right, including Mises and Hayek, but also Ayn Rand, Milton Friedman, and James M. Buchanan, did not shy away from the seedy underbelly of democratic cynicism. Ayn Rand's 1943 book, *The Fountainhead*, signaled an opening salvo for an entire economic-political philosophy that shows where oligarchy can end up. Later, *Atlas Shrugged* (1957) became one of the most important books of the century, second only to the Bible in its stated impact on thought leaders in the twentieth century (Aune, *Selling the Free Market*, 59). It was a polemical dedicated to the idea that there was no morality higher than pursuing one's own self-interest. A close textual analysis of each is beyond my scope here, but one theme is relevant: for Rand, like Hayek, most people were losers. And their mere existence represented a threat to their oligarchic aspirations (see Doherty, *Radicals for Capitalism*, 146).

101. Slobodian, *Globalists*, Kindle Location 4521.

102. Hayek, "Friedrich von Hayek Prize Lecture."

103. Zeitz, *Building the Great Society*, Kindle Location 891.

104. Juan Gabriel Valdes, *Pinochet's Economists*, 59; Klein, *The Shock Doctrine*, 25; Phillips-Fein, *Invisible Hands*, Location 715, 2745; Martha J. Bailey and Sheldon Danziger, eds., *Legacies of the War on Poverty* (New York: Russell Sage Foundation, 2013), 3.

105. Marchand, *Creating the Corporate Soul*, 239; MacLean, *Democracy in Chains*, 52; Phillips-Fein, *Invisible Hands*, Location 1099, 2745; St. Onge, "Neoliberalism as Common Sense," 297–98.

106. Freeland, *Plutocrats*, Kindle Location 284; see also Hacker and Pierson, *American Amnesia*, and MacLean, *Democracy in Chains*, 46, Location 1205; Teles, *The Rise*, 58.

107. Richard A. Posner, "The Future of Law and Economics: Looking Forward," 64 *University of Chicago Law Review 1132* (1997): 1144.

108. Appelbaum, *The Economists' Hour*, Location 170; Mayer, *Dark Money*, 78; Phillips-Fein, *Invisible Hands*, Location 151, 536, 580.

CHAPTER 5

1. Erwin Chemerinsky, *Worse Than Nothing: The Dangerous Fallacy of Originalism* (New Haven, CT: Yale University Press), 184.

NOTES

2. "Lochner v. New York," *Oyez*; see also Cohen, *Supreme Inequality*, Kindle Location 876; Winkler, *We the Corporations*, 182.

3. Joan Biskupic, *The Chief: The Life and Turbulent Times of Chief Justice John Roberts* (New York: Basic, 2019), Location 3790; William P. Hustwit, "From Caste to Color Blindness: James J. Kilpatrick's Segregationist Semantics," *Journal of Southern History* 77, no. 3 (2011).

4. See Biskupic, *The Chief*, Location 3790; Leonard, *Kochland*, Location 1554; Sitaraman, *The Crisis of the Middle-Class Constitution*, 264.

5. B. Friedman, *Religion*, 5263.

6. Peck, *Constructions of Neoliberal Reason*, 42.

7. Catherine Chaput, "Rhetorical Circulation in Late Capitalism: Neoliberalism and the Overdetermination of Affective Energy," *Philosophy & Rhetoric* 43, no. 1 (February 2010): 4; Magnuson, *For Profit*, Kindle Location: 2,889.

8. Fraser and Gerstle, *Ruling America*, Location 1539; Magnuson, *For Profit*, Kindle Location: 2,057.

9. Magnuson, *For Profit*, Kindle Location: 4669.

10. Teles, *The Rise of the Conservative Legal Movement*, 44.

11. Putnam, *The Upswing*, 318.

12. Corey Robin, *The Enigma of Clarence Thomas* (New York: Metropolitan Books, 2019), Kindle location 2984; Jane Mayer and Jill Abramson, *Strange Justice: The Selling of Clarence Thomas* (New York: Graymalkin Media, 2018), Kindle location 2445.

13. Phillips-Fein, *Invisible Hands*, Location 715.

14. Cohen, *Supreme Inequality*, Kindle Location 110.

15. Cohen, *Supreme Inequality*, Kindle Location 113.

16. Chemerinsky, *Worse Than Nothing*, 35.

17. Hustwit, *James J. Kilpatrick*, 32; James R. Sweeney, "Postscript to Massive Resistance: The Decline and Fall of the Virginia Commission on Constitutional Government," *Virginia Magazine of History and Biography* 121, no. 1 (2013): 46.

18. Hustwit, "From Caste to Color Blindness," 654; George, Lewis, "Virginia's Northern Strategy: Southern Segregationists and the Route to National Conservatism," *Journal of Southern History* 72, no. 1 (2006): 118.

19. Hustwit, *James J. Kilpatrick*, 186; Klein, *Why We're Polarized*, Kindle Location 307.

20. Theodore R. Johnson, "The Monolith," *New York Times Magazine*, September 20, 2020, 31.

21. See Buccola, *The Fire*; Hart, *The Making of the Conservative Mind*; Johnson, *I The People*, 5; Lee, *Creating Conservatism*; Lewis, "Virginia's Northern Strategy," 114; MacLean, *Democracy in Chains*, 88; Osnos, *Wildland*, 169; Phillips-Fein, *Invisible Hands*.

22. Hustwit, *James J. Kilpatrick*, 90; Sweeney, "Postscript to Massive Resistance," 46.

23. Hustwit, *James J. Kilpatrick*, 91.

24. Buccola, *The Fire*.

25. Hustwit, *James J. Kilpatrick*, 20–21.

26. Hustwit, *James J. Kilpatrick*, 1–2.

27. Hustwit, *James J. Kilpatrick*, 5, 73.
28. Hustwit, "From Caste to Color Blindness," 645.
29. Hustwit, "From Caste to Color Blindness," 654; Lewis, "Virginia's Northern Strategy," 118.
30. Lewis, "Virginia's Northern Strategy," 144.
31. Hustwit, *James J. Kilpatrick*, 5.
32. Sweeney, "Postscript to Massive Resistance," 47.
33. Kilpatrick, *Richmond News Leader*, September 25, 1954, cited in Hustwit, *James J. Kilpatrick*, 45; see also Lewis, "Virginia's Northern Strategy," 145.
34. Kilpatrick, cited in Sweeney, "Postscript to Massive Resistance," 49.
35. Hustwit, *James J. Kilpatrick*, 53, 97.
36. Hustwit, *James J. Kilpatrick*, 66.
37. Kilpatrick, James J. Kilpatrick Papers, July 1962, cited in Hustwit, *James J. Kilpatrick*, 99.
38. VCCG pamphlet, General Collection, JK 2439, M45, in David J. Mays Papers, cited in Hustwit, *James J. Kilpatrick*, 93.
39. Hustwit, *James J. Kilpatrick*, 93–95; 103; Sweeney, "Postscript to Massive Resistance," 51.
40. Virginia Commission on Constitutional Government, "Did the Court Interpret or Amend?: The Meaning of the Fourteenth Amendment, in Terms of a State's Power to Operate Racially Separate Public Schools, as Defined by the Courts," (1962).
41. ". . . On the Fixing of Boundary Lines."
42. Lee J. Strang, *Originalism's Promise: A Natural Law Account of the American Constitution* 2 (2019); Jamal Greene, *Selling Originalism, GEO L. J.* 657, no. 716 (2009); Chemerinsky, *Worse Than Nothing*, 37.
43. James Kilpatrick proclaimed to interpret the law in its original context long before Bork, Scalia, and Thomas. Beyond whining about progressive tax rates or burdensome protections for their labor force, oligarchy resonated with strict constitutionalism because it could justify Keynesian dissent through more legitimate public arguments. Strict constitutionalism could offer a constitutional rationale of Keynesianism's equality orientation, and the regulations, protections, and support for labor it produced, as partisan, ideological, unconstitutional—and worse, unnatural. Strict constitutionalism met those aims. Notice how strict constitutionalism aligns with legal realism, textualism, and constitutional originalism today.
44. David A. Kaplan, *The Most Dangerous Branch: Inside the Supreme Court's Assault on the Constitution* (New York: Crown, 2018), 13. There is some conceptual daylight between originalism and textualism, but as a source of public argument and for the sake of clarity I lump the exclusionary emphasis of textualism under the broader conceptualization of originalism in this chapter.
45. Decades later, legal scholars would trace the popular emergence of constitutional originalism in the scholarship of Robert Bork; see Robert J. Delahunty and John Yoo, "Saving Originalism," *Michigan Law Review* 113, no. 6 (2015): 1081–1113; Robert Bork, *Neutral Principles and Some First Amendment Problems*, 47, *IND. L.J.* (1971): 1, 2–3; Jack Balkin, *Living Originalism* (2011). "If contemporary originalism can be assigned a definite starting point, that point must be the publication

NOTES

of Robert Bork's Neutral Principles and Some First Amendment Problems," write Robert J. Delahunty and John Yoo in the *Michigan Law Review*. Since Bork, originalism grew into the mainstream legal theory, espoused by three of the nine Supreme Court justices, including Clarence Thomas, Neil Gorsuch, and Amy Coney Barrett, who each describe themselves as originalists. John Roberts, Samuel Alito, and Brett Kavanaugh often justify their opinions in originalist arguments, reflecting the overlap between conservative legal thought and originalist legal interpretation. But originalism aligns with mid-century conservatism because Kilpatrick first located a potent response to *Brown* in strict constitutionalism.

46. See Putnam, *The Upswing*, 186–87.
47. Buccola, *The Fire*, 84.
48. VCCG, "Report of the Conference," 7.
49. VCCG, "Report of the Conference."
50. VCCG, "... On the Fixing of Boundary Lines," 1.
51. VCCG, "... On the Fixing of Boundary Lines," 2
52. Hustwit, "From Caste to Color Blindness," 645.
53. Cohen, *Supreme Inequality*, Kindle Location 1736.
54. Strang, *Originalism's Promise*, 2.
55. In *Brown*, Kilpatrick defended the local communities' right to control their local schools without federal interference, but later in life, when Seattle and Louisville instituted a voluntary busing program, Kilpatrick urged the Supreme Court to intervene in ways anathema to his previous concerns about Warren and *Brown*. In response to *Brown*, James Kilpatrick complained federal overreach contradicted the will of local communities (see Hustwit, "From Caste to Color Blindness," 668). But later, when Kilpatrick emerged as a conservative thought leader, he applauded the John Roberts court overturning desegregation efforts of local communities in Seattle and Louisville. States' rights and local control are applied based on the political demands they produce—but often incoherently, inconsistently, and opportunistically. Likewise, the judicial activism of the Lochner-era Supreme Court to combat democratically supported legislation took on an unconstitutional and unnatural hue when the Warren Court ruled against segregated schools.
56. Hustwit, *James J. Kilpatrick*, 71.
57. Hustwit, *James J. Kilpatrick*, 71.
58. Chemerinsky, *Worse Than Nothing*, xiii.
59. Chemerinsky, *Worse Than Nothing*, xi, 114.
60. Kilpatrick, "My Journey from Racism," cited in Hustwit, *James J. Kilpatrick*, 1.
61. Kilpatrick, James J. Kilpatrick Papers, 29 June 1961, cited in Hustwit, *James J. Kilpatrick*, 164.
62. Hustwit, "From Caste to Color Blindness," 662.
63. Kilpatrick, James J. Kilpatrick Papers, March 27, 1961, cited in Hustwit, *James J. Kilpatrick*, 143, Ch 5.
64. Hustwit, *James J. Kilpatrick*, 112.
65. Hustwit, *James J. Kilpatrick*, 31.
66. See Isaac Kramnick, *The Rage of Edmund Burke: Portrait of an Ambivalent Conservative* (New York: Basic: 1977), 34.

NOTES

67. Cited in Hustwit, *James J. Kilpatrick*, 35.
68. Hustwit, "From Caste to Color Blindness," 662.
69. Cited in Hustwit, *James J. Kilpatrick*, 35.
70. Kilpatrick, *Richmond News Leader*, October 9, 1957, cited in Hustwit, *James J. Kilpatrick*, 81.
71. Hustwit, *James J. Kilpatrick*, 164, 18.
72. Rodney D. Coates, "If a Tree Falls in the Wilderness: Reparations, Academic Silences, and Social Justice," *Social Forces* 83, no. 2 (2004): 848.
73. Coates, "If a Tree Falls in the Wilderness," 848.
74. VCCG citation, Thomas Jefferson 1776:1964, cited in Coates, "If a Tree Falls in the Wilderness," 860.
75. "Report of the Conference," 35; ". . . On the Fixing of Boundary Lines."
76. "The Right Not to Listen," 5.
77. Forward, "The Right Not to Listen."
78. Kilpatrick, *James J. Kilpatrick*, "New National Nightmare," November 12, 1963, cited in Hustwit, *James J. Kilpatrick*, 32.
79. "The Kentucky-Virginia Resolutions."
80. Hustwit, *James J. Kilpatrick*, 49.
81. Kilpatrick, *Richmond News Leader*, November 21, 1955, cited in Hustwit, *James J. Kilpatrick*, 50–51.
82. VCCG, "Did the Court Interpret or Amend?" 3.
83. VCCG charter, cited in Sweeney, "Postscript to Massive Resistance," 46.
84. VCCG, "Did the Court Interpret or Amend?" 4.
85. "Did the Court Interpret or Amend?"
86. "Did the Court Interpret or Amend?"
87. "Did the Court Interpret or Amend?"
88. VCCG, "Did the Court Interpret or Amend?" 4, cited in Hustwit, *James J. Kilpatrick*, 94; see the 1967 tome *The Reconstruction Amendments' Debates*, a 743-page investigation of the congressional debates and legislation leading up to the passage of the Thirteenth, Fourteenth, and Fifteenth Amendments, the CCG divined the framers' true intentions. Hustwit, *James J. Kilpatrick*, 98.
89. "Did the Court Interpret or Amend?" 43.
90. Kilpatrick, *Richmond News Leader*, January 25, 1957, cited in Hustwit, *James J. Kilpatrick*, 52.
91. Kilpatrick, *National Review*, July 14, 1964, cited in Hustwit, *James J. Kilpatrick*, 139–40.
92. Kilpatrick, cited in Sweeney, "Postscript to Massive Resistance," 54.
93. Hustwit, *James J. Kilpatrick*, 148.
94. Hustwit, *James J. Kilpatrick*, 121.
95. Hustwit, *James J. Kilpatrick*, 69.
96. Sweeney, *The Virginia*, 301.
97. Hustwit, *James J. Kilpatrick*, 155.
98. Hustwit, *James J. Kilpatrick*, 1–2.
99. In a 1968 "A Conservative View" column: "Liberty demands order. It demands discipline. It demands a sense of hierarchy" in which people "are inferior to their masters." Hustwit, *James J. Kilpatrick*, 166.

100. Hustwit, *James J. Kilpatrick*, 145.

101. Kilpatrick, *Southern Case for School Segregation*, 42, cited in Hustwit, *James J. Kilpatrick*, 145.

102. Hustwit, *James J. Kilpatrick*, 156.

103. Kilpatrick, "A Conservative View," February 19/20, 1966, cited in Hustwit, *James J. Kilpatrick*, 156.

104. Kilpatrick, *James J. Kilpatrick Papers*, February 16, 1965, cited in Hustwit, *James J. Kilpatrick*, 157.

105. Hustwit, *James J. Kilpatrick*, 180.

106. Adam Smith, *The Theory of Moral*, cited in Kramnick, *The Rage*, 192.

107. Kilpatrick, *The Southern Case for Segregation*, 97–101, cited in Hustwit, *James J. Kilpatrick*, 148.

108. Hustwit, *James J. Kilpatrick*, 171.

109. VCCG, "Report of the Conference," 36.

110. VCCG, "Did the Court Interpret or Amend?" 3.

111. VCCG, ". . . On the Fixing of Boundary Lines," 3.

112. Kilpatrick, *Richmond News Leader*, January 25, 1957, cited in Hustwit, *James J. Kilpatrick*, 53.

113. Cited in Hustwit, *James J. Kilpatrick*, 33.

114. James R. Sweeney, ed., *Race, Reason, and Massive Resistance: The Diary of David J. Mays, 1954–1959* (Athens: University of Georgia Press, 2008), 219–20; see also MacLean, *Democracy in Chains*, 82.

115. Hustwit, *James J. Kilpatrick*, 174–75. See also MacLean, *Democracy in Chains*, 82.

116. Kilpatrick, *James J. Kilpatrick Papers*, January 18, 1966, cited in Hustwit, *James J. Kilpatrick*, 174–75.

117. Hustwit, *James J. Kilpatrick*, 10.

118. James R. Sweeney, *The Virginia Magazine of History and Biography* 121, no. 3 (2013): 299.

119. Hustwit, *James J. Kilpatrick*, 155.

120. Hustwit, *James J. Kilpatrick*, 158.

121. Hustwit, *James J. Kilpatrick*, 30.

122. Hustwit, *James J. Kilpatrick*, 161.

CHAPTER 6

1. Teles, *The Rise of the Conservative Legal Movement*, 14; see also Gill, "The Evolution of Organizational Archetypes," 332–33.

2. Piketty, *Capital and Ideology*, Location 763; see also Naomi Klein, *This Changes Everything: Capitalism vs. The Climate* (New York: Simon & Schuster, 2014), 10; Benjamin Kunkel, *Utopia or Bust: A Guide to the Present Crisis* (New York: Verso Books, 2014), 43.

3. Hacker and Pierson, *American Amnesia*.

4. Hacker and Pierson, *American Amnesia*.

5. David Harvey, *The Condition of Postmodernity: An Enquiry into the Origins of Cultural Change* (Cambridge, MA: Basil Blackwell, 1989), 125–40.

6. John Clarke, *New Times and Old Enemies: Essays on Cultural Studies in America*

NOTES

(New York: Routledge, 1992), 50; Ronald Walter Greene, "Y Movies: Film and the Modernization of Pastoral Power," *Communication and Critical/Cultural Studies* 2 (2005): 30–31.

7. Greene, "Y Movies," 30; Jürgen Habermas, *The Structural Transformation of the Public Sphere*, trans. Thomas Burger (Cambridge, MA: MIT Press, 1989), 129–40.

8. Peck and Tickell, "Neoliberalizing Space."

9. Hacker and Pierson, *American Amnesia*.

10. Saez and Zucman, *The Triumph of Injustice*, Kindle Location 159.

11. Timothy Noah, *The Great Divergence: America's Growing Inequality Crisis and What We Can Do about It* (New York: Bloomsbury, 2012), 135; Hedrick Smith, *Who Stole the American Dream?* (New York: Random House, 2013), 434.

12. Clarke, *New Times and Old Enemies*, 113, 117–18; Ronald Walter Greene and Sara Holiday Nelson, "Struggle for the Commons: Communicative Labor, Control Economics, and the Rhetorical Marketplace" in *Communication and the Economy*, ed. Hanan and Hayward, 264.

13. Dana Cloud, "Fighting Words: Labor and the Limits of Communication at Staley, 1993 to 1996," *Management Communication Quarterly* 18 (2005): 510–11; Bethany Moreton, *To Serve God and Wal-Mart: The Making of Christian Free Enterprise* (Cambridge, MA: Harvard, 2009): 75, 103; Noah, *The Great Divergence*, 138.

14. Freeland, *Plutocrats*, Kindle Location 17.

15. David George, cited in cited in Hacker and Pierson, *American Amnesia*.

16. Meyer, *Dark Money*, 375.

17. Kunkel, *Utopia or Bust*, 129.

18. Phillips-Fein, *Invisible Hands*, Location 544.

19. Phillips-Fein, *Invisible Hands*, Location 330.

20. Ellis, *American Dialogue*, 109; MacLean, *Democracy in Chains*, 52; Slobodian, *Globalists*, Kindle Location 3190.

21. Marchand, *Creating the Corporate Soul*, 239, 319.

22. Andersen, *Evil Geniuses*, Kindle location 1338. "Long" because the era begins in 1954 with the Supreme Court's *Brown v. Board of Education* ruling and stretches to the Court's 1973 *Roe v. Wade* ruling.

23. Rick Perlstein, *Nixonland: The Rise of a President and the Fracturing of America* (New York: Scribner, 2008), 95.

24. Bethany E. Moreton, "Make Payroll, Not War: Business Culture as Youth Culture," in *Rightward Bound: Making America Conservative in the 1970s*, ed. Bruce Schulman and Julian Zelizer (Cambridge, MA: Harvard University Press, 2008), 54.

25. Phillips-Fein, *Invisible Hands*, Location 2984.

26. Fitzgerald, *The Evangelicals*, Kindle Location 155; Giroux, *Stormy Weather*, 21; Margolis, *From Politics to the Pews*, Kindle Location 251.

27. Perlstein, *Nixonland*, 41.

28. Leonard, *Kochland*, 1549

29. MacLean, *Democracy in Chains*, xxx.

30. Sandra Day O'Connor would describe him as "a model of human kindness, decency, exemplary behavior, and integrity"; see Sandra Day O'Connor, *The Majesty of the Law* (New York: Random House, 2003).

NOTES

31. Andersen, *Evil Geniuses*, Kindle location 1259; Osnos, *Wildland*, 170.
32. Andersen, *Evil Geniuses*, Kindle location 1259.
33. Cohen, *Supreme Inequality*, Kindle Location 1284.
34. Lewis F. Powell Jr., "Attack on American Free Enterprise System," 1, para. 1.
35. Powell, "Attack on American Free Enterprise System," p. 34, para 1.
36. Powell, "Attack on American Free Enterprise System," p. 8, para. 4.
37. Powell, "Attack on American Free Enterprise System," p. 1, para. 2.
38. Powell, "Attack on American Free Enterprise System," p. 2–3, Para. 4; See also Cohen, *Supreme Inequality*, Kindle Location 1991.
39. Powell, "Attack on American Free Enterprise System," p. 1–2, para. 3.
40. Powell, "Attack on American Free Enterprise System," p. 2, para. 2.
41. Powell, "Attack on American Free Enterprise System," p. 1, footnote.
42. Powell, "Attack on American Free Enterprise System," p. 2, para. 3.
43. Powell, "Attack on American Free Enterprise System," p. 5, para. 4.
44. Powell, "Attack on American Free Enterprise System," p. 10, para. 2.
45. Powell, "Attack on American Free Enterprise System," p. 32, para. 2.
46. Powell, "Attack on American Free Enterprise System," p. 10; Para. 3.
47. Powell, "Attack on American Free Enterprise System," p. 24, para. 5.
48. Powell, "Attack on American Free Enterprise System," p. 33, para. 2.
49. Powell, "Attack on American Free Enterprise System," p. 25, para. 3.
50. Powell, "Attack on American Free Enterprise System," p. 27, para. 4.
51. Powell, "Attack on American Free Enterprise System," p. 32, para. 1.
52. Powell, "Attack on American Free Enterprise System," p. 24, para 3.
53. Powell, "Attack on American Free Enterprise System," p. 2, para. 4.
54. Powell, "Attack on American Free Enterprise System," p. 15, Para. 1.
55. Moreton, "Make Payroll."
56. Powell, "Attack on American Free Enterprise System," p. 3; para. 3.
57. Powell, "Attack on American Free Enterprise System," p. 5, para. 5.
58. Powell, "Attack on American Free Enterprise System," p. 8, para. 1.
59. Powell, "Attack on American Free Enterprise System," p. 3, para. 3.
60. Powell, "Attack on American Free Enterprise System," p. 28, para. 1.
61. Powell, "Attack on American Free Enterprise System," p. 8, para. 3.
62. Powell, "Attack on American Free Enterprise System," p. 5, para. 2; p. 7, para. 2; p. 14, para. 3.
63. Powell, "Attack on American Free Enterprise System," p. 13, para. 1.
64. Powell, "Attack on American Free Enterprise System," p. 6, footnote #2.
65. Powell, "Attack on American Free Enterprise System," p. 8, para. 2.
66. Appelbaum, *The Economists' Hour*, Location 1701; Harvey, *A Brief History of Neoliberalism*, 43; Sitaraman, *The Crisis of the Middle-Class Constitution*, 218; Mayer, *Dark Money*, 81–87; "Introduction: The Powell Memo (AKA the Powell Manifesto)," *Reclaim Democracy!*, accessed May 6, 2023.
67. Andersen, *Evil Geniuses*, Kindle location 1317.
68. Powell Memo, 1971; see also Sitaraman, *The Crisis of the Middle-Class Constitution*, 218.
69. Powell, "Attack on American Free Enterprise System," p. 11, para. 2.
70. Powell, "Attack on American Free Enterprise System," p. 30, para. 1.

NOTES

71. Powell, "Attack on American Free Enterprise System," p. 26, para. 3.
72. Powell, "Attack on American Free Enterprise System," p. 6. Para. 1.
73. Powell, "Attack on American Free Enterprise System," p. 23, para. 1.
74. Powell, "Attack on American Free Enterprise System," p. 15, para. 3.
75. Sweeney, "Postscript to Massive Resistance," 50.
76. Powell, "Attack on American Free Enterprise System," 21, para. 2.
77. Powell, "Attack on American Free Enterprise System," 15, para. 2.
78. Powell, "Attack on American Free Enterprise System," 17, para. 3.
79. Powell, "Attack on American Free Enterprise System," 29, para. 4.
80. Paul Boyer, "The Evangelical Resurgence in 1970s American Protestantism," in *Rightward Bound: Making America Conservative in the 1970s*, ed. Bruce Schulman and Julian Zelizer (Cambridge, MA: Harvard University Press, 2008), 49; Zeitz, *Building the Great Society*, Kindle Location 4380.
81. Teles, *The Rise of the Conservative Legal*, 71.
82. Zeitz, *Building the Great Society*, Kindle Location 4386.
83. Zeitz, *Building the Great Society*, Kindle Location 4386.
84. Amadae, *Prisoners of Reason*, 183.
85. Gershberg and Illing, *The Paradox of Democracy*, 161.
86. Andersen, *Evil Geniuses*, Kindle location 1317; Sitaraman, *The Crisis of the Middle-Class Constitution*, 218.
87. Amadae, *Prisoners of Reason*, 178; Appelbaum, *The Economists' Hour*, Kindle Location 1390; 1388; Thomas Byrne Edsall and Mary D. Edsall, *Chain Reaction: The Impact of Race, Rights and Taxes on American Politics* (New York: W. W. Norton, 1991), 15.
88. Phillips-Fein, *Invisible Hands*, Location 3036; see also Harvey, *A Brief History of Neoliberalism*; Timothy A. Gibson, "Primitive Accumulation, Eminent Domain, and the Contradictions of Neo-Liberalism," *Cultural Studies* 24, no. 1 (2010): 135; Jean Parker and Damien Cahill, "The Retreat from Neoliberalism that Was Not: Australia's Building the Education Revolution," *Australian Journal of Political Science* 52 (2017): 258; Peck and Tickell, "Neoliberalizing Space."
89. Zeitz, *Building the Great Society*, Kindle Location 4380.
90. Mounk, *The Age of Responsibility*, Location: 2,762; see also Wendy S. Hesford, Adela C. Licona, and Christa Teston, *Precarious Rhetorics: New Directions in Rhetoric and Materiality* (Columbus: Ohio State University Press, 2018), Location 131.
91. Aihwa Ong, *Neoliberalism as Exception: Mutation in Citizenship and Sovereignty* (Durham, NC: Duke University Press, 2006), 11; Anderson, cited in Jason Hackworth, *The Neoliberal City: Governance, Ideology, and Development in American Urbanism* (Ithaca, NY: Cornell University Press, 2007), 2.
92. Bill Grantham and Toby Miller, "The End of Neoliberalism," *Popular Communication* 8, no. 3 (July 2010): 174.
93. Harvey, *A Brief History of Neoliberalism*; see also Rob Van Horn and Philip Mirowski, "The Rise of the Chicago School of Economics and the Birth of Neoliberalism," in *The Road from Mont Pèlerin: The Making of the Neoliberal Thought Collective*, ed. Philip Mirowski and Dieter Plehwe.
94. See Amadae, *Prisoners of Reason*, 8; Roei Davidson and Amit M. Schejter,

"'Their Deeds are the Deeds of Zimri; but They Expect a Reward Like Phineas': Neoliberal and Multicultural Discourses in the Development of Israeli DTT Policy," *Communication, Culture & Critique* 4, no. 1 (March 2011): 2; Adam Fish, "Participatory Television: Convergence, Crowdsourcing, and Neoliberalism," *Communication, Culture & Critique* 6, no. 3 (September 2013): 377–78; Gibson, "Primitive Accumulation, Eminent Domain, and the Contradictions of Neo-Liberalism," 134; Giridharadas, *Winners Take All*, Location 302; Jones and Mukherjee, "From California to Michigan," 405–6; Ashley Noel Mack, "The Self-Made Mom: Neoliberalism and Masochistic Motherhood in Home-Birth Videos on YouTube," *Women's Studies In Communication* 39, no. 1 (January 2016): 51; Bryan J. McCann, "Redemption in the Neoliberal and Radical Imaginations: The Saga of Stanley 'Tookie' Williams," *Communication, Culture & Critique* 7, no. 1 (March 2014): 94; Neubauer, "Dialogue, Monologue, or Something in Between?" 2178; Peck, *Constructions of Neoliberal Reason*, 31.

95. See Rob Van Horn and Philip Mirowski, "The Rise of the Chicago School of Economics and the Birth of Neoliberalism," in *The Road from Mont Pèlerin: The Making of the Neoliberal Thought Collective*, ed. Philip Mirowski and Dieter Plehwe; Teles, *The Rise of the Conservative Legal*, 92.

96. Amadae, *Prisoners of Reason*, 291.

97. Chaput, "The Rhetorical Situation," 194; Jones and Mukherjee, "From California to Michigan," 407; see also Edgar, "Commenting Straight," 225.

98. Russell Kirk, *The Conservative Mind, from Burke to Santayana* (Chicago: H. Regnery, 1953), 3, 4, 8; Lepore, *These Truths*, Location, 10,555.

99. Asen, "Neoliberalism, the Public Sphere," 3; Brown, *Undoing the Demos*, 28; Abraham Iqbal Khan, "A Rant Good For Business: Communicative Capitalism and the Capture of Anti-Racist Resistance," *Popular Communication* 14, no. 1 (January 2016): 41; Parker and Cahill, "The Retreat from Neoliberalism," 267.

100. Mounk, *The Age of Responsibility*, Location 59.

101. For example, see Asen, "Neoliberalism, the Public Sphere," 3; Brown, *Undoing the Demos*, 173; Jones and Mukherjee. "From California to Michigan," 407; Sean Phelan, "The Rise and Fall of Neo-Liberalism: The Collapse of an Economic Order?" *Critical Discourse Studies* 10, no. 1 (2013): 117–19.

102. Asen, "Neoliberalism, the Public Sphere," 2; Phillips-Fein, *Invisible Hands*, Kindle Location 138. Neoliberalism's presence and detrimental effect is illustrated in deteriorating standards of workplace safety and national infrastructure; see Mary Douglas Vavrus, "Postfeminist Redux?" *Review of Communication* 12, no. 3 (July 2012): 230. Neoliberalism illustrates why more full-time workers don't have health benefits (Fish, "Participatory Television," 390). Neoliberalism illustrates the durability of American racism; see Henry A. Giroux, "Spectacles of Race and Pedagogies of Denial: Anti-Black Racist Pedagogy Under the Reign of Neoliberalism," *Communication Education* 52, no. 3/4 (July 2003): 191. Neoliberalism has helped bolster anti-affirmative action movements and the sexualization of women of color (Jones and Mukherjee, "From California to Michigan," 401; Amy Adele Hasinoff, "Fashioning Race for the Free Market on America's Next Top Model," *Critical Studies In Media Communication* 25, no. 3 (August 2008): 330). Cady and Oates fault neoliberal social organization for de-radicalizing LGBTQ rights, and

LeMaster finds that the economic interests of neoliberalism neutralize the radical political movement in queer critiques of social exclusions (Kathryn A. Cady and Thomas Oates, "Family Splatters: Rescuing Heteronormativity from the Zombie Apocalypse," *Women's Studies in Communication* 39, no. 3 (July 2016): 312; Benny LeMaster, "Discontents of Being and Becoming Fabulous on RuPaul's Drag U: Queer Criticism in Neoliberal Times," *Women's Studies in Communication* 38, no. 2 (2015): 170.

103. Wendy Brown, "American Nightmare: Neoliberalism, Neoconservatism, and De-Democratization," *Political Theory* 34 (2006): 690–92, 714; see also Jones and Mukherjee, "From California to Michigan," 407.

104. Peck, *Constructions of Neoliberal Reason*, 31.

105. Harvey, *A Brief History of Neoliberalism*, 2.

106. Gibson, "Primitive Accumulation, Eminent Domain, and the Contradictions of Neo-Liberalism," 135; Jones and Mukherjee, "From California to Michigan," 406; see Robert McChesney in Bradford Vivian, "Neoliberal Epideictic: Rhetorical Form and Commemorative Politics on September 11, 2002," *Quarterly Journal Of Speech* 92, no. 1 (2006): 8; Mahuya Pal and Patrice M. Buzzanell, "Breaking the Myth of Indian Call Centers: A Postcolonial Analysis of Resistance," *Communication Monographs* 80, no. 2 (2013): 216; Helene A. Shugart, "Consuming Citizen: Neoliberating the Obese Body," *Communication, Culture & Critique* 3, no. 1 (2010): 112. Clarke illustrates this trend, writing, "Yet the pristine clarity of its ideological apparition, the free market, coupled with the inevitable failure to arrive at this elusive destination, confer a significant degree of forward momentum on the neoliberal project"; see John Clarke, "In Search of Ordinary People: The Problematic Politics of Popular Participation," *Communication, Culture & Critique* 6, no. 2 (2013): 218. One may wonder if Clarke is being ironic in his use of the term "pristine clarity" because the free market is so far from pristine.

107. Terry Eagleton, *Ideology: An Introduction*, chapter 4, "From Lukas to Gramsci."

108. See Nikolas Rose and Peter Miller, *Governing the Present: Administering Economic, Social and Personal Life* (Malden, MA: Polity Press, 2008); Jones and Mukherjee, 405–8; Klein, *The Shock Doctrine*, 204; MacLean, *Democracy in Chains*, xxvii, 5, 208, 223.

109. Lepore, *These Truths*, Kindle Location 10, 240; Lisa McGirr, *Suburban Warriors: The Origins of the New American Right* (Oxford: Princeton University Press, 2001) 7. A useful line of research has expanded neoliberalism's market logics and lean government boundaries. Foucault said neoliberalism's theoretical distinctiveness lay in its ability to take "the formal principles of a market economy and project them onto a general art of government" (Foucault, *The Birth of Biopolitics*, 131–32). Following Foucault's lead, Wendy Brown showed that neoliberal political rationality requires the economy to be supported and maintained by the state (Brown, *Undoing the Demos*, 62). Scholars of economic rhetoric have also expanded the definition and application of neoliberalism. Greene and Nelson describe neoliberalism as a bundle of techniques transforming the government to influence capital accumulation (Greene and Nelson, "Struggle," 263). Kaplan described the state as the "locus for the articulation and pursuit of commercial objectives," and thus,

quite distinct from the shrunken, austere government we associate with the political Right (Kaplan, "The Communicative Efficacy of Markets," 137). Jones and Mukherjee describe how the political project of neoliberalism requires a powerful state to regulate corporate interests, absorb market risk, provide corporate welfare, and suppress organized labor and regulatory attempts (Jones and Mukherjee, "From California to Michigan," 406). Hanan analyzed the 2008 housing bubble to show the irrelevance of neoliberalism's free market/small government links after the Great Recession. Hanan went on to urge economic rhetoricians to pay more attention to state efforts organizing labor (Hanan, "Home Is Where the Capital Is," 181). Likewise, Gibson analyzed eminent domain laws to encourage us to locate other instances where the state regularly intervenes directly in the market, including the privatization of land rights, agribusiness and pharmaceuticals, and multinational media firms (Gibson, "Primitive Accumulation, Eminent Domain, and the Contradictions of Neo-Liberalism," 135).

110. Jones and Rowland, "Redefining the Proper Role of Government," 695.

111. Crowley, *Toward a Civil Discourse*, 47–48.

112. Crowley, *Toward a Civil Discourse*, 47–48.

113. Kenneth Burke, *The Philosophy of Literary Form* (Berkeley: University of California Press, 1974), 164.

114. Barry Brummett, *Rhetorical Homologies: Form, Culture, Experience* (Tuscaloosa: University of Alabama Press, 2004), 29.

115. Kiewe and Houck, "Introduction," in *The Effects of Rhetoric*, 9.

116. Kiewe and Houck, "Introduction," in *The Effects of Rhetoric*, 16.

117. Zarefsky, "Presidential Rhetoric and the Power of Definition," 610.

118. Jones and Rowland, "Redefining the Proper Role of Government," 694.

119. Crowley, *Toward a Civil Discourse*, 47–48.

120. Tali Sharot, *The Influential Mind: What the Brain Reveals About Our Power to Change Others* (New York: Henry Holt, 2017), 33.

121. Crowley, *Toward a Civil Discourse*, 59.

122. Amadae, *Prisoners of Reason*, 183; Friedman, *Free to Choose*, vol. 10; Ellis and Stimson, *Ideology in America*, xv, 85; Zeitz, *Building the Great Society*, Kindle 4369.

CHAPTER 7

1. Chaput, *Market Affect and the Rhetoric of Political Economic Debates*, 113–14.

2. George Shultz, cited in Appelbaum, *The Economists' Hour*, Location 351.

3. Appelbaum, *The Economists' Hour*, Location 351.

4. Chaput, *Market Affect and the Rhetoric of Political Economic Debates*, 123.

5. Friedman, *Capitalism and Freedom*, 285; see also Appelbaum, *The Economists' Hour*, Location 6584; Chaput, *Market Affect and the Rhetoric of Political Economic Debates*, 124; Alan O. Ebenstein, *Milton Friedman* (New York: Palgrave Macmillan, 2007), esp. 156–57. Friedman articulated both the limits of rational persuasion and his confidence in an intellectual climate shifting in his direction when he admitted on his PBS program, "I can't change their opinions. You can't change their opinions, but experience is changing their opinions. Is there anybody, anywhere now who believes that government is an efficient way to run an industrial enterprise?" (Friedman, *Free to Choose*, vol. 3).

6. Friedman, *Capitalism and Freedom*, xiii–xiv.

7. Friedman writes in the forward to Hayek's book, "I use the term liberal, as Hayek does—in the original nineteenth-century sense of limited government and free markets, not in the corrupted sense it has acquired in the United States, in which it means almost the opposite" (Hayek, *Road to Serfdom*).

8. Friedman, *Free to Choose*, vol. 4; see also Luke Winslow, Alec Baker, and Charles Goehring, "The Neoliberal Conquest of the Supreme Court," *Communication & The Public* 3, no. 3 (2018): 205–17.

9. Friedman, *Free to Choose*, vol. 10.

10. In a debate with his liberal guests about *Free to Choose*, Friedman offered a summary of their—and his entire opposition's—affinity for government programs when he said, "I have never yet known anybody who was trying to defend a government program who didn't say all its evils came from the fact that it wasn't big enough (Friedman, *Free to Choose*, vol. 6). See also Kristen Hoerl, "Cinematic Jujitsu: Resisting White Hegemony through the American Dream in Spike Lee's *Malcolm X*," *Communication Studies* 59, no. 4 (2008): 355–70.

11. Doherty, *Radicals for Capitalism*, 588; Friedman, *Free to Choose*, vol. 10.

12. Friedman, *Free to Choose*, vol. 10.

13. Friedman, *Capitalism and Freedom*, 1–2.

14. Friedman, *Capitalism and Freedom*, 5

15. Friedman, *Capitalism and Freedom*, 5. See also Asen, "Neoliberalism, the Public Sphere," 9.

16. MacLean, *Democracy in Chains*, xxiv.

17. Phillips-Fein, *Invisible Hands*, Location 2737.

18. Will, *The Conservative Sensibility*, xxxiii. According to Will, Goldwater got crushed because he was ahead of his time. Goldwater concurred, writing in his journal: "Today as I sit in the Senate in the year 1979 it is interesting to me to watch liberals, moderates and conservatives fighting each other to see who can come out on top the quickest against those matters that I talked so fervently and so much about in 1964. . . . Now that almost every one of the principles I advocated in 1964 have become the gospel of the whole spread of the spectrum of politics, there really isn't a heck of a lot left"; see Phillips-Fein, *Invisible Hands*, Location 3824.

19. Friedman, *Why Government Is the Problem*, 14; Milton Friedman and Rose Friedman, *Free to Choose: A Personal Statement* (San Diego: Harcourt, 1980), 64.

20. Friedman, *Free to Choose*, vol. 7.

21. Gordon Tullock, for example, described the Chicago economics department to the *National Review* as "a very small but growing movement of scholars" doing research on a "science of politics" with important lessons for the world. On his PBS program, Friedman was adamant, telling his guests, "I am not a partisan, I am not a partisan," and criticizing both Republicans and Democrats for adopting the Socialist Party platform (Friedman, *Free to Choose*, vol. 5).

22. Friedman, *Free to Choose*, vol. 7.

23. Phillips-Fein, *Invisible Hands*, Location 1024; Doherty, *Radicals for Capitalism*, 18. Recall from the previous chapter, however, that Friedrich Hayek was torn. He initially assumed the label of economic scientist, but he ultimately rejected it as a misguided ruse. But as a result of Friedman's work, economic science became

seesaw-simple. Bleeding heart liberals sat on the Left and serious economic scientists sat on the Right. Nuance is lost, and as a result the oligarchic political logics at the foundation of the American political economy remain uncontested.

24. Phillips-Fein, *Invisible Hands*, Location 1024.

25. Doherty, *Radicals for Capitalism*, 18.

26. Chaput, *Market Affect and the Rhetoric of Political Economic Debates*, 116.

27. In 2020, as the coronavirus pandemic ravished the country, Americans were surveyed about which presidential candidate was better equipped to lead. Donald Trump trailed Joe Biden in every dimension except one: the economy; see Patricia Cohen, "Trump's Biggest Economic Legacy Isn't About the Numbers," *New York Times*, October 24, 2020. Despite decades of contradictory economic research, and even in the face of such brazen and self-inflicted political and economic incompetence, most Americans continued to link economic expertise with Trump and the political Right; see Michael Tomasky, "Why Recent Republican Presidents Have Been Economic Failures," *New York Times*, August 20, 2020.

28. Friedman, *Free to Choose*, vol. 2.

29. Friedman, *Free to Choose*, vol. 1.

30. Milton Friedman, "Value Judgments in Economics," Collected Works of Milton Friedman Project records, Hoover Institution Library & Archives, 92; see Chaput, *Market Affect and the Rhetoric of Political Economic Debates*, 118.

31. Slobodian, *Globalists*, Kindle Location 3576. In Friedman's *Free to Choose* series, he summarized his whole critique by locating the real culprit for not having the liberating economy he desired: "Well I want to—I want to go and make a very different point. I sit here and berate you and you, as government officials, and so on, but I understand very well that the real culprits are not the politicians, are not the central bankers, but it's I and my fellow citizens. I always say to people when I talk about this, 'If you want to know who's responsible for inflation, look in the mirror.' It's not because of the way you spend your money. Inflation doesn't arise because you got consumers who are spendthrift; they've always been spendthrift. It doesn't arise because you've got businessmen who are greedy. They've always been greedy. Inflation arises because we as citizens have been asking you as politicians to perform an impossible task. We've been asking you to spend somebody else's money on us, but not to spend our money on anybody else" (Friedman, *Free to Choose*, vol. 9). In episode 10, he also urged not to directly fault government bureaucrats, saying, "The deals made here affect all of us, and sometimes in ways we don't like. But don't blame the people making the deals. They're just pursuing their own self-interests, which may be as narrow as making a buck or as broad as trying to reform the world. We the citizens are to blame, because we've handed over so much of our lives, our personal decision-making, to government, and we now find that what government does severely limits our freedom" (Friedman, *Free to Choose*, vol. 10).

32. Milton Friedman, cited in Slobodian, *Globalists*, Kindle Location 3589.

33. Friedman, *Free to Choose*, vol. 5.

34. Friedman, *Free to Choose*, vol. 5.

35. Milton Friedman, "Capitalism and Freedom," in *New Individualist Review*, ed. Ralph Raico (1961) 1, no. 1. See also Peck, *Constructions of Neoliberal Reason*, 106.

NOTES

36. Aune, *Selling the Free Market*, 37; Valdes, *Pinochet's Economists*, 6.

37. Appelbaum, *The Economists' Hour*, Location 990.

38. Friedman, *Free to Choose*, vol. 2; see also Appelbaum, *The Economists' Hour*, Location 990 and 2302.

39. Margaret O'Mara in *The Code* offered an updated link: Milton Friedman's grandson, who, in 2020, was proposing to build a libertarian utopia where he can "escape the tentacles of bureaucratic control," according to O'Mara (385). The ancestral link reveals the rhetorical and political purpose of the public argument: Friedman dreamed of an unrealizable utopia that must be conceived before it could be implemented.

40. Friedman, *Free to Choose*, vol. 2.

41. See Milton Friedman, "Monetarism in Rhetoric and in Practice," keynote paper presented at the First International Conference of the Institute for Monetary and Economics Studies, Tokyo, June 22, 1983. Friedman's if/only logic has a long and distinguished history: Alan Greenspan, during the Great Recession echoed a consistent purge vocabulary that can be traced back to Andrew Mellon, Herbert Hoover's secretary of treasury who wanted to let the economic crisis run its course, telling Hoover to "Liquidate labor, liquidate stocks, liquidate the farmers, liquidate real estate. It will purge the rottenness out of the system. People will work harder, live a more moral life" and in the end "enterprising people will pick up the pieces from less competent people"; see Alan S. Blinder, *After the Music Stopped: The Financial Crisis, the Response, and the Work Ahead* (New York: Penguin Group US, 2013. Kindle edition), 353. During the Great Depression, when Mellon's advice was rejected and Hoover, instead, supported government interventions in farm policy, public works, and tariffs, neoliberal proponents now had vivid examples of state intervention adulterating the natural purifying force of the market. Rothbard, of course, complained that such efforts "stymied the necessary and proper economic adjustments that would have ended the crisis soon enough"; see Murray Rothbard, *Left and Right: A Journal of Libertarian Thought (Complete, 1965–1968)* (Auburn: Ludwig von Mises Institute, 2007). In Chile, as Chicago policies allowed unemployment to surge to 30 percent, poverty rates to climb to 50 percent, and the collapse of the banking sector, voters not surprisingly rejected neoliberalism, the Chicago boys can return to the US with their heads high and self-righteously lament that "If only . . ." More recently, the TARP bailouts of the Obama era were similarly criticized—not for bringing the entire global economy back from the brink of collapse—but for slowing the recovery by not letting natural market forces work to purge General Motors and Wells Fargo from the system.

42. Chaput, *Market Affect and the Rhetoric of Political Economic Debates*, 117.

43. Chaput, *Market Affect and the Rhetoric of Political Economic Debates*, 118; Zeitz, *Building the Great Society*, Kindle Location 891.

44. Friedman, *Free to Choose*, vol. 7.

45. Friedman, *Free to Choose*, vol. 8.

46. MacLean, *Democracy in Chains*, 67.

47. MacLean, *Democracy in Chains*, 90.

48. Friedman and Friedman, *Free to Choose*, 298.

49. Friedman and Friedman, *Free to Choose*, 124.

50. Friedman, *Why Government Is the Problem*, 10.

51. Friedman, *Free to Choose*, vol. 10.

52. Lessl, *Rhetorical Darwinism*, 23.

53. Lessl, *Rhetorical Darwinism*, 16.

54. Lessl, *Rhetorical Darwinism*, xi.

55. For further support for the link between public cynicism and arrogance as a central feature of the oligarchic/intellectual outlook, see MacLean, *Democracy in Chains*, 116.

56. Credit to T. M. Luhrmann for the metaphor; see T. M. Luhrmann, *When God Talks Back: Understanding the American Evangelical Relationship with God* (New York: Knopf, 2012). Following Lessl and Goodnight, Friedman's "relaxed" methodological standards were well-suited to linking lay audiences, technical expertise, and public policy (Lessl, *Rhetorical Darwinism*, 22). James Aune argues that quasi-scientific language is influential because it allows rhetors like Friedman to assume a persona the scientific method forbids (Aune, *Selling the Free Market*, 166). Rather than remain confined to the methodological imperatives of his technical spheres, Friedman reflected what Roberts-Miller described as the "assurances of certainty" that affectively accompany facts, statistics, and data (Roberts-Miller, *Rhetoric and Demagoguery*, 24).

57. See Chaput, *Market Affect and the Rhetoric of Political Economic Debates*, 125.

58. Friedman and Friedman, *Free to Choose*, 127; Friedman, *Capitalism and Freedom*, 35. See Winslow, Baker, and Goehring, "The Neoliberal."

59. Friedman, *Capitalism and Freedom*, xi–xiii. See also Klein, *The Shock Doctrine*, 21.

60. Chaput, *Market Affect and the Rhetoric of Political Economic Debates*, 125.

61. Milton Friedman and Rose Friedman, *Two Lucky People* (Chicago: University of Chicago Press, 1999), 220. See also Appelbaum, *The Economists' Hour*, Location 335; Neubauer, "Dialogue, Monologue, or Something in Between?" 2189; Peck, *Constructions of Neoliberal Reason*, 70. On his PBS program, Friedman assured viewers and his guests he was "not proposing [to] dismantle anything"; he was "only proposing that there be a wider range of alternatives"; see Friedman, *Free to Choose*, vol. 6. See also Mark Hlavacik, "Milton Friedman Blames the Bureaucrats," in *Assigning Blame: The Rhetoric of Education Reform* (Cambridge, MA: Harvard Education Press, 2016), 42.

62. Friedman, cited in Appelbaum, *The Economists' Hour*, Location 335; Chaput, *Market Affect and the Rhetoric of Political Economic Debates*, 125; Doherty, *Radicals for Capitalism*, 2.

63. For example, Andrew Ross Sorkin says Friedman laid "the groundwork for laissez-faire revolution" and Sorkin called Friedman's 1970 essay in the *New York Times Magazine* a "call to arms for free market capitalism"; see "Greed Is Good. Except When It Is Bad," *New York Times Magazine*. September 13, 2020. Kurt Andersen calls Friedman "an avatar of the ultra-conservative economic strain" (Andersen, *Evil Geniuses*, Kindle location 999). S. A. Amadae links Friedman to "the mid-century faith in free markets" (Amadae, *Prisoners of Reason*, 12). Aihwa Ong linked Friedman to the wave of "attacks on big government and the bureaucratic welfare state" (Ong, *Neoliberalism as Exception*, 10). Robert Asen links Friedman to

NOTES

the Right's skepticism of coordinated action as an infringement on individual prerogatives (Asen, "Neoliberalism, the Public Sphere," 9). Catherine Chaput opens her book chapter on Friedman by contrasting his aversion to government intervention to liberal economist John Kenneth Galbraith (Chaput, *Market Affect and the Rhetoric of Political Economic Debates*, 113). And Binyamin Appelbaum says Friedman was "the forceful prophet of a conservative counterrevolution" (Appelbaum, *The Economists' Hour*, Location 333).

64. Fish, "Participatory Television," 377–78. For more examples, see Amadae, *Prisoners of Reason*, 12; Doherty, *Radicals for Capitalism*, 15, 67; MacLean, *Democracy in Chains*, 36.

65. Friedman, *Free to Choose*, vol. 2; see also Andersen, *Evil Geniuses*, Kindle location 2560; Appelbaum, *The Economists' Hour*, Location 230.

66. Friedman, *Free to Choose*, vol. 5.

67. Milton Friedman, "Policy Forum: 'Milton Friedman on Business Suicide,'" Cato Institute, March/April 1999. Accessed November 23, 2020. See also Andersen, *Evil Geniuses*, Kindle location 5873, 1115.

68. Andersen, *Evil Geniuses*, 139.

69. Henry Simons, "Introduction: A Political Credo," in *Economic Policy for a Free Society*, ed. Ekkehard Köhler and Stefan Kolev (Chicago: University of Chicago Press, 1948), 18.

70. Peck, *Constructions of Neoliberal Reason*, 42. See also Asen, "Neoliberalism, the Public Sphere," 12.

71. Friedman, "Neo-liberalism and its prospects," 3; see also Chaput, *Market Affect and the Rhetoric of Political Economic Debates*, 124.

72. Friedman, *Free to Choose*, vol. 5.

73. Friedman and Friedman, *Free to Choose*, 130.

74. He told his PBS audience, "All I am saying is: Don't kid yourself into thinking that there is some painless way to do it. There just is not" (Friedman, *Free to Choose*, vol. 9).

75. Friedman, *Capitalism and Freedom*, 24.

76. Friedman, *Free to Choose*, vol. 7. Notice the links between Friedman's warnings and Spencer's concern that once the state is allowed to enforce mine safety regulations and fund public libraries, a state inspector will soon be knocking on our doors to monitor our exercise and diets (Spencer, *Proper Sphere of Government* 46, 54; see also Francis, *Herbert Spencer and the Invention of Modern Life*, 268).

77. Friedman, *Free to Choose*, vol. 2. Friedman disdained welfare because he claimed it sapped "self-pride," for example; when you force people off welfare and give them a job, they can regain their pride (Friedman, *Free to Choose*, vol. 4). He also highlighted the undeserving comfort and security of government workers when he visited a Washington, DC, suburb to open episode 8 of *Free to Choose*. Standing in front of a row of large houses with manicured lawns, Friedman said, "Half an hour's drive out of Washington you come to Montgomery County, where many very senior civil servants live. It has the highest average family income of any county in the United States. Of the people who live here who are employed, one out of every four works for the federal government. Like all civil servants, they have job security, salaries linked to the cost of living, a fine retirement plan

also linked to the cost of living, and many manage to qualify for Social Security as well, becoming double-dippers. Many of their neighbors are also here because of the federal government: congressmen, lobbyists, top executives of corporations with government contracts. As government expands, so does this neighborhood. Government protects its workers just as trade unions protect their members. But both do it at someone else's expense. It doesn't have to be that way (Friedman, *Free to Choose*, vol. 8). Decades later, Tucker Carlson would reflect the same bureaucratic disdain in his bestselling book, *Ship of Fools*, writing, "Washington isn't like everywhere else. The city's economy is tied directly to the size of the federal budget, which has grown virtually without pause since the attack on Pearl Harbor in 1941. The District of Columbia and its surrounding suburbs are now the wealthiest metro region in the country. Washington's job market is effectively bulletproof. Political figures cycle in and out of government, from lobbying to finance to contracting and back, growing richer at every turn. In Washington, prosperity is all but guaranteed. To the rest of the country, this looks like corruption, because, essentially, it is. But if you live there, it's all upside" (Carlson, *Ship of Fools*, Location 1280.)

78. Andersen, *Evil Geniuses*, Kindle Location 2904.

79. Stewart, *The 9.9 Percent*, 133.

80. Daniel Schulman, *Sons of Wichita: How the Koch Brothers Became America's Most Powerful and Private Dynasty* (New York: Grand Central, 2014), 94.

81. Friedman, cited in Klein, *The Shock Doctrine*, 25, 60, 203. See also MacLean, *Democracy in Chains*, 175; Mayer, *Dark Money*, 53.

82. Amadae, *Prisoners of Reason*, 248.

83. Friedman, *Free to Choose*, vol. 5. See also Amadae, *Prisoners of Reason*, 186.

84. Brown, *Undoing the Demos*, 215.

85. Friedman, *Free to Choose*, vol. 4.

86. For the libertarian rationale for pain-as-policy, see Doherty, *Radicals for Capitalism*, 409. For an example of pain-infliction as governing philosophy from the Supreme Court, see Cohen, *Supreme Inequality*, Kindle Location 5402.

87. Meese, cited in Cohen, *Supreme Inequality*, Kindle Location 1485.

88. MacLean, *Democracy in Chains*, 212.

89. Amadae, *Prisoners of Reason*, 223; Binmore, *Natural Justice*.

90. Zeitz, *Building the Great Society*, Kindle Location 4393.

91. Milton Friedman, *Why Government Is the Problem* (Stanford, CA: Hoover Press, 1993).

92. Friedman, *Capitalism and Freedom*, xiii.

93. Friedman on Rhodesia, cited in Slobodian, *Globalists*, Kindle Location 3576.

94. For a precise delineation of racism, bigotry, and prejudice, see Kendi, *Stamped from the Beginning*, 43.

95. Chaput, *Market Affect and the Rhetoric of Political Economic Debates*, 135.

96. Slobodian, *Globalists*, Kindle Location 4521.

97. Valdes, *Pinochet's Economists*, 10.

98. Appelbaum, *The Economists' Hour*, Location 230; Hart, *The Making of the Conservative Mind*, 263; Burns, *Goddess of the Market*, 247–48; Chaput, *Market Affect and the Rhetoric of Political Economic Debates*, 111; Lee, *Creating Conservatism*,

NOTES

11, 68; MacLean, Democracy in Chains, xviii; Neubauer, "Dialogue, Monologue, or Something in Between?" 2177; Phillips-Fein, *Invisible Hands*, Location 3337.

99. Foucault, *The Birth of Biopolitics*, 247.

100. Giroux, *Stormy Weather*, 21.

101. Friedman, *Capitalism and Freedom*, 14; Friedman and Friedman, *Free to Choose*, 34; see also Robert Asen, *Visions of Poverty: Welfare Policy and Political Imagination* (East Lansing: Michigan State University Press, 2002); Brown, *Undoing the Demos*, 215; Giroux, *Stormy Weather*, 22–25; Mayer, *Dark Money*, 88; Mounk, *The Age of Responsibility*, Location 59, 2,762; Arlie Russell Hochschild, *Strangers in Their Own Land: Anger and Mourning on the American Right* (New York: New Press, 2016), Kindle Location: "Chapter 14: The Fires of History."

102. For example, Barry Goldwater said, "We must and shall return to proven ways—not because they are old, but because they are true." See Peck, *Constructions of Neoliberal Reason*, 105; MacLean, *Democracy in Chains*, 90; for more nostalgic references from Milton Friedman, see *Free to Choose*, vol. 1, vol. 10.

103. Giroux, *Stormy Weather*, 22; Klein, *The Shock Doctrine*, 204.

104. Mayer, *Dark Money*, 53.

105. Foucault, *The Birth of Biopolitics*, 145–47, 218; see also Chaput, "Rhetorical Circulation in Late Capitalism," 4; Catherine Chaput, "Trumponomics, Neoliberal Branding, and the Rhetorical Circulation of Affect," *Advances in the History of Rhetoric* 21, no. 2 (2018): 194–209; William Davies, "What Is 'Neo' about Neoliberalism?" in *Liberalism in Neoliberal Times: Dimensions, Contradictions, Limits*, ed. Alejandro Abraham-Hamanoiel, Des Freedman, Gholam Khiabany, Kate Nash, and Julian Petley (London: Goldsmiths Press, 2017), 18; Grantham and Miller, "The End of Neoliberalism," 175.

106. Chaput, "Rhetorical Circulation in Late Capitalism," 4; Harvey, *A Brief History of Neoliberalism*; Neubauer, "Dialogue, Monologue, or Something in Between?" 2179.

107. Jennifer Wingard, "Branding Citizens: The Logic(s) of a Few Bad Apples," in *Rhetoric in Neoliberalism*, ed. Kim Hong Nguyen (London: Palgrave Macmillan, 2017), 136.

108. Formisano, *American Oligarchy*, 58.

109. Andersen, *Evil Geniuses*, Kindle location 5528. See also Frank, *What's the Matter with Kansas?* 6; Neubauer, "Dialogue, Monologue, or Something in Between?" 2179.

110. Frank, *What's the Matter with Kansas?*, 6.

111. For example, Chaput describes how neoliberal appeal "functions through a series of political and cultural interventions designed to implement competition as an economic rationality that counters purportedly irrational social practices" (Chaput, "Rhetorical Circulation in Late Capitalism," 4). Davies uses Hayek to focus on "competition determining who and what is valuable" (Davies, "What Is 'Neo' about Neoliberalism?"). And Grantham and Miller use Foucault to highlight how competition "was imposed to regulate everyday life in the most subtly comprehensive statism imaginable" (Grantham and Miller, "The End of Neoliberalism," 175).

112. Andersen, *Evil Geniuses*, Kindle location 2206.

113. Mounk, *The Age of Responsibility*, Location 2,927. Heather McGhee, in *The Sum of Us: What Racism Costs Everyone and How We Can Prosper Together* (New York: One World, 2021), leverages the "drained-pool" metaphor to insightfully illuminate the pernicious idea that many Americans seem willing to make their lives more difficult just to ensure the (perceived) unworthy do not have access to resources they do not "deserve." More specifically, southern racists during the Civil Rights era preferred to drain the local community swimming pool, so that no one—white or Black—could swim, than to integrate it and swim together.

114. Piketty, *Capital and Ideology*, Kindle Location 763; see also Asen, "Neoliberalism, the Public Sphere."

CHAPTER 8

1. MacLean, *Democracy in Chains*, xxiii.
2. Amadae. *Prisoners of Reason*, 176; MacLean, *Democracy in Chains*, xxi, 142, 206, 248.
3. MacLean, *Democracy in Chains*, xviii.
4. Amadae, *Prisoners of Reason*, 26, 60.
5. Asen, "Neoliberalism, the Public Sphere," 3.
6. Peck, *Constructions of Neoliberal Reason*, 88.
7. Mounk, *The Age of Responsibility*, Location 2,762.
8. MacLean, *Democracy in Chains*, 212.
9. Mayer, *Dark Money*, 232. See also Foley, "From Infantile," 400; Fraser and Gerstle, *Ruling America*, Location 1767.
10. Milton Friedman also criticized the Civil Rights Act as government coercion (MacLean, *Democracy in Chains*, 32–35, 90, 223).
11. Mounk, *The Age of Responsibility*, Location 480; MacLean, *Democracy in Chains*, 134.
12. MacLean, *Democracy in Chains*, 170.
13. MacLean, *Democracy in Chains*, 171.
14. MacLean, *Democracy in Chains*, 32.
15. MacLean, *Democracy in Chains*, 108; see also Teles, *The Rise of the Conservative Legal Movement*.
16. MacLean, *Democracy in Chains*, 101.
17. MacLean, *Democracy in Chains*, 48.
18. MacLean, *Democracy in Chains*, 170.
19. MacLean, *Democracy in Chains*, 170.
20. MacLean, *Democracy in Chains*, 171–73.
21. James M. Buchanan, cited in Amadae, *Prisoners of Reason*, 183.
22. Amadae, *Prisoners of Reason*, 183.
23. MacLean, *Democracy in Chains*, 32.
24. Buchanan, "The Samaritan's Dilemma," 83.
25. James M. Buchanan, *The Limits of Liberty: Between Anarchy and Leviathan* (Chicago: University of Chicago, 1975), 96.
26. Ludwig von Mises, *Human Action: A Treatise on Economics* (Ludwig von Mises Institute, 1949), chapter 34: The Economics of War.
27. James M. Buchanan, "The Samaritan's Dilemma," in *Altruism, Morality,*

and Economic Theory, ed. Edmund S. Phelps (New York: Russell Sage Foundation, 1975), 84.

28. Buchanan, "The Samaritan's Dilemma," 71.

29. Buchanan, "The Samaritan's Dilemma," 84.

30. Luke Winslow, "'Not Exactly a Model of Good Hygiene': Theorizing an Aesthetic of Disgust in the Occupy Wall Street Movement," *Critical Studies in Media Communication* 34 (2017): 278–92.

31. Buchanan, "The Samaritan's Dilemma," 83.

32. Asen, *Visions of Poverty*; Luke Winslow, *Economic Injustice and the Rhetoric of the American Dream* (Lanham, MD: Lexington Books, 2017).

33. Buchanan, "The Samaritan's Dilemma," 78–79.

34. Buchanan, "The Samaritan's Dilemma,"83.

35. Buchanan, "The Samaritan's Dilemma," 79.

36. Buchanan, "The Samaritan's Dilemma," 80.

37. Andrew Carnegie, "The Gospel of Wealth" (New York: Carnegie Corporation of New York, 2017, first published in 1889), 90; Milton Friedman, *Free to Choose*, vol. 4, From Cradle to Grave (PBS, 1980); MacLean, *Democracy in Chains*, 213; Mayer, *Dark Money*, 315, 360.

38. Economist Tyler Cowen illustrates this perverse appeal when he imagines his ideal social contract marked by increased burdens on the working class and poor being mediated by their enhanced geographical mobility. Because the working class and poor have less, they can more easily move to lower-cost states like Texas (MacLean, *Democracy in Chains*, 212). Likewise, Friedman's "cut it off" offers the welfare recipient the motivation to earn a living with his or her dignity intact. Or starve. Either outcome is preferable to the state aiding exploitive laziness.

39. Edward F. McClennen, "Comment," in *Altruism, Morality, and Economic Theory*, ed. Edmund S. Phelps (New York: Russell Sage Foundation, 1975), 138.

40. Buchanan, "The Samaritan's Dilemma," 81.

41. Buchanan, "The Samaritan's Dilemma," 81.

42. Hacker and Pierson, *American Amnesia*; Phillips-Fein, *Invisible Hands*, Kindle Location 120.

43. Amadae, *Prisoners of Reason*, 176; MacLean, *Democracy in Chains*, 143.

44. James M. Buchanan, "Afraid to Be Free: Dependency as Desideratum," *Public Choice* 124 (2005): 24.

45. Buchanan, "The Samaritan's Dilemma," 83–84.

46. Buchanan, "The Samaritan's Dilemma," 74.

47. Buchanan, "The Samaritan's Dilemma," 83–84.

48. Buchanan, "The Samaritan's Dilemma," 84n6.

49. Buchanan, "The Samaritan's Dilemma," 83–84.

50. Buchanan, "The Samaritan's Dilemma," 81.

51. Buchanan, "The Samaritan's Dilemma," 83.

52. Buchanan, "The Samaritan's Dilemma," 82.

53. The history of conservatism is marked by a paradoxical relationship between the desire for a lean government and the desire for a robust nation-state capable of maintaining order by policing original sin and evil, but without mediating adversity and suffering. I explore this paradox in chapters 1 and 10. Edmund Burke provided

the clearest distillation of this paradox, as he argued for government as a positive tool of repressing evil passions while also idealizing a reduced and streamlined governmental apparatus. For conservatives, the rhetoric of democratic oligarchy is especially resonant because it offers a discursive reconciliation of this paradox in its naturalist, consequentialist, and realist points of formal correspondence. Edmund Burke, "Reflections on the Revolution in France," in *Works*, 320–22, 327; See also Kramnick, *The Rage*, 30, 49.

54. MacLean, *Democracy in Chains*, 142.

55. Maurice Charland, "Constitutive Rhetoric: The Case of the Peuple Québécois," *Quarterly Journal of Speech* 73 (1987): 133–50; Bonnie J. Dow, "Response Criticism and Authority in the Artistic Mode," *Western Journal of Communication* 65, no. 3 (2001): 343; Amos Kiewe and David W. Houck, eds., *The Effects of Rhetoric and the Rhetoric of Effects* (Columbia: University of South Carolina Press, 2015).

56. Asen, "Neoliberalism, the Public Sphere," 12; Darrel Enck-Wanzer, "Barack Obama, the Tea Party, and the Threat of Race: On Racial Neoliberalism and Born Again Racism," *Communication, Culture & Critique* 4, no. 1 (2011): 25.

57. Buchanan's rhetoric illustrates the gap oligarchy can fill in conceptualizations of a "neoliberal" political economy, which I discuss in relation to Lewis Powell in chapter 6. Consider how many scholars have responded to the ubiquitous and undeniable spatial and temporal positionality of the state by stretching the conceptual parameters of neoliberal capitalism. Sean Phelan notes how the discipline has done well in connecting neoliberalism to the transformation of individual identities according to market logics but less well in theorizing how the affluent can enjoin the state to defend, enhance, and maximize their wealth and power. After Timothy Gibson describes the "fairly serious contradictions" marking neoliberalism's state/market conceptualization, he goes on to describe a "world of actually-existing neoliberalism" where the government intervenes directly in the market on a routine basis. Jones and Mukherjee also highlight neoliberalism's conceptual bind: after detailing neoliberalism's associations with free markets and smaller government, they described how the political project of neoliberalism actually requires a powerful government to regulate corporate interests, absorb market risk, provide corporate welfare, and suppress organized labor and regulatory attempts; see Sean Phelan, "The Discourses of Neoliberal Hegemony: The Case of The Irish Republic," *Critical Discourse Studies* 4, no. 1 (2007): 34; Gibson, "Primitive Accumulation, Eminent Domain, and the Contradictions of Neo-Liberalism," 135; Jones and Mukherjee, "From California to Michigan," 406. Many scholars do acknowledge the conceptual incongruity, but then they too often move on to lumping neoliberalism with austerity and diminished government interventions into economic affairs; for examples, see McCann, "Redemption in the Neoliberal," 94; and Michael J. Steudeman, "Indeterminacy, Incipiency, and Attitudes: Materialist Oscillation in the 2012 Chicago Teachers' Strike," *Quarterly Journal of Speech* 101 (2015): 516–17. Henry Giroux illustrates the scholarly challenge that comes with this stretching when he says that under American neoliberalism, "all levels of government have been hollowed out and largely reduced either to their policing functions *or* to maintaining the privileges of the rich and the interests of corporate power" (Giroux, "Spectacles of Race," 207). Buchanan's oligarchic implications allow us to highlight the "*or*" in

NOTES

Giroux's sentence. Halliburton won a $39 billion defense contract when we invaded Iraq in 2003; Koch Industries used their Pine Bend refinery in Minnesota as a cash cow by exploiting a loophole that allowed unlimited oil imports from Canada. And as I discuss in the introduction, FedEx reduced its effective tax rate from 34 percent in 2017 to zero in 2018 because it influenced how Donald Trump's 2017 Tax Cuts and Jobs Act was crafted. The American economic-political condition is replete with examples like these. The Import/Export bank, licensing and patent laws, ethanol subsidies, trade barriers, price supports for agricultural industries, and regressive regulations protecting drug makers, oil companies, car dealers, hospitals, tech companies, and funeral directors are defining features of our liberal democracy; see Brink Lindsey and Steven M. Teles, *The Captured Economy: How the Powerful Enrich Themselves, Slow Down Growth, and Increase Inequality* (New York: Oxford University Press, 2017), Location 533. Giroux's neoliberal economy defined by "maintaining the privileges of the rich and the interests of corporate power" strains under its conceptual contradictions and practical exceptions. Buchanan's rhetoric explains, in part, how those contradictions are reconciled.

58. Amadae, *Prisoners of Reason*, 173.

59. Amadae, *Prisoners of Reason*, 48, 60190, 239; Binmore, *Natural Justice*, 66; Doherty, *Radicals for Capitalism*, ii; Slobodian, *Globalists*, Kindle Location 2120.

60. Winters, *Oligarchy*, 6.

61. Amadae, *Prisoners of Reason*, Location 8847.

62. Roy Child, cited in Doherty, *Radicals for Capitalism*, 559.

63. Doherty, *Radicals for Capitalism*, 559.

64. A. P. Carnevale and B. Cheah, *From Hard Times to Better Times* (Washington, DC: Georgetown University Center on Education and the Workforce); A. P. Carnevale, B. Cheah, and A. R. Hanson, *The Economic Value of College Majors* (Washington, DC: Georgetown University Center on Education and the Workforce, 2015).

65. Friedman, "The Role of Government in Education," 123–44, cited in MacLean, *Democracy in Chains*, 68; See also Friedman, *Free to Choose*, vol. 6.

66. MacLean, *Democracy in Chains*, 106.

67. See Leonard, *Kochland*, Location 8279; MacLean, *Democracy in Chains*, xxii; Mayer, *Dark Money*, 150; Saez and Zucman, *The Triumph of Injustice*, Kindle Location 894.

68. Zucman and Wezerek, "Shut Down," 2021.

69. Duhigg and Kocieniewski, "How Apple Sidesteps Billions in Taxes," April 28, 2012; Kocieniewski, "At G.E. on Tax Day," September 23, 2015.

70. Buchanan, "The Samaritan's Dilemma," 84–85.

71. Buchanan's closing argument reflects larger cultural touchstones, such as Yoda's retort to Luke Skywalker when he expresses doubt about the power of the force ("And that is why you failed"), and the children's book and movie *The Polar Express*, in which one's ability to hear Santa Claus's bell hinges on the ability to believe. Buchanan also reflects American prosperity theology, connecting material wealth to belief in God's blessings. Belief symbolizes entrance into the community. Doubt symbolizes ignorance and complicity.

72. James Darsey, *The Prophetic Tradition and Radical Rhetoric in America* (New York: New York University Press, 1997), 27–28; Jonathan J. Edwards, *Superchurch:*

The Rhetoric and Politics of American Fundamentalism (East Lansing: Michigan State University Press, 2015), 127–28.

73. Page, Seawright, and Lacombe, *Billionaires and Stealth Politics*, 2.

CHAPTER 9

1. Page, Seawright, and Lacombe, *Billionaires and Stealth Politics*, 132–33, 136, 143.
2. Page, Seawright, and Lacombe, *Billionaires and Stealth Politics*, 7, 76.
3. Page, Seawright, and Lacombe, *Billionaires and Stealth Politics*, 47.
4. Ralph Miliband, writing in 1969, described the mindset that normally prevented the ultra-rich from running for office: "Businessmen have often tended to stress their remoteness from, even their distaste for 'politics': and they have also tended to have a poor view of politicians as men, who, in the hallowed phrase, have never had to meet a payroll and therefore know very little of the *real* world—yet who seek to interfere in the affairs of the hard-headed and practical men whose business it is to meet a payroll, and who therefore do know that the world is about" (Miliband, *The State in Capitalist Society*, 41).
5. In 2014, the Koch brothers assembled $300 million to elect sympathetic politicians, and over the next two years they contributed $3 million to the Republican Governors Association. Theda Skocpol has detailed the links between the Kochs and their foundations, including Americans For Prosperity and ALEC, to highlight how the Kochs have developed a network of 2.5 million conservative activists in influential state and local political positions, charged with raising money, producing political ads, leading voter turnout operations, and assuming the duties of conventional political parties—without the diffused power concentrations (Theda Skocpol, cited in Page, Seawright, and Lacombe, *Billionaires and Stealth Politics*, 2, 104–15).
6. Charles G. Koch, *The Science of Success: How Market-Based Management Built the World's Largest Private Company* (Hoboken, NJ: John Wiley & Sons, 2007), vii–viii.
7. Page, Seawright, and Lacombe, *Billionaires and Stealth Politics*, 20, 47, 139. In *The Science of Success*, Koch attributes his ability to merge with Union Oil as hinged on convincing J. Howard the deal "could be done tax-efficiently" (Koch, *The Science of Success*, 14).
8. Page, Seawright, and Lacombe, *Billionaires and Stealth Politics*, 8.
9. Andersen, *Evil Geniuses*, Kindle location 1317.
10. Leonard, *Kochland*, Location 3134. To enhance readability, I focus on Charles Koch, but most of my claims also apply to his late brother, David, as well.
11. Schulman, *Sons of Wichita*, 94.
12. Schulman, *Sons of Wichita*, 252.
13. Formisano, *American Oligarchy*, 90.
14. Matea Gold, "Koch-backed Political Network, Built to Shield Donors, Raised $400 Million In 2012 Elections," *Washington Post*, January 5, 2014.
15. Leonard, *Kochland*, Location 702; Mayer, *Dark Money*, Location 7140.
16. Charles Koch, "1974 Charles Koch Speech: Anti-Capitalism and Big Business and How the Powell Memo Did Not Go Far Enough," *KochDocs*; see also

NOTES

Christopher Leonard, "Charles Koch's Big Bet on Barrett," *New York Times*, Oct 12, 2020.

17. Charles Koch, "The Business Community: Resisting Regulation," *Libertarian Review* (August 1978), 34.

18. Charles Koch, "The Business Community: Resisting Regulation," *Libertarian Review* (August 1978), 33.

19. Charles Koch, *Anti-Capitalism and Business* (Menlo Park: Institute for Humane Studies, 1974), 5. See also Nicholas Confessore, "Quixotic '80 Campaign Gave Birth to Kochs' Powerful Network," *New York Times*, May 14, 2014; Mayer, *Dark Money*, Location 2304; Leonard, *Kochland*, Location 109.

20. Mayer, *Dark Money*, Location 1672.

21. Leonard, *Kochland*, Location 147.

22. Koch, *The Science of Success*, vii.

23. Koch, *The Science of Success*, vii.

24. Koch, *The Science of Success*, 152.

25. Koch, *The Science of Success*, 25. The intergenerational origins of Charles Koch's wealth is, understandably, avoided in his public messaging. For example, Koch wrote, without a trace of irony, "A truly free society rewards people according to their individual merits, not by what they are associated with" (Koch, *The Science of Success*, 84). And Jane Mayer notes that when Koch promoted his son Chase to the presidency of Koch Fertilizer, he said "every step, he's done it on his own" (Mayer, *Dark Money*, 360).

26. Koch, *The Science of Success*, ix.

27. Leonard, *Kochland*, Location 692.

28. Koch, *The Science of Success*, viii.

29. Koch, *The Science of Success*, x.

30. Koch, *The Science of Success*, 117.

31. Koch, *The Science of Success*, 31.

32. Leonard, *Kochland*, 2595.

33. Koch, *The Science of Success*, 25.

34. Koch, *The Science of Success*, 128.

35. Koch, *The Science of Success*, 16; Koch, *The Science of Success*, 29.

36. Koch, *The Science of Success*, 29.

37. Koch, *The Science of Success*, 90.

38. Koch, *The Science of Success*, 109.

39. Koch, *The Science of Success*, 36.

40. Koch, *The Science of Success*, 45–46.

41. Schulman, *Sons of Wichita*, 94. In *The Science of Success*, Koch offers a more palatable account, writing, "Value creation is the role of business in a market economy. Businesses that don't create value are not enhancing people's lives. In fact, businesses that destroy value are detrimental to our lives. When businesses make unprofitable products, they are drawing resources away from higher-valued uses, and when businesses waste resources, they prevent them from being beneficially used at all. In either case, a business with unattractive returns should be restructured, sold to a better owner or shut down" (Koch, *The Science of Success*, 55–56).

42. Leonard, *Kochland*, Location 7885.

43. Leonard, *Kochland*, Location 5965.

44. Leonard, *Kochland*, Location 1537.

45. Charles Koch said this in an interview with Brian Doherty. See Doherty, *Radicals for Capitalism*, 606.

46. Leonard, *Kochland*, Location 4407.

47. Amadae, *Prisoners of Reason*, 180.

48. Leonard, *Kochland*, Location 9452. Jane Mayer offers another useful example in detailing the initial reluctance of the Kochs' Americans for Prosperity to support the TARP bailouts of 2008 and 2009. That reluctance faded, as it is wont to do, when the bottom began to fall out of the stock market threatening the Kochs' massive investment portfolio. Americans for Prosperity reversed its position (Mayer, *Dark Money*, 21).

49. Leonard, *Kochland*, Location 5965.

50. Leonard, *Kochland*, Location 3577.

51. Leonard, *Kochland*, Location 3157.

52. Leonard, *Kochland*, Location 3113.

53. Leonard, *Kochland*, Location 2196.

54. Mayer, *Dark Money*, 16, 140; MacLean, *Democracy in Chains*, xxvii.

55. On delusional voters, see Leonard, *Kochland*, Location 5965. Fraser and Gerstle, *Ruling America*, Location 1539, cite the historical precedent for such actions.

56. Leonard, *Kochland*, Location 8310.

57. Leonard, *Kochland*, Location 4537.

58. Leonard, *Kochland*, Location 2311.

59. The Kochs were not the first to exploit the judiciary in similar ways. In 1971, Chicago economist Henry Mann used money donated from companies like GE, IBM, and Exxon to lure law professors to similar "boot camps." Appelbaum described how, by 1990, 40 percent of all federal judges had attended one of Mann's boot camps, with clear impact: Appelbaum cited an examination of the judges' rulings before and after attending and found a significant shift in favor of Mann and his allies' preferences. See Appelbaum, *The Economists' Hour*, Location 2474.

60. Doherty, *Radicals for Capitalism*, 16.

61. Doherty, *Radicals for Capitalism*, 16.

62. Mayer, *Dark Money*, Location 1672.

63. Justin Miller, "Kansas, Sam Brownback, and the Trickle-Down Implosion," *American Prospect* (blogs), June 28, 2017.

64. Sam Brownback, "Q&A with Sam Brownback," by Brian Lamb, CSPAN (December 15, 2005); on Moore and Laffer, see Miller, "Kansas, Sam Brownback," June 28, 2017.

65. Michael Mazerov, "Kansas Provides Compelling Evidence of Failure of 'Supply-Side' Tax Cuts," States News Service, January 22, 2018.

66. Miller, "Kansas, Sam Brownback," June 28, 2017; "Do Tax Cuts Spur Growth? What We Can Learn from the Kansas Budget Crisis," *PBS NewsHour*, December 7, 2017.

67. Mazerov, "Kansas Provides Compelling Evidence of Failure of 'Supply-Side' Tax Cuts."

68. Mazerov, "Kansas Provides Compelling Evidence of Failure of 'Supply-Side' Tax Cuts."

69. Milton Friedman, "The Limitations of Tax Limitation," *Heritage Foundation Policy Review* (Summer 1978), 11; Edward Nelson, *Milton Friedman and Economic Debate in the United States, 1932–1972* (Chicago: University of Chicago Press, 2020), 222; see also Appelbaum, *The Economists' Hour*, Location 1775.

70. Brad Cooper, "Brownback Signs Big Tax Cut in Kansas," *Kansas City Star*, May 23, 2012.

71. Kevin D. Williamson, "Starving the Beast in Kansas," *National Review*, May 3, 2016.

72. Mazerov, "Kansas Provides Compelling Evidence of Failure of 'Supply-Side' Tax Cuts"; John Milburn, "Brownback Imposing Kan. Budget Cuts," Associated Press State and Local Wire, March 11, 2011.

73. Dan Balz, "Will Conservative Kansas Vote Out Its Conservative Governor, Sam Brownback?" *Washington Post* (blogs), October 28, 2014; Mazerov, "Kansas Provides Compelling Evidence of Failure of 'Supply-Side' Tax Cuts."

74. "Kansas Gov. Sam Brownback on MSNBC's Morning Joe," YouTube, June 19, 2020.

75. Appelbaum, *The Economists' Hour*, Location 1726; Peck and Tickell, 2002.

76. Appelbaum, *The Economists' Hour*, Location 1726.

77. Sam Brownback, "A Midwest Renaissance Rooted in the Reagan Formula," *Wall Street Journal*, May 29, 2014.

78. Frank, *What's the Matter with Kansas?*, 136.

79. Miller, "Kansas, Sam Brownback."

80. Frank, *What's the Matter with Kansas?*, 71.

81. A bill Brownback signed in April 2015 that hardened a work requirement for able-bodied welfare recipients without dependents was also praised: "Poverty is subdued not when liberals throw money at an issue, but when Kansans are able to stand independently—without the confining shackles of artificial government assistance," Brownback's deputy director of communications Melika Willoughby wrote in an email. "With work, comes dignity, self-respect, and a boundless future"; see "Gov. Sam Brownback's Office Sends Email on Welfare Policies," Associated Press State and Local Wire, September 25, 2015.

82. Philippon, *The Great Reversal*, 159. Thomas Piketty, *Capital in the Twenty-First Century* (Cambridge, MA: Belknap/Harvard University Press, 2014), 6.

83. Kenneth Burke, *Permanence and Change: An Anatomy of Purpose* (Berkeley: University of California Press, 1954).

84. "Do Tax Cuts," *PBS NewsHour*; "Kansas Provides," States News Service.

85. Balz, "Will Conservative Kansas Vote Out Its Conservative Governor, Sam Brownback?," October 28, 2014.

86. Justin Miller, "Kansas, Sam Brownback," June 28, 2017.

87. "Do Tax Cuts," *PBS NewsHour*.

88. Miller, "Kansas, Sam Brownback," June 28, 2017.

89. Miller, "Kansas, Sam Brownback," June 28, 2017.

90. Miller, "Kansas, Sam Brownback," June 28, 2017.

91. Miller, "Kansas, Sam Brownback," June 28, 2017.

92. It is. See "Laffer Curve Napkin," *Smithsonian: National Museum of American History*.

93. Mazerov, "Kansas Provides Compelling Evidence of Failure of 'Supply-Side' Tax Cuts"; Jason Matthew DeBacker, Bradley Heim, Shanthi Ramnath, and Justin M. Ross, "The Impact of State Taxes on Pass-Through Businesses: Evidence from the 2012 Kansas Income Tax Reform," *SSRN* (September 1, 2017).

94. Mazerov, "Kansas Provides Compelling Evidence of Failure of 'Supply-Side' Tax Cuts"; DeBacker, Heim, Ramnath, and Ross, "The Impact of State Taxes on Pass-Through Businesses"; see also Barrow, *Critical Theories of the State*, 76.

95. Blinder, *After the Music Stopped*, 394; Edsall and Edsall, *Chain Reaction*, 6; Hacker and Pierson, *American Amnesia*; Pinker, *Enlightenment Now*, 109.

96. MacLean, *Democracy in Chains*, xxxi.

97. Friedman, *Free to Choose*, vol. 2.

98. Appelbaum, *The Economists' Hour*, Location 1936.

99. Friedman, "Monetarism in Rhetoric and in Practice."

100. Ty Masterson, interviewed on "Do Tax Cuts," *PBS NewsHour*.

101. Miller, "Kansas, Sam Brownback."

102. Balz, "Will Conservative Kansas Vote Out Its Conservative Governor, Sam Brownback?"; Miller, "Kansas, Sam Brownback."

103. DeBacker, Heim, Ramnath, and Ross, "The Impact of State Taxes on Pass-Through Businesses."

104. Jeff Glendening, "Historic Tax Hike Won't Fix Spending Problem," *Wichita Eagle*, July 2, 2017; "Kansas Provides," *States News Service*.

105. "Kansas Provides," *States News Service*.

106. Jonathan Williams and Ben Wilterdink, "Lessons from Kansas: A Behind the Scenes Look at America's Most Discussed Tax Reform Effort," *American Legislative Exchange Council* (February 2017).

107. "Do Tax Cuts," *PBS NewsHour*.

108. Milburn, "Brownback Imposing."

109. Miller, "Kansas, Sam Brownback."

110. Miller, "Kansas, Sam Brownback."

111. Mazerov, "Kansas Provides Compelling Evidence of Failure of 'Supply-Side' Tax Cuts."

112. Miller, "Kansas, Sam Brownback."

113. Mazerov, "Kansas Provides Compelling Evidence of Failure of 'Supply-Side' Tax Cuts."

114. Miller, "Kansas, Sam Brownback."

115. Miller, "Kansas, Sam Brownback."

116. Burke, *Permanence and Change*.

CHAPTER 10

1. E. J. Dionne, *Why the Right Went Wrong: Conservatism—From Goldwater to Trump And Beyond* (New York: Simon & Schuster, 2016), 14; MacLean, *Democracy in Chains*, 52; Phillips-Fein, *Invisible Hands*, Location 1099; Craig R. Smith, "Ronald Reagan's Rhetorical Re-Invention of Conservatism," *Quarterly Journal of Speech* 103, no. 1/2 (2017): 33–65.

NOTES

2. Tucker Carlson, *The Long Slide: Thirty Years in American Journalism* (New York: Threshold, 2021), Kindle Location 1006.

3. Carlson, *The Long Slide*, Kindle Location 1006.

4. Carlson, *The Long Slide*, Kindle Location 1027.

5. Carlson, *The Long Slide*, Kindle Location 1027.

6. Carlson, *The Long Slide*, Kindle Location 1056.

7. Carlson, *The Long Slide*, Kindle Location 1086.

8. Carlson, *The Long Slide*, Kindle Location 1086.

9. "User Clip: Tucker Carlson Criticizes Pat Buchanan (1999)," CSPAN.

10. Nicholas Confessore, "American Nationalist," (Part I) *New York Times*, May 1, 2022.

11. Klein, *Why We're Polarized*, Kindle Location 3548.

12. "CPAC: Tucker Carlson Tries to Defend the New York Times, Gets Booed," YouTube, February 26, 2009.

13. Confessore, "American Nationalist," May 1, 2022.

14. Klein, *Why We're Polarized*, Kindle Location 3584.

15. Nicholas Confessore, "American Nationalist," (Part II) *New York Times*, May 2, 2022.

16. Karen Yourish, Weiyi Cai, and Larry Buchanan, "Inside the Apocalyptic Worldview of 'Tucker Carlson Tonight,'" *New York Times*, May 1, 2022.

17. Confessore, "American Nationalist" Part II. May 2, 2022. In May 2022, the *New York Times* wrote a series of three massive articles based on their reporter's analysis of fifteen hundred episodes of Tucker Carlson's television appearances. In general, the *Times*'s analysis affirms my findings, and I integrated their textual evidence throughout this chapter to add texture and nuance. However, the *Times* also reflects the larger discursive challenges of properly categorizing Carlson's impact on American liberal democracy. Carlson's oligarchic impact is neglected, and instead, he is described as "the ideological enforcer of conservative populism." See "Inside the Apocalyptic," *New York Times*, May 1, 2022.

18. Stanley, cited in Nathan Crick, "Introduction: The Rhetorical Devises of Fascism," in *The Rhetoric of Fascism*, ed. Nathan Crick (Tuscaloosa: University of Alabama Press, 2022), 1.

19. Crick, "Introduction," in *The Rhetoric of Fascism*, 8.

20. Crick, "Introduction," in *The Rhetoric of Fascism*, 7.

21. Nathan Crick, "Remaking Shit: The Carnage and Utopias of Twentieth-Century Fascists," in *The Rhetoric of Fascism*, ed. Nathan Crick (Tuscaloosa: University of Alabama Press, 2022), 13.

22. *Tucker Carlson Tonight*, November 19, 2020.

23. *Tucker Carlson Tonight*, November 19, 2020.

24. *Tucker Carlson Tonight*, November 19, 2020.

25. Roderick P. Hart and E. Johanna Hartelius, "The Political Sins of Jon Stewart," *Critical Studies in Media Communication* 24, no. 3 (2007): 270.

26. Farhad Manjoo, "Tucker Carlson 2024," *New York Times*, September 21, 2019.

27. Miliband, *The State in Capitalist Society*, 135–36.

28. Miliband, *The State in Capitalist Society*, 135–36.

29. McKay Coppins, *Romney: A Reckoning* (New York: Scribner, 2023), 133–34.
30. Ellis, *American Dialogue*, 88.
31. Miliband, *The State in Capitalist Society*, 13.
32. Barrow, *Critical Theories of the State*, 18; Miliband, *The State in Capitalist Society*, 34.
33. Yourish, Cai, and Buchanan, "Inside the Apocalyptic," May 1, 2022.
34. Carlson, *The Long Slide*, Kindle Location 2997.
35. Carlson, *The Long Slide*, Kindle Location 1430; see also Friedman, *Free to Choose*, Vol. 7.
36. Carlson, *The Long Slide*, Kindle Location 1744.
37. Carlson, *The Long Slide*, Kindle Location 295.
38. Carlson, *The Long Slide*, Kindle Location 1049.
39. Jonathan Chait, "Tucker Carlson Has Seen the Future, and It Is Fascist," *New York*, August 4, 2021.
40. Carlson, *Ship of Fools*, Location 2727, 2713, 2807.
41. Carlson, *Ship of Fools*, Location 2408.
42. Carlson, *Ship of Fools*, Location 2435. On an October 11, 2018, episode, Carlson claimed, "Actual male testosterone levels have fallen dramatically in the past 20 years" (see Yourish, Cai, and Buchanan, "Inside the Apocalyptic," May 1, 2022).
43. Gina Kolata, "Tucker Carlson Has a Cure for Declining Virility," *New York Times*, April 22, 2022; Confessore, "American Nationalist," May 1, 2022.
44. Carlson, *The Long Slide*, Kindle Location 1919.
45. Carlson, *The Long Slide*, Kindle Location 1919.
46. Carlson, *The Long Slide*, Kindle Location 887.
47. Carlson, *Ship of Fools*, Location 1280.
48. Friedman, *Free to Choose*, vol. 10.
49. Carlson, *The Long Slide*, Kindle Location 637.
50. Carlson, May 4, 2019, cited in Manjoo, "Tucker Carlson 2024."
51. Yourish, Cai, and Buchanan, "Inside the Apocalyptic," May 1, 2022.
52. Carlson, *Ship of Fools*, Location 1685.
53. Carlson, *The Long Slide*, Kindle Location 77.
54. Carlson, *The Long Slide*, Kindle Location 303.
55. Carlson, May 4, 2019, cited in Manjoo, "Tucker Carlson 2024."
56. Carlson, *Ship of Fools*, Location 167.
57. Tucker Carlson, May 31, 2019, cited in Manjoo, "Tucker Carlson 2024."
58. Carlson, *The Long Slide*, Kindle Location 149.
59. Carlson, May 31, 2019, cited in Manjoo, "Tucker Carlson 2024."
60. See Stewart, *The 9.9 Percent*, 277.
61. Carlson, *Ship of Fools*, Location 1691.
62. See Barrow, *Critical Theories of the State*, 24–25.
63. Carlson, *Ship of Fools*, Location 181.
64. Carlson, *The Long Slide*, Kindle Location 26.
65. Carlson, *The Long Slide*, Kindle Location 1073.
66. Carlson, May 4, 2019, cited in Manjoo, "Tucker Carlson 2024."
67. Carlson, *Ship of Fools*, Location 844.

NOTES

68. Carlson, May 4, 2019, cited in Manjoo, "Tucker Carlson 2024."
69. *Tucker Carlson Tonight*, August 5, 2021
70. *Tucker Carlson Tonight*, August 6, 2021.
71. Chait, "Tucker Carlson Has Seen the Future"; Confessore, "American Nationalist" Part II, May 2, 2022.
72. *Tucker Carlson Tonight*, August 5, 2021.
73. *Tucker Carlson Tonight*, August 6, 2021.
74. Confessore, "American Nationalist" Part II, May 2, 2022.
75. *Tucker Carlson Tonight*, August 6, 2021.
76. *Tucker Carlson Tonight*, August 5, 2021.
77. Miliband, *The State in Capitalist Society*, 18.
78. Miliband, *The State in Capitalist Society*, 56.
79. Miliband, *The State in Capitalist Society*, 17.
80. Charles Homans, "Americans Think 'Corruption' Is Everywhere: Is That Why We Vote for It?" July 10, 2018. *New York Times Magazine*; see also Joshua Gunn, "On Political Perversion," *Rhetoric Society Quarterly* 48, no. 2 (2018): 177.
81. Yourish, Cai, and Buchanan, "Inside the Apocalyptic," May 1, 2022.
82. Carlson, *Ship of Fools*, Location 2807.
83. Naomi Oreskes and Erik M. Conway, *The Big Myth: How American Business Taught Us to Loathe Government and Love the Free Market* (New York: Bloomsbury, 2023).
84. Barrow, *Critical Theories of the State*, 13, 87; Stewart, *The 9.9 Percent*, 115.
85. Barrow, *Critical Theories of the State*, 31; Stewart, *The 9.9 Percent*, 157.
86. Barrow, *Critical Theories of the State*, 44.
87. Ellis, *American Dialogue*, 112; Henry George in *Progress and Poverty*, cited in Stewart, *The 9.9 Percent*, 115; Stewart, *The 9.9 Percent*, 157; Skocpol, cited in Barrow, *Critical Theories of the State*, 126.
88. Miliband, *The State in Capitalist Society*, 4, 193.
89. The empirical data affirm America's distrustful turn: in 1960, 70–80 percent of the US population answered "Yes" when asked if they trusted the government of the United States. By 1975, those numbers were nearly reversed and have remained distrustful since (Ellis, *American Dialogue*, 104, 112).
90. Anita Sreedhar and Anand Gopal, "Behind Low Vaccination Rates Lurks a More Profound Social Weakness," *New York Times*, December 2, 2021.
91. Miliband, *The State in Capitalist Society*, 127.
92. Barrow, *Critical Theories of the State*, 57, 124.
93. Hart and Hartelius, "The Political Sins," 267, 271–72; Michael Lewis, *The Fifth Risk: Undoing Democracy* (New York: W. W. Norton, 2018).
94. Corruption Perception Index, in Homans, "Americans Think 'Corruption' Is Everywhere."
95. Gallup, cited in Homans, "Americans Think 'Corruption' Is Everywhere."
96. Homans, "Americans Think 'Corruption' Is Everywhere."
97. Lewis, *The Fifth Risk*, Kindle Location 99.
98. Pinker, *Enlightenment Now*, 88.
99. Asen, "Neoliberalism, the Public Sphere," 4.

CONCLUSION

Engels, *The Politics of Resentment*, 9, 127; see also Chaput, *Market Affect and the Rhetoric of Political Economic Debates*, 141; Cintron, *Democracy as Fetish*, 35.

2. Brown, *Undoing the Demos*, 202–3.
3. Barrow, *Critical Theories of the State*, 76, 126–27.
4. Brown, *Undoing the Demos*, 204–5; Engels, *The Politics of Resentment*, 10.
5. Robin, *The Reactionary Mind*, 15.
6. Piketty, *Capital and Ideology*, Kindle Location 236.
7. Ellis, *American Dialogue*, 108–9.
8. Katherine M. Gehl and Michael E. Porter, *The Politics Industry: How Political Innovation Can Break Partisan Gridlock and Save Our Democracy* (Cambridge, MA: Harvard Business Review Press, 2020). This is not to suggest that elite political influence is unique to the twenty-first century. One of the primary objectives of the US Constitution was to prioritize the economic interests of the wealthy plantation owners above the interests of small farmers; see Martin Gilens and Benjamin I. Page, "Testing Theories of American Politics: Elites, Interest Groups, and Average Citizens," *Perspectives on Politics* 12, no. 3 (2014): 572; also see Lindsey and Teles, *The Captured Economy*, Kindle Location 1297; Mayer, *Dark Money*, 343. As Engels wrote, "The Constitution was designed to temper and control democratic movements" (Engels, *The Politics of Resentment*, 136; see also Cintron, *Democracy as Fetish*, 58). During the second half of the twentieth century, a symbiotic relationship developed among corporate elites and "conservative" economists. Lynde and Harry Bradley, Adolph Coors, Earhart, Sarah Scaife, Smith Richardson, and the John M. Olin foundation began to influence electoral politics by focusing their efforts upstream. These efforts reflect the potent combination of extremely wealthy, well-connected, and bitter oligarchs translating their democratic dissatisfaction into a flurry of idea-influencing enterprises, including powerful, well-funded policy-influencing networks, PACs, and think tanks that have come to dominate political conversations. Appelbaum and Phillips-Fein detailed the decision by economists like Friedman and Stigler to make "common cause" with ruling elites. Rockefeller endowed the University of Chicago. Drugstore magnate Charles Walgreen encouraged George Stigler to join the Chicago faculty by offering a massive salary and research endowment. More recently, the Koch brothers and their oligarchic allies have created think tanks like the Cato Institute, the Heritage Foundation, and the Mercatus Center to develop and spread oligarchic ideas, ranging from op-ed articles, books and position papers, media appearances, and educational tool kits to crafting model legislation and restricting the available Supreme Court nominees. Also see Appelbaum, *The Economists' Hour*, Kindle Location 230, 2369; Carey, *Taking*, 27; Doherty, *Radicals for Capitalism*, 407, 449; Neubauer, "Dialogue, Monologue, or Something in Between?" 2179; O'Connor, "Financing the Counterrevolution," 152; Phillips-Fein, *Invisible Hands*, Kindle Location 3881.
9. Gilens and Page, "Testing Theories of American Politics," 572; See also Luigi Zingales, "Towards a Political Theory of the Firm," *Journal of Economic Perspective* 31, no. 3 (2017): 113–30.
10. Gilens and Page, "Testing Theories of American Politics," 575.
11. Page, Seawright, and Lacombe, *Billionaires and Stealth Politics*, 30, 135.

NOTES

12. Page, Seawright, and Lacombe, *Billionaires and Stealth Politics*, 127, 135–37.
13. Page, Seawright, and Lacombe, *Billionaires and Stealth Politics*, 1.
14. Stewart, *The 9.9 Percent*. See also Lindsey and Teles, *The Captured Economy*, Kindle Location 1638; Matthew Stewart, "The Birth of a New American Aristocracy," *Atlantic*, June 2018, 61.
15. Lindsey and Teles, *The Captured Economy*, Location 2105. See also Seth Stephen-Davidowitz, "The Rich Are Not Who We Think They Are. And Happiness Is Not What We Think It Is, Either," *New York Times*, May 14, 2022.
16. Philippon, *The Great Reversal*, Kindle Location 1122; Matthew Smith, Danny Yagan, Owen Zidar, and Eric Zwick, "Capitalists in the Twenty-First Century," *Quarterly Journal of Economics* 134, no. 4 (2019): 1675–1745.
17. Philippon, *The Great Reversal*, 283.
18. Formisano, *American Oligarchy*, 25, 41; Lindsey and Teles, *The Captured Economy*, Location 533; Stewart, "The Birth," 61.
19. Mariana Mazzucato, *The Entrepreneurial State: Debunking Public vs. Private Sector Myths* (New York: Public Affairs, 2015), Location 2336.
20. Mayer, *Dark Money* 16, 203. For an illustration on how large energy companies rely on government intervention, see Jeffrey Ball's article comparing the tax breaks and subsidies of renewable energy companies in Texas versus fossil fuel companies; see Jeffrey Ball, "Texas's Oil and Gas Industry Is Defending Its Billions in Subsidies Against a Green Energy Push," *Texas Monthly*, June 2021.
21. Lindsey and Teles, *The Captured Economy*, Location 533, 1870; Mazzucato, *The Entrepreneurial State*, Location 2336; Robert Reich, *Saving Capitalism: For the Many, Not the Few* (New York: Knopf, 2015), 22, 32.
22. Stewart, "The Birth," 61.
23. Saez and Zucman, *The Triumph of Injustice*, Kindle Location 2547.
24. Colleen Cunningham, Florian Ederer, and Song Ma, "Killer Acquisitions," *Journal of Political Economy* 129, no. 3 (February 2021): 649–702. See also Philippon, *The Great Reversal*, Kindle Location 1610.
25. Reich, *Saving Capitalism*, 30.
26. Philippon, *The Great Reversal*, Kindle Location 88; David Leonhardt, "A Lack of Competition, and a Plan to Fix it," *New York Times*. July 10, 2021.
27. Stewart, *The 9.9 Percent*, 157.
28. Sitaraman, *The Crisis of the Middle-Class Constitution*, 236.
29. Philippon, *The Great Reversal*, Kindle Location 1862.
30. David Leonhardt, "A Lack of Competition," July 20, 2012.
31. Philippon, *The Great Reversal*, Kindle Location 1610.
32. Leonhardt, "A Lack of Competition," July 20, 2012.
33. Philippon, *The Great Reversal*, 258.
34. Philippon, *The Great Reversal*, Kindle Location 2880; Piketty, *Capital and Ideology*, Kindle Location 236.
35. Sitaraman, *The Crisis of the Middle-Class Constitution*, 236.
36. Osnos, *Wildland*, 36; see also Frank, *Pity the Billionaire*, 34.
37. Packer, "We Are Living in a Failed State," 2020.
38. Robert Draper, "The Arizona Republican Party's Anti-Democracy Experiment," *New York Times Magazine*, August 15, 2022, 42.

39. Amber Phillips, "'Oh, We'd Fill It': How McConnell Is Doing a 180 on Supreme Court Vacancies in an Election Year," *Washington Post*, May 29, 2019.
40. Gershberg and Illing, *The Paradox of Democracy*, 252.
41. Gershberg and Illing, *The Paradox of Democracy*, 252.
42. Osnos, *Wildland*, 404.
43. McCarthy, cited in Osnos, *Wildland*, 398.
44. Pence, cited in Osnos, *Wildland*, 398.
45. Draper, "The Arizona Republican Party's Anti-Democracy Experiment," 47.
46. Draper, "The Arizona Republican Party's Anti-Democracy Experiment," 47.
47. Draper, "The Arizona Republican Party's Anti-Democracy Experiment," 43.
48. Gershberg and Illing, *The Paradox of Democracy*, 273–74; Osnos, *Wildland*, 392.
49. Trump 2016 victory speech, cited in Gershberg and Illing, *The Paradox of Democracy*, 245.
50. Osnos, *Wildland*, 404.
51. Osnos, *Wildland*, 404.
52. Osnos, *Wildland*, 401.
53. See Stewart, *The 9.9 Percent*, 178, 280.
54. Page, Seawright, and Lacombe, *Billionaires and Stealth Politics*, 138; Stewart, *The 9.9 Percent*, 139–41.
55. Page, Seawright, and Lacombe, *Billionaires and Stealth Politics*, 143.
56. Fraser and Gerstle, *Ruling America*, Location 189.
57. Martha J. Bailey and Sheldon Danziger, eds., *Legacies of the War on Poverty* (New York: Russell Sage Foundation, 2013).

APPENDIX

1. Cintron, *Democracy as Fetish*, 14; Gershberg and Illing, *The Paradox of Democracy*, 1; Johnson, *I The People*, 19.
2. Engels, *The Politics of Resentment*, 11.
3. Luke Winslow, *Economic Injustice and the Rhetoric of the American Dream* (Lanham, MD: Lexington Books, 2017).
4. Kenneth Burke, *Attitudes Toward History* (Berkeley: University of California Press, 1937/1984), 92.
5. Burke, *Attitudes Toward History*, 27.
6. Burke, *Attitudes Toward History*, 4.
7. Burke, *Attitudes Toward History*, 92.
8. Burke, *Attitudes Toward History*, 4.
9. Burke, *Attitudes Toward History*, 34.
10. Burke, *Attitudes Toward History*, 192.
11. Burke, *Attitudes Toward History*, 193.
12. Burke, *Attitudes Toward History*, 5.
13. Burke, *Attitudes Toward History*, 20.
14. Burke, *Attitudes Toward History*, 20.
15. Osnos, *Wildland*, 169.
16. Burke, *Attitudes Toward History*, 193.
17. McGee, cited in Johnson, *I The People*, 154.

18. Lee, *Creating Conservatism*, 11.
19. Lee, *Creating Conservatism*, 38.
20. Engels, *The Politics of Resentment*, 141.
21. Cintron describes language as "a clinching force from which our thoughts cannot escape—indeed, our thinking cannot *become thinking* without some sort of language" (Cintron, *Democracy as Fetish*, 18). Raymond Williams notes how complicated concepts can be better understood by "recovering the substance from which their forms were cast"; Raymond Williams, *Marxism and Literature* (Oxford: Oxford University Press, 1977), 11. See also Barrow, *Critical Theories of the State*, 12, 57, 97, 117. Both Barrow's and Williams's approaches affirm the theory-building assumptions of my home discipline. In this way, I also follow the methodological guidance of Catherine Chaput who suggests that complicated signifying structures can be better understood by beginning with effects and then working backward to appeals, lines of argument, and rhetorical frames (Chaput, *Market Affect and the Rhetoric of Political Economic Debates*, 3). See also Robert Hariman, *Political Style: The Artistry of Power* (Chicago: University of Chicago Press, 1995), 11; Michael McGee, "Text, Context, and the Fragmentation of Contemporary Culture," *Western Journal of Communication* 54 (1990): 274–89; and Patricia Roberts-Miller, *Rhetoric and Demagoguery* (Carbondale: Southern Illinois University Press, 2019), 282.
22. Burke, *Attitudes Toward History*, 94.
23. Burke, *Attitudes Toward History*, 291.
24. Burke, *Attitudes Toward History*, 93.
25. Burke, *Attitudes Toward History*, 93–94.
26. Garver, *Aristotle's Politics*, 14.
27. Kenneth Burke, *Counter-Statement* (Los Altos, CA: Hermes, 1931/1953).
28. James Aune, "Democratic Style and Ideological Containment," *Rhetoric & Public Affairs* 11, no. 3 (2008): 483.
29. Aune, "Democratic Style," 482.
30. Davis, *Inessential Solidarity*, 33.
31. Catherine Chaput, "The Rhetorical Situation and the Battle for Public Sentiment," in *Communication and the Economy*, ed. Joshua Hanan and Mark Hayward (New York: Peter Lang, 2014), 191.
32. Melissa Gregg and Gregory J. Seigworth, *The Affect Theory Reader* (Durham, NC: Duke University Press, 2010), Kindle Location 71.
33. Chaput, *Market Affect and the Rhetoric of Political Economic Debates*, 18.
34. Chaput urges us to explore the "vibrant materiality moving through each of these layers to constitute an invisibly entangled infrastructure that merges myriad moments into a single, though dynamic and differentiated force." Hanan and St. Onge deploy "primordial infrastructure" similarly to explain how performative economies materialize. Affirming Hanan and St. Onge, I assume economic rhetoric maintains an immanent capacity to "intercept and overdetermine the performative production of meaning" becoming "the material and discursive constitution of meaning and identity at different moments in history" (see Chaput, *Market Affect and the Rhetoric of Political Economic Debates*, 17–18; Hanan and St. Onge, "Beyond the Dialectic," 167–68).

35. Chaput, *Market Affect and the Rhetoric of Political Economic Debates*, 12, 17. Kaplan's description of affect as "the circulation between objects and signs" is illuminated for communication and rhetorical scholars trained in analyzing the symbolic exchange of meaning. See Michael Kaplan, "The Communicative Efficacy of Markets," in *Communication and the Economy*, ed. Hanan and Hayward, 130.

36. Joshua Gunn, *Political Perversion: Rhetorical Aberration in the Time of Trumpeteering* (Chicago: University of Chicago Press, 2020), Kindle Location 318.

37. Burke, *Attitudes Toward History*, 191–92.

38. Chaput, *Market Affect and the Rhetoric of Political Economic Debates*, 23.

39. Joshua S. Hanan, "The Oikos as Economic Rhetoric: Toward an Ontological Investigation of Rhetorical Biopolitics," in *Rhetorics Change / Rhetoric's Change*, ed. Jenny Rice, Chelsea Graham, and Eric Detweiler (Parlor Press, 2018).

40. Chaput, *Market Affect and the Rhetoric of Political Economic Debates*, 53.

41. Hanan and St. Onge, "Beyond the Dialectic," 166; see also Dilip P. Gaonkar, "The Idea of Rhetoric in the Rhetoric of Science," *Western Journal of Communication* 58 (1993): 258–95; Joshua S. Hanan and Catherine Chaput, "A Rhetoric of Economics Beyond Civic Humanism: Exploring the Political Economy of Rhetoric in the Context of Late Neoliberalism," *Journal of Cultural Economy* 8, no. 1 (2015), 16–24.

42. Deirdre McCloskey, *Bourgeois Virtues: Ethics for an Age of Commerce* (John Wiley & Sons, 2006), 91; Deirdre McCloskey, *The Rhetoric of Economics*, 2nd ed. (Madison: University of Wisconsin Press, 1998), 44.

43. Johnson, *I The People*, 142; Roberts-Miller, *Rhetoric and Demagoguery*, 28–30.

44. Chaput, *Market Affect and the Rhetoric of Political Economic Debates*, 51.

45. Chaput, *Market Affect and the Rhetoric of Political Economic Debates*, 3.

46. Chaput, *Market Affect and the Rhetoric of Political Economic Debates*, 18.

47. Cintron, *Democracy as Fetish*, 21.

48. Chaput, *Market Affect and the Rhetoric of Political Economic Debates*, 18.

49. Chaput, *Market Affect and the Rhetoric of Political Economic Debates*, 124–25; see also Milton Friedman, *Free to Choose*, vol. 10.

50. Chaput, *Market Affect and the Rhetoric of Political Economic Debates*, 98.

51. Cintron, *Democracy as Fetish*, 21; Davis, *Inessential Solidarity*, 36.

52. Lee, *Creating Conservatism*, 5.

53. Lee, *Creating Conservatism*, 16; see also Johnson, *I The People*, 24.

54. Lee, *Creating Conservatism*, 35.

55. Lee, *Creating Conservatism*, 103–4.

56. Burke, *Attitudes Toward History*, 195.

57. Burke, *Attitudes Toward History*, 196.

58. Engels, *The Politics of Resentment*, 140.

59. Burke calls style "the ritualistic projection of manners" (Burke, *Attitudes Toward History*, 201). Hariman links style, politics, and culture, arguing that a certain political style lights up "a coherent set of symbols giving meaning to the manifest activities of common living" (Hariman, *Political Style*; see also Lee, *Creating Conservatism*, 138). As Brummett argues, style includes a certain way of walking and also how that way of walking branches out to larger symbol systems (*The Rhetoric of Style*).

60. Thomas M. Lessl, *Rhetorical Darwinism: Religion, Evolution, and the Scientific Identity* (Waco, TX: Baylor University Press 2012), 16.

61. For example, Hanan's use of *oikos* to illuminate the political potency of Donald Trump offers a cogent and timely example of the synthetic approach upon which I will explore democratic oligarchy. Hanan describes oikos as "a material-discursive locus of rhetorical biopolitics" relying on "primitive and peripheral spheres of subject formation" and daily "practices and processes" to co-constitute a political economic outlook far beyond rational argumentation (Hanan, "The Oikos as Economic Rhetoric"). Hanan details the capacity of oikos to rationalize hierarchy and inequality by first establishing "assumptions of value based on difference of kind" through the construction of a neutral background space that served as "a moral foundation for Athenian society and culture." The superiority of white male property-owning citizens within the economic household was expanded to create "the normative expectations of the nation-state." Hanan locates similar normative expectations in the Trump administration's use of racist, sexist, classist, and ableist enthymemes to rationalize Trump's domestic and international policies. Hanan uses the affective and biopolitical function of oikos to connect an American public willing to overlook such obviously and blatantly bigoted appeals to the continued affirmation of a nation-state "predicated on the same logic of xenophobia, sexism, and speciesism that made possible the articulation of the oikos in Ancient Greece" (Hanan, "The Oikos as Economic Rhetoric"). Notice also how Chaput describes Adam Smith as "the adopted father of the free market" (*Market Affect and the Rhetoric of Political Economic Debates*, 1, 39). *Adopted* is the operative term, because there was no free market—no single rhetor could have created it anyway—and Smith would eschew today's discursive links between his famous invisible hand and the policies of the political Right in America. Chaput also describes how Friedrich Hayek absorbed a discrete intellectual class into his conversation by "giving them the language" to describe economic freedom and government corruption in a way that might "persuade the masses" (101). Third, Chaput describes how Milton Friedman shifted public blame from the inherent limitations of capitalism to "its mismanagement by the federal government" not only by circulating persuasive arguments but also by "changing the all-encompassing structure of opinion so that one can later persuade people to make policy changes consonant with that structure" (123). In *Creating Conservatism*, Michael Lee details the "popular narratives, standard idioms, dominant lines of argument, de rigueur tropes, and god and devil terms" that both "formulated a doctrinal inventory for conservatives" and also "taught them how to think" (38). Lee traces conservative arguments "to a small set of postwar texts and the reverential discourse each has inspired" by analyzing the "general political language" in books like Goldwater's *The Conscience of Conservatism*, Hayek's *The Road to Serfdom*, and Chambers's *Witness*. But Lee supplements his focus on "general political language" by positioning the emergence of canonical status for the author and book within the correct kairotic moment of its emergence (149). Lee notes how conservatism cannot be understood as a preexisting and referential concept popularized by potent rhetors alone. Instead, he analyzes the "long lives" of each book as a product of conservatives constantly "mining these texts" to make them appropriate for a specific historical moment—from anti-communists in 1955 to Tea Party activists in

NOTES

2010 (103–4). Jennifer Burns in *Goddess of the Market* notices how readers of Ayn Rand felt her "words could penetrate to the core, stirring secret selves and masked dreams" into a subjectivity defined by the defense of individualism, the celebration of capitalism, and the morality of selfishness; Jennifer Burns, *Goddess of the Market: Ayn Rand and the American Right* (Oxford: Oxford University Press, 2009, 1–2. And yet, Burns also traces how Rand's influence must be "understood only against the backdrop of her historical moment," especially as incongruities and changing cultural dynamics set Objectivism "loose in the world" far beyond Rand's control (248). Patricia Roberts-Miller and Jennifer Mercieca, in separate books, each develop demagoguery by first locating it in the public arguments of rhetors like Pat Buchanan and Donald Trump. But Roberts-Miller and Mercieca each theorize the "constituted discourse" of demagoguery far beyond one influential rhetor or political party. Demagoguery was positioned within "the constraints set by the current beliefs of the ideal audience, and how much those beliefs can be moved," Roberts-Miller wrote (*Rhetoric and Demagoguery*, 28). Likewise, Jeremy Engels developed *resentment* as a discrete category describing the rhetoric "used in the contemporary United States to uphold unjust hierarchies of rich and poor." He first observed the shared features of powerless political rhetoric and violent speech in the American populace (*The Politics*, 4). He then positions resentment's emergence into a specific kairotic moment marked by affective and discursive expressions of victimization and powerlessness in an audience faced with changes they could not control.

62. Chaput, *Market Affect and the Rhetoric of Political Economic Debates*, 3. I also follow the methodological guidance of Hariman *Political Style*, 11; see McGee, "Text, Context"; and Roberts-Miller, *Rhetoric and Demagoguery*, 282.

63. With regard to the various *personas* following Edwin Black, I want to use *textual persona* here to affirm and extend this critical approach by drawing attention to the free-floating signifying potential of public rhetors like Spencer, Hayek, Friedman, and Buchanan. As I will show, a critical approach that emphasizes textual persona carves out valuable rhetorical space for understanding how the arguments of these influential rhetors evolve and shift over time, as well as carving out space for disagreements within scholarly interpretations.

64. Barry Brummett, *Rhetoric in Popular Culture* (Thousand Oaks, CA: Sage, 2006).

65. James Jasinski, *Sourcebook of Rhetoric: Key Concepts in Rhetorical Studies* (Thousand Oaks, CA: Sage, 2001).

66. Michel Foucault, "What Is an Author?" in *The Foucault Reader*, ed. Paul Rabinow (New York: Pantheon, 1984), 101–20; see also Engels, *The Politics of Resentment*, 139.

67. Stephen Howard Browne, "Response Context in Critical Theory and Practice," *Western Journal of Communication* 65, no. 3 (Summer 2001): 330; Kirt H. Wilson, "Theory/Criticism: A Functionalist Approach to the 'Specific Intellectual' Work of Rhetorical Criticism," *Western Journal of Communication* 84, no. 3 (May 2020): 280–96; Bonnie Dow, "Criticism and Authority in the Artistic Mode," *Western Journal of Communication* 65, no. 3 (2001): 345–46; and Stephanie Houston Grey, "Conceptually-Oriented Criticism," in *Rhetorical Criticism: Perspectives in Action*, ed. Jim A. Kuypers (Lanham, MD: Lexington, 2009), 341.

NOTES

68. There are a few examples of where my reading departs from the extant literature. Chaput says Hayek endorses "a state in which government actions are strictly delimited by a few universally agreed upon rules" (Chaput, *Market Affect and the Rhetoric of Political Economic Debates*, 87–88). Chaput places Milton Friedman and John Kenneth Galbraith on opposite ideological axes (Chaput, *Market Affect and the Rhetoric of Political Economic Debates*, 113). And she summarizes Friedman and his Chicago school interlocutors as extending "free-market practices into every nook and cranny of society" (Chaput, *Market Affect and the Rhetoric of Political Economic Debates*, 135–36). Lee includes "individual humility" as a classical conservative value, and he suggests Hayek's political philosophy was infused with a predictable skepticism toward concentrating power (Lee, *Creating Conservatism*, 38, 83). Longaker describes Hayek "spinning an approaching libertarian-anarchist utopia where the law resides within each person's emotionally edified breast," and he notes an enduring consistency across Spencer's decades of research and advocacy in "the individual—not the government—[as] the drum major leading humanity toward industry" (Longaker, *Rhetorical Style and the Bourgeois Virtue*, 108, 117). I will note disagreements about an imprecise use of terms like "free market" and "small government"—and even the more prosaic but taken-for-granted rhetorical potency of aligning economic rhetors with terms like "tradition," "order," "individual rights." I will hope to complicate the extant literature's assumptions about the criteria for what counts as empirical and scientific economic research. For example, Chaput describes how Friedman "mined statistical data from historical episodes, ones he equated with scientific experiments, to uncover economic reality," and she notes how Friedman transforms a philosophical (and affective) defense of capitalism into a scientific one (Chaput, *Market Affect and the Rhetoric of Political Economic Debates*, 114).

References

Agamben, Giorgio. *State of Exception*. Translated by Kevin Attell. Chicago: University of Chicago Press, 2005.

———. *Homo Sacer: Sovereign Power and Bare Life*. Translated by Daniel Heller-Rozen. Palo Alto, CA: Stanford University Press, 1998.

Amadae, S. M. *Prisoners of Reason: Game Theory and Neoliberal Political Economy*. Cambridge: Cambridge University Press, 2016.

Andersen, Kurt. *Evil Geniuses: The Unmaking of America; A Recent History*. New York: Random House, 2020.

Appelbaum, Binyamin. *The Economists' Hour: False Prophets, Free Markets, and the Fracture of Society*. New York: Little, Brown, 2019.

Aristotle. *The Politics*. Translated by Carnes Lord. Chicago: University of Chicago Press, 1984.

Asen, Robert. "Neoliberalism, the Public Sphere." *Quarterly Journal of Speech* 103, no. 4 (2007): 329–49.

———. *Visions of Poverty: Welfare Policy and Political Imagination*. East Lansing: Michigan State University Press, 2002.

Aune, James Arnt. *Selling the Free Market: The Rhetoric of Economic Correctness*. New York: Guilford Press, 2001.

———. "Democratic Style and Ideological Containment." *Rhetoric & Public Affairs* 11, no. 3 (2008): 482–90.

Bailey, Martha J., and Sheldon Danziger, eds. *Legacies of the War on Poverty*. New York: Russell Sage Foundation, 2013.

Balkin, Jack. *Living Originalism*. Cambridge, MA: Harvard University Press, 2011.

Ball, Jeffrey. "Texas's Oil and Gas Industry Is Defending Its Billions in Subsidies Against a Green Energy Push." *Texas Monthly*, June 2021.

Balmer, Randall. *Mine Eyes Have Seen the Glory*. New York: Oxford University Press, 1993.

Balz, Dan. "Will Conservative Kansas Vote Out Its Conservative Governor, Sam Brownback?" *Washington Post Blogs*, October 28, 2014.

Barnes, Sandra L. *Live Long and Prosper: How Black Megachurches Address HIV/Aids and Poverty in the Age of Prosperity Theology*. New York: Fordham University Press, 2013.

REFERENCES

Barrow, Clyde W. *Critical Theories of the State: Marxist, Neo-Marxist, Post-Marxist.* Madison: University of Wisconsin Press, 1993.

Bertrand, Marianne, Matilde Bombardini, and Francesco Trebbi. "Is It Whom You Know or What You Know? An Empirical Assessment of the Lobbying Process." *American Economic Review* 104, no. 12 (2014): 3885–3920.

Bertrand, Marianne, Matilde Bombardini, Raymond Fisman, and Francesco Trebbi. "Tax-Exempt Lobbying: Corporate Philanthropy as a Tool for Political Influence." *American Economic Review* 110, no. 7 (2020): 2065–2102.

Binmore, Ken. *Natural Justice.* Oxford: Oxford University Press, 2005.

Biskupic, Joan. *The Chief: The Life and Turbulent Times of Chief Justice John Roberts.* New York: Basic, 2019.

Blinder, Alan S. *After the Music Stopped: The Financial Crisis, the Response, and the Work Ahead.* New York: Penguin, 2013.

Bork, Robert. "Neutral Principles and Some First Amendment Problems." *IND. L.J.* 47 (1971): 1–35.

Boyer, Paul. "The Evangelical Resurgence in 1970s American Protestantism." In *Rightward Bound: Making America Conservative in the 1970s*, edited by Bruce Schulman and Julian Zelizer, 29–51. Cambridge, MA: Harvard University Press, 2008.

Brown, Wendy. "American Nightmare: Neoliberalism, Neoconservatism, and De-Democratization." *Political Theory* 34, no. 6 (2006): 690–714.

———. *In the Ruins of Neoliberalism: The Rise of Antidemocratic Politics in the West.* New York: Columbia University Press, 2019.

———. *Undoing the Demos: Neoliberalism's Stealth Revolution.* Brooklyn: Zone, 2015.

Brownback, Sam. "A Midwest Renaissance Rooted in the Reagan Formula." *Wall Street Journal*, May 29, 2014.

———. "Q&A with Sam Brownback." By Brian Lamb. CSPAN (December 15, 2005).

Browne, Stephen Howard. "Response Context in Critical Theory and Practice." *Western Journal of Communication* 65, no. 3 (Summer 2001): 330–35.

Brummett, Barry. "Rhetorical Theory as Heuristic and Moral: A Pedagogical Justification." *Communication Education* 33, no. 2 (1984): 97–107.

———. *Rhetoric in Popular Culture.* Thousand Oaks, CA: Sage, 2006.

———. *Rhetorical Homologies: Form, Culture, Experience.* Tuscaloosa: University of Alabama Press, 2004.

Buccola, Nicholas. *The Fire Is Upon Us: James Baldwin, William F. Buckley Jr., and the Debate Over Race in America.* Princeton, NJ: Princeton University Press, 2019.

Buchanan, James M. *The Limits of Liberty: Between Anarchy and Leviathan.* Chicago: University of Chicago Press, 1975.

———. "The Samaritan's Dilemma." In *Altruism, Morality, and Economic Theory*, edited by Edmund S. Phelps, 71–86. New York: Russell Sage Foundation, 1975.

Buettner, Russ, and Susanne Craig. "Decade in the Red: Trump Tax Figures Show Over $1 Billion in Business Losses." *New York Times*, May 8, 2019.

Burke, Edmund. *Reflections on the Revolution in France*, edited by J. C. D. Clark. Stanford, CA: Stanford University Press, 2001.
Burke, Kenneth. *Attitudes Toward History*. Berkeley: University of California Press, 1937/1984.
———. *Grammar of Motives*. Berkeley: University of California Press, 1945/1969.
———. *Permanence and Change: An Anatomy of Purpose*. Berkeley: University of California Press, 1954.
———. *The Philosophy of Literary Form*. Berkeley: University of California Press, 1974.
Burns, Jennifer. *Goddess of the Market: Ayn Rand and the American Right*. Oxford: Oxford University Press, 2009.
Bush, George H. W. "Remarks on Presenting the Presidential Medal of Freedom Awards." November 18, 1991.
Cady, Kathryn A., and Thomas Oates. "Family Splatters: Rescuing Heteronormativity from the Zombie Apocalypse." *Women's Studies in Communication* 39, no. 3 (July 2016): 308–25.
Caldwell, Bruce. *Hayek's Challenge: An Intellectual Biography of F. A. Hayek*. Chicago: University of Chicago Press, 2005.
Campbell, Karlyn Kohrs. "Rhetorical Criticism 2009: A Study in Method." In *The Handbook of Rhetoric and Public Address*, edited by Shawn. J. Parry-Giles and J. Michael Hogan, 86–108. Hoboken, NJ: Wiley-Blackwell, 2010.
Carey, Alex. *Taking the Risk Out of Democracy: Corporate Propaganda Versus Freedom and Liberty*. Urbana: University of Illinois Press, 1995.
Carnegie, Andrew. "The Gospel of Wealth." New York: Carnegie Corporation of New York, 1889/2017.
Carnevale, Anthony P., and Ban Cheah. *From Hard Times to Better Times*. Washington, DC: Georgetown University Center on Education and the Workforce, 2015.
Carnevale, Anthony P., Ban Cheah, and A. R. Hanson. *The Economic Value of College Majors*. Washington, DC: Georgetown University Center on Education and the Workforce, 2015.
Caro, Robert. *Master of the Senate: The Years of Lyndon Johnson III*. New York: Vintage, 2009.
Carrington, Ben. *Race, Sport, and Politics: The Sporting Black Diaspora*. New York: Sage, 2010.
Chait, Jonathan. "Tucker Carlson Has Seen the Future, and It Is Fascist." *New York*, August 4, 2021.
Chaput, Catherine. "Rhetorical Circulation in Late Capitalism: Neoliberalism and the Overdetermination of Affective Energy." *Philosophy & Rhetoric* 43, no. 1 (February 2010).
———. "The Rhetorical Situation and the Battle for Public Sentiment." In *Communication and the Economy*, edited by Joshua Hanan and Mark Hayward, 187–208. New York: Peter Lang, 2014.
———. "Trumponomics, Neoliberal Branding, and the Rhetorical Circulation of Affect." *Advances in the History of Rhetoric* 21, no. 2 (2018): 194–209.

REFERENCES

———. *Market Affect and the Rhetoric of Political Economic Debates.* Columbia: University of South Carolina Press, 2019.

Charland, Maurice. "Constitutive Rhetoric: The Case of the Peuple Québécois." *Quarterly Journal of Speech* 73 (1987): 133–50.

Chemerinsky, Erwin. *Worse Than Nothing: The Dangerous Fallacy of Originalism.* New Haven, CT: Yale University Press, 2022.

Chernow, Ron. *Alexander Hamilton.* New York: Penguin, 2005.

Cintron, Ralph. *Democracy as Fetish.* University Park: Pennsylvania University Press, 2020.

Clarke, John. "In Search of Ordinary People: The Problematic Politics of Popular Participation." *Communication, Culture & Critique* 6, no. 2 (2013): 208–26.

———. *New Times and Old Enemies: Essays on Cultural Studies in America.* New York: Routledge, 1992.

Cloud, Dana. "Fighting Words: Labor and the Limits of Communication at Staley, 1993 to 1996." *Management Communication Quarterly* 18, no. 4 (2005): 509–42.

Coates, Rodney D. "If a Tree Falls in the Wilderness: Reparations, Academic Silences, and Social Justice." *Social Forces* 83, no. 2 (2004): 841–64.

Cohen, Adam. *Supreme Inequality: The Supreme Court's Fifty-Year Battle for a More Unjust America.* New York: Penguin, 2020.

Cohen, Patricia. "Trump's Biggest Economic Legacy Isn't About the Numbers." *New York Times,* October 24, 2020.

Confessore, Nicholas. "American Nationalist." (Part I) *New York Times,* May 1, 2022.

———. "American Nationalist." (Part II) *New York Times,* May 2, 2022.

———. "Quixotic '80 Campaign Gave Birth to Kochs' Powerful Network." *New York Times,* May 14, 2014.

Cook, Eli. *The Pricing of Progress: Economic Indicators and the Capitalization of American Life.* Cambridge, MA: Harvard University Press, 2017.

Cooper, Brad. "Brownback Signs Big Tax Cut in Kansas." *Kansas City Star,* May 23, 2012.

Coppins, McKay, *Romney: A Reckoning.* New York: Scribner, 2023.

"CPAC: Tucker Carlson Tries to Defend the New York Times, Gets Booed." YouTube. February 26, 2009.

Crick, Nathan. "Introduction: The Rhetorical Devices of Fascism." In *The Rhetoric of Fascism,* edited by Nathan Crick, 1–11. Tuscaloosa: University of Alabama Press, 2022.

———. "Remaking Shit: The Carnage and Utopias of Twentieth-Century Fascists." In *The Rhetoric of Fascism,* edited by Nathan Crick, 12–33. Tuscaloosa: University of Alabama Press, 2022.

Crowley, Sharon. *Toward a Civil Discourse: Rhetoric and Fundamentalism.* Pittsburgh: University of Pittsburgh Press, 2006.

Cunningham, Colleen, Florian Ederer, and Song Ma. "Killer Acquisitions." *Journal of Political Economy* 129, no. 3 (February 2021): 649–702.

Darsey, James. *The Prophetic Tradition and Radical Rhetoric in America.* New York: New York University Press, 1997.

Darwin, Charles. *On the Origin of Species by Means of Natural Selection.* London: John Murray, 1859.

Davidson, Roei, and Amit M. Schejter. "'"Their Deeds Are the Deeds of Zimri; but They Expect a Reward Like Phineas': Neoliberal and Multicultural Discourses in the Development of Israeli DTT Policy." *Communication, Culture & Critique* 4, no. 1 (March 2011): 1–22.

Davies, William. "What Is 'Neo' about Neoliberalism?" In *Liberalism in Neoliberal Times: Dimensions, Contradictions, Limits*, edited by Alejandro Abraham-Hamanoiel, Des Freedman, Gholam Khiabany, Kate Nash, and Julian Petley, 13–22. London: Goldsmiths Press, 2017.

Davis, Diane. *Inessential Solidarity: Rhetoric and Foreigner Relations.* Pittsburgh: University of Pittsburgh Press, 2010.

DeBacker, Jason Matthew, Bradley Heim, Shanthi Ramnath, and Justin M. Ross. "The Impact of State Taxes on Pass-Through Businesses: Evidence from the 2012 Kansas Income Tax Reform." *SSRN.* September 1, 2017: 1–62.

Delahunty, Robert J., and John Yoo. "Saving Originalism." *Michigan Law Review* 113, no. 6 (2015): 1081–1113.

Dionne, E. J. *Why the Right Went Wrong: Conservatism—From Goldwater to Trump and Beyond.* New York: Simon & Schuster, 2016.

"Do Tax Cuts Spur Growth? What We Can Learn from the Kansas Budget Crisis." *PBS NewsHour*, December 7, 2017.

Doherty, Brian. *Radicals for Capitalism: A Freewheeling History of the Modern American Libertarian Movement.* New York: PublicAffairs, 2007.

Dow, Bonnie. "Criticism and Authority in the Artistic Mode." *Western Journal of Communication* 65, no. 3 (2001): 336–48.

Draper, Robert. "The Arizona Republican Party's Anti-Democracy Experiment." *New York Times Magazine*, August 15, 2022.

Duhigg, Charles, and David Kocieniewski. "How Apple Sidesteps Billions in Taxes." *New York Times*, April 28, 2012.

Duncan, David. *The Life and Letters of Herbert Spencer.* London: Methuen, 1908.

Earle, Timothy K. "A Reappraisal of Redistribution: Complex Hawaiian Chiefdoms." In *Exchange Systems in Prehistory*, edited by Timothy K. Earle and Jonathan E. Ericson, 213–29. New York: Academic Press, 1977.

Earle, Timothy K., and Jonathan E. Ericson. "Exchange Systems in Archaeological Perspective." In *Exchange Systems in Prehistory*, edited by Timothy K. Earle and Jonathan E. Ericson, 3–12. New York: Academic Press, 1977.

Ebenstein, Alan O. *Milton Friedman.* New York: Palgrave Macmillan, 2007.

Edgar, Amanda Nell. "Commenting Straight from the Underground: N.W.A., Police Brutality, and YouTube as a Space for Neoliberal Resistance." *Southern Communication Journal* 81, no. 4 (September 2016): 223–36.

Edsall, Thomas Byrne, and Mary D. Edsall. *Chain Reaction: The Impact of Race, Rights and Taxes on American Politics.* New York: W. W. Norton, 1991.

Edwards, Jonathan J. *Superchurch: The Rhetoric and Politics of American Fundamentalism.* East Lansing: Michigan State University Press, 2015.

Ellis, Christopher, and James A. Stimson. *Ideology in America.* Cambridge: Cambridge University Press, 2012.

REFERENCES

Ellis, Joseph J. *American Dialogue: The Founders and Us.* New York: Knopf, 2018.
Enck-Wanzer, Darrel. "Barack Obama, the Tea Party, and the Threat of Race: On Racial Neoliberalism and Born Again Racism." *Communication, Culture & Critique* 4, no. 1 (2011): 23–30.
Engels, Jeremy. *The Politics of Resentment: A Genealogy.* University Park: Pennsylvania State University Press, 2015.
Farrell, Thomas B. "Practicing the Arts of Rhetoric: Tradition and Invention." *Philosophy & Rhetoric* 24, no. 3 (1991): 183–212.
Fischer, Karin. "The Influence of Neoliberals in Chile Before, During, and After Pinochet." In *The Road from Mont Pèlerin: The Making of the Neoliberal Thought Collective*, edited by Philip Mirowski and Dieter Plehwe, 305–46. Cambridge, MA: Harvard University Press, 2009.
Fish, Adam. "Participatory Television: Convergence, Crowdsourcing, and Neoliberalism." *Communication, Culture & Critique* 6, no. 3 (September 2013): 372–95.
Fitzgerald, Frances. *The Evangelicals: The Struggle to Shape America.* New York: Simon & Schuster, 2017.
Foley, Megan. "From Infantile Citizens to Infantile Institutions: The Metaphoric Transformation of Political Economy in the 2008 Housing Market Crisis." *Quarterly Journal of Speech* 98 (2012): 386–410.
Formisano, Ron. *American Oligarchy: The Permanent Political Class.* Urbana: University of Illinois Press, 2017.
Foucault, Michel. *Discipline and Punish: The Birth of the Prison.* Translated by A. Sheridan. London: Tavistock, 1977.
———. *Security, Territory, Population: Lectures at the College De France, 1977–1978.* Translated by Graham Burchell. New York: Picador, 2007.
———. *The Birth of Biopolitics.* Translated by Graham Burchell. New York: Picador, 2008.
———. "What Is an Author?" In *The Foucault Reader*, edited Paul Rabinow, 101–20. New York: Pantheon, 1984.
Francis, Mark. *Herbert Spencer and the Invention of Modern Life.* Ithaca, NY: Cornell University Press, 2007.
Frank, Robert H. *Success and Luck: Good Fortune and the Myth of Meritocracy.* Princeton, NJ: Princeton University Press, 2016.
Frank, Thomas. *Pity the Billionaire: The Hard-Times Swindle and the Unlikely Comeback of the Right.* New York: Metropolitan Books, 2012.
———. *What's the Matter with Kansas? How Conservatives Won the Heart of America.* New York: Metro, 2004.
Fraser, Steve, and Gary Gerstle, eds. *Ruling America: A History of Wealth and Power in a Democracy.* Cambridge, MA: Harvard University Press, 2005.
Freeland, Chrystia. *Plutocrats: The Rise of the New Global Super-Rich and the Fall of Everyone Else.* New York: Penguin Press, 2012.
Friedman, Benjamin. *Religion and the Rise of Capitalism.* New York: Knopf, 2021.
Friedman, Milton. "Capitalism and Freedom." In *New Individualist Review*, edited by Ralph Raico 1, no. 1 (1961).
———. "Free to Choose, Vol. 4 - From Cradle to Grave." *PBS*, 1980.

---. "Monetarism in Rhetoric and in Practice." Keynote paper presented at the First International Conference of the Institute for Monetary and Economics Studies, Tokyo, June 22, 1983.
---. "Policy Forum: 'Milton Friedman on Business Suicide.'" *Cato Institute*, March/April 1999.
---. "The Limitations of Tax Limitation." *Heritage Foundation Policy Review*, Summer 1978.
---. "Value Judgments in Economics." Collected Works of Milton Friedman Project records, Hoover Institution Library & Archives.
---. *Capitalism and Freedom*. Chicago: University of Chicago Press, 1962.
Friedman, Milton, and Rose Friedman. *Two Lucky People*. Chicago: University of Chicago Press, 1999.
---. *Free to Choose: A Personal Statement*. San Diego: Harcourt, 1980.
Gaonkar, Dilip P. "The Idea of Rhetoric in the Rhetoric of Science." *Western Journal of Communication* 58 (1993): 258–95.
Garver, Eugene. *Aristotle's Politics: Living Well and Living Together*. Chicago: University of Chicago Press, 2011.
Gehl, Katherine M., and Michael E. Porter. *The Politics Industry: How Political Innovation Can Break Partisan Gridlock and Save Our Democracy*. Cambridge, MA: Harvard Business Review Press, 2020.
---. "Fixing U.S. Politics." *Harvard Business Review*, July–August 2020.
Gershberg, Zac, and Sean Illing. *The Paradox of Democracy: Free Speech, Open Media, and Perilous Persuasion*. Chicago: University of Chicago Press, 2022.
Gibson, Timothy A. "Primitive Accumulation, Eminent Domain, and the Contradictions of Neo-Liberalism." *Cultural Studies* 24, no. 1 (2010): 133–60.
Gilens, Martin, and Benjamin I. Page. "Testing Theories of American Politics: Elites, Interest Groups, and Average Citizens." *Perspectives on Politics* 12, no. 3 (2014): 564–81.
Gill, Rebecca. "The Evolution of Organizational Archetypes: From the American to the Entrepreneurial Dream." *Communication Monographs* 80, no. 3 (September 2013): 331–53.
Giridharadas, Anand. *Winners Take All: The Elite Charade of Changing the World*. New York: Vintage, 2018.
Giroux, Henry A. *Stormy Weather: Katrina and the Politics of Disposability*. Boulder, CO: Paradigm, 2006.
Glendening, Jeff. "Historic Tax Hike Won't Fix Spending Problem." *Wichita Eagle*, July 2, 2017.
Gold, Matea. "Koch-backed Political Network, Built to Shield Donors, Raised $400 Million In 2012 Elections." *Washington Post*, January 5, 2014.
Goodnight, G. Thomas. "The Personal, Technical, and Public Spheres of Argument: A Speculative Inquiry into the Art of Public Deliberation." *Argumentation & Advocacy* 48 (2012): 198–210.
"Gov. Sam Brownback's Office Sends Email on Welfare Policies." *Associated Press State & Local*, September 25, 2015.
Gramsci, Antonio. *Selections from the Prison Notebooks of Antonio Gramsci*, edited

REFERENCES

and translated by Quintin Hoare and Geoffrey Nowell Smith. New York: International Publishers, 1971.

Grantham, Bill, and Toby Miller. "The End of Neoliberalism." *Popular Communication* 8, no. 3 (July 2010): 174–77.

Greene, Jamal. "Selling Originalism." *Geo. L. J.* 97 (2009): 657–721.

Greene, Ronald Walter, and Sara Holiday Nelson. "Struggle for the Commons: Communicative Labor, Control Economics, and the Rhetorical Marketplace." In *Communication and the Economy*, edited by Joshua Hanan and Mark Hayward, 259–84. New York: Peter Lang, 2014.

Greene, Ronald Walter. "Y Movies: Film and the Modernization of Pastoral Power." *Communication and Critical/Cultural Studies* 2 (2005): 20–36.

Gregg, Melissa, and Gregory J. Seigworth. *The Affect Theory Reader*. Durham, NC: Duke University Press, 2010.

Grey, Stephanie Houston. "Conceptually-Oriented Criticism." In *Rhetorical Criticism: Perspectives in Action*, edited by Jim A. Kuypers, 341–62. Lanham, MD: Lexington, 2009.

Gunn, Joshua. "On Political Perversion." *Rhetoric Society Quarterly* 48, no. 2 (2018): 161–86.

Habermas, Jürgen. *The Structural Transformation of the Public Sphere*. Translated by Thomas Burger. Cambridge, MA: MIT Press, 1989.

Hacker, Jacob S., and Paul Pierson. *American Amnesia: How the War on Government Led Us to Forget What Made America Prosper*. New York: Simon & Schuster, 2016.

Hackworth, Jason. *The Neoliberal City: Governance, Ideology, and Development in American Urbanism*. Ithaca, NY: Cornell University Press, 2007.

Haidt, Jonathan. *The Righteous Mind: Why Good People Are Divided by Politics and Religion*. New York: Vintage, 2012.

Hanan, Joshua S. "Home Is Where the Capital Is: The Culture of Real Estate in an Era of Control Societies." *Communication & Critical/Cultural Studies* 7, no. 2 (June 2010): 176–201.

———. "The Oikos as Economic Rhetoric: Toward an Ontological Investigation of Rhetorical Biopolitics." In *Rhetorics Change / Rhetoric's Change*, edited by Jenny Rice, Chelsea Graham, and Eric Detweiler. Anderson, SC: Parlor Press, 2018.

Hanan, Joshua S., and Catherine Chaput. "A Rhetoric of Economics Beyond Civic Humanism: Exploring the Political Economy of Rhetoric in the Context of Late Neoliberalism." *Journal of Cultural Economy* 8, no. 1 (2015):16–24.

Hanan, Joshua, and Jeffrey St. Onge. "Beyond the Dialectic Between Wall Street and Main Street: A Materialist Analysis of *The Big Short*." *Advances in the History of Rhetoric* 21, no. 2 (2018): 163–77.

Hariman, Robert. "Norms of the Rhetorical Theory." *Quarterly Journal of Speech* 80, no. 3 (1994): 329–32.

———. *Political Style: The Artistry of Power*. Chicago: University of Chicago Press, 1995.

Hart, Jeffrey. *The Making of the Conservative Mind: National Review and Its Times*. Wilmington, DE: ISI Books, 2005.

Hart, Roderick P., and E. Johanna Hartelius. "The Political Sins of Jon Stewart." *Critical Studies in Media Communication* 24, no. 3 (2007): 263–72.

Harvey, David. *A Brief History of Neoliberalism.* Oxford: Oxford University Press, 2005.

———. *The Condition of Postmodernity: An Enquiry Into the Origins of Cultural Change.* Cambridge, MA: Basil Blackwell, 1989.

Hasinoff, Amy Adele. "Fashioning Race for the Free Market on America's Next Top Model." *Critical Studies in Media Communication* 25, no. 3 (August 2008): 324–43.

Hay, James, Stuart Hall, and Lawrence Grossberg. "Interview with Stuart Hall." *Communication & Critical/Cultural Studies* 10, no. 1 (2013): 10–33.

Hayek, Friedrich von. *The Constitution of Liberty.* Edited by Ronald Hamowy. Chicago: University of Chicago Press, 2011.

———. "Friedrich von Hayek Prize Lecture." December 11, 1974. Nobel Prize (website).

———. "The Pretense of Knowledge." In *New Studies in Philosophy, Politics, Economics, and the History of Ideas,* edited by F. A. Hayek. Chicago: University of Chicago Press, 1978.

———. *The Road to Serfdom: Text and Documents—The Definitive Edition: Text and Documents—The Definitive Edition (The Collected Works of F. A. Hayek,* Volume 2). Chicago: University of Chicago Press, 2009.

Herrnstein Smith, Barbara. *Belief and Resistance: Dynamics of Contemporary Intellectual Controversy.* Cambridge, MA: Harvard University Press, 1997.

Hesford, Wendy S., Adela C. Licona, and Christa Teston. *Precarious Rhetorics: New Directions in Rhetoric and Materiality.* Columbus: Ohio State University Press, 2018.

Hlavacik, Mark. *Assigning Blame: The Rhetoric of Education Reform.* Cambridge, MA: Harvard Education Press, 2016.

Hochschild, Arlie Russell. *Strangers in Their Own Land: Anger and Mourning on the American Right.* New York: New Press, 2016.

Hoerl, Kristen. "Cinematic Jujitsu: Resisting White Hegemony through the American Dream in Spike Lee's *Malcolm X.*" *Communication Studies* 59, no. 4 (2008): 355–70.

Holloway, John, and Sol Picciotto. "Introduction: Toward a Materialist Theory of the State." In *State and Capital: A Marxist Debate,* edited by John Holloway and Sol Picciotto, 1–31. Austin: University of Texas Press, 1978.

Homans, Charles. "Americans Think 'Corruption' Is Everywhere. Is That Why We Vote for It?" *New York Times Magazine,* July 10, 2018.

Hustwit, William P. "From Caste to Color Blindness: James J. Kilpatrick's Segregationist Semantics." *Journal of Southern History* 77, no. 3 (2011): 639–70.

———. *James J. Kilpatrick: Salesman for Segregation.* Chapel Hill, NC: University of North Carolina Press, 2013.

"Introduction: The Powell Memo (AKA the Powell Manifesto)." *Reclaim Democracy!* Accessed May 6, 2023.

Jameson, Fredric. *The Political Unconscious: Narrative as a Socially Symbolic Act.* Ithaca, NY: Cornell University Press, 1971.

REFERENCES

Jasinski, James. *Sourcebook of Rhetoric: Key Concepts in Rhetorical Studies.* Thousand Oaks, CA: Sage, 2001.

Johnson, Paul Elliot. *I The People: The Rhetoric of Conservative Populism in the United States.* Tuscaloosa: University of Alabama Press, 2022.

Johnson, Theodore R. "The Monolith." *New York Times Magazine*, September 20, 2020.

Jones, Bradley, and Roopali Mukherjee. "From California to Michigan: Race, Rationality, and Neoliberal Governmentality." *Communication & Critical/Cultural Studies* 7, no. 4 (2010): 401–22.

Jones, John M., and Robert C. Rowland. "Redefining the Proper Role of Government: Ultimate Definition in Reagan's First Inaugural." *Rhetoric & Public Affairs* 18 (2015): 691–718.

"Kansas Gov. Sam Brownback on MSNBC's Morning Joe." YouTube (website). June 19, 2020.

Kaplan, David A. *The Most Dangerous Branch: Inside the Supreme Court's Assault on the Constitution.* New York: Crown, 2018.

Kaplan, Michael. "The Communicative Efficacy of Markets." In *Communication and the Economy*, edited by Joshua Hanan and Mark Hayward, 121–46. New York: Peter Lang, 2014.

Kendi, Ibram X. *How to Be an Antiracist.* New York: One World, 2019.

———. *Stamped from the Beginning: The Definitive History of Racist Ideas in America.* New York: Nation Books, 2016.

Khan, Abraham Iqbal. "A Rant Good for Business: Communicative Capitalism and the Capture of Anti-Racist Resistance." *Popular Communication* 14, no. 1 (January 2016): 39–48.

Kiewe, Amos, and David W. Houck, eds. *The Effects of Rhetoric and the Rhetoric of Effects.* Columbia: University of South Carolina Press, 2015.

———. "Introduction." In *The Effects of Rhetoric and the Rhetoric of Effects*, edited by Amos Kiewe and David W. Houck, 1–30. Columbia: University of South Carolina Press, 2015.

Kirk, Russell. *The Conservative Mind, from Burke to Santayana.* Chicago: H. Regnery, 1953.

Klein, Ezra. "Robert Frank's Radical Idea." *Vox*, May 26, 2020.

Klein, Naomi. *The Shock Doctrine: The Rise of Disaster Capitalism.* Picador: New York, 2007.

———. *This Changes Everything: Capitalism vs. The Climate.* New York: Simon & Schuster, 2014.

Koch, Charles. *Anti-Capitalism and Business.* Menlo Park: Institute for Humane Studies, 1974.

———. "The Business Community: Resisting Regulation." *Libertarian Review* (August 1978).

———. "1974 Charles Koch Speech: Anti-Capitalism and Big Business and How the Powell Memo Did Not Go Far Enough." KochDocs (website).

———. *The Science of Success: How Market-Based Management Built the World's Largest Private Company.* Hoboken, NJ: John Wiley & Sons, 2007.

Kocieniewski, David. "At G.E. on Tax Day, Billions of Reasons to Smile." *New York Times*, September 23, 2015.
Kolata, Gina. "Tucker Carlson Has a Cure for Declining Virility." *New York Times*, April 22, 2022.
Kramnick, Isaac. *The Rage of Edmund Burke: Portrait of an Ambivalent Conservative*. New York: Basic: 1977.
Krugman, Paul. "Trump's Big Libertarian Experiment." *New York Times*, January 11, 2019.
Kunkel, Benjamin. *Utopia or Bust: A Guide to the Present Crisis*. New York: Verso Books, 2014.
Lears, Jackson. *Something for Nothing: Luck in America*. New York: Viking, 2003.
Lee, Michael J. *Creating Conservatism: Postwar Words that Made an American Movement*. East Lansing: Michigan State University Press, 2014.
LeMaster, Benny. "Discontents of Being and Becoming Fabulous on RuPaul's Drag U: Queer Criticism in Neoliberal Times." *Women's Studies in Communication* 38, no. 2 (2015): 167–86.
Leonard, Christopher. *Kochland: The Secret History of Koch Industries and Corporate Power in America*. New York: Simon & Schuster, 2019.
Lepore, Jill. *These Truths: A History of the United States*. New York: W. W. Norton, 2018.
Lessl, Thomas M. *Rhetorical Darwinism: Religion, Evolution, and the Scientific Identity*. Waco, TX: Baylor University Press, 2012.
Lewis, George. "Virginia's Northern Strategy: Southern Segregationists and the Route to National Conservatism." *Journal of Southern History* 72, no. 1 (2006): 111–46.
Lloyd, Henry Demarest. "The Story of a Great Monopoly." *Atlantic*, March 1881.
"Lochner v. New York." *Oyez*. Accessed May 22, 2023.
Longaker, Mark Garrett. *Rhetorical Style and the Bourgeois Virtue. Capitalism and Civil Society in the British Enlightenment*. University Park: Pennsylvania State University Press, 2015.
Lowe, Jamie. "With 'Stealth Politics,' Billionaires Make Sure Their Money Talks." *New York Times Magazine*, April 10, 2022.
Luhrmann, T. M. *When God Talks Back: Understanding the American Evangelical Relationship with God*. New York: Knopf, 2012.
Lukianoff, Greg, and Jonathan Haidt. *The Coddling of the American Mind: How Good Intentions and Bad Ideas Are Setting up a Generation for Failure*. New York: Penguin, 2018.
Mack, Ashley Noel. "The Self-Made Mom: Neoliberalism and Masochistic Motherhood in Home-Birth Videos on YouTube." *Women's Studies in Communication* 39, no. 1 (January 2016): 47–69.
MacLean, Nancy. *Democracy in Chains: The Deep History of the Radical Right's Stealth Plan for America*. New York: Penguin, 2017.
Magnuson, William. *For Profit: A History of Corporations*. New York: Basic, 2022.
Manjoo, Farhad. "Tucker Carlson 2024." *New York Times*, September 21, 2019.

REFERENCES

Marchand, Roland. *Creating the Corporate Soul.* Berkeley: University of California Press, 1996.

Marchese, David. "Thomas Piketty Thinks America Is Primed for Wealth Redistribution." *New York Times Magazine,* April 10, 2022.

Mayer, Jane. *Dark Money: The Hidden History of the Billionaires behind the Rise of the Radical Right.* New York: Doubleday, 2016.

Mayer, Jane, and Jill Abramson. *Strange Justice: The Selling of Clarence Thomas.* New York: Graymalkin Media, 2018.

Mazerov, Michael. "Kansas Provides Compelling Evidence of Failure of "Supply-Side" Tax Cuts." *States News Service,* January 22, 2018.

Mazzucato, Mariana. *The Entrepreneurial State: Debunking Public vs. Private Sector Myths.* New York: PublicAffairs, 2015.

McCann, Bryan J. "Redemption in the Neoliberal and Radical Imaginations: The Saga of Stanley 'Tookie' Williams." *Communication, Culture & Critique* 7, no. 1 (March 2014): 92–111.

McChesney, Robert W. *Rich Media, Poor Democracy: Communication Politics in Dubious Times.* Urbana: University of Illinois Press, 1999.

McChesney, Robert, cited in Bradford Vivian. "Neoliberal Epideictic: Rhetorical Form and Commemorative Politics on September 11, 2002." *Quarterly Journal of Speech* 92, no. 1 (2006): 1–26.

McClennen, Edward F. "Comment." In *Altruism, Morality, and Economic Theory,* edited by Edmund S. Phelps, 133–40. New York: Russell Sage Foundation, 1975.

McCloskey, Deirdre. *Bourgeois Virtues: Ethics for an Age of Commerce.* Hoboken, NJ: John Wiley & Sons, 2006.

———. *The Rhetoric of Economics.* 2nd edition. Madison: University of Wisconsin Press, 1998.

McGee, Michael. "Text, Context, and the Fragmentation of Contemporary Culture." *Western Journal of Communication* 54 (1990): 274–89.

McGhee, Heather. *The Sum of Us: What Racism Costs Everyone and How We Can Prosper Together.* New York: One World, 2021.

McGirr, Lisa. *Suburban Warriors: The Origins of the New American Right.* Princeton, NJ: Princeton University Press, 2001.

Mercieca, Jennifer. *Demagogue for President: The Rhetorical Genius of Donald Trump.* College Station: Texas A&M University Press, 2019.

Milburn, John. "Brownback Imposing Kan. Budget Cuts." Associated Press (state and local wire), March 11, 2011.

Miliband, Ralph. *The State in Capitalist Society.* Pontypool, Wales: Merlin Press, 1969/2009.

Miller, Justin. "Kansas, Sam Brownback, and the Trickle-Down Implosion." *American Prospect Blogs,* June 28, 2017.

Mills, Charles W. *The Racial Contract.* Ithaca, NY: Cornell University Press, 1997.

Mises, Ludwig von. *Human Action: A Treatise on Economics.* Ludwig von Mises Institute, 1949.

Moreton, Bethany E. "Make Payroll, Not War: Business Culture as Youth Culture." In *Rightward Bound: Making America Conservative in the 1970s,* edited by Bruce Schulman and Julian Zelizer, 52–70. Cambridge, MA: Harvard University Press, 2008.

———. *To Serve God and Wal-Mart: The Making of Christian Free Enterprise*. Cambridge, MA: Harvard University Press, 2009.

Mosco, Vincent. *The Political Economy of Communication*. Los Angeles: Sage, 2009.

Mounk, Yascha. *The Age of Responsibility: Luck, Choice, and the Welfare State*. Cambridge, MA: Harvard University Press, 2017.

Musgrave, Kevin. *Persons of the Market: Conservatism, Corporate Personhood, and Economic Theology*. East Lansing: Michigan State University Press, 2022.

Nasaw, David. "Gilded Age Gospels." In *Ruling America*, edited by Steve Fraser and Gary Gerstle, 123–48. Cambridge, MA: Harvard University Press, 2005.

Neiman, Susan. *Learning from the Germans: Race and the Memory of Evil*. New York: Farrar, Straus and Giroux, 2019.

Nelson, Edward. *Milton Friedman and Economic Debate in the United States, 1932–1972*. Chicago: University of Chicago Press, 2020.

Neubauer, Robert J. "Dialogue, Monologue, or Something in Between? Neoliberal Think Tanks in the Americas." *International Journal of Communication* 6 (2012): 2173–98.

Nietzsche, Friedrich. *Thus Spake Zarathustra*. Translated by Walter Kaufmann. New York: Vintage, 1966.

Nixon, Richard. "Transcript of David Frost's Interview with Richard Nixon." 1977. Teaching American History (website), Ashland, OH.

Noah, Timothy. *The Great Divergence: America's Growing Inequality Crisis and What We Can Do About It*. New York: Bloomsbury, 2012.

O'Connor, Alice. "Financing the Counterrevolution." In *Rightward Bound: Making America Conservative in the 1970s*, edited by Bruce Schulman and Julian Zelizer, 148–67. Cambridge, MA: Harvard University Press, 2008.

O'Connor, Sandra Day. *The Majesty of the Law*. New York: Random House, 2003.

O'Mara, Margaret. *The Code: Silicon Valley and the Remaking of America*. New York: Penguin, 2019.

Oliver, Eric J., and Thomas Wood. "Conspiracy Theories of the Paranoid Styles(s) of Mass Opinion." *American Journal of Political Science* 58, no. 4 (2014): 952–66.

Ong, Aihwa. *Neoliberalism as Exception: Mutation in Citizenship and Sovereignty*. Durham, NC: Duke University Press, 2006.

Oreskes, Naomi, and Erik M. Conway. *The Big Myth: How American Business Taught Us to Loathe Government and Love the Free Market*. New York: Bloomsbury, 2023.

Osnos, Evan. *Wildland: The Making of America's Fury*. New York: Farrar, Straus, and Giroux, 2021.

Packer, George. "We Are Living in a Failed State." *Atlantic*, June 2020.

Page, Benjamin I., Jason Seawright, and Matthew J. Lacombe. *Billionaires and Stealth Politics*. Chicago: University of Chicago Press, 2019.

Pal, Mahuya, and Patrice M. Buzzanell. "Breaking the Myth of Indian Call Centers:

REFERENCES

A Postcolonial Analysis of Resistance." *Communication Monographs* 80, no. 2 (2013): 199–219.

Panitch, Leo. "Forward: Reading *The State in Capitalist Society*." In *The State in Capitalist Society*, Ralph Miliband, ix–xxvii. Pontypool, Wales: Merlin Press, 1969/2009.

Parker, Jean, and Damien Cahill. "The Retreat from Neoliberalism That Was Not: Australia's Building the Education Revolution." *Australian Journal of Political Science* 52 (2017): 257–71.

Peck, Jamie. *Constructions of Neoliberal Reason*. Oxford: Oxford University Press, 2010.

Peck, Jamie, and Adam Tickell. "Neoliberalizing Space." *Antipode* 34 (2002): 380–404.

Peel, J. D. Y. *Herbert Spencer: The Evolution of a Sociologist*. New York: Basic, 1971.

Perelman, Chaïm. *Realm of Rhetoric*. South Bend, IN: University of Notre Dame Press, 1982.

Perlstein, Rick. *Nixonland: The Rise of a President and the Fracturing of America*. New York: Scribner, 2008.

Phelan, Sean. "The Discourses of Neoliberal Hegemony: The Case of the Irish Republic." *Critical Discourse Studies* 4, no. 1 (2007): 29–48.

———. "The Rise and Fall of Neo-Liberalism: The Collapse of an Economic Order?" *Critical Discourse Studies* 10, no. 1 (2013): 117–19.

Philippon, Thomas. *The Great Reversal: How America Gave Up on Free Markets*. Cambridge, MA: Harvard University Press, 2019.

Phillips-Fein, Kim. *Invisible Hands: The Businessmen's Crusade Against the New Deal*. New York: Norton, 2010.

Phillips, Amber. "'Oh, We'd Fill It': How McConnell Is Doing a 180 on Supreme Court Vacancies in an Election Year." *Washington Post*, May 29, 2019.

Piketty, Thomas. *Capital and Ideology*. Cambridge, MA: Belknap/Harvard University Press, 2020.

———. *Capital in the Twenty-First Century*. Cambridge, MA: Belknap/Harvard University Press, 2014.

Piketty, Thomas, and Steven Rendall. *A Brief History of Equality*. Cambridge, MA: Belknap/Harvard University Press, 2022.

Pinker, Steven. *Enlightenment Now: The Case for Reason, Science, Humanism, and Progress*. New York: Viking, 2018.

Posner, Eric. "You Deserve a Bigger Paycheck: Here's How You Might Get It." *New York Times*, September 23, 2021.

Posner, Richard A. "The Future of Law and Economics: Looking Forward." *University of Chicago Law Review* 64, no. 4 (1997): 1129–165.

Powell, Lewis F., Jr. "Attack on American Free Enterprise System." Accessed June 1, 2021.

Purdy, Jedediah. *Two Cheers for Politics: Why Democracy Is Flawed, Frightening, and Our Best Hope*. New York: Basic, 2022.

Putnam, Robert D. *The Upswing: How America Came Together a Century Ago and How We Can Do It Again*. New York: Simon & Schuster, 2020.

REFERENCES

Reich, Robert. *Saving Capitalism: For the Many, Not the Few*. New York: Knopf, 2015.
Roberts-Miller, Patricia. *Rhetoric and Demagoguery*. Carbondale: Southern Illinois University Press, 2019.
Robin, Corey. *The Enigma of Clarence Thomas*. New York: Metropolitan Books, 2019.
———. *The Reactionary Mind: Conservatism from Edmund Burke to Donald Trump*. 2nd edition. Oxford: Oxford University Press, 2018.
Rose, Nikolas, and Peter Miller. *Governing the Present: Administering Economic, Social and Personal Life*. Malden, MA: Polity Press, 2008.
Rothbard, Murray. *Left and Right: A Journal of Libertarian Thought (Complete, 1965–1968)*. Auburn, AL: Ludwig von Mises Institute, 2007.
Rothkopf, David. *American Resistance: The Inside Story of How the Deep State Saved the Nation*. New York: PublicAffairs, 2022.
Saez, Emmanuel, and Gabriel Zucman. *The Triumph of Injustice: How the Rich Dodge Taxes and How to Make Them Pay*. New York: W. W. Norton, 2019.
Said, Edward W. *Orientalism*. New York: Pantheon, 1978.
Schreckinger, Ben. "Reagan's Supply-Side Warriors Blaze Comeback Under Trump." *Politico Magazine*, April 22, 2019.
Schulman, Daniel. *Sons of Wichita: How the Koch Brothers Became America's Most Powerful and Private Dynasty*. New York: Grand Central, 2014.
Sharot, Tali. *The Influential Mind: What the Brain Reveals About Our Power to Change Others*. New York: Henry Holt, 2017.
Shugart, Helene A. "Consuming Citizen: Neoliberating the Obese Body." *Communication, Culture & Critique* 3, no. 1 (2010): 105–26.
Simons, Henry. "Introduction: A Political Credo." In *Economic Policy for a Free Society*, edited by Ekkehard Köhler and Stefan Kolev. Chicago: University of Chicago Press, 1948.
Sitaraman, Ganesh. *The Crisis of the Middle-Class Constitution: Why Economic Inequality Threatens Our Republic*. New York: Vintage, 2017.
Slobodian, Quinn. *Globalists: The End of Empire and the Birth of Neoliberalism*. Cambridge, MA: Harvard University Press, 2018.
Smith, Craig R. "Ronald Reagan's Rhetorical Re-Invention of Conservatism." *Quarterly Journal of Speech* 103, no. 1/2 (2017): 33–65.
Smith, Hedrick. *Who Stole the American Dream?* New York: Random House, 2013.
Smith, Matthew, Danny Yagan, Owen Zidar, and Eric Zwick. "Capitalists in the Twenty-First Century." *Quarterly Journal of Economics* 134, no. 4 (2019): 1675–1745.
Somers, Margaret. *Genealogies of Citizenship: Markets, Stateless, and the Right to Have Rights*. Cambridge: Cambridge University Press, 2008.
Sorkin, Andrew Ross. "Greed Is Good. Except When It Is Bad." *New York Times Magazine*, September 13, 2020.
Spencer, Herbert. "Over-Regulation." *Westminster Review*, July 1853.
———. *Essays: Scientific, Political and Speculative*. England: Williams and Norgate, 1891.
———. *The Complete Works of Herbert Spencer: Essays. Scientific, Political, and Speculative*. Volume 1. HardPress, 2013.

REFERENCES

———. *The Principles of Biology*, Vol. II (1867), Part VI: Laws of Multiplication, Ch. 8: Human Population in the Future.
Sreedhar, Anita, and Anand Gopal. "Behind Low Vaccination Rates Lurks a More Profound Social Weakness." *New York Times*, December 2, 2021.
St. Onge, Jeffrey. "Neoliberalism as Common Sense in Barack Obama's Health Care Rhetoric." *Rhetoric Society Quarterly* 47 (2017): 295–312.
Stephen-Davidowitz, Seth. "The Rich Are Not Who We Think They Are: And Happiness Is Not What We Think It Is, Either." *New York Times*, May 14, 2022.
Steudeman, Michael J. "Indeterminacy, Incipiency, and Attitudes: Materialist Oscillation in the 2012 Chicago Teachers' Strike." *Quarterly Journal of Speech* 101 (2015): 509–33.
Stewart, Charles J., Craig Allen Smith, and Robert E. Denton. *Persuasion and Social Movements*, 6th edition. Long Grove, IL: Waveland Press, 2014.
Stewart, Matthew. "The Birth of a New American Aristocracy." *Atlantic*, June 2018.
———. *The 9.9 Percent: The New Aristocracy That Is Entrenching Inequality and Warping Our Culture*. New York: Simon & Schuster, 2021.
Strang, Lee J. *Originalism's Promise: A Natural Law Account of the American Constitution*. Cambridge: Cambridge University Press, 2019.
Stuckey, Mary E. "American Elections and the Rhetoric of Political Change: Hyperbole, Anger, and Hope in U.S. Politics." *Rhetoric & Public Affairs* 20, no. 4 (2017): 667–94.
Sweeney, James R. "Postscript to Massive Resistance: The Decline and Fall of the Virginia Commission on Constitutional Government." *Virginia Magazine of History and Biography* 121, no. 1 (2013): 44–86.
———, ed. *Race, Reason, and Massive Resistance: The Diary of David J. Mays, 1954–1959*. Athens: University of Georgia Press, 2008.
Tankersley, Jim, Peter Eavis, and Ben Casselman. "How FedEx Cut Its Tax Bill to $0." *New York Times*, November 17, 2019.
Tankersley, Jim. "A Broken Promise on Taxes." *Daily* (podcast), *New York Times*, November 19, 2019.
Teles, Steven M. *The Rise of the Conservative Legal Movement: The Battle for Control of the Law*. Princeton, NJ: Princeton University Press, 2012.
Tomasky, Michael. "Why Recent Republican Presidents Have Been Economic Failures." *New York Times*, August 20, 2020.
"User Clip: Tucker Carlson Criticizes Pat Buchanan (1999)," CSPAN. Accessed May 22, 2023.
Valdes, Juan Gabriel. *Pinochet's Economists: The Chicago School in Chile*. Cambridge: Cambridge University Press, 1995.
Van Horn, Rob, and Philip Mirowski. "The Rise of the Chicago School of Economics and the Birth of Neoliberalism." In *The Road from Mont Pèlerin: The Making of the Neoliberal Thought Collective*, edited by Philip Mirowski and Dieter Plehwe, 139–78. Cambridge, MA: Harvard University Press, 2009.
Virginia Commission on Constitutional Government. "Did the Court Interpret or Amend?: The Meaning of the Fourteenth Amendment, in Terms of a

State's Power to Operate Racially Separate Public Schools, as Defined by the Courts." (1962).

Vivian, Bradford. "Neoliberal Epideictic: Rhetorical Form and Commemorative Politics on September 11, 2002." *Quarterly Journal of Speech* 92, no. 1 (2006): 1–26.

Ward, Lester F. "Herbert Spencer's Autobiography," *Science* 19, no. 493 (1904): 873–79.

Weaver, Richard. *The Ethics of Rhetoric*. South Bend, IN: Regnery/Gateway, 1953.

Wilkerson, Isabel. *The Warmth of Other Sons: The Epic Story of America's Great Migration*. New York: Vintage, 2011.

Will, George. *The Conservative Sensibility*. New York: Hachette, 2019.

Williams, Jonathan, and Ben Wilterdink. "Lessons from Kansas: A Behind the Scenes Look at America's Most Discussed Tax Reform Effort." *American Legislative Exchange Council* (February 2017).

Williams, Raymond. *Marxism and Literature*. Oxford: Oxford University Press, 1977.

Williamson, Kevin D. "Starving the Beast in Kansas," *National Review*, May 3, 2016.

Wilson, Kirt H. "Theory/Criticism: A Functionalist Approach to the 'Specific Intellectual' Work of Rhetorical Criticism." *Western Journal of Communication* 84, no. 3 (May 2020): 280–96.

Wingard, Jennifer. "Branding Citizens: The Logic(s) of a Few Bad Apples." In *Rhetoric in Neoliberalism*, edited by Kim Hong Nguyen, 135–55. London: Palgrave Macmillan, 2017.

Winkler, Adam. *We the Corporations: How American Businesses Won Their Civil Rights*. New York: Liveright, 2018.

Winslow, Luke. *American Catastrophe: Fundamentalism, Climate Change, Gun Rights, and the Rhetoric of Donald J. Trump*. Columbus: Ohio State University Press, 2020.

———. *Economic Injustice and the Rhetoric of the American Dream*. Lanham, MD: Lexington Books, 2017.

———. "Not Exactly a Model of Good Hygiene": Theorizing an Aesthetic of Disgust in the Occupy Wall Street Movement." *Critical Studies in Media Communication* 34 (2017): 278–92.

Winslow, Luke, Alec Baker, and Charles Goehring. "The Neoliberal Conquest of the Supreme Court." *Communication & The Public* 3, no. 3 (2018): 205–17.

Winters, Jeffrey A. *Oligarchy*. New York: Cambridge University Press, 2018.

Winters, Jeffrey A., and Benjamin I. Page. "Oligarchy in the United States?" *Perspectives on Politics* 7, no. 4 (2009): 731–51.

Wulf, Andrea. *The Invention of Nature: Alexander von Humboldt's New World*. New York: Vintage, 2015.

Yourish, Karen, Weiyi Cai, and Larry Buchanan. "Inside the Apocalyptic Worldview of 'Tucker Carlson Tonight.'" *New York Times*, May 1, 2022.

Zarefsky, David. "Presidential Rhetoric and the Power of Definition." *Presidential Studies Quarterly* 34, no. 4 (2004): 607–19.

REFERENCES

Zeitz, Joshua. *Building the Great Society: Inside Lyndon Johnson's White House.* New York: Penguin, 2018.

Zingales, Luigi. "Towards a Political Theory of the Firm." *Journal of Economic Perspective* 31, no. 3 (2017): 113–30.

Zucman, Gabriel, and Gus Wezerek. "This is Tax Evasion, Plain and Simple." *New York Times*, July 7, 2021.

Index

Adams John, 15, 17–19, 42, 43, 55, 56, 87, 96
affect, ix, 2, 11, 25, 38, 39, 43, 52, 68, 73, 83, 121–22, 125, 126, 143, 147, 197, 205–6, 207, 209, 210, 251n56, 252n63, 270n21, 270–71nn34–35, 272–73n61, 274n68
affirmative action, 29, 57; affirmative action, opposition to, 86, 89, 95, 130, 245n102
Ailes, Roger, 110
Almond, J. Lindsay, 82
Amadae, S. A., 143, 251n63
Amazon, 5, 129
American Dream, 48, 49, 50. See also Carnegie, Andrew
American Legislative Exchange Council (ALEC), 152, 160, 161, 167, 259n5
American Liberty League, 101
Americans for Prosperity, 151, 167, 259n5, 261n48
Andersen, Kurt, 108, 128, 133, 152, 153, 251n63
Anderson, Perry, 112
Appelbaum, Binyamin, 126, 152, 215n32, 251n63, 261n59, 267n8
Apple, 9, 58, 191, 217–18n59
Aristotle, 6, 15–17, 21, 22, 35, 42, 43, 45, 55, 71, 72, 115, 143, 216n44, 221n37, 221n39, 224n88
Asen, Robert, 55, 251–52n63
Aune, James, 205, 207, 251n56

Barrett, Amy Coney, 96, 239n45
Barrow, Clyde, 4, 19–20, 198, 212n13, 213n16, 270n21
Bazelon, Emily, 87
Beck, Glenn, 13, 63, 208
Bezos, Jeff, ix, 5, 51, 147, 182
Biden, Joe, 152, 178, 195, 228n47, 249n27
Biden, Hunter, 180
Black Americans, 17, 27–28, 81, 89, 92–93, 94, 124, 136–37. See also race
Black, Edwin, 273n63
Bloomberg, Michael, 6
Boeing, 58, 100
Brandeis, Louis D., 189, 193
Brown v. Board of Education, 80–85, 86–87, 88, 89, 90–92, 95, 96, 239n45, 239n55, 242n22
Brown, Wendy, 189, 215n31, 246n109
Brownback, Sam, 161–69, 262n81
Brummett, Barry, 116, 209, 271n59
Buchanan, James McGill, 99, 135–50, 154, 186, 257–58n57, 258n71, 273n63; conjoint depletion, 135–38, 143; conservatism, 135, 142, 146; democracy, 139, 141, 143, 145, 236n100; education, 148–49; post-constitutionalism, 138; private property, 147–48; race, 136–37; the Samaritan's dilemma, 138–42, 143, 149–50; the state, 136, 138, 141, 144–46; tax policy, 149; and violence, 149

INDEX

Buchanan, Patrick, 172, 176, 273n61
Buckley, William F., 8, 22, 49, 81, 82, 179, 204
Buffett, Warren, 54
Burke, Edmund, 7, 17, 88–89, 95, 122, 171, 221n37, 256–57n53
Burke, Kenneth, 10, 23, 24, 28, 116, 163, 169, 203–6, 208, 271n59
Burr, Aaron, 27
Bush, George H. W., 68
Bush, George W., 171, 182, 215n32, 225n115

Caldwell, Bruce, 70
Calvinist-Puritanism, 24, 35. *See also* Christianity
Carlson, Tucker, 10, 92, 171–88, 253n77, 264n17; conservatism, 171, 173, 175, 176, 181, 182, 264n17; conspiracy theories, 175, 179; corruption, 179, 180, 184, 185, 186–87; democracy, 183, 188; and Donald Trump, 171–72, 174, 176, 179, 185, 188; gender 178, 181, 265n42; Hungary, 182–84; meritocracy, 177; realism, 175; *Tucker Carlson Tonight*, 173–74
Carnegie, Andrew, 45, 48–60, 63, 66, 77, 142; and the American Dream, 48, 50, 67; and Darwinism, 49, 51, 58; natural law, 48, 49, 50, 52–54, 55–57, 58; philanthropy, 48, 49–50, 52, 57; the state, 53, 57, 70, 72
Caro, Robert, 47
Cato Institute, 111, 135, 160, 161, 215n32, 267n8
Chaput, Catherine, 35, 68, 121, 127, 207, 252n63, 254n111, 270n21, 270n34, 272n61, 274n68
Cheers, 53
Chemerinsky, Erwin, 87–88
Chernow, Ron, 15–16, 19
Chicago school of economics, 70, 76, 77, 121, 125, 131, 137, 248n21, 267n8, 274n68
Child, Roy, 147–48
Chile, 72, 131, 162, 165, 250n41

Chodorov, Frank, 82
Christianity, 12, 25, 59–60, 85, 89, 139–41, 145, 182, 183, 226n18, 231–32n45; non-Christians, 80; white Christian Nationalism, 174. *See also* oligarchy: religion
Cintron, Ralph, 13, 207, 212n12, 215n31, 218n61, 226n33, 270n21
Civil Rights Movement, 11, 73, 81, 82, 86, 88–89, 90, 92, 93, 95, 124, 126, 139, 255n113 (chap 7), 255n10 (chap. 8)
Civil War, American 46, 79, 90
Clark, Jim, 83
Clarke, John, 246n106
class consciousness, 4–5, 7, 8, 20, 31, 172, 175–76, 179, 182, 185. *See also* Carlson, Tucker
Clayton Antitrust Act, 58–59
Clinton, Hillary, 178, 182, 184, 195, 196–97, 228n47
Cloud, Dana, 207
Connor, Bull, 25, 81, 83, 86
conservatism, 3, 5, 6–8, 9. 12–13, 25, 30, 33, 39, 64, 77, 78, 80, 87, 95, 120, 121, 126, 133, 142, 145, 164, 167, 171, 176, 182, 194–95, 204, 208, 210, 213n22, 225n115, 256n53, 272n61
constitutional originalism. *See* originalism
Coors, Adolph, 77, 80, 98, 115, 267n8; Joseph Coors, 111
Coronavirus. *See* COVID-19
corruption, 172, 187, 189, 252n77
COVID-19, 130, 187, 193, 194, 223n81, 249n27
Cowen, Tyler, 130, 256n38
Crane, Jasper, 62, 77
Crick, Nathan, 174
Crowley, Sharon, 21, 54, 116–17

Darwin, Charles, 23, 32–34, 36, 37–38
Darwinian evolutionary theory, 24, 32–34, 35, 36, 37–38, 41, 42, 43, 48, 49, 51, 52, 58, 129, 138, 146, 156, 227n38
Davis, Diane 207
Declaration of Independence, 81, 89

294

INDEX

democracy: American x, 4, 18–19, 26–27, 30, 44, 56, 185–86, 188, 189, 194–96, 205; folk theory of, 12, 14–16, 29, 30, 223n76; and spectacle 26; and voting 34, 39, 62, 217n55
Director, Aaron, 121
distrust of government. *See* trust in government / democracy, Americans'
Doherty, Brian, 121, 148, 160
doxa, 115–16, 205
Draper, Robert, 194, 196
du Pont family, 66, 188
du Pont, Irénée, 61, 66, 70, 80, 98, 188
du Pont, Pete, 6
du Pont, Pierre, 77, 80, 98, 101, 188

economics, the academic discipline, 67–68, 69, 74–76, 206, 234n57
education, 17, 25, 40, 44, 59, 100, 130, 148–49, 187
Eisenhower, Dwight D., 81, 96, 101
Ellis, Joseph, 19
Engels, Jeremy, x, 8, 13, 20–21, 203, 204–5, 208, 212n12, 218n61, 223n81, 267n8, 273n61
Enlightenment, x, 25, 35, 136, 174
Environmental Protection Agency (EPA), 96, 150,
Equal Employment Opportunity Commission (EEOC), 94, 95, 96
equality orientation, 64, 77, 80, 85, 86, 89, 113, 117, 122, 127–28, 156, 174, 221n33, 226n33. *See also* inequality
ethos, 208
eugenics movement, 58
exceptionalism, 30

false consciousness, 207, 220n14. *See also* oligarchy
Falwell, Jerry, 81
fascism, 174, 184
FDR. *See* Roosevelt, Franklin (FDR)
Federal Election Commission, 198
Federalist Papers, The, 16, 17
Federalist Society, 23, 92, 111, 113, 185
Fleming, David, 207
Flynn, Michael, 196

Foley, Megan, 7
Fordist-Keynesian. *See* Keynesian welfare state
Formisano, Ron, 153, 215n32
Foucault, Michel, 35, 66, 70, 131, 209, 246n109, 254n111
Foundation for Economic Education, 61, 62
Fourteenth Amendment. *See* Kilpatrick, James J.
Fox News, 173, 178
frames of acceptance, 204. *See also* Burke, Kenneth
Francis, Mark, 34, 40
Frank, Thomas, 12–13, 163, 215n32, 225n115
Fraser, Steve, 214n27, 217n55
free enterprise. *See* free market
free market, 3, 4, 7, 9, 26, 29, 30, 33, 35, 46, 49–50, 53, 62, 68, 69, 70, 123, 128, 145, 157, 191, 198
Freeland, Chrystia, 3, 100
French Revolution, 15, 17–18, 89
Friedman, Benjamin, 32, 62–63, 68, 219n3
Friedman, Milton, 68, 85, 99, 106, 113, 117, 118–33, 142, 145, 148, 154, 157, 161, 164, 165, 169, 176, 179, 181, 207, 234n59, 236n100, 247n5, 248n7, 248n10, 248n21, 248n23, 249n31, 250n39, 250n41, 251n56, 251n61, 251–52n63, 252–53nn76–77, 255n10, 267n8, 272n61, 273n63, 274n68; antitrust laws, 127; and Barry Goldwater, 120, 126; conservatism, 120, 121, 123–24, 126, 133, 251n63, 274n68; democracy, 118, 123, 126, 128; Keynesianism 118, 119, 122, 128, 129, 130, 132, 249n31; millenarianism, 123; race, 124, 130–31; and Ronald Reagan, 118, 120, 121, 126, 130, 132, 133; the state, 120, 122, 127–28, 131–32, 134, 248n10, 252n76, 256n38

Garland, Merrick, 194
Garver, Eugene, 22, 35, 42, 221n37

295

INDEX

Gates, Bill, ix
General Electric (GE), 58, 100, 128
George Mason University, 137
Gershberg, Zac, 12, 111, 195, 196
Gerstle, Gary, 40, 48, 214n27, 217n55
Gilded Age, 11, 18, 44, 46–48, 49, 51, 57, 229n94
Giroux, Henry, 131–32, 257–58n57
Goldwater, Barry, 68, 81, 82, 101, 120, 126, 248n18, 254n102, 272n61
Goodnight, Thomas, 38–39, 251n56
Google, ix, 9, 191
Gorsuch, Neil, 96, 239n45
Gospel of Wealth. *See* Carnegie, Andrew
Gould, Jay, 45, 50
Gramsci, Antonio, 216n47
Great Depression, 59, 60, 61, 66, 77, 80, 99, 101, 186, 220n21, 250n41
Great Society, 77, 81, 86, 95, 119, 120, 143
Gregg, Melissa, 207
Gunn, Joshua, 10, 11, 206

Haidt, Jonathan, 25
Hamilton, Alexander, 15, 16–18, 19, 27, 42, 55, 78, 87, 96, 221n35
Hanan, Joshua, 68, 247n109, 270n34, 272n61
Hannity, Sean, 92, 174, 182
Hariman, Robert, 231n29, 271n59, 273n62
Harvey, David, 99, 112–15
Hayek, Friedrich, 62–77, 80, 85, 104, 113, 119, 154, 155, 161, 164, 207–8, 233n27, 233n36, 234n57, 234n59, 248n23, 254n111, 272n61, 274n68; conservatism, 63, 68, 69, 70, 71–72, 74; democracy, 65, 71, 73; equality, 64–66, 73; individualism, 63, 67; Keynesianism, 63, 64, 65, 66, 69; the law, 63–64, 66, 72–73, 74; and Milton Friedman, 68, 120, 121, 122–23, 124, 157, 236n100, 248n7, 273n63; Nobel Prize, 74–76, 77; socialism, 64–65, 66, 69; violence 72–73
Heritage Foundation, 92, 111, 160, 161, 267n8

Hitler, Adolph, 65, 69, 73, 102
Humboldt, Alexander von, 23. *See also* Darwinian evolutionary theory
Hustwit, William, 82, 83, 87, 88, 96

Icahn, Carl, 54
illiberalism, 4
Illing, Sean 12, 111, 195, 196
inequality, 7, 29, 44, 52, 53–54, 56, 65, 96, 127–28, 133, 189, 192, 222n41, 228n78, 240n99. *See also* equality orientation
Internal Revenue Service (IRS), 96. *See also* oligarchy: taxes
invention. *See* rhetoric
Ireland 9, 31

January 6 insurrection, 197
Jefferson, Thomas, 15, 18, 19, 78, 87, 89, 90, 175
John Birch Society, 61, 82, 101
Johnson, Lyndon B., 76, 95, 96
Johnson, Paul, 8, 13–14, 220n14, 225n115
Johnson, Samuel, 221n37

kairotic, 10, 35, 126, 131
Kansas, 12–13, 150, 152, 159, 160, 161–70, 220n14. *See also* Koch, Charles: Kansas Experiment
Kaplan, David A., 87
Kaplan, Michael, 246n109, 271n35
Kemp, Jack, 162
Kendi, Ibram X., 27, 223n84, 253n94
Kennedy, John F., 76, 96
Keynes, John Maynard, 59, 60, 61–66, 69, 73, 77, 80, 86, 113, 124, 164
Keynesian welfare state, 60, 61, 62, 65, 69, 77, 81, 99, 111, 112, 113, 117, 118–19, 122, 125, 128, 129, 130, 131, 132, 145, 146, 162, 238n43
Kilpatrick, James J., 81–97, 98, 103, 130; conservatism, 82–83, 85–86, 87, 93, 95, 142, 239n55, 240n99; the Constitution, 84–86, 90, 91, 92, 94; the Fourteenth Amendment, 84, 87, 90, 91, 240n88; natural law 93–94;

INDEX

states' rights, 86, 90; strict constitutionalism, 85–87, 91, 92, 238n43, 238–39n45, and segregation, 83–84, 87, 88; the Virginia Commission on Constitutional Government (VCCG), 83–84, 89, 90, 91, 110, 131. 240n88
King, Martin Luther, Jr., 88–89, 93
Kirk, Russell, 7, 81
Knight, Frank, 121
Koch Industries, 9, 149, 152, 153, 155–56, 157, 158–59, 217–18n59, 258n57, 259n5
Koch family, 13, 135, 152, 164, 186, 215n32, 220n14, 225n115, 259n5, 261n48, 261n59, 267n8. *See also* Koch Industries; Koch, Charles; Koch, David
Koch, Charles, ix, 22, 49, 51, 111, 113, 115, 126, 132, 135, 145, 150–61, 167, 169, 186, 188, 198, 225n115, 259n7, 259n10, 260n25, 260n41, 261n45; conservatism, 152, 153–54, 157, 159, 161, 164–65, 167–68, 215n32, 260n25; democracy, 157, 158, 165; Kansas Experiment, 161–68; lawbreaking, 158–59; legal influence 160, 261n59; Market-Based Management (MBM), 154–57; political influence, 159–60, 259n5, 267n8; the state, 152–53, 154, 155–58; "10,000 Percent Compliance", 159; voters, Koch's assumption that they are delusional, 158, 217n55, 261n55
Koch, David, 6, 151–52, 259n10
Ku Klux Klan, 61, 95

labor. *See* organized labor
Laffer, Arthur, 161, 165; Laffer Curve, the, 162–63
laissez-faire, 7, 13, 41, 42, 78, 79, 127, 132, 251n63
Lee, Michael, 63, 68, 70, 72, 204, 208, 229n78, 272n61, 274n68
Leo, Leonard, 185
Leonard, Christopher, 152, 153, 157, 158

Leonhardt, David, 193
Lessl, Thomas, 38–39 125, 209, 227n40, 227n46–47, 251n56
Lewis, Michael, 198
liberalism, 3, 138
liberation theology. *See* Christianity
libertarianism, 3, 8, 30, 39, 41, 63, 68, 142, 147–48, 150, 152, 157, 158, 169–70, 210, 250n39, 252n86, 253n86. *See also* conservatism
Limbaugh, Rush, 63, 182, 208
Lippman, Walter, 62, 221n33
Lloyd, Henry Demarest, 46
Lochner era, 78–80, 81, 239n55, 239n55
Lochner v. New York, 78, 79, 80
Loeffler, Kelly, 194
Longaker, Mark, 38, 39, 207, 226n18, 274n68
Luhnow, Harold, 62

MacLean, Nancy, 135, 137, 143, 145
Madison, James, 17, 19, 78, 87, 90
Magnuson, William, 79
Malthus, Thomas, 23
Marchand, Roland, 101
Marx, Karl, 34, 182, 204; Marxist theory, 212n13
Masterson, Ty, 166, 167
Mayer, Jane, 152, 160, 225n115, 260n25, 261n48
Mays, David J., 82
McCarthy, Joseph, 25
McCarthy, Kevin, 195
McCloskey, Deirdre, 206
McConnell, Mitch, 182, 194, 195
McGee, Michael, 204, 207
Meese, Edwin, 130
Mercieca, Jennifer, 273n61
Mercier, Ernest, 62
Meyer, Frank, 82
Miliband, Ralph, 175, 186, 214n26, 217n59, 259n4
Mills, Charles W., 28
Mises, Ludwig von, 62, 138, 154, 234n59, 236n100
monopolies, 33, 46–47, 48, 57, 59, 78, 127, 197–98

INDEX

Mont Pèlerin Society, 62, 114, 135
Moore, Stephen, 161
Morgan, J. P., 9, 50, 66, 70
Mounk, Yascha, 114

Nader, Ralph, 31, 102, 104, 107, 109, 111
Nasaw, David, 47
National Association of Manufacturers, 62
National Review, 82, 92, 248n21
National Rifle Association (NRA), *154*
natural law, 23, 16, 29, 30, 31, 32, 30, 43, 44, 46, 54, 55, 61, 66, 141, 193
natural selection, 33–34, 53. *See also* Darwinian evolutionary theory
neoliberalism, 8, 62, 69, 70, 74, 112–15, 131–32, 135, 142, 146, 169–70, 182, 210, 245n102, 246n109, 257n57
New Deal, 12, 59, 60, 61, 62, 63, 77, 78, 79–80, 81, 86, 102, 119, 120, 139, 143, 175, 176, 234n59
Nixon, Richard, 27, 81, 82, 100, 102, 110
Norquist, Grover, 132, 161
nostalgia, 47, 132, 171, 176
Nye, Bill ("the Science Guy"), 178, 184–85, 186

Oath Keepers, 196
Obama, Barack, 31, 152, 161, 164, 168, 250n41
O'Connor, Sandra Day, 242n30
oikonomon, 7
oligarchy: alternatives to, 98–99, 100–101, 184, 187–88, 190, 197–99; aristocracy, 3–4, 18, 31, 71, 88; and culture, 4, 8, 145; and cynicism, 73, 74, 76–77, 105, 138, 146, 158, 171, 176, 180, 184, 186, 236n100, 251n55; definition of, ix, 2–9, 126, 138–39, 210, 212n12, 215n31; and democracy, 4–6, 14–16, 18–21, 42, 45, 56, 78–79, 188, 194, 203–4, 212n12, 218n61, 221n33; history of, 213n16; impact on consumers, 192–93; justice, 21–22, 23, 24, 45, 134, 146–47, 174, 223n84; licensing, 190–92, 197; merit, 22–23, 27 55–56, 63, 87, 89, 113, 156, 222n41, 222n41, 260n25; plutocracy, 3–4, 8, 31; public opinion, 150, 190; religion, 25, 28, 44, 59, 219n3, 231n45, 258n71; the state, 3, 4–5, 7, 8, 9, 18–20, 28–29, 33, 40–41, 56–57, 67, 133, 136, 146, 158, 176, 185, 187, 196, 198, 206, 212n13, 214n27, 217n56, 217n59, 218n61, 225n115, 268n20; and style, 208–9; taxes, 2, 9, 29, 44, 54, 85, 100, 128, 132, 146, 149, 161, 165–66, 167–68, 181, 190; and the US Constitution, 15–16, 138, 267n8; violence, 8, 16–17, 20, 30, 72–73, 149, 221n39, 228n73; and wealth, 3, 4–6, 51, 52, 199, 213n22
Olin, John M., 98, 267n8
Ong, Aihwa, 112, 251n63
Orbán, Victor, 182–84
ordoliberalism, 70
organized labor, 19, 51, 53, 57, 59, 74, 81, 100, 113, 124, 130, 133, 187
originalism, 87, 88, 91, 238n43, 238n44, 238n45
Osnos, Evan, 8, 22, 194, 197, 215n32

Packer, George, 194, 212n5, 223n81
Parks and Recreation, 53
Peck, Jamie, 70, 127, 213n21
Pence, Mike, 195–96
Perelman, Chaïm, 68
Pew, J. Howard, 61
Philip Morris, 102, 107
Philippon, Thomas, 191, 192–93
Phillips-Fein, Kim, 80, 101, 121, 215n32, 232n45, 267n8
Piketty, Thomas, 60, 63, 216n44, 221–22n39, 222n41
Pinochet, Augusto, 72
Plato, 14, 17, 55, 88, 89, 182
Polanyi, Karl, 59, 69, 124, 164
Polanyi, Michael, 155
political economy, 2, 4, 5, 7, 11, 33, 63, 64, 66, 67, 70, 121, 146, 157, 205, 207–8, 210
political right. *See* conservatism